PRECIOUS CARGO

PRECIOUS CARGO

HOW FOODS FROM THE AMERICAS
CHANGED THE WORLD

Dave DeWitt

COUNTERPOINT

BERKELEY

Library of Congress Cataloging-in-Publication data is available
ISBN 978-1-61902-309-3

Book design by Lois Manno

COUNTERPOINT
1919 Fifth Street
Berkeley, CA 94710
www.counterpointpress.com

Distributed by Publishers Group West
Printed RR Donnelley in China

10 9 8 7 6 5 4 3 2 1

Illustration on previous page: Three Maize Cobs (India Corn).
Engraving by Anga Bottione-Rossi, 1835. Sunbelt Archives.

"Hypotheses about past events are not susceptible to scientific proofs, and the historian can never hope to have a hypothesis certified as anything better than reasonable. He must lope along where scientists fear to tread."

—*Alfred W. Crosby, Jr., in* The Columbian Exchange, *1972*

To my favorite food historians: Sophie Coe, Karen Hess, Mark Kurlansky, Waverly Root, and Andrew F. Smith.

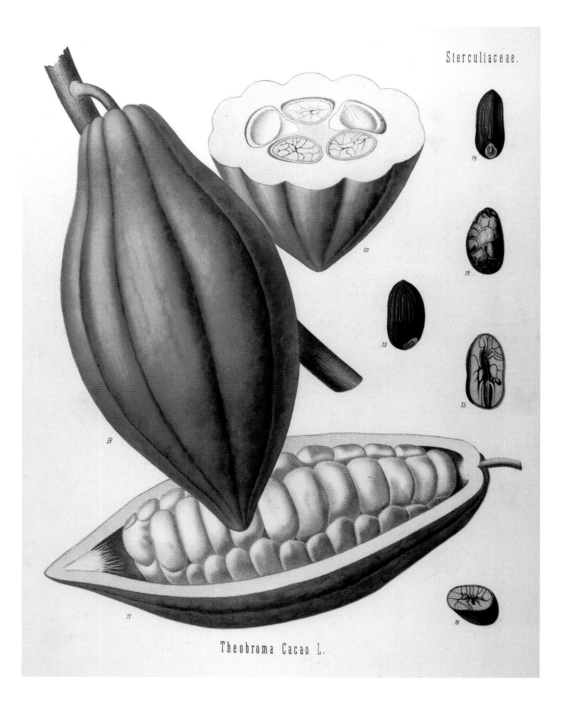

Sterculiaceae.

Theobroma Cacao L.

CONTENTS

Opposite: Theobroma cacao *(Chocolate), by Franz Eugen Köhler, 1897. Sunbelt Archives.*

ACKNOWLEDGMENTS

I was mostly on my own for this project, but I did receive a lot of help from Dean Elizabeth Titus and her staff at the New Mexico State University Library, along with assistance from Rick Browne, Pat Chapman, Marco Del Freo, Lois Manno, Richard Sterling, and Harald Zoschke. A special thanks to my agent, Scott Mendel, who never gives up. And a big *abrazo* to editor Jack Shoemaker of Counterpoint, who really believed in this book from his first reading of it.

Chile Peppers. Botanical illustration by Ernst Benary, 1876. Sunbelt Archives.

PREFACE

For the past quarter century, I've been just a little bit preoccupied with chile peppers, and that obsession has driven me to create two magazines, more than thirty books, a major trade show now in its twenty-sixth year, and a large online archive that is the Fiery Foods & Barbecue SuperSite. After I completed my part of *The Complete Chile Pepper Book* (2009), I searched for a food history project with a broader scope than my previous two books in that genre had—namely an alternative history of Italian cuisine and then the story of the historical food lovers who launched what is now American cuisine. My work on the first one, *Da Vinci's Kitchen* (2006), which I'm proud to say has been published in fourteen languages so far, got me thinking about how New World crops beyond chile peppers influenced other worldwide cuisines. This time, my new project involved chile peppers as only one crop among all the New World foods transferred to the Old World that were destined to change the history of civilization.

So this book is not about American food but rather American *foods*—the lowly crops that became commodities, and one gobbling protein source, the turkey—and how these foreign and often suspicious temptations were transported around the world and eventually changed not only cuisines but the very fabric of human life on the planet. Many books have been written on each and every food topic I'm covering, but the entire story has never been properly told. To tell it, I had to dig rather deeply into food and popular history, plus numerous other disciplines, a task that would not have been possible without two invaluable resources: Google Books and the New Mexico State University Library and its connections to libraries all over the world.

What I enjoyed the most about researching this book was discovering the cross-disciplinary nature of food history. It's a lot more than just history and recipes, so I had to delve into botany, zoology, anthropology, and archeology, to name the more important disciplines I investigated to complete the research. For example, the archaeological excavations Cerén, the "American

Pompeii," proved that most of the early Spanish descriptions of the crops and foods of the New World—often derided throughout time—were dead-on accurate. I also loved telling the tales of those surprising individuals who were caught up in the spread and influence of American foods, including a slave trader, a physician and African explorer, several brutish conquerors, the "Indiana Jones of Southeast Asia," a Scottish millionaire obsessed with a single fruit, and a British Lord and colonial governor with a passion for peppers, to name a few.

Enjoy the journey.

PROLOGUE

Discovery, Botany, and Food Evolution

Proponents of localized food production, often called "locavores," are opposed to food globalization, and many of them believe that this spread and exchange of foods is a trend unique to the modern era. This is simply not true. The subtitle of Kenneth F. Kiple's book *A Movable Feast* is "Ten Millennia of Food Globalization," and he notes that food globalization "began with the invention of agriculture some ten thousand years ago in at least seven independent centers of plant and animal domestication."

In one example that I discussed in depth in *Da Vinci's Kitchen,* were it not for food globalization and the introduction of durum wheat, maize, rice, tomatoes, and sugar into Italy at different times, the cuisine of that country would be far different from what it is today, lacking pasta, polenta, risotto, marinara sauce, and tiramisu. But arguably the most significant globalization event in history was the "Columbian exchange" of New World and Old World foods and culinary techniques, which made an enormous impact on population growth, famine avoidance, and a new direction in the evolution of major cuisines of the world's diverse regions. This transfer of plants, animals, foods, slaves, settlers, diseases, and culture between the hemispheres is one of the most significant worldwide events in human history concerning ecology, agriculture, and culture. And these momentous events began with what is called "The Age of Discovery."

The quest for spices and the need to eliminate Arab middlemen from that lucrative trade were the motivating factors driving the search for alternative routes to "the Indies" so that European traders could deal directly with the spice sources. The Portuguese led the way by exploring the Atlantic coast of Africa from 1418, under the sponsorship of Prince Henry the Navigator, and reached the Indian Ocean by 1488. The Treaty of Tordesillas in 1494 divided the world into two parts, the western part for

Spain and the eastern section, including Brazil, for Portugal. Although that treaty prevented war between Spain and Portugal, it eventually backfired, according to historian Stephen R. Bown. "It was to have a profound influence on world history," he wrote in *1494: How a Family Feud in Medieval Spain Divided the World in Half* (2011), "steering European nations on a collision course and insidiously emerging as the central grievance that stimulated nearly two centuries of espionage, piracy, smuggling, and warfare."

In 1497–99, Vasco da Gama led a Portuguese expedition to India for the first time by sailing around Africa, opening up trade with one of the major spice centers of the world. It was a remarkable trip of 28,000 miles, and at one point his three ships were out of sight of land for ninety-five days, as compared to Columbus's first voyage of 1492 from the Canary Islands to the Bahamas, when he didn't spot land for thirty-six days. Despite da Gama's navigational ability—he missed his target of Calicut on the Indian coast by a mere seven miles—he was a completely naive trader who had not brought enough merchandise (such as fine linen) to trade for spices, so, like any European trader, he resorted to robbery, kidnapping, and murder to accomplish his goal of filling the holds of his ship with black pepper, cinnamon, and cloves. And, with the help of Arab pilots, he was enormously successful. The Portuguese reached the next spice center, the Spice Islands, or Moluccas, in 1512, and they arrived in China in 1513. Magellan's circumnavigation of the world in 1522 proved that Portugal and Spain could sail anywhere they wanted, and worldwide trade, including the Columbian exchange, began.

Technology played a large role in the globalization process, particularly new maritime inventions like the caravel, which was developed by mariners supported by Henry the Navigator. This round-hulled ship with lateen (triangular) rigging carried more cargo and sailed closer to the wind than any other ship of its time. By sailing as close as possible to the direction from which the wind was blowing, mariners took better advantage of it and reduced the zigzag tacking distances. The caravel, according to William Bernstein, author of *A Splendid Exchange* (2008), "improved the speed and cargo-carrying capacities of Portuguese merchants to the point where they were able to divert the trade in Africa's two most profitable exports, slaves and gold, to their North African ports and away from the Muslim-controlled trans-Saharan camel routes."

Columbus's three ships were caravels, but he sailed west rather than south and east as da Gama had, and he did not have the same measure of financial success. And, half of da Gama's men died of scurvy. "No matter," Bernstein concluded. "Da Gama's crews had loaded enough pepper, cinnamon, and cloves in Calicut to pay the expedition's cost sixty times over, and when the sorry remains of the expedition limped into Lisbon, no one questioned the awful human toll." According to Stephen Bown, author of *Scurvy*, a history of that disease, "Scurvy was responsible for more deaths at sea than storms, shipwrecks, combat, and all other diseases combined. Historians have conservatively estimated that more than two million sailors perished from scurvy during the Age of Sail."

Running parallel with the Age of Discovery was the Age of Botany, led by two men who were contemporaries but who never met, Carolus Clusius and John Gerard. Florike Egmond, author of *The World of Carolus Clusius*, notes: "In the sixteenth century—precisely during the lifetime of Clusius—a number of new phenomena emerged which together are known as the Botanical Renaissance and produced the greatest changes in the European knowledge of living nature before the age of Linnaeus, or perhaps even before Darwin." Clusius holds the title of the first scientific botanist because his knowledge was based more upon observation and experimentation than on the out-of-date beliefs of the past botanical writers.

Right on the heels of Clusius was John Gerard, whose *Herball or General Historie of Plantes* (1597) was one of the most remarkable books produced in Europe during the sixteenth century. It was published at the same time England was expanding its boundaries and when voyages of discovery asserted England's claims on the New World. New lands, plants, and animals were being discovered; science, literature, and the arts flourished; and poets, playwrights, scientists, and scholars (think Shakespeare, Cervantes, Bacon, and Galileo) were producing master works of literature and science.

Top: Carolus Clusius. Engraving by J. J. Boissard, 1598. Sunbelt Archives. Bottom: John Gerard. Frontispiece to The Herball, 1636, engraving by John Payne. Sunbelt Archives.

Botany was still in its infancy, and Gerard's *Herball,* much like Clusius's *Rariorum plantarum historia* (1601), reveals his early process of scientific thought by replacing information passed down through the ages and using instead what he found to be true from experimentation. The *Herball or General Historie of Plantes,* with 1,800 woodcuts of the plants described, became required reading for botany students for the next two centuries and was part of the essential education of botanists well into the nineteenth century. Gerard's contribution to the advancement of botany and plant knowledge during the time of the Botanical Renaissance set a precedent that inspired most later herbals and catalogs of plants.

Both Clusius and Gerard were heavily influenced by the introduction of vast numbers of exotic plants brought back by the explorers from the Middle East, Africa, the Far East, and the Americas. The change in the knowledge about the natural world was astonishing, as Egmond comments: "The passion for gardening and the cultivation of rare plants spread like wildfire throughout Europe; the first university botanical gardens and academic chairs in medicinal botany were created; and the first richly illustrated surveys of the world of plants and the world of animals were published." For the first time, the world of nature was the center of interest for European intellectuals, which of course affected their beliefs about the radical new foods of the Columbian exchange.

As I researched and wrote this book I kept noticing similarities between Darwinian evolutionary theory and the insertion of New World foods into the Old World. As organisms in nature find ecological niches and adapt to them, they flourish, reproduce, and evolve; likewise, the New World crops, with the cooperation of humans, filled niches around the world where they proliferated and guaranteed the success not only of their species but also the humans who were depending upon them for sustenance. This type of mutual benefit is termed "coevolution," and the perfect example is bees evolving to pollinate plants and the plants returning the favor by providing food for the bees in terms of nectar and pollen. They both enhanced the other's ability to survive and reproduce. Thus New World foods enabled human populations to grow, thrive, and further evolve in environmental niches where they never could have survived without them.

PART I

SPANISH INVASIONS AND STRANGE FOODS OF THE NEW WORLD

"The First Voyage," (Columbus Bids Farewell to Queen Isabella), Chromolithograph by L. Prang & Co., Published by The Prang Educational Co., Boston, 1893. Sunbelt Archives.

*Remains of the Maya
village of Joya de
Cerén buried by a
volcanic eruption
around A.D. 600 in El
Salvador. Tamazcal
(Structure 9) was
excavated at Area
2. By Mario Roberto
Durán Ortiz.*

ROUGHLY A MILLENNIUM BEFORE THE AGES OF DISCOVERY AND BOTANY, AN IMPORTANT GEOLOGICAL EVENT OCCURRED IN A WORLD COMPLETELY UNKNOWN TO ANYONE WHO LIVED IN WHAT LATER WAS KNOWN AS EUROPE. THIS EVENT PRESERVED AN ANCIENT CULTURE SO PERFECTLY THAT ARCHAEOLOGISTS WHO COULDN'T BELIEVE THEIR LUCK LITERALLY WERE TRANSFORMED INTO FOOD HISTORIANS, ILLUSTRATING HOW IMPORTANT SCIENCE IS TO FOOD HISTORY.

Out of the Ash:
The Prehistoric Village of Cerén

On an August evening in the year 595, the Loma Caldera in what is now El Salvador erupted, sending clouds of volcanic ash into the Maya agricultural village of Cerén, burying it twenty feet deep and turning it into the New World equivalent of Pompeii. Miraculously, all the villagers escaped, but what they left behind gives us a good idea of the life they led, the food they ate, and the maize, squash, beans, chile peppers, and cacao they grew or harvested in the wild.

In 1976, while leveling ground for the erection of grain silos, a Salvadoran bulldozer operator believed that he had accidentally plowed into an ancient building. He immediately notified the national museum, but a museum archaeologist thought that the building was of recent vintage and allowed the bulldozing to continue. Several buildings were destroyed. Two years later, Payson Sheets, an anthropologist from the University of Colorado, led a team of students on an archaeological survey of the Zapotitan Valley. He was taken to the bulldozer site by local residents and quickly began a test excavation, and radiocarbon dating of artifacts proved that they were very ancient. He received permission from the government to do a complete excavation of Cerén, and the site was saved.

Dr. Sheets and his students returned for five field sessions at Cerén, and their discoveries are detailed on their website, http://ceren.colorado.edu. One of the most interesting things they discovered was, well, how civilized these people were. In the

Chile Stem at Cerén.
University of Colorado.

words of Dr. Sheets, "We had no idea that people in the region lived so well fourteen centuries ago." The ash preserved the crops in the field, leaving impressions of the plants. The plants then rotted away, leaving perfect cavities, or molds.

Using techniques that were developed at Pompeii, the archaeologists poured liquid plaster into the cavities. By removing the ash, the ancient crops in the fields were revealed and could be studied. Interestingly, the agriculturists of Cerén used row and furrow techniques similar to those still utilized today; corn was grown in elevated rows, and beans and squash were grown in the furrows in between. In a courtyard of a building, "We even found a series of four mature chile plants with stem diameters over 5 centimeters (2 inches)," wrote Dr. Sheets. Chile peppers are rarely found in archaeological sites in Mesoamerica, so imagine the surprise of the researchers when they discovered painted ceramic storage vessels that contained large quantities of chile seeds. "One vessel had cacao seeds in the bottom, and chiles above, separated by a layer of cotton gauze," Dr. Sheets revealed. "It is possible that they would have been prepared into a kind of *mole* sauce." Also found were corn kernels, beans, squash seeds, cotton seeds, and evidence of manioc plants and small agave plants, which were used for their fiber to make rope rather than being fermented for an alcoholic beverage, *pulque*, as was done in Mexico. I emailed Dr. Sheets, hoping to discover the shape and size of the chiles and thus deduce the variety being grown. But no whole pods were found, just the seeds and some pod fragments. The size of the chile stem indicated that the plant had been grown as a perennial, but all chile plants are perennials in tropical climates and can grow to considerable size.

Dr. Sheets wrote me back about an article by Dr. David Lentz, the botanist who had studied the plant remains, and I tracked it down in the journal *Latin American Antiquity*, which I found in Zimmerman Library at the University of New Mexico. Dr. Lentz wrote about the seeds and the pod fragments, "It appears that many of these fell from the rafters of buildings where they would have been hung for drying or storage." He added that the chile seeds from the site were the first in Central America found outside Mexico, and he speculated that those seeds in vessels were probably being saved for future planting.

The Taming of the Wild Chile

For a researcher with a chile obsession like me, of course I wanted to know what kind of chile was grown in Cerén. There was an intriguing clue in the article: a photograph of a chile seed compared with a bar indicating the lengths in millimeters. The seed was 3.5 millimeters wide. Since the size of the seed is directly related to the size of the pod (generally speaking, the larger the pod, the larger the seed), perhaps it was possible to guess the size of the pod by comparing that ancient seed to seeds I had stored in my greenhouse.

Paleoethnobotanists, the scientists who study the plants used by ancient civilizations, have theorized that chiles were first used as "tolerated weeds." They were not cultivated but rather collected in the wild when the fruits were ripe. The wild forms had small, erect fruits that were deciduous, meaning that they separated easily from the calyx and fell to the ground. During the domestication process, whether consciously or unconsciously, the pre-Columbian farmers selected seeds from plants with larger, non-deciduous, and pendant fruits. The reasons for these selection criteria are a greater yield from each plant and protection of the pods from chile-hungry birds. The larger the pod, the greater its tendency to become pendant rather than to remain erect. Thus the pods became hidden amid the leaves and did not protrude above them as beacons for birds. The selection of varieties with the tendency to be non-deciduous ensured that the pods remained on the plant until fully ripe and thus were resistant to dropping off as a result of wind or physical contact. The domesticated chiles gradually lost their natural means of seed dispersal by birds and became dependent upon human intervention for their continued existence.

Because chiles cross-pollinate, hundreds of varieties of the five domesticated chile species were developed by humans over thousands of years in South and Central America. The color, size, and shape of the pods of these domesticated forms varied enormously. Ripe fruits could be red, orange, brown, yellow, or white. Their shapes could be round, conic, elongate, oblate, or bell-like, and their size could vary from the tiny fruits of chiltepins or tabascos to the large pods of the anchos and pasillas. But very little archaeological evidence existed to support these theories until the finds at Cerén.

It was exciting to think that perhaps we had a window into the ancient chile domestication process. Because their seeds were collected, and the plants were growing in a courtyard, the chile plants at Cerén were obviously cultivated and were more than just "tolerated weeds." It was time to break out my metric ruler and start measuring seeds. I devised the following table, ranked by seed width:

Variety	Pod Length	Seed Width
Ancho	12 cm	6 mm
Serrano	7 cm	5 mm
Jalapeño	6.5 cm	5 mm
de Arbol	4,5 cm	4.5 mm
Habanero	4.5 cm	4 mm
Piquin	1.3 cm	4 mm
Cerén Chiles	?	3.5 mm
Chiltepin	0.5 cm	3 mm

The first conclusion I reached was that the Cerén chiles were small-podded. They certainly were not as large as anchos, whose seeds are twice the width of those of the Cerén chiles. They could, of course, have been chiltepins, because the seeds were only half a millimeter wider than chiltepin seeds. But if they were somewhere between the size of chiltepins and piquins, that would have made the pods about 1 centimeter long, less than half an inch. And since there is evidence that the chile pods had been hung up to dry with agave twine, that process would not have been necessary for such small-podded plants. Note that the habanero, which is nine times the length of the chiltepin, has seeds only 1 millimeter wider. Also note that the de árbol variety, which is also 4.5 cm long but much thinner, has seeds only 1 millimeter wider than the Cerén chiles. I believe that the domestication of chiles from chiltepins to serranos and anchos would not be completed until the Aztec culture of nearly a millennium after AD 595, and perhaps this was a window into the domestication process. I repeat that this is my personal theory and that I am not a paleoethnobotanist, though sometimes I wish I had studied that discipline.

The Cuisine of Cerén

In addition to the vegetable crops of corn, chiles, beans, manioc, cacao, and squash, the archaeologists found evidence that the Cerén villagers also harvested wild avocados, palm fruits and nuts, and certain spices such as *achiote*, or annatto seeds. In fact, Dr. Sheets observed, "[t]he villagers ate better and had a greater variety of foodstuff than their descendants. Traditional families today eat mostly corn and beans, with some rice, squash, and chiles, but rarely any meat. Cerén's residents ate deer and dog meat." They also consumed peccary, mud turtle, duck, and rodents, but deer was their primary meat. Fully 50 percent of the total bones found on the site belonged to white-tailed deer, and many of those deer were immature animals—giving rise to a very interesting theory.

Linda Brown, who wrote the 1996 Field Season Preliminary Report entitled "Household and Village Animal Use," noted, "Cerén residents may have practiced some form of deer management. One of the deer procurement strategies the Cerén villagers may have utilized is 'garden hunting.' Garden hunting consists of allowing deer to browse in cultivated fields and household gardens where they can be hunted. While some vegetation is lost to browsing, the benefits include easy access to deer when needed." Expanding upon that theory, she wrote, "The ethnohistoric data make many references to the Maya partially taming white-tailed deer. Specifically, historical sources note that it was women who were responsible for taking in, semi-taming, and raising deer. [Diego de] Landa mentioned that women raise other domestic animals and let the deer suck their breasts, by which means they raise them and make them so tame that they never will go into the woods, although they take them and carry them through the woods and raise them there. Apparently, during historic times, there was a designated place in the woods where women would take deer to browse until they needed them. Scholars have argued that pre-Columbian women may have raised deer, dogs, peccary, and fowl much like contemporary Maya women raise pigs and fowl for food, trade, and special occasion feasts. Perhaps the Cerén women raised dog, fowl (a duck was tethered inside the Household 1 *bodega*), and semi-tamed deer as a contribution to the domestic and ceremonial economy."

It is always a challenge for archaeologists to reconstruct ancient cuisines and cooking techniques. The Cerén villagers did not have metal utensils, but they did have fired ceramics that could be used to boil foods. They could grill over open flames and perhaps fry foods in ceramic pots using cottonseed oil or animal fat. They had obsidian knives that could cut as cleanly as metal. They had *metates* for grinding corn into flour and *mocaljetes* for grinding fruits, vegetables, chiles, and spices together into sauces. The next step in the evolution of Latin American cuisine and its influence on the Old World came with the arrival of the Spanish and Portuguese, but the excavations at Cerén have since corroborated their food observations by providing physical evidence in addition to their eyewitness accounts.

Columbus and Peppers

Eight hundred and ninety-seven years after the volcano exploded, Columbus and his men were aboard ship headed to "the Indies" and not eating nearly as well as those simple villagers in Cerén. Salt pork and beef, ship's biscuit, dried fish, cheese, and beer don't seem all that bad when you read the words on paper, but in reality the sailors were forced to eat food that was moldy, maggot-infested, and spoiled. The salt pork and beef, known as sea junk or sea horse, was so salty it had to be towed behind the ship for half a day to reduce the salt, and then it was cooked in a copper pot of sea water. It burned the sailors' mouths as they ate it, and the "best" part of it, the fatty dregs of boiled meat called slush, had so much copper acetate from the pot that it prevented the body from absorbing nutrients—including the all-important vitamin C, which could be reduced up to 75 percent. The result? Deadly scurvy.

The ship's biscuit was ridden with weevils and maggots, and the cheese, in the words of historian Stephen Bown, author of *Scurvy*, "quickly went rancid, cloaking the entire ship in a cloying cloud of noxious stench." The beer soon went stale, forcing the sailors to drink hard liquor, so alcoholism was rampant. But the good news was that they regularly ate some fresh protein, namely rats, "full as good as rabbits, although not so large," according to Bown.

Considering these delicacies that Columbus and his men were eating during their voyage to "the Indies" in 1492, their resistance to many of the New World crops and animals is surprising. After all, just what is wrong with a dog meat tamale after you've dined on stewed rat? Hernando Colón, Columbus's son who chronicled the voyages of "The Admiral," admitted that the sailors survived on a daily ration of "a pound of rotten biscuit and a pint of wine" but still thought that the Indians had a strange diet, commenting, "They eat many such things that would not only make any Spaniard vomit but would poison him if he tried them." Some of the Spaniards "rashly tried" some fruit from a tree that resembled the familiar apple in shape, leaf, and fruit, most likely the manchineel, or "death apple," and "no sooner did they taste them than their faces swelled, growing so inflamed and painful that they almost went out of their minds," according to Dr. Diego Chanca, the court physician who accompanied Columbus on the voyage.

Christopher Columbus. Engraving by André Thevet, 1676. Sunbelt Archives.

Colón continued, "The Indians are accustomed to eating unclean things, such as large, fat spiders and white worms that breed among wood and other rotting matter." About fish, he observed: "Before they boil them they tear out their eyes and eat them on the spot." No wonder the Spaniards were suspicious of the strange foods they were encountering on a daily basis.

Maize, the central ingredient in tamales and the dominant crop of the Americas, was given mixed reviews by Columbus and his peers. The two Spaniards Columbus sent to explore the interior of Cuba returned with a report that they had seen "a sort of grain they called maize." Hernando Colón wrote, "This grain has a very good taste when cooked, either roasted or ground and made into a gruel which was well tasted, bak'd, dry'd and made into flour." Yet it was hardly "well tasted" for the chronicler of the exploits of Cortés, Bernal Díaz del Castillo, author of *The True History of the Conquest of New Spain,* who described the "misery of maize cakes." Even the botanists didn't like it very much, with Gerard writing that it was "a more convenient food for swine than for men." Columbus, though, bragged about it: "It is a cereal with an ear like that of wheat," he wrote in 1500. "I have brought some back and there is now much in Castile. The best is apparently considered excellent and most highly prized." Columbus tried maize and pronounced, "It tasted very good." I would imagine that he ate a lot of it during his four voyages to the center of world maize consumption.

The Spaniards seemed to like sweet potatoes, with Colón writing that "they tasted like chestnuts." Chanca also described them: "They all bring yams [sweet potatoes], which are like turnips, and we prepare them for eating in a variety of ways. They are so nourishing that we are all greatly restored by them, for we have been living on the smallest possible rations during our months at sea." As we shall see in Europe, it was the New World foods that most closely resembled familiar Old World foods that were first accepted by the Europeans. Maize was obviously a grain that looked like large wheat to Columbus, and sweet potatoes closely resembled yams, an unrelated tuber.

Another crop they immediately appreciated was the local spice. Columbus commented about it while in Puerto Rico on January 15, 1493: "The land was found to produce much *ají,* which is the pepper of the inhabitants, and more valuable than the common sort; they deem it very wholesome and eat nothing without it. Fifty caravels might be loaded every year with this commodity at Española." This spice, of course, was chile peppers. Columbus in his letter of February 15, 1493, noted: "It was very cold this winter but the natives are used to this and withstand the weather, thanks to their food, which they eat heavily seasoned with very hot spices." Chanca added that "[t]hey use as a seasoning a spice called *agi* [*ají*], with which they also season their fish and birds when they can get them."

There are several mentions in the writings of Columbus and his son about the fact that the Spaniards liked cassava bread, but overall, the comments dealt with the problems of adaptability: "Their hardships were increased by the fact that they were not yet accustomed to eating the food of the Indians, as people do now who live and travel in these parts."

Columbus was the first European to taste a pineapple. One of his men described it as being "in the shape of a pinecone, twice as big, which fruit is excellent and it can be cut with a knife, like a turnip and it seems to be wholesome." Columbus noted that the cultivated pineapple was better than the wild ones, which is confusing because there were no wild pineapples. Like maize, they depended upon mankind for reproduction, in this case from clones by cutting and planting the tops or from sprouts at the bottom of the plants, much like agaves.

In addition to the pineapple, Columbus was also the first European to see cacao beans. In 1502, on his final voyage to the New World, he noticed a large Maya trading canoe in the Gulf of Honduras. In the canoe, he saw some objects that looked like almonds and the natives scrambling to pick them up "as if their eyes had fallen out of their heads." But to Columbus and his men, the cacao beans were not a food but rather a form of currency. Columbus admitted bringing maize back to Spain, and most food historians surmise that he did the same with the other foods he encountered, such as chile peppers and sweet potatoes. But documentary evidence supporting these claims is lacking, so it may have been other explorers who followed Columbus. In the long run, it really doesn't matter who gets the credit, because once the foods were established in the Old World, their movement around the world was a certainty.

Three Ships of Columbus. Engraving by F. E. Wright, 1892. Sunbelt Archives.

And the Columbian exchange went in both directions. In addition to the new foods Columbus and his men were discovering and bringing back to Europe, the Europeans were determined to re-create the familiar foods of the Old World in the New. On his second voyage, Columbus brought sugarcane, wheat, melons, onions, radishes, grape vines, and fruit trees. The addition of pigs, cattle, horses, and sheep forever changed the foods and cuisines of the Americas. Columbus was only visiting the frontiers of the New World settlements. Deep within Mexico, which had not yet been discovered, the top evolution of sophisticated Native American culture awaited the conquerors.

Cortés and Turkeys

Bernal Díaz was excited as the Cortés expedition marched along the causeway to the principal city of the Aztecs, Tenochtitlán, what is now Mexico City. They were approaching one of the largest cities in the world, with a population estimated at 100,000 to 200,000. By comparison, the Spanish cities of Madrid and Seville had only about 40,000 inhabitants each. Historian Buddy Levy, author of *Conquistador,* writes that the population was probably 200,000 to 300,000 and states that "many scholars agreed that at the time, Tenochtitlán was the largest city in the world." Hugh Thomas begs to differ. In his history of the same era, *Conquest,* he devotes five pages to a discussion of the population of Mexico, with estimates of the size of Tenochtitlán varying from a low of 70,000 to a high of one million and concludes, in the words of Nicolás Sánchez-Albornoz in 1976, it was "the largest city on the American continent . . . the precise size is still disputed, but it was unusually large for that age."

Díaz gushes, "With such wonderful sights to gaze on we did not know what to say, or if this was real what we saw before our eyes." He was writing nearly fifty years after he witnessed the sights and sounds of Mexico. "On the land side there were great cities, and on the lake many more." He described meeting "the great Montezuma" and detailed how Cortés gave him a necklace of colored glass beads and Montezuma's response: a necklace for Cortés crafted from carved crabs of solid gold. The date was November 8, 1519.

The Aztec world revolved around maize, from religion to the highest levels of government to the humblest houses. Friar

Bernardino de Sahagún, in his great work on the Aztecs, *General History of the Things of New Spain*, also called the *Florentine Codex* (1580), described eight varieties of maize, with white maize being, as the Aztecs put it, "our flesh and bones." Beans were also important to the Aztec diet, with twelve different kinds, and other significant crops were amaranth, cassava, chía, squash, agave, and cacti. But one of the most important of all was chile peppers.

"The chile seller . . . sells mild red chiles, broad chiles, hot green chiles, yellow chiles . . . water chiles, smoked chiles, small chiles, tree chiles, thin chiles, those like beetles. He sells

Chronicler of Conquest: Bernal Díaz del Castillo

We owe our knowledge and understanding of the exploits of Hernán Cortés to the eyewitness who accompanied the conqueror to Tenochtitlán, Bernal Díaz. Born the same year as Columbus's first voyage, Díaz didn't even finish his *True History of the Conquest of New Spain* until he was seventy-six and supposedly deaf and blind. Although criticized for being a poor stylist, he nevertheless made quite an impression on W. H. Prescott, who wrote the classic history *The History of the Conquest of Mexico*, in 1843: "He is among chroniclers what Defoe is among novelists. . . . All the picturesque scenes and romantic incidents of the campaign are reflected in his page as in a mirror."

Díaz was inspired to write the story of Cortés after reading two accounts of the conquest that he hated, one by Cortés's chaplain, Francisco López de Gómara, and the other by Gonzalo de Illescas. Of the latter, he wrote that de Illescas spoke the truth "neither in the beginning, nor the middle, nor the end." At this time he was in Guatemala, living out his life as the "oldest Conquistador of New Spain" in mostly impoverished conditions. He died there at the age of eighty-nine.

Bernardino de Sahagún, c. 1600. Artist Unknown. Sunbelt Archives.

hot chiles, the early variety, the hollow-based kind. He sells green chiles, sharp-pointed red chiles, a late variety. . . . Separately he sells strings of chiles, chiles cooked in an *olla*, fish chiles, white fish chiles." It's not too difficult to figure out what modern varieties he might be referring to. Mild red chiles are probably *guajillos*, one of the progenitors of the New Mexican pod type. Broad chiles are *anchos*, which means broad or wide in Spanish, while hot green chiles may be anything from *serranos* to immature *piquins*. Yellow chiles are probably the modern *güeros*, and blonde chiles and water chiles simply means irrigated chiles, much like the *chile de agua* in Oaxaca today. Smoked chiles are chipotles, smoke-dried red jalapeños, while tree chiles have not changed in four hundred-plus years—they are still *chiles de árbol*. The beetle chiles are *chiltepins*, and surprisingly, there is a modern variety with a very wavy skin that is called fish chile, although Sahagún is probably referring to a specific chile used in preparing fish ceviche of some sort. Every province in Aztec-controlled Mexico was required to provide an annual tribute of 1,600 bales of chiles to Montezuma.

Tomatoes had a similar number of varieties: "Leaf tomatoes, thin tomatoes, sweet tomatoes, large serpent tomatoes . . . coyote tomatoes, sand tomatoes, those which are yellow, very yellow, quite yellows, red, very red, quite ruddy, bright red, reddish, rosy dawn-colored." A quick glance at the tomato section of a large commercial seed catalog will reveal the same variation in tomato shapes, sweetness, and colors. That said, I'm still trying to decipher what a "serpent tomato" might be. And ever the budding historical humorist, Sahagún also wrote about the "bad" chile and tomato sellers, who sold produce that was "evil-smelling . . . insipid . . . spoiled . . . sour . . . [and] those which cause diarrhea."

Aztec chile and tomato breeders had evidently developed the progenitors of most of the "heirloom" varieties that we see today. The process began with wild forms that were "tolerated weeds," but their fruits were harvested and used mostly to spice up or flavor bland staple foods like cassava pudding. The invention of agriculture allowed growers to collect and save seed of their favorite forms and colors, which were continually replanted and rogue plants culled until a specific variety was developed. This selective breeding technique is still used today.

Chiles were added to many seafood dishes that were common in ancient Mexico. "They would eat another kind of stew, with frogs and green chile," Sahagún recorded, "and a stew of those fish called *axolotl* [salamander] with yellow chile. They also used to eat a lobster stew which is very delicious." Apparently the Aztecs utilized every possible source of protein. The friar noted such exotic variations as maguey worms with a sauce of small chiles, newt with yellow chiles, and tadpoles with *chiltecpitl*. Sahagún classified chiles according to their pungency, as evidenced by the following chart.

Nahuatl	Spanish	English
cococ	*picantes*	hot
cocopatic	*muy picantes*	very hot
cocopetzpatic	*muy, muy picantes*	very, very hot
cocopetztic	*brillantemente picantes*	brilliantly hot
cocopetzquauitl	*extremadamente picantes*	extremely hot
cocopalatic	*picantisimos*	hottest

Sahagún, one of the first behavioral scientists, also noted that chiles were revered as much as sex by the ancient Aztecs. While fasting to appease their rather bloodthirsty gods, the priests required two abstentions by the faithful: sexual relations and chile peppers. Chocolate and chiles were commonly combined in a drink called *chicahuatl*, which was usually reserved for the priests and the wealthy. Sahagún also discovered the earliest examples of dishes that have since become classics of Mexican cuisine: *tamales* and *moles*. The early versions of tamales often used banana leaves as a wrapper to steam combinations of masa dough, chicken, and the chiles of choice. Sahagún wrote that there were two types of "chilemollis": one with red chile and tomatoes, and the other with yellow chile and tomatoes. These *chilemollis* eventually became the savory *mole* sauces for which Mexican cuisine is justly famous.

Aztec cookery was the basis for the Mexican food of today, and, in fact, many Aztec dishes have lasted through the centuries virtually unchanged. Since oil and fat were not generally used in cooking, the foods were usually roasted, boiled, or cooked in sauce. Aztecs living close to either coast were fond of drinking *chilote*, a liquor made with *pulque* (fermented agave pulp), ancho chiles, and herbs. Since pork was not available until the Spanish arrived, the Aztecs would have used peccary (wild pig) meat. The main meal was served at midday and usually consisted of tortillas with beans and a salsa made with chiles and tomatoes.

Totollin-Chile Stew

Exact recipes did not appear in any of the works of Sahagún, Díaz, Motolinia, or Peter Martyr, but based upon a close reading of the food descriptions, I have re-created a probable Aztec turkey stew. Culantro is a New World herb that tastes much like cilantro.

Take four dried broad chiles (anchos) and soak them in water until soft. Combine them with three chopped hot green chiles (serranos), three ripe red tomatoes, and a half-handful of culantro *in a stone* molcajete. *Grind all together to make a paste. In a cooking vessel, place the paste, fresh turkey slices from a small bird with the skin removed, and water as needed. Cook for one hour or until the turkey is tender.*

The salsas were usually made by grinding the ingredients between two hand-held stones, the *molcajetes*. Even today, the same technique is used in Indian villages throughout Central America. A remarkable variety of tamales were also served for the midday meal. They were stuffed with fruits such as plums, pineapple, or guava; with game meat such as deer or turkey; or with other items such as snails or frogs. Whole chile pods were included with the stuffing, and after steaming, the tamales were often served with a cooked chile sauce. It was this highly sophisticated, chile-based cuisine that the Spanish encountered during their conquest of the New World.

Montezuma's feasts took Aztec cuisine to another level, that of royalty. "For each meal his servants prepared him more than thirty dishes cooked in their native style," Díaz wrote, "which they put over earthenware braziers to keep them from getting cold. They cooked more than three hundred plates of food the great Montezuma was going to eat, and more than a thousand for the guard. . . . Every day they cooked fowls, turkeys, pheasants, local partridges, quail, tame and wild duck, venison, wild boar, marsh birds, pigeons, hares and rabbits, also many other kinds of birds and beasts native to their country, so numerous that I cannot quickly name them. . . . Then four very clean and beautiful girls brought water for his hands in one of those deep basins that they call *xicales* [gourds]. They held others like plates beneath it to catch the water, and brought him towels. . . . Montezuma's food was served on Cholula ware, some red and some black. . . . Sometimes they brought him in cups of pure gold a drink from the cocoa-plant, which they said he took before visiting his wives. We did not take much notice of this at the time, though I saw them bring in fifty large jugs of this chocolate, all frothed up, of which he would drink a little. . . . They also placed on the table three tubes, much painted and gilded, in which they placed some liquid amber [gum from a native tree] mixed with some herbs, which are called tobacco. When Montezuma had finished his dinner, and the singing and dancing were over and the cloths had been removed, he would inhale the smoke from the tubes. He took very little of it, then fell asleep." This scenario must have been viewed by the Spanish as highly civilized.

One of the most popular meats in the Aztec kitchens was the turkey, one of the few domesticated animals (others were Mus-

Aztec Turkey: Chalchiuhtotolin, "Precious Night Turkey," as depicted in the Codex Telleriano-Remensis, c. 1550. Sunbelt Archives.

German Artist and Cookbook Author Marx Rumpolt's Turkey Illustration, 1581. Sunbelt Archives.

covy ducks, dogs, bees, and the cochineal insect used as a dye). Sahagún carefully described the turkey: "The native hens and cocks are called *totollin*. These are well known domestic birds having a round tail and feathers on the wings but they do not fly. They eat corn as mash when small, also cooked, ground pig-weed, and other plants. . . . The males are called *huex-olotl* and have a large dew-lap, a large breast and a large neck which has red tubercles. The female fowl is smaller than the cock and has tubercles on the head and throat. She submits to the cock, lays eggs, sits on them and hatches the poults."

Peter Martyr, who wrote a history of Cortés's siege of Mexico in 1525, never saw a turkey but said that a priest, Benito Martin, told him an "incredible" story that "the male has a deformation of the claws, making it difficult for him to mate unless someone lifts up the female for him. The hen does not mind being held and the male is not afraid of man. Therefore the moment he sees someone hold up his favorite hen, the peacock runs toward her, eager to copulate." This could be the ultimate domestication story.

Sahagún wrote that turkeys are "very good to eat, having the best meat of all birds." He preferred the hens, which were "very savory and fat." Gonzalo Fernández de Oviedo, in his natural history of the West Indies and Mexico in 1525, added that the turkeys, which he called peacocks for lack of a better term, were excellent: "The flesh of these peacocks is very good, and incomparably better and more tender than that of the peacocks of Spain."

The turkey was honored in a festival held every two hundred days. The Aztecs used turkey eggshells that they had saved and spread them on the roads "in memory of the goodness of the god who had given them fowl." An entire turkey was cooked, chopped, mixed with corn meal to make a tamale, and served with chile sauce. Turkey raising, like dog breeding, was hugely popular. Toribio de Benavente Motolinia, a Franciscan friar who wrote a history of the Aztecs in the mid-1500s, claimed that the market of Tepeyacac, outside of Tenochtitlán, sold eight thousand turkeys every five days, year-round. Another source claims that five hundred turkeys a day were used to feed the hawks and eagles in Montezuma's zoo. Turkeys were also required as a tribute by Montezuma and other lords. Since the people in towns like Mixquiahuala were required to give Montezuma a turkey every twenty days, hundreds of thousands of turkeys were given as tribute each year.

Food historian Andrew F. Smith believes that the turkey was domesticated in central Mexico prior to the Aztecs' arrival from the north and not long before the Europeans arrived. The Aztec word for the male turkey, *huexolotl*, was transformed into the modern Mexican Spanish term *guajolote* for turkey. Not only did the Aztecs roast the turkeys over fire, they combined them with dog meat and covered the slices with a sauce. Writes Smith, "The Aztecs also made a turkey stew," *totolmolli*, which is similar to today's *mole de guajolote*. Except, that is, for the fact that the Aztecs did not use chocolate in their foods—it was strictly a drink. Many versions of *mole* today, especially those from Puebla, contain turkey, chiles, and unsweetened chocolate. Aztec merchants gave turkey heads as religious offerings to celebrate a safe return to Tenochtitlán, and the turkey's wattle was thought to cause impotence. They were ground up and given to rivals or even enemies as a prank.

If we are surprised by the urban sophistication of the Aztecs in Mexico, equally stunning revelations occurred in South America. When one mentions the word "Amazon," we conjure up a vision of a relatively unspoiled wilderness half the size of the United States that from the beginning of time has been primeval and barely touched by mankind. The concept that at one time the Amazon Basin was tamed by man and consisted of settled towns interspersed with agricultural fields is shocking to say the least, but just such a scenario was proposed by Charles C. Mann in his 2005 book, *1491*.

In 1541, Francisco de Orellana, under orders from Gonzalo Pizarro, set off in a large boat with a crew of fifty-nine to explore the Napo River, near Quito, which flows into the Amazon River near Iquitos. Of course, he was searching for El Dorado.

Don Francisco Pizarro,
1728. Sunbelt Archives.

EL MARQUEZ DON FRANCISCO PISARRO
de Truxillo.

The five-month journey was documented by Gaspar de Carvajal, and his description "depicts a crowded and prosperous land." The farther they traveled down the Amazon, the more populous it became, with one 180-mile stretch "all inhabited, for there was not from village to village a crossbow shot." But because Carvajal also described tall, topless women who attacked them, starting the legend of Amazons, he was not believed and historians dismissed him as "*mentiroso*," full of lies.

Mann explains: "Physical scientists were unwilling to accept his depiction of the Amazon. To ecologists, the great tropical forest in South America was and is the planet's greatest wilderness, primeval and ancient, an Edenic zone touched lightly by humankind, if at all. Constrained by its punishing climate, poor soil, and lack of protein, these scientists argue, large-scale societies have never existed—can never exist—in the river basin. Amazonia thus could not have been the jostling, crowded place described by Cavajal." But anthropology tells a different story. "Far from being the timeless, million-year-old wilderness portrayed on calendars . . . today's forest is the product of a historical interaction between the environment and human beings—human beings in the form of the populous, long-lasting Indian societies described by Cavajal."

Of course, diseases were part of the Columbian exchange, and some estimates show that up to 95 percent of the indigenous population of the Americas were killed by them. After a disaster of that magnitude, the jungle reclaimed the Amazon Basin. And then there were the Incas.

Pizarro and Potatoes

"This city is the greatest and finest that has ever been seen in this realm or even in the Indies," wrote the Spaniards to King Charles V after their first sight of the city of Cuzco, astounded by its size and beauty much in the same manner as Cortés's men when they saw Tenochtitlán. One Spanish estimate gave the population of Cuzco as two hundred thousand, most likely an exaggeration, but the Incas controlled about eight million people over 1,500 square miles. And finally, the search for gold finally paid off in the New World. "These buildings were sheathed on the side where the sun rises with large plates of gold," wrote an amazed Cristóbal de Mena. And it didn't take the Spaniards long to figure out how to take it. Pizarro kidnapped the Incan emperor Atahualpa and held him for a modest ransom: eleven tons of pure gold and silver ingots. This was the beginning of the fabulous wealth that began flowing into the Spanish court and profoundly affected the economies of Europe. Food historian John Reader adds, "So too would another treasure which the Spaniards almost entirely overlooked: the potato."

At the heart of the Incan Empire was farming, which determined nearly every aspect of their society: the calendar, religion, law, and even war. The Incas were farmer-soldiers, likely to be called out of their elaborately terraced and irrigated fields at any time to defend the empire or extend its boundaries. But farming took precedence over fighting, and some later uprisings against the Spanish failed because the Incan soldiers left the battlefront to return to their fields.

Although farming was the top vocation, the economic system of the Incan Empire was a well-oiled engine that also included herding, fishing, mining, craft manufacture, and state service. Historian Kim MacQuarrie also noted: "Peasants were a crop, a crop that could be harvested through periodic taxation. Docile, obedient workers who created surpluses, in fact, were a crop more valuable than the five thousand varieties of potatoes that the Incas cultivated in the Andes." MacQuarrie exaggerates the number of cultivated varieties (the International Potato Center estimates 3,800), but his point about the peasants is well taken. The Incan system worked very well . . . until the Spaniards arrived.

It has been estimated that more kinds of foods and medicinal plants were systematically cultivated in the Andes than any-

Top: Atahualpa, Last Incan Ruler. Engraving by Eberhard Happel, 1688. Sunbelt Archives.
Bottom: Incan Chile Pepper Jar, c. 1500. Sunbelt Archives.

where else in the world at any time. The result of the Incan agricultural expertise included at least 240 varieties of cultivated potatoes, nearly as many kinds of beans, 20 types of maize, plus sweet potatoes, peanuts, pineapples, chocolate, avocados, papayas, tomatoes, and—of course—several varieties of the beloved chile pepper.

Maize, an ancient crop imported from Mexico and found in Incan graves dating to 3,000 BC, was grown in the lower altitudes while potatoes dominated in the mountains above the altitude of eight thousand feet, where it's too cold for all but the hardiest varieties of maize. Maize was easily transported after harvest and was the basis of a beer called *chicha*—still made and as nutritious as it is alcoholic. As vital as maize was to the Incan Empire, it was merely a supplement to the most valuable subsistence crop grown: potatoes.

The potato is a very tough survivor and probably sets the record for altitude at which crops can be grown, fifteen thousand feet. It grows in the poorest soil, is easy to harvest and store, and it will keep for months without rotting. It provides starch, needed calories and vitamins (especially C), and can be grown in rotation with other crops, such as quinoa. Its bitterness when immature is the result of glycoalkaloid compounds that are especially present in the wild forms of potatoes, and their more palatable cultivated forms required a twenty-fold reduction of those chemicals during the domestication process.

Potatoes might store well, but their preservation can be increased by turning them into *chuño,* a freeze-drying method that results in potatoes that can be stored for up to a decade. The freshly harvested potatoes are exposed to several nights of freezing temperatures, then rinsed for weeks in cold streams. Then they are refrozen and stomped on to remove the skins and excess water. The final process is to spread them out to dry in direct sunlight for two weeks. The result can be rehydrated and cooked in oil or butter with herbs and spices, like chiles, or just added to soups and stews as a thickening agent.

The great Incan civilization came to depend upon the chiles as their principal spice to improve the flavor of the bland potato, and chiles were a major crop by themselves. The half-Incan historian Garcilaso de la Vega, known as El Inca, wrote in detail about chile peppers and their place in Incan culture. In his *Royal Commentaries of the Incas* (1609), he noted that chiles were the favorite fruit of the Indians, who ate it with everything they cooked, "whether stewed, boiled, or roasted." He traced the nomenclature of the plant: The pods were called *uchu* by the Incas, *pimiento de las Indias* by the Spaniards, and *ají* by the people of the West Indies, a name that became quite common in the Andes in later times.

The Incas worshipped the chile pepper as one of the four brothers of their creation myth. "Agar-Uchu," or "Brother Chile Pepper," was believed to be the brother of the first Incan king. Garcilaso de la Vega observed that the chile pods were perceived to symbolize the teachings of the early Incan brothers. Chile peppers were thus regarded as holy plants, and the Incas' most rigorous fasts were those prohibiting all chiles.

According to El Inca, the Incas raised three types of chile. The first was called *rocot uchu,* "thick pepper," which described the long, thick pods that matured to yellow, red, and purple. The most likely identification of these chiles would be the ají type, *Capsicum baccatum.* Garcilaso forgot the name of the next type but wrote that it was used exclusively by the royal household.

The third chile he described was *chinchi uchu*, which "resembles exactly a cherry with its stalk." This type, with its name and cherry-like pods both still intact, has survived to this day in Peru and Bolivia; it is *rocoto, Capsicum pubescens*, a species with no wild form. El Inca noted that the *chinchi uchu* was "incomparably stronger than the rest and only small quantities of it are found."

Garcilaso also collected some chile anecdotes. Chiles were reputedly good for the sight, were avoided by poisonous creatures, and had been offered as one of the gifts to appease Pizarro and his invading soldiers. As a final culinary note, El Inca unconsciously predicted the spread of the chile around the world when he noted, "All the Spaniards who come to Spain from the Indies are accustomed to it and prefer it to all Oriental spices." Thus the invaders were conquered by the fiery foods of the Incas!

Most Incan dishes were vegetarian because fish and meat were luxuries—at least for the commoners. The Incan royalty, however, did consume fish caught in the rich coastal waters and Lake Titicaca and also ate deer, wild llama, guanaco, and a large rodent known as *vizcacha*. But the royalty would not consume dogs, domesticated ducks, and *cui* (guinea pigs)—meat sources beloved by the peasants when they could obtain them.

The Incas' morning meal was extremely simple: leftovers from the previous evening and a cup of *chicha*, the mildly intoxicating beverage made from fermented corn. Around noon, an Incan family would gather for the midday meal, which was prepared by boiling or baking because cooking oils and frying were unknown. Corn was often boiled with chile peppers, potatoes, and herbs to make a stew called *mote*. A similar dish has survived the test of time and is still prepared in the Andes today, and another midday meal of the Incas was *locro*, a stew made from sun-dried llama meat, dehydrated potatoes, and chiles. The evening meal was eaten at about five o'clock in the afternoon and was usually a soup or stew similar to the midday feast. Potatoes are still ubiquitous in Andean cookery.

But food was not the only use for the beloved chiles. According to historian L. E. Valcárcel, chile peppers were so highly valued in Incan society that they were probably used as currency. Since there were no coins or bills in those days, certain preferred products like chiles became part of a rudimentary monetary system. He noted that until the mid-twentieth century, shoppers in the plaza of Cuzco could buy goods with *rantii*, a handful of chiles.

The Incas decorated bowls and dishes with chile pepper designs, and one exquisite dish that was found near Cuzco and is dated circa 1400 to 1532 is painted with fish swimming amid two types of chiles. The fish appear to be catfish, and the chiles closely resemble Garcilaso de la Vega's description of *rocot uchu* and *chinchi uchu*, mentioned above. Chiles also were the subject of embroidery designs. One example of textile art of the early Nazca period is a cotton cloth with twenty-three figures of farmers carrying their crops embroidered in yarn. One of the farmer figures is wearing chile pods around his neck and is carrying a plant bearing pods.

About AD 900, a sculptor of the Chavín culture in Peru carved elaborate designs into a sharp-pointed granite shaft measuring eight feet long and a foot wide that has become known as the Tello Obelisk. The principal figure on this obelisk is a mythical creature, the black caiman. The sharp point of the stone corresponds to a real caiman's narrow snout, and the end of the stone is carved with the feet and claws of the reptile, which are holding the leaves and pods of a chile plant. As yet, no scholar has deciphered the meaning of a magical caiman grasping chile peppers in its claws, but the image is suggestive of the magical powers that the people of the Andes believed were inherent in the powerful pods.

Tello Obelisk, Peru, c. 500–200 BC. Sunbelt Archives.

The Lord of Sipán and His Golden Peanuts

The peanuts of South America are mostly ignored by food historians and cookbook authors who have been dazzled by the wealth of Peruvian potatoes. But in another example of archaeology's playing a major role in food history, the excavation of Moche royal tombs in northwestern Peru has revealed the importance of the peanut in pre-Incan culture—and it's a weird tale. The tomb robbers known as the Bernal brothers began their dig at Huaca Rajada ("cracked pyramid") in February 1987 after threatening Ricardo Zapata—a squatter who lived there—at gunpoint. Emil Bernal, the leader of the brothers, was an unemployed truck mechanic. Huaca Rajada was a large, unguarded adobe structure associated with the Chimu culture, but what Bernal found twenty-three feet down was from the Moche culture, which existed eight hundred years before the Chimus. Bernal had spotted some gold beads in the roof of his little tunnel and started digging them out when the tunnel collapsed on top of him. He screamed for help, and his two brothers and several other conspirators began to dig him out, in doing so discovering a treasure trove of gold and silver artifacts that represented some of the finest examples of Moche metallurgy ever found. For our purposes here, the most significant finds were gold and silver peanuts that never had been found before.

The peanuts were three-dimensional, perfect replicas that were several times larger than the underground legumes, with one side silver and the other half gold. Bernal sold the peanuts to buy cocaine, and soon they made their way into the illicit trade in Peruvian artifacts. More beads were unearthed later by an archaeologist named Walter Alva after Emil Bernal, who, completely stoned, resisted the police raiding his house to recover the peanuts, was shot in the liver, and soon died.

Alva, who was the director of the nearby Bruning National Archaeological Museum, was called by police and at the station inspected a rice sack with twenty-three beautiful gold and silver artifacts. Alva knew he had to visit the Huaca Rajada site, but when he arrived the next morning, the site was crawling with hundreds of villagers searching for anything of value. As Daniel Radthorne wrote in his article "Poverty, Pots and Golden Peanuts," "Most archaeologists assumed that the tomb was sacked and anything of value would be long gone, but Alva's intuition told him there was more to find." His intuition was right, and it made Alva's career.

El Inca, the Historian

Garcilaso de la Vega, "El Inca," was one of the first Peruvian mestizos, born of the union between an Incan princess, Isabel Suarez Chimpu Ocllo, and the prominent conquistador captain Sebastiàn Garcilaso de la Vega y Vargas. As a child he first learned Quechua and then Spanish before studying Latin in Cuzco. He studied in Spain but soon learned that his mixed parentage prevented him from  achieving the status he thought he deserved, and he did not succeed in the military and was refused royal patronage. But after inheriting a small fortune from his paternal uncle, he turned to scholarship and soon established himself as a European humanist of the highest caliber, calling himself *El Inca* on the title pages of his books. He wrote *La Florida del Inca* (1605) and the *Comentarios Reales de los Incas,* part 1 in 1609 and part 2, the *Historia General del Peru,* published posthumously in 1617.

The first volume of his history tells the story of the origins and rise of the Incan Empire, using accounts sent by native friends in Peru combined with his own own childhood memories, which recounted stories handed down by his Incan relatives. His message was that the Incas were a noble people deserving respect and perhaps a role in the governing of their own land.

The second volume describes the violent events of early colonial Peru and suggests that the Spanish takeover was a disaster for the region. In an age of Inquisition, racial intolerance, and banned books, he argued that the region needed a new, enlightened regime that understood the language and traditions of both the Incas and the Spanish. The response from the government in Spain was the seizure of all known copies of his history, and they were hidden away until colonial independence in the nineteenth century.

El Inca died on April 23, 1616. He was buried in Córdoba's cathedral and is remembered with pride in both Spain and Peru.

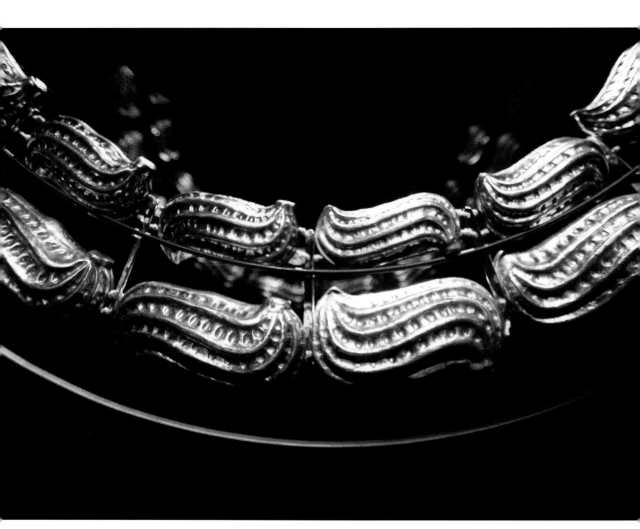

Gold and Silver Peanut Necklace Found in the Tomb of the Lord of Sipán. Displayed at the Museo Tumbas Reales de Sipán (Royal Tombs of Sipán Museum), Lambayeque, Peru. Photograph © Peter Langer/ DanitaDelmont.com.

The police chased away the villagers, seized the site, and soon Alva and his team were excavating the tomb of the Lord of Sipán under the twenty-four-hour-a-day protection of an armed guard. Three and a half months later, in June 1987, Alva's men found two more tombs next to the looters' main shaft. These were the tombs of Sipán's rulers and had more gold and silver beads, which were soon determined to be part of a complete peanut necklace with ten golden peanuts on the right side and ten silver peanuts on the left. The necklace was positioned on the chest of the skeleton of the Lord of Sipán. But what did the peanut necklace signify?

Archaeologists, of course, have their theories. Steve Bourget, author of *Sex, Death, and Sacrifice in Moche Religion and Visual Culture* (2006), believes that "the use of symbolic dualities linking life and death, humans and beings with supernatural attributes, and fertility and social reproduction allowed the Moche to create a complex system of reciprocity between the world of the living and the afterworld." The anonymous author of the Wikipedia article "The Lord of Sipán" suggests that "the peanuts symbolized that men came from the land, and that when they die, they return back to the earth; the Moches harvested peanuts for food. The necklace has . . . kernels to the right, which are gold, signifying masculinity and the sun god, while the kernels on the left side are silver, to represent femininity and the moon god." These interpretations may well be true, but I prefer the more practical and food-related theory of archaeologist Rebecca Stone-Miller, author of *Art of the Andes: From Chavín to Inca* (1995): "The peanut necklaces is one of many half-gold, half-silver ornaments found in the tombs, expressing duality in yet another form. . . . They are sheet metal beaten into fully three-dimensional hollow forms, the largest peanut being 3.5 inches (9 cm) long. Peanuts may seem an unlikely subject for such an important personage to flaunt, but scientists have determined that around this point, AD 300, a new type of peanut was domesticated. The premium on protein sources in a marginal environment made such a foodstuff politically valent, its representation symbolizing a leader's power over natural fertility and people."

Supporting Stone-Miller's interpretation are other peanut-decorated finds that are definitely food-related. One is a bottle in the shape of a human being in the form of a peanut with its head on a potato, with the spout contained on the top of the semicircular handle—it resides in the collection of the National Museum of Anthropology, Archaeology, and History in Lima. Another fascinating bottle with a spout in the handle was what's called a stirrup-spout bottle, with two gourd plates on top of each other. A plate that looks more like a shallow bowl filled with peanuts is resting atop an identical plate filled with ají chiles, showing the connection of peanuts and chiles in early Peruvian cuisine. The combination still exists today in the *ocopa* sauces served over potatoes. Margaret Ann Jackson, author of *Moche Art and Visual Culture in Ancient Peru* (2008), believes these pots represent a form of ritual offerings by humans to supernatural beings at certain times of the year, like when peanuts and chiles were harvested. Both the remains of peanuts themselves and their "extraordinarily life-like representations" on jars and textiles show how much the Moche depended on peanuts, according to Margaret A. Towle, author of *The Ethnobotany of Pre-Columbian Peru* (2007), and she notes that earthenware pans with painted peanuts on the handle were probably used to parch peanuts.

In 1988, Alva's findings in Sipán were described by the National Geographic Society as the richest, intact pre-Columbian tomb in the Western Hemisphere. Alva received the Orden del Sol del Peru (Order of the Sun of Peru) in 1990. It is the highest award bestowed by Peru to commend notable civil and military merit. The prize is the oldest civilian award in the Americas, dating back to 1821, and Alva owes this award to the tomb robbers.

Another peanut theory was unknowingly advanced by A. Hyatt Verrill in his 1937 book, *Foods America Gave the World*. Verrill, who is hardly remembered today, was an excellent researcher and writer whom one critic called "one of the most prolific and successful writers of our time," with 115 books to his credit. I knew of him because I had read *Smugglers and Smuggling* (1924), one of the better books on that subject. Since he was a solid researcher and an amateur archaeologist, it didn't surprise me to read these lines: "Almost every mummy of the Incan and pre-Incan people is provided with its ration of peanuts on its journey to Hamack, the Incans' Heaven. As a rule, these peanuts, interred with the dead hundreds or even thousands of years ago, are in an excellent state of preservation. Indeed, in many cases, they are scarcely changed after being buried for centuries, and I have even roasted and eaten peanuts taken from the tombs of Incan mummies." If ordinary peanuts would last that long, perhaps the priests who buried the Lord of Sipán gave him gold and silver peanuts so that his journey to Hamack would go on forever, granting him immortality because symbolically he was not deceased until he arrived. Before I go too far out on this hypothetical limb, I have to ask the question: Why were the peanuts hollow?

Peanuts, completely ignored in Europe (except for France) after the Columbian exchange, were a boom crop in Africa—particularly Senegal—in the late 1890s, and their importance to African cuisines along with maize, chiles, avocados, and cassava is recounted in Part 5. They also had flings of importance in India and China in various centuries, and I report on those along with the importance of maize and sweet potatoes in Parts 6 and 7.

Between New World and Old

People who want to rewrite history and blame Columbus solely for spreading diseases and importing Old World foods and livestock should do some research and understand that Columbus was merely the tip of the iceberg, the explorer who started the New World fad. Many others who followed were strictly driven by profit motives and the desire to find treasure in the New World, regardless of whether it was gold, silver, or crops that could be grown in the Americas and sold in Europe or to the new settlers. And one of the first of these profit-hungry adventurers was not Columbus but rather Cortés. William Dunmire, author of *Gardens of New Spain* (2004), maintains that "Cortés, too often identified solely as an infamous conqueror, was a man of multiple interests." And one of his main interests "was an ambition to oversee development of a Mexican economy based on integrating Old World Agriculture with what was then being practiced in the New." Cortés, now a major land owner, first planted sugar cane on his estates for refining into much-needed sugar, then directed his laborers to plant maize, beans, and chiles, and additionally, his favorite Old World crops. The result? "In no time, apple, peach, pear, plum, and citrus orchards had been established and were starting to bear fruit," Dunmire writes. And the Mediterranean vegetables such as carrots, cauliflowers, turnips, horseradish, and lettuce "were not only grown on various estates, but as early as 1526, surplus produce was available and for sale in the markets of Mexico City."

But what the Spanish settlers of Mexico missed most of all was bread made from wheat, not native corn. "Fortunately," adds Dunmire, "cool, moist winters and warm summers of the Valley of Mexico proved productive, if not ideal, for growing wheat, and Cortés had his Indian laborers planting it shortly after receiving his first shipment of seed grain. From then on most Spaniards were able to enjoy fresh leavened bread, and wheat bread regained its accustomed culinary prominence as the colonial empire swelled." John Super, author of *Food, Conquest, and Colonization in Sixteenth-Century Spanish America* (1998), adds: "Despite the expense and obstacles, Spaniards planted wheat with an intensity lacking with other crops. Wheat was a cultural imperative, a driving force that shaped the social and physical landscape. Where wheat was planted and survived, Spanish society took root and grew."

The next Spanish food necessity was meat. Columbus is also blamed for importing Old World livestock to the New and causing the environmental destruction wrought by pigs and cattle. It is true, as Alfred Crosby writes in *The Columbian Exchange*, that "the first contingent of horses, dogs, pigs, cattle, chickens, sheep, and goats arrived with Columbus on the second voyage in 1493."

Old World Foods in the Americas

Grains: barley, rice, wheat, rye.

Nuts: almonds, pistachios.

Fruits: apples, bananas, cherries, citrus fruits, eggplant, grapes, olives, melons, peaches, pears, plums, mangos.

Vegetables: cabbage, capers, carrots, celery, cucumber, spinach, lettuce.

Legumes: soybeans, fava beans, peas.

Herbs, Spices, Flavorings: basil, bayleaf, black pepper, cilantro, cinnamon, cumin, garlic, ginger, mint, mustard seed, nutmeg, parsley.

Tubers: beets, onions, turnips.

Meats: pigs, cattle, sheep, chicken, goats.

But Columbus alone did not cause the enormous livestock population increases—all of the Spanish and Portuguese explorers were doing exactly the same thing. As early as 1514, Diego Velásquez de Cuéllar wrote the King that the pigs he had brought to Cuba had increased to 30,000. And four years later, Alonzo de Zuazo in Hispaniola wrote that if thirty or forty cattle stray from the farm, they will grow to three or four hundred in three or four years, "breeding in the salubrious environment of the New World," as Crosby put it.

Pork was the first Old World meat to have a price set for it in Mexico City. In 1525, the price of fresh or salt pork was set at one *real* per pound. But the pigs bred faster than people could eat them, becoming

Hernán Cortés. Engraving by André Thevet, 1676. Sunbelt Archives.

a real nuisance in Mexico City, and increased supplies of beef and mutton caused the price of pork to drop by three-quarters of that a year later. Livestock devastated native crops, causing friction between the Spanish settlers and the Indians, and the Spaniards ridiculously accused the Indians of deliberately planting their crops where they *knew* that they would be destroyed by pigs and cattle.

Cortés, Party Animal of New Spain

After the news of peace between Spain and France reached Mexico City in 1538, the two most important men in Mexico, Cortés, the Marqués del Valle, and Antonio de Mendoza, the Viceroy, celebrated by settling their differences and throwing two parties described by Bernal Díaz as more elaborate than any he had seen in Castile and ones that rival similar feasts in Europe (especially Italy) of the same era that I describe in detail in *Da Vinci's Kitchen.* The celebration went on for days and had all the pageantry possible in Mexico at that time, and the food was all European except for now-sweetened chocolate drinks.

On the morning of the first party day, citizens awoke to find that the great plaza in Mexico City had been transformed into a forest, complete with trees, wild animals, and birds, all controlled

Rudolf II, Holy Roman Emperor Painted as Vertumnus, Roman God of the Seasons. Painting by Giuseppe Arcimboldo, c. 1590. Sunbelt Archives.

by Indians supervised by Luis de León, who apparently had the same skill as Da Vinci in producing large feasts. There were staged hunts and disputes between the Indian hunters, and even a black king and queen made an appearance. But that was just the beginning.

The next day the plaza became the island of Rhodes, seat of the knights of the Crusades, and Cortés played the role of the grand master of the Knights Hospitallers of Saint John of Jerusalem. The show featured four ships with sails and working cannons, and Indians dressed as Dominican monks from Spain. The Turks, played by Indians dressed in finery, tried to capture the Indians playing shepherds, and fake fighting broke out. The only way to stop the fighting, of course, was to release wild bulls into the plaza to separate the combatants.

Marzipan, candied citron, almonds, and confits were served to the great ladies watching the fray and dressed in their crimson, silk, and damask. The best wines were provided, as well as mead, spiced wine, and hot chocolate served with *suplicaciones,* sweet wafers. This was the prelude for the two banquets, one by Cortés (which Díaz says was very solemn, but with a lot of food), and one by the Viceroy that featured some kind of automatons in a skit that involved four Indians stealing the wineskins of a sleeping muleteer. The meal started with three salads, then roasted kids and hams, then pies of quail and doves, then stuffed chickens, then more fowl in *escabeche* (a vinegar-based sauce). The women were served empanadas stuffed with live rabbits and birds, which was undoubtedly influenced by a recipe from the first great chef and food writer of Italy. That would be Maestro Martino's Fluttering Pie (c. 1465), in which the very birds cooked in the pie (without feathers) were contrived to escape and fly to freedom. All of this food was carried by servants to the Spanish houses in the city so that everyone could enjoy the largess of Cortés and the Viceroy. Following this were bullfights, horse races, and a woman's foot race with gold jewelry as a prize. At last, the Spanish had succeeded in re-creating Europe in the New World.

In summary, then, because the Spanish and the Portuguese took charge of the New World and drove the natives into submission, their European foodstuffs were readily adopted everywhere and were rapidly assimilated into a mixed ethnic culture. But it was vastly different for the major New World crops headed east.

PART 2

THE CULINARY CENTURY: TURKISH WHEAT, INDIAN CHICKENS, AND FALSE PEPPER

"Turkish Wheat," New World Maize Varieties in Europe. Artist Unknown. Sunbelt Archives.

THE ENSLAVED PEOPLES OF THE NEW WORLD HAD NO CHOICE ABOUT WHETHER OR NOT TO ACCEPT THE OLD WORLD FOODS BROUGHT BY THE SPANISH AND PORTUGUESE. HOWEVER, AS NELSON FOSTER AND LINDA S. CORDELL WRITE IN *CHILIES TO CHOCOLATE* (1996): "THE OLD WORLD RECEPTION OF NEW WORLD CROPS WAS FAR FROM REGULAR OR PREDICTABLE. SOME STRUCK THE EUROPEAN FANCY AND WERE SOON SUCCESSFULLY TRANSPLANTED INTO ROYAL HOT HOUSES AND EXPERIMENTAL GARDENS, INCORPORATED INTO EXISTING CUISINES, AND APPRECIATED AS WORTHY ADDITIONS TO THE FOOD SUPPLY AND THE PANOPLY OF FLAVORS. . . . [BUT] SOME EQUALLY FINE AMERICAN CROPS WERE REJECTED OR WENT UNAPPRECIATED UNTIL THEIR VIRTUES WERE LATER DISCOVERED, OFTEN AS A RESULT OF ECONOMIC NECESSITY." HOWEVER ERRATIC AND INEXPLICABLE THE PROCESS, IN THE ENSUING CENTURIES NEW WORLD CROPS RADICALLY TRANSFORMED OLD WORLD EATING.

Opposite page: Red Pepper Plant with Insects. Botanical Illustration by Maria Merian, 1719. Sunbelt Archives.

What was Europe like during the "Culinary Century"? Raymond Sokolov, writing in *Why We Eat What We Eat* (1991), explains: "The national cuisines we find in European countries today evolved out of a pan-European medieval way of eating at about the same time that France, Italy, and Spain were defining themselves as nations in the modern sense of the word. New World ingredients influenced the growth of these cuisines every step of the way. They were not oddities grafted onto a full-grown, gnarly tradition of national cooking stretching back to the Caesars. Rather, they were naturalized into everyday cooking in an atmosphere of universal experimentation and invention."

An Exchange Becomes Globalization

The sixteenth century and a little beyond were a time of scientific, culinary, and entrepreneurial advancement as strange new crops and foods were introduced to the Old World from the New and vice versa. The momentous event of the cultural exchange of the most basic of human needs has produced two radically different opinions. On one hand there are the historians who—rather absurdly, in my opinion—wish it had never happened. One is Alfred W. Crosby, who coined the term "Columbian exchange" and believes that "the Columbian exchange has left us with not a richer but a more impoverished genetic pool. We, all of the life on this planet are the less for Columbus, and the impoverishment will increase." This negativity was published in *The Columbian Exchange* in 1972 and was fervently believed by a vast number of environmentalists—and perhaps an entire generation of Columbus-haters.

On the other hand, there are historians who take a much more positive view of the Columbian exchange. "American foods did much more for the world than merely provide a bonanza of calories and new crops for fields that had been only marginally productive in the past," wrote Jack Weatherford in *Indian Givers* in 1988, disagreeing with Crosby but not confronting him. "American food and spices made possible the development of national and local cuisines to a degree not previously imagined."

Gradually, scholarly opinion has shifted to a more positive and pragmatic view. In 2007, Kenneth F. Kiple, the distinguished editor of *The Cambridge World History of Food*, wrote: "Truly, the Columbian exchange was revolutionary in every sense of the word. It reversed an evolutionary tendency for the world's biota to grow ever more distinctive, even as it began rearranging available foods around the globe." And beyond that, he added: "It lay behind swelling populations and their renewed migrations, and gave rise to undreamed of commerce and enterprise. It ushered in the modern world." So much for Crosby's "impoverished genetic pool."

These days, the term "Columbian exchange" has been supplanted by a single word: globalization. Seemingly innocuous, the word is often used disparagingly. Historian Raymond Grew, author of *Food in Global History* (1999), notes: "An ungainly term, globalization often suggests a troubling determinism, a juggernaut that destroys rain forests, while multinational agribusinesses plow under family farms and capitalism forces peasants to move into cities and work for wages, thereby eroding social relations, undermining local customs, and subverting taste in culture and food." Another historian, William J. Bernstein, adds "'Globalization,' it turns out, was not one event or even a sequence of events; it is a process that has been evolving for a very, very long time."

So, again, we need a new term, and Kiple suggests that since in the West diets are no longer tied to regional food production, eventually global food will become homogenized. "Such food homogenization means that for the first time in human history, political will alone can eliminate global inequalities in the kinds and quantities of food available," he writes. "The next big question is whether the phenomenon of greater food availability will be canceled out by swelling numbers of food consumers." I would add to that another question: In the age of McDonald's and KFC being worldwide brands, will regional cuisines survive? Hopefully, they will. After all, since all of America is flooded with fast food franchises, Southern food is still popular in the region, and New Mexicans are not giving up their green and red chile peppers anytime soon. In fact, McDonald's sells green chile cheeseburgers now in Albuquerque. Perhaps it's not a question of survival for regional cuisines around the world but one of adaptation. By adding green chile to its condiment list, McDonald's is supporting New Mexico chile farmers. And with the growing popularity of regional foods, many fast food operations around the world are increasingly using locally produced foodstuffs.

The Maize Mystery in Europe

The word "corn" was a generic term in Europe that referred to whichever grain was the primary crop in a given place—so corn could mean barley or wheat, which makes a lot of references to "corn" suspect in older sources. Maize is a much more precise term, as it specifically refers to the species *Zea mays* L. and all its hybrids—specifically, New World corn.

There is a commonly held belief that when maize was first introduced into Europe, it was primarily grown as animal fodder and was thought to be an inferior food for mankind because it was somehow cruder than wheat or millet. It is true that it took maize hundreds of years to become accepted by elite diners and that some Europeans today disdain it. But historian William Langer, who studied the ties between American foods and Europe's population growth from 1750 to 1850, notes that "[b]y the eighteen century, it [maize] was grown everywhere south of a line from Bordeaux to Alsace, and had become the chief food of the peasantry." It was also grown extensively in northern Italy, where it also was the food of the peasant class, as we shall see. "In the more northern areas," Langer continues, "where only smaller varieties were planted, maize was used largely as fodder, having proved its popularity with horses, cattle, pigs and poultry."

Thus maize was eaten, as Waverly Root observed, "where it was accepted because there was nothing else to eat, as in Russia." It was eaten in Africa, too, where it was grown specifically to provide food for slaves on their voyages to the New World. "Among history's many ironies," wrote food historian Reay Tannahill, "is the fact that a cheap food designed to feed African slaves on their way to America should have resulted, in Africa itself, in a population increase substantial enough to ensure that the slavers would never sail empty of human cargo." This subject will be covered in more detail in Part 5.

Chile pepper expert Jean Andrews believes that the introduction of chile peppers around the world coincided with the spread of maize and that the Portuguese started growing maize and chiles in the Azores, Cape Verde Islands, and Guinea on the Gold Coast of Africa "as soon as they acquired the seed from a yet undetermined Spanish source late in the fifteenth century." She goes on to point out that "[w]hen maize was introduced to the island of São Tomé in 1502, the seed could not have come from the first Columbian landfall on the North American continent (1502–1504). She is somewhat supported by Pieter de Marees's *Description and Historical Account of the Gold Kingdom of Guinea* published in 1602 (some say 1604 or 1607), which has an illustration showing maize and peppers in the same engraving.

Andrews's findings add more speculation about the complex questions surrounding the introduction of maize into Europe. There is little doubt that Christopher Columbus returned to Europe with New World maize in 1493. However, a few scholars believe that maize was already growing in Europe and Africa at the time. In 1494, maize was introduced into Italy by the Cardinal Ascanio Sforza, brother of Leonardo's patron, Ludovico Sforza, after he was given the seeds by the diplomat and historian Pietro Martire d'Anghiera, also known as Peter Martyr, who received them directly from Columbus.

In the fall of 1495, in the Sforza Court at Milan, while working on *The Last Supper*, Leonardo wrote in his notebook a shopping list that included "white maize" and "red maize." It is difficult to confuse this with any other grain because he also mentioned millet, buckwheat, and wheat. The word used for maize is "melica," which in Latin means sorghum, but in Italian of the time it meant maize.

The appearance of maize in Leonardo's notebook just over two years after Columbus brought it back raises a number of questions. Was Leonardo referring to the maize seeds of Ascanio Sforza, or was maize already established as a crop near Milan? If we accept the first possibility, what was Leonardo doing with the maize seeds, along with the beans, millet, buckwheat, and peas that are mentioned along with the white maize and red maize? If maize was an established crop, did that really happen in only two growing seasons, 1494 and 1495? Was there enough time to plant the few seeds, do a seed increase in 1494, and have a significant crop in 1495? And another question demands to be answered: Did Ludovico Sforza encourage the planting of maize like he did the planting of rice, and is that one of the reasons that Lombardy became the largest maize-producing region in Italy and the center of the love of polenta?

Or, was maize already established in some parts of Europe? Interestingly, in 1498, Vasco da Gama, while sailing up the coast of East Africa, wrote of capturing a *barca,* or ocean-going vessel. "In the one we took we found seventeen men, besides gold, silver, an abundance of maize [*milho*] and other provisions." This seems to support the arguments of Andrews, above, who thinks that the Portuguese introduced maize to Africa prior to Columbus.

M.D.W. Jeffreys, in his article "Pre-Columbian Maize in the Old World," believes that these "widespread reports" of maize prior to 1500 "can only be explained by earlier introductions. His article, which he admits is a "linguistic study," cites reports of maize in Castile, Andalusia, Milan, and Portugal, plus extensive cultivation in Morocco and West and East Africa. This evidence, he concludes, "is only compatible with an introduction into Africa about the twelfth century and an introduction into Spain about the thirteenth century." Unfortunately for his theory, he cites no archaeological or ethnobotanical evidence to support the linguistic references.

Jeffreys believes that five years is too short a period of time for maize to move from Spain to East Africa and become established there, and he may be right. Food historian Alan Davidson seems to be somewhat swayed by Jeffrey's argument, pointing out the

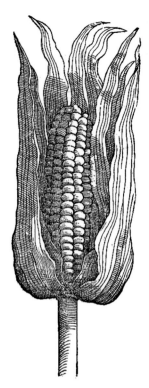

One of the Earliest Depictions of Maize in the Old World. Engraving by Giovanni Battista Ramusio, c. 1606. Sunbelt Archives.

*"Turkie Wheat,"
Different Colored
Maize Varieties
from* The Herball,
*or Generall Historie
of Plantes, by John
Gerard. First
Published 1597.
Sunbelt Archives.*

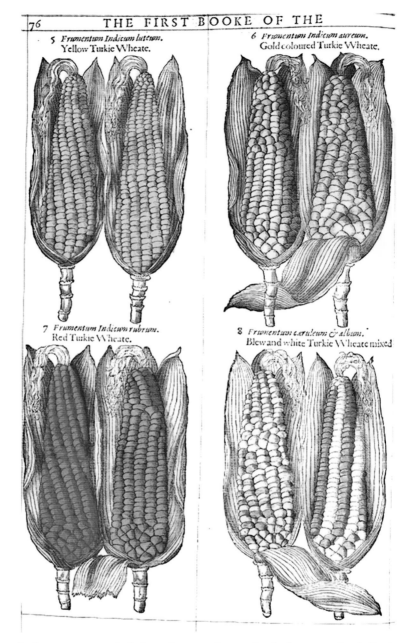

5 *Frumentum Indicum luteum.*
Yellow Turkie Wheate.

6 *Frumentum Indicum aureum.*
Gold coloured Turkie Wheate.

7 *Frumentum Indicum rubrum.*
Red Turkie Wheate.

8 *Frumentum cæruleum & album.*
Blew and white Turkie Wheate mixed

"inherent improbability that a plant which first reached Spain in 1492 could have been under cultivation in the E. Indies in 1496 and in China by 1516." However, once in Italy, it became established quickly in Lombardy and flourishes there to this day, along with rice.

"Turkish Wheat" Enters Society

It took longer for maize to be recognized by the herbalists and historians. In 1539, maize is mentioned in the herbal of Hieronymus Bock, and in 1543 in the herbal of Leonhard Fuchs. By 1554 maize was extensively cultivated in Polesina de Rovigo and Basso Veronese in Italy, but Waverly Root suggests that it was first grown in the Maccarese region, north of the Tiber River, where it was known as "Roman wheat." Botanical lists of garden plants grown in Europe during the 1500s referred to it as "Turkish wheat," "Asian wheat," and "Barbary corn." All of these names implied a foreign, or exotic, crop. In Turkey, it was called "*Roums* corn," or "foreign corn."

Initially, farmers grew maize because it produced more food (and thus more calories) per acre than did other grains. Another reason they grew it was that they could avoid paying taxes on it—the authorities simply did not consider it to be food for humans and did not want to accept it as in-kind taxes or rent. Because of this situation, there were no tax records for maize and its early spread across Italy and the rest of Europe was not well tracked. Only after maize attracted the attention of travelers and tax collectors did written records reveal its dispersion.

Maize gradually arrived in other regions of Italy as well as Lombardy. Luigi Messedaglia, author of *Il mais e la vita rurale italiana* (*The Maize in Italian Rural Life*, 1927), states that Andrea Navagero, a Venetian diplomat, visited another Venetian living in Seville, a botanist named Giovanni Ramusio, in the 1520s. Ramusio showed him maize under cultivation, and Navagero carried some maize seeds with him when he returned to Venice. Eventually, in 1545, Cosimo de' Medici and his wife, Eleonora di Toledo, acquired maize seeds that they called *grano indiano* (Indian corn, yet another name, probably referring to India rather than America) and grew them on their estate, Villa di Castello, near Naples. Meanwhile, up north, it took a while for maize to catch on around Venice, but by 1554, farmers in Polesine, southwest of Venice, were cultivating entire fields of maize.

Surprisingly, maize quickly entered the realm of Italian frescoes and decorative sculpture even before it was commonly grown in fields or served at meals. As early as 1515, the sculpture *Tentazione di Adamo* (*Temptation of Adam*), by Giovanni della Robbia, depicted images of maize plants in the Garden of Eden. A fresco decorating the walls of the hunting lodge of Emo Capodilista, painted around 1540, shows ears of green maize among the fruits and vegetables. And in 1550, marble decorations on the canal portal constructed below the Bridge of Sighs near the Palazzo Ducale also had ears of maize among the usual fruits and vegetables of the Italian garden. As food historian James C. McCann observes, "The early presence of maize as an iconographic symbol of abundance and exoticism suggests an expanding worldview within the Venetian consciousness."

Maize was being eaten by peasants, but what did chefs think when maize started commonly appearing in fields? Not much. In the seventeenth-century cookbooks of Stefani and Latini, it is called animal fodder. There is a single reference to it as "coarse wheat" in a soup in Scappi's *Opera* (1570), but at least he included a recipe, which he would not have done if he hadn't liked the new crop. He was, of course, one of the best chefs Italy ever produced and the personal chef to Pope Pius V. More on his contributions to the popularity of American foodstuffs in the turkey section of this part.

Scappi's Recipe for Maize Soup

"Coarse wheat" is a grain much larger than the one used to make bread, and in Lombardy one finds it in quantity. Select it and wash the dirt off of it, and soak it in water for ten hours, changing the water several times. Place it in a pot to cook with fatty meat broth. Add Milanese sausage or a piece of salted pork to give it flavor. Add cinnamon and saffron; cover the pot and cook it for no less than two and a half hours. Serve with cheese and cinnamon on top. This soup should be very thick and can be enriched with cheese, eggs, and pepper.

The Power of Polenta

Initial resistance to America crops was sometimes overcome by the familiarity factor. Food historian Waverly Root comments: "Europe resisted this strange new grain [maize] except where it borrowed familiarity by resembling foods already known, as in Italy, where it became the chief cereal from which polenta is made, the last in a series dating from Etruscan times." Thus the

history of maize in Italy is really the story of the transformation of the ultimate peasant dish, polenta into what is now considered to be a gourmet delicacy. Originally, before maize, it was a type of porridge or gruel was made with ground chestnuts, acorns, barley, or wheat. Then millet was the grain of choice (which gave it a golden color), or foxtail (*panico*), which was not cultivated as extensively.

After the introduction of buckwheat around the beginning of the sixteenth century, northern Italians began to use it to make polenta, and the result was a grainy, gray gruel with a sharper flavor. (It is still made this way in the Alpine valleys, where it is known as *polenta taragna*.) After maize was introduced and was widely grown around the middle of the sixteenth century, it was used to make polenta and was accepted not only because

La Polenta. Painting by Pietro Longhi, c. 1740. Sunbelt Archives.

it was easy to grow, but it returned polenta to its familiar golden coloration.

But there was a downside to the peasant polenta. Because it was the major part of the diet in the eighteenth and nineteenth centuries, consuming it almost exclusively in the diet resulted in outbreaks of pellagra, a vitamin-deficiency disease caused by a dietary lack of niacin and protein. Symptoms of pellagra are red skin lesions, diarrhea, dermatitis, weakness, mental confusion, and eventually dementia. Corn kernels that were treated with lime to remove the tough skin of the kernels in the New World made niacin available to the body and prevented pellagra, but this technique was not transmitted to Europe. But in reality, the polenta did not *cause* pellagra; the narrow diet of eating only polenta did. Eating a more varied diet would have prevented it, but during lean times, maize was all the commoners had to eat. This was particularly true during the food shortages of the eighteenth century, when peasants had no choice but to grow the most productive food crop available. This is a perfect example of the ability of maize to combat famines, but at a terrible cost if it is the only food to eat.

Polenta is an extremely simple dish that can take on many dimensions. It is a still a tradition, and in the words of Anna del Conte, author of *Gastronomy of Italy*, "Making it and serving it are a hallowed ritual." The dish is still so popular in Lombardy that Root notes that the "properly equipped family" owns a copper polenta pot (a *paiolo*), which is a special device used only for the cooking of polenta. And, of course, there must be a favorite carved stick or spoon to stir the basic mixture.

And that's what it is—basic, just cornmeal and salted water with the proportion of ground grain to water one to two. You pour the cornmeal into the boiling water and stir it constantly for an hour or so, and you have polenta. If you thin it out to make a breakfast gruel, that's *polentina*, which is often served with sugar and milk. Root notes that the quality of the final dish results from the particular grind of the cornmeal, coarse or fine; whether or not the polenta is removed from the heat or allowed to thicken over it; and the instincts and experience of the individual cook. Anna Del Conte adds: "In Veneto, polenta is also made with very fine powder which is sometimes white. It is called *polentina bianca*, and being thinner, it is spooned rather than cut. Although equally good, it is not as striking in appearance as the golden mountain that is proudly placed on a board in the middle of the table."

Noted northern Italian chef Lidia Bastianich observes, "When you shop for the makings of polenta, I'd recommend a medium- or coarse-grind, but a trip to an ethnic grocery for a coarser, unlabeled meal is worth the time it takes. A successful batch of polenta requires about forty minutes of close attention, which may account for its scarcity on Italian menus in the United States."

When the polenta is thick and creamy, it can be eaten with a little butter and a favorite spice (why not sugar?), or it can turn hard as it dries out. In dry form, polenta is similar to but not as grainy as cornbread, but it can serve a similar purpose. It can be flavored with pan juices from roasts, tomato sauces, and commercial sauces of all kinds, and the slices can be roasted, toasted, or fried (in butter and olive oil). The slices can then be used as sandwich bread, with fillings of cheese, tomatoes, meat sauce, and sausages, as with *torta di polenta* or as part of a casserole that could include sausage, mushrooms, and grated cheese.

Other polenta variations include *polenta e ciccioli,* which has pork cracklings (fried pork fat) and onions added to the polenta near the end of the cooking, which makes it stiff enough for slicing. It is served, of course, with grated cheese. *Polenta con bagna d'infern* has a very spicy sauce served over it, and the variations go on and on. The most unusual polenta recipe recounted by Root is *polenta coi osei,* a Venetian specialty that consists of very small songbirds—probably thrushes—that have been wrapped in fat and spit-roasted. Each bird is placed on its own slice of polenta that has been flavored with the drippings from the spit. Root could not resist in observing that the birds are caught in wire nets because they are too small to shoot.

With polenta, all that changes somehow stays the same, and even the older traditions are still intact. *Paniccia*, the traditional dish of the Feast of Saint Anthony the Abbot, is a polenta still made with millet on the day of the feast. In Abruzzo, a large cauldron of millet-based polenta is stirred with wooden paddles, and large chunks of pecorino cheese are added until the mass turns dark and creamy. Then the polenta is blessed by the priest and the feast begins.

But like many Italian dishes, polenta has entered the realm of the exotic, if not downright erotic. The phrase "stirring the polenta" is "sexually explicit," according to Elena Kostioukovitch, author of *Why Italians Love to Talk About Food*. She comments that *La Polenta*, by Pietro Longhi, painted around 1740, with "hot, scantily dressed serving maids can be seen pouring soft polenta from a cauldron onto a white cloth spread on the table. Both the seductive allure of the female body as well as the fervor of the collective movement, the stirring and ladling, are rendered in the painting." Well, perhaps these maids were considered "scantily clad" in 1740, but they look rather tame in the twenty-first century.

Europeans Adopt the "Indian Chicken"

The 2009 statistics from the Food and Agriculture Organization of the United Nations reveal that three European countries—France, Germany, and Italy—are among the top five countries in the world for turkey meat production. The U.S. is by far number one, but France is in second place with 468,000 metric tons produced. The story of how this happened is a tale of adventurers, chefs, politicians, and protein. The latter is particularly important because the Columbian exchange was one-sided in the protein department, with the Old World supplying the New with cattle, pigs, chickens, sheep, and goats and the New supplying the Old with just a single protein source: turkeys. (Cod doesn't count because they ranged all over the Atlantic Ocean, including Europe.)

Historians endlessly debate about when turkeys arrived in Europe and who brought them. One side, led by Sabine Eiche, author of *Presenting the Turkey* (2004), argues that in 1511, King Ferdinand of Spain ordered his chief treasurer in the West Indies, Miguel de Pasamonte, to send ten turkeys to Seville (five of each gender) on each ship sailing back from Spain. Food historian Andrew F. Smith begs to differ, noting, "It seems unlikely that he was referring to turkeys, however, because in 1511 few Spanish ships visited Central America, and no evidence for turkey raising in the West Indies before 1520 has surfaced."

Rather, Smith continues, the first turkeys were sent by Alessandro Geraldini, bishop of the island of Hispaniola, to Cardinal Lorenzo Pucci in Rome in 1520. "Turkeys were raised in Spain during the 1520s," Smith notes, "and quickly became an important food for the upper class." Seemingly, no documentation exists that explains whether the Spanish turkeys came from Rome

Wild Turkey. Male and Female.
Meleagris Gallopavo.

or from the New World. Such are the mysteries of the Columbian exchange.

Further complicating this issue is the fact that there was no common nomenclature for the birds in the various languages of Europe. For example, de Pasamonte used the word *pabo*, meaning *pavo*, or peafowl, by far the most prestigious bird eaten in Europe, though not the tastiest. *Pavo* could be a reference to a number of New World birds other than the turkey, including curassows, horned guans, and chachalacas, notes Smith, because many of them were tamed and kept in cages. All are large, turkey-like birds.

Once turkeys arrived in Europe, traders, breeders, and chefs called them whatever they wanted to, which yielded *galle d'India* or "Indian chicken" (Italy, referring to India); *tacchino* or "gob-

Wild Turkey, Male and Female, by Alexander Lawson. Plate from Charles Lucian Bonaparte, American Ornithology; Or The Natural History of Birds Inhabiting the United States, 1825-33. *Sunbelt Archives.*

bler" (Italy); *poules d'Indes* or "Indian fowl," shortened to *dinde* (France); *Indianischen Hanen* or "Indian rooster" (Germany); *pavo de las Indias* or "Indian peafowl" (Spain, referring to the West Indies); *gallina de la tierra* or "country hen" (Spain); and, finally, "turkey" (England). Precisely why the turkey is called that in English is extensively discussed in an entire chapter in Karen Davis's food history, *More Than a Meal* (2001), and is really not our main topic here. "In the history of avian nomenclature and species identification," she notes in an understatement, "the turkey has borne a burden of confusion."

That said, the simplest explanation why a turkey is called a turkey is found on the website World Wide Words: "This bird had been brought to England by merchants trading out of that area of the eastern Mediterranean called the Levant but whom the English called 'Turkey merchants' because that whole area was then part of the Turkish empire. The new bird was therefore called a 'Turkey bird,' or 'Turkey cock.'" Of course, the tale of the turkey would not be true food history if there weren't some controversy involved, and food writer Vivien Devlin asserts that the turkey was "first introduced to Britain from America in 1526 by William Strickland, a Yorkshire landowner."

Despite the fact that no one knew exactly what the turkey was, or what to call it, the bird itself was as spectacular as a peacock and a lot larger. One amazed Italian, Giovanmaria della Porta, described the bird in 1531 as "some sort of Indian peacock, stranger than anything an artist could ever imagine drawing." When the Indian chicken finally reached India, the Moghul Emperor Jahangir attempted to describe its iridescent feathers: "Its head, neck, and wattle constantly change color. When it is mating they are as red as can be—you'd think it had all been set with coral. After a while these same places become white and look like cotton. Sometimes they look turquoise. It keeps changing color like a chameleon." And Sabine Eiche concluded, "Here, then, was a creature even more bizarre than the ancient Roman *grotteschi* [fantastic human and animal figures in Roman grottoes and, later, tapestries], an example of nature producing something that surpassed manmade art in weirdness." She continues, "Although it was in Spain that the turkey first stepped onto European soil, it was in Italy that it was first portrayed in art. The Renaissance was at its height in Italy in the sixteenth century, and the turkey could not have entered the scene at a more auspicious moment."

That said, it is no wonder that artists simply loved to depict it in every form of art imaginable, including tapestries, paintings, etchings, sculptures, cartoons, and even serving dishes such as tureens in the shape of turkeys. Eiche, in her book, has an entire chapter that traces the representation of the turkey through the history of art, and some of the more noted artists that have portrayed the bird in various symbolic situations include Pieter Brueghel (*Invidia*, 1558), Vincenzo Campi (*The Poulterers*, c. 1580), Anne-Louis Girodet (*Mademoiselle Lange as Danaë*, 1799), John James Audubon (*Wild Turkey*, 1827), Claude Monet (*Les Dindons*, 1876), and Pablo Picasso (*Le Dindon*, 1942).

These artists portray the turkey as envy, anger, vanity, warmth (as in turkey-down feathers for stuffing pillows), pomposity, and nobility. One famous turkey bronze was commissioned by Cosimo de' Medici in the 1560s, who chose famous sculptor Giambologna to make a life-size bronze sculpture to be displayed in his grotto at Villa Castello near Florence. One art critic commented on the turkey's "ridiculous pomposity" and wrote that it lampooned a human figure dressed in a formal ruff and heavy robes. But the oddest portrayal (and most charming, in my opinion) is Girodet's *Mademoiselle Lange as Danaë*.

In this gorgeous and satirical painting, Mlle. Lange, a notorious Parisian actress who had once humiliated the artist, is portrayed as Danaë, who in Greek mythology was the mother

of Perseus by Zeus, who impregnated her in the form of golden rain (the gold coins in the painting, which also imply that she's a common whore). The mask of the satyr with extra large horns at bottom right (get it?) is one of Lange's lovers; the winged putto (a representation of a naked child in Renaissance paintings) is her daughter, fathered by yet another lover. The turkey, with the strange expression and a tail with an odd cherub in peacock feathers, represents her cuckolded husband, who is not only staring directly and wistfully at his wife's pudendum but is, as Eiche puts it, "foolish and vain." In other words, he is a real turkey. Do I need to point out the significance of Girodet's calling her "mademoiselle" when she is really "madame"?

They're Also Good To Eat

The flavor of turkey meat was first mentioned by Europeans when the Spanish historian Bernardino de Sahagún (see Part 1) described it in his *General History of the Things of New Spain*, written between 1545 and 1590. "[It] leads the meats; it is the master," he wrote. "It is tasty, fat, savory." Of course, other Spaniards were not reading this because it remained an untranslated,

De Gallopavo. Engraving by Conrad Gessner, 1555. Sunbelt Archives.

unpublished manuscript until centuries later. Meanwhile, other Europeans were discovering turkey's taste delights. In 1529, the banquet honoring the ascension of Charles V of Spain to Holy Roman Emperor featured a barbecued ox stuffed with sheep, hares, geese, and turkeys, and a contemporary illustration of the feast shows a turkey's head protruding from a cut in the belly of the ox.

Eiche wrote that her research indicated that between 1534 and 1542, turkeys were becoming common in French aristocrats' kitchens. Rabelais's second edition of *Gargantua*, published in 1542, has a new element in the elaborate feasts he described: the turkey. And his later book, *Pantagruel* (1548), mentions turkey cocks, hens, and poults that were served at the fictional feast of "The Gastrolaters," a group of court gluttons who worship the belly as a god.

In 1549, Catherine de' Medici hosted a banquet at the bishopric of Paris (a diocese of the Catholic church) where she served seventy "Indian chickens" that were actually less expensive than the peacocks, herons, pheasants, bustards, and cranes usually served. According to food historian Jean-Louis Flandrin, "[T]he turkey was accepted almost from the moment it arrived because all sorts of large birds were already served on aristocratic tables, including some that we consider inedible." In contrast to, say, a cormorant or a stork, the turkey must have been gourmet fare.

But not everyone was as enthusiastic about the turkey as Catherine de' Medici. Charles Estienne, who wrote a book on animal husbandry in France in 1564, *L'Agriculture et maison rustique,* commented caustically that the importer of the turkey "has done more for our gullet than for our profit." This is

Meleagris en Grec, Gibber en Latin, Coc d'Inde en Francoys.

Coc d'Inde. Turkeys, Thought to Originate in India. Illustration by Pierre Belon, 1555. Sunbelt Archives.

because "this bird is a regular oat bin, and abyss for foodstuffs," he wrote, and contrary to others who praised the beauty of the bird, Estienne sniffed, "[M]oreover, they are filthy and hideous to look at because of their deformed heads." And he was not impressed by their flavor. "While it is true that the meat of the turkey is delicate," he acknowledged, "it is also tasteless and difficult to digest." Finally, he wrote that they ate as much as a mule, certainly a gross exaggeration. Perhaps he had once been attacked by a turkey cock in heat.

However, Estienne was in the minority, and the turkey continued to gain favor in Europe. In 1570, turkeys were served at the banquet for the marriage of Charles IX of France and Elizabeth of Austria, which led lords who attended the feast to begin raising turkeys on their estates. During such banquets, the roasted turkeys were presented at the table in full plumage, much as peacocks were, but Root points out that the bird displaced by the turkey was not the peacock but the goose. In the same year, the finest chef in Europe was featuring the turkey in a soon-to-be-famous cookbook.

Bartolomeo Scappi, the personal chef for Pope Pius V and the manager in charge of the Vatican kitchens, published *Opera dell'arte del cucinare* (*Works of the Art of Cooking,* 1570), with more than a thousand recipes of mostly Italian Renaissance cuisine with techniques and tools, including the first known picture of a fork. Turkeys and recipes with them are mentioned dozens of times in contrast to the goose, referenced but once. Scappi recommends blanching or brining the turkey first and then, if it is not fat, larding it with pork fat and studding it with a few whole cloves. It can be stuffed with goat liver and mint, marjoram, egg yolks, pepper, cinnamon, plus prunes, cherries, gooseberries, or grapes. He also suggests another stuffing of grated cheese, garlic cloves, and sautéed spring onions and another consisting of "marbled prosciutto," herbs, raisins, and either artichoke hearts or field mushrooms.

After Scappi's book appeared, cooks and writers in other countries quickly popularized the turkey. In 1581, Marx Rumpolt published *Ein New Kochbuch*, with an entire section on *Indianischen Hanen* with forty-plus turkey recipes borrowed from Scappi. The appearance of a cookbook so heavily turkey-oriented indicated that turkeys, which had been introduced around 1530, were common in Germany by this time. Meanwhile, in Spain in 1599, the first Spanish turkey recipes were published in Diego Granado's *Libro del arte de cocina* (*Book of the Art of Cooking*). These recipes included roast turkey, a sauce, and wine-marinated turkey.

The National Bird and Tales of Truffled Turkeys

Benjamin Franklin was a champion of American foodstuffs and wrote essays praising maize and defending American corn against Europeans who called it "pig food." While in Paris as an American ambassador during the later stages of the American Revolution, he also praised the turkey, which of course was already popular in France. Probably influenced by memories of delicious Thanksgiving dinners, he was particularly fond of the American turkey, writing to his daughter, Sarah Franklin Bache, from Paris in 1784: "For my own part I wish the Bald Eagle had not been chosen as the Representative of our Country. He is a Bird of bad moral Character. . . . For in Truth the Turkey is in Comparison a much more respectable Bird, and withal a true original Native of America. Eagles have been found in all Countries, but the Turkey was peculiar to ours, the first of the Species seen in Europe being brought to France by the Jesuits from Canada, and serv'd up at the Wedding Table of Charles the ninth. He is besides, tho' a little vain and silly, a Bird of Courage, and would not hesitate to attack a Grenadier of the British Guards who should presume to invade his Farm Yard with a red Coat on."

Benjamin Franklin. Portrait by Joseph Siffred Duplessis, 1798. Sunbelt Archives.

But Franklin was a lightweight when compared to France's most influential proponent of the bird, Jean Anthelme Brillat-

Savarin, author of *Physiologie du goût* (*The Physiology of Taste*), published in 1825. He called the turkey "certainly one of the most glorious presents made by the new world to the old" and then discussed his favorite bird:

> The turkey is the largest, and if not the finest, at least the most highly flavored of the gallinaceous family. It has also the advantage of collecting around it every class of society. When the virgin dresses, and farmers of our countries wish to regale themselves in the long winter evenings, what do they roast before the fire of the room in which the table is spread? A turkey. When the mechanic, when the artist, collects a few friends to enjoy a relief which is the more grateful because it is the rarer; what is one of the dishes *always* put on the table? A turkey stuffed with Lyons sausage and with chestnuts of Lyons. In the highest gastronomical circles, in the most select reunions, where politics yield to dissertations on the taste, for what do people wait? What do they wish for? A *dinde truffée* [truffled turkey] at the second course. My secret memoirs tell me that its flavor has more than once lighted up most diplomatic faces.

In his essay on truffles, Brillat-Savarin noted, "About 1780 truffles were very rare in Paris, and they were to be had only in small quantities at the *Hotel des Americans,* and at the *Hotel de Provence.* A *dindon truffée* [truffled turkey] was a luxury only seen at the tables of great nobles and of kept women." In the forty-five years between 1780 and his book's publication, the situation had radically changed, and truffles and turkeys were everywhere: "I have reason to believe, that between the first of November and the end of February, three hundred *dindon truffées* are consumed *per diem.* The sum total is 30,000 turkeys."

And that's an astonishing figure considering the relative newness of the bird, but it probably reflects the rise of the restaurant in nineteenth-century France, and in Paris in particular. In 1835, two new words entered the *Dictionnaire de l'Académie française* (*Dictionary of the French Academy*), "gastronomy" and "restaurant," and this is probably not a coincidence, as dining out was becoming the rage in France. At this time, there were more than two thousand restaurants in Paris, up from about a thousand ten years earlier. Prior to the Revolution, there were fewer than a hundred restaurants, so a boom was happening that was triggered by the concept of gastronomy. "Gastronomy," wrote Brillat-Savarin, "is the analytical knowledge of everything related to man's eating. Its aim is to ensure the preservation of mankind by means of the best possible nutrition."

Besides these noble aims, gastronomy was, according to French food historian Alain Drouard, "a means of legitimizing the new social hierarchy that had emerged from the French Revolution." He noted that gastronomy joined the old ruling class, the aristocracy, and the new, the bourgeoise, by subjecting both of them to the same culinary laws. What resulted was "French" cuisines, whether it was *cuisine de province* (regional cooking), *cuisine de bourgeoise* (domestic cooking), or *grande* or *haute cuisine* (fine dining), and all three variations were reflected in Parisian restaurants of the nineteenth century and the rise of *chefs de cuisine*.

Chefs de cuisine originally worked for the nobility. But with the rise of the middle class and urban centers in the early nineteenth century, these chefs moved from private venues to oversee open restaurants and their kitchens. An example is Antoine Beauvilliers, who was the head chef for several noble houses but eventually moved to Paris and opened a hallmark fine dining restaurant, La Grande Taverne de Londres, in 1782. Beauvilliers was a friend of Brillat-Savarin, who wrote that the chef was "the first to combine the four essentials of an elegant room, smart waiters, a choice cellar, and superior cooking." Perhaps foreshadowing the celebrity chefs of today, Beauvilliers wrote a cookbook, *L'Art du cuisinier* (*The Art of the Cook,* 1814), that was republished in a British edition in 1827, in which the truffled turkey was prominently featured.

Thus the turkey played a key role in the development of Parisian fine dining restaurants, and its prevalence caught the attention of French novelists as well as food writers. In Alphonse Daudet's *Three Low Masses* (1866), Father Balaguère and his sacristan (church curator of sacred objects) are momentarily possessed by the devil and commit the sin of gluttony by envisioning "two magnificent turkeys stuffed with truffles. . . . The skin had been stretched so tightly you would have thought it was going to burst as it was roasting."

And Alexander Dumas, the famous author of *The Three Musketeers, The Count of Monte Cristo,* and *The Man in the Iron Mask,* was also a gourmand of the highest repute who was fascinated by truffled turkeys. In his culinary dictionary, *Le Grand dictionnaire de cuisine,* published posthumously in 1873, he told a funny story.

> Avignon has always been a place where one ate marvelously well; it has traditionally been so since the time it was a papal town. A worthy president of the tribunal in that town appreciated the qualities of the turkey. One day he said:
>
> "Really, we have just eaten a superb turkey. It was excellent, crammed with truffles up to its beak, tender as a fat pullet, plump as an ortolan [a bunting], fragrant as a thrush. To be sure, we left only the bones."
>
> "How many were you?" inquired someone curiously.
>
> "We were two, sir!" he replied.
>
> "Two? . . ."
>
> "Yes, the turkey and me."

Dumas did not stop with simply laughing about and exaggerating truffled turkeys; he included a detailed recipe for the dish and insisted that previous cooks who wrote that the turkeys should not be plucked before being truffle-stuffed were dead wrong. That way, "the truffles lose what they give," he wrote; "all the pores remain closed and there is no evaporation." He did note that not too many people could spend forty francs (roughly $100 today) on the number of truffles needed to stuff a large turkey, so he included a recipe for Artists' Turkey, in which the turkey was stuffed with veal, chicken, partridge, sausage, celery, chestnuts, and parsley. Dumas hated the technique of basting a roasting turkey with broth and admonished, "Above all, do not baste your roasts, whatever they are, except with butter into which you have worked salt and pepper. Any cook who puts a single drop of bouillon into his dripping pan deserves to be thrown out on the spot, and banned from France."

Even musicians were reduced to tears by this classic, expensive poultry roast. "I have wept three times in my life," the Italian composer Gioachino Rossini admitted. "Once when my first opera failed. Once again, the first time I heard Paganini play the violin. And once when a truffled turkey fell overboard at a boating picnic."

Turkey Traditions Today

The United Kingdom is seventh in the world in what the FAO, the Food and Agriculture Organization of the United Nations, terms "Indigenous Turkey Meat Production," and much of that production is holiday-related. The turkey first appeared on Christmas dining tables in England in the sixteenth century, and popular

---

Turkey Roasted with Truffles (*Dinde aux Truffes et a la Broche*), by Antoine Beauvilliers

Note that as early as 1814, only the neck of the turkey was stuffed with the truffles, and the cavity of the bird was apparently empty. My theory holds that the cost of truffles grew so high that it was ridiculous to think of stuffing the cavity of a twelve-pound hen with just truffles. Because France had excellent chestnut harvests, they replaced truffles in the stuffing except as an occasional flavoring, and today chestnuts are the base for holiday turkey stuffings in France.

Take a white fat turkey hen; prepare and open it at the craw; take care not to break the gall; if that should happen, it will be necessary to wash it, by putting several waters through the body; take three or four pounds of truffle, clean it with care; take out any musty ones, and hash those that are defective; pound a pound of fat lard, put it into a stew-pan with the minced truffles, as also the whole ones; season with salt, large pepper, fine spices, and a bay leaf; pass the whole upon a slow fire, and let them simmer from a half to three quarters of an hour, take them off the fire and shake them well; let them be nearly cold when the turkey is stuffed with them, which must be to the throat sew it up; truss and cover it with slices of bacon leave it three or four days to take the perfume; spit it wrap it in strong paper; give it two hours; take the paper off, and let it take a good colour.

A Domestic Male Turkey Displaying. It's Easy to See Why Turkey Was A Favored Bird of the Nobility. Photograph by Hatmatbbat10, 2005. Sunbelt Archives.

history recounts that King Henry VIII was the first English monarch to have turkey for Christmas dinner. This tradition of dining on turkey at Christmas rapidly spread quickly throughout England in the seventeenth century, when turkeys were brought to London in large numbers from Cambridgeshire, Suffolk, and Norfolk. And how did they get there? "They were driven to the city on foot," writes British food historian C. Anne Wilson, "beginning their journey in August at the end of the harvest, and taking three months along the way." By arriving in early November, there was enough time to fatten them up for Christmas dinner.

These days, approximately 90 percent of U.K. families will serve roast turkey as the centerpiece of their Christmas dinner. As with cooks in the U.S., the main variation is the type of stuffing used. I searched dozens of online sources to determine which stuffings were the most popular and found that the recipes varied enormously. The stuffings ranged from simple breadcrumbs with apples to sausage variations or minced pork to dressings based upon chestnuts, cashews, or pine nuts. Other stuffings included gingerbread, cornbread, or apricots, and some cooks stuffed the main cavity, some stuffed the neck cavity only and placed an orange or slices or a whole onion in the main cavity, and some stuffed both cavities. In Scotland, some cooks stuff their Christmas turkeys with haggis.

For Christmas in 2008, holiday revelers in the U.K. consumed about ten million turkeys, 25 million Christmas puddings, two hundred and fifty million pints of beer, and thirty-five million bottles of wine. The average family spends £170 on their Christmas dinner, and the average turkey weighs twelve pounds and costs around £60, about $94 in the U.S. Compare that to the cost of a twelve-pound turkey in the U.S., the world's largest producer of Indigenous Turkey Meat: about $19, or £12.

In Italy, the world's fifth largest producer of Indigenous Turkey Meat, the turkey goes by several names. As *dindo*, derived from the French *dinde,* there are two main dishes, *dindo alla schiavono* (turkey stuffed with celery hearts, prunes, and chestnuts and grill-roasted) and *dindietta col pien*, which is stuffed with a mixture of salami, prosciutto, Parmesan, spices, and crumbled molasses-lard cookies. When known as *paeta*, the local word for turkey in the province of Vincenza, a saying goes *"Quando in novembre el vin no xe più, la oaeta xe pronto par el rosto,"* which means "When the wine has stopped fermenting in November, the turkey is ready for roasting."

A town in the province Castelgomberto has a turkey fair each year, and prizes are award to the breeders of the best birds. The main turkey recipe in the region is a Venetian specialty, *paeta al malgaragno*, which is prepared in October and November when pomegranates are ripe. A *pancetta*-covered turkey is half-roasted and then basted with crushed pomegranate seeds. It is served with a sauce made from sautéing the giblets in olive oil and pomegranate juice.

In northern Italy, the turkey is known as *tacchino* mostly, but specifically as *polin* in Milan. It is traditional Christmas fare and is sometimes boiled with vegetables and served with *mostarda di frutta*, a very sweet preserve from Lombardy featuring candied fruits, honey, spices, and mustard. More commonly, its holiday incarnation is *tacchino ripieno alla milanese*, turkey stuffed with sausage, ground veal, spices, prunes, chestnuts, apples, pears, and Marsala.

Perhaps the most interesting turkey roasting is done in Nereto, Abruzzo. There a *sagra* (market festival) on November

11 each year features turkeys raised on walnut shells, a process that hardens the meat and greatly reduces the fat in the birds. During the *sagra*, a special turkey dish is prepared, *tacchino alla porchetta*, which means turkey cooked in the manner of roasted pig. If you've never tasted porchetta in Italy, you have missed perhaps the best pork in the world, so it makes sense to attempt such a dish with turkey. Essentially, the turkey is heavily seasoned with fresh rosemary and lots of garlic, and then roasted. But halfway through the roasting process, the unstuffed turkey is cut in half along the breastbone and put back in the oven so that the entire bird becomes a golden brown.

Since turkey breasts are far more common in Italian markets than the whole bird, it's not surprising that some wonderful recipes for it appear in restaurants. *Involtini alla salvia*, or roulades with sage, is quite popular in restaurants in Florence, and turkey breasts are the meat of choice for preparing it. The breasts are flattened and then covered with sage leaves, slices of mortadella, and slices of Edam cheese, then rolled up and secured with toothpicks. They are fried in olive oil and butter until golden and served (of course) with dry white wine. There are many variations on this recipe, including adding some garlic *frittata* to the roulades or substituting fresh parsley for the sage.

Moving on to the number three Indigenous Turkey Meat producer, Germany, the first fact that surfaces is that their total annual production is thirty million birds per year, according to the Zentralverband der Deutschen Geflügelwirtschaft, or poultry producers association. And all are "free range" in the sense that they are raised on the ground, not in cages.

German food expert Harald Zoschke notes that *putenschnitzel* is a simple and highly popular German lunch entrée. Slices of turkey breast are sautéed in vegetable oil, then cooked in a mixture of cream, tomato sauce, and balsamic vinegar. Slices of mozzarella are placed on the breast slices and, when melted, the dish is served topped with chopped fresh basil.

We can trace the heritage of a recipe like this back to Marx Rumpolt's 1581 German cookbook, *Ein New Kochbuch*, mentioned earlier, which has an entire section devoted to turkey recipes, more than forty of them. Like the *putenschnitzel*, they are mostly simple, like turkey roast, dumplings, pie, wings, fritters, and tortes. The turkey-roast concept in Germany has been passed down for 430 years, and has become, as Zoschke

Opposite: Cover of
Ein new Kochbuch, *by*
Marx Rumpolt, 1581.
Sunbelt Archives.

Ein new Kochbuch/

Das ist Ein

gründtliche beschreibung

wie man recht vnd wol / nicht allein von vierfüssigen / heymischen
vnd wilden Thieren / sondern auch von mancherley Vögel vnd Federwildpret / dar-
zu von allem grünen vnd dürren Fischwerck / allerley Speiß / als gesotten / gebraten / gebacken / Pre-
solen / Carbonaden / mancherley Pasteten vnd Füllwerck / Gallrat / etc. auff Teutsche / Vngerische / Hispanische / Ita-
lianische vnnd Frantzösische weiß / kochen vnd zubereiten solle: Auch wie allerley Gemüß /
Obß / Salsen / Senff / Confect vnd Latwergen / zuzurichten seye.

Auch ist darinnen zu vernemmen / wie man herrliche grosse Pancketen / sampt
gemeinen Gastereyen / ordentlich anrichten vnd bestellen soll.

Allen Menschen / hohes vnd nidriges Standts / Weibs vnd Manns Personen / zu nut
jetzundt zum ersten in Druck gegeben / dergleichen vor nie ist außgegangen:
Durch

M. Marxen Rumpolt / Churf. Meintzischen Mundtkoch.

Mit Röm. Keyserlicher Maiestat special Priuilegio.

1 5   8 1.

Sampt einem gründtlichen Bericht / wie man alle Wein vor allen zufällen
bewaren / die bresthafften widerbringen / Kräuter vnd andere Wein / Bier /
Essig / vnd alle andere Getränck / machen vnd bereiten soll / daß sie natür-
lich / vnd allen Menschen vnschädlich / zu trin-
cken seindt.

Gedruckt zu Franckfort am Mayn / In verlegung M.
Marx Rumpolts / Churf. Meintz. Mundtkochs /
vnd Sigmundt Feyerabendts.

puts it, "*The* Christmas dinner classic in Deutschland." He says that because he won't eat goose, because his mother and father kept geese, which were family pets when he was growing up in Hamburg. When I asked him if turkeys were now challenging the traditional goose as the favored Christmas bird, he replied, "They're neck and neck." Actually, the necks are not served but rather used to make the stocks for gravy. (Harald and his wife lived for a decade in Treasure Beach, Florida, where he learned American slang and puns.)

He went on to tell me that stuffing the turkeys was not particularly popular in Germany, and no one deep-fried them as adventurous cooks do in the States. "Gallons of hot oil and people drinking beer? Not a good combination," he wrote. More Germans are cooking Christmas turkeys (*Weihnachtspute*) on the grill or in a smoker as barbecues grow in popularity. The "pute" in the word comes from *puter,* a regional term for turkey that was first used in 1559 and is believed to have originated as an imitation of the turkey's call, much like the English word "gobbler."

Ever since 150 turkeys were consumed during a wedding feast in Arstadt in 1560, the turkey has been a feast bird in Germany, and the bird has also had a number of appellations, including *Indianisch han* (mentioned above), *Kalekutisch hun* ("Calicut hen," associating it with the Portuguese trade with that city in India), *Welsch hun* (linking it with Italy), and *Truthahn,* a regional named derived from *drohen* (to threaten), a probable allusion to the turkey cock's aggressive behavior.

But they're not so aggressive when they're strutting down the "turkey catwalk" in the town of Licques, France. Turkeys are prized in France, the number two producer of Indigenous Turkey Meat in the world, where the per capita consumption of the bird nearly equals that of the U.S. On the second Saturday of every December, Licques opens its Marché du Terroir, or regional market, in the Nord Pas-de-Calais region, where turkey lovers vote on their favorite birds, no doubt helped along by some of their *licques*, the potent local liquor that is similar to pastis or pernod. After the vote, the "winning" birds stroll through the streets before being slaughtered, plucked, stuffed with chestnuts, and roasted for the feast.

However, Licques is not the epitome of French turkeydom. Maybe that's in the region of Bresse, in France's "gastronomic heartland," where the turkey has its own *Appellation d'origine* contrôlée (AOC), or protected designation of origin exactly like champagne, roquefort cheese, and Dijon mustard. These turkeys carry the Poulet de Bresse label, and they are free-range and are fattened on, of course, formerly American maize. During the third week in December the region holds a movable feast called the Trois Glorieuses that travels between the towns of Montrevel-en-Bresse, Bourg-en-Bresse, and Pont-de-Vaux. The purpose is for, once again, turkey fanciers to select their favorite birds (chickens and capons also compete) for the upcoming Christmas holidays.

But even that event is not the epitome of turkey worship in France. That is reserved for the awarding of the *Dinde d'Honneur*, or Honorable Turkey, in the town of Jaligny-sur-Bresbre in the Allier department of the Auvergne during the largest turkey market in the country. Here the turkeys are dressed up like beloved pets, with ribbons and little crowns above their wattles, and during this market, the award is not given to the bird but rather to human dignitaries like local firefighters. Previous Honorable Turkey recipients have been Winston Churchill, Queen Elizabeth II, and Pope Paul VI, each of whom received a premium turkey.

During the 1960s, when French cooking became the rage in the U.S., and even before Julia Child's *The French Chef Cookbook* (Knopf, 1969), Collier Books published *The French Provincial Cookbook* (1963) with two regional turkey recipes. *Dinde à Strasbourgeoise* (Roast Stuffed Turkey, Strasbourg Style) calls for the turkey to be stuffed with chicken livers, ground pork, and truffles (!), while *Dindonneau à La Bretonne* (Turkey Bretonne

Advertisement Promoting the 64th Annual Turkey Fair in Jaligny-sur-Besbre, France, 2013. Sunbelt Archives.

Style) has the bird stuffed with sausage, raisins, prunes, and turkey livers.

Bantam Books published *The Art of French Cooking*, by Fernande Garvin, in 1958, and it went through at least ten printings as a mass market paperback through 1965. The copy I have in my library I purchased in 1967. Garvin wrote, "Everybody who can afford it has turkey for the two 'réveillons.' *'Réveillon de Noël'* and *'Réveillon du Jour de l'An'* are the dinner suppers served at midnight at the 24th and 31st of December." On Christmas Eve, the family eats a very light snack at dinnertime, then goes to a midnight mass at their church. Afterward, family and friends sit down for an elaborate turkey feasts with appropriate toasts that lasts into the early morning hours. New Year's Eve is the same minus the churchgoing.

Dinde aux marrons, or turkey stuffed with chestnuts, is the focus of the feast, and it's served with braised celery and a "great Bordeaux." The chestnuts are baked, shelled, and then simmered in consommé for twenty minutes. Then they are chopped in half and mixed with ground lean pork, sausage meat, and brandy and stuffed into the main cavity of the turkey. After roasting for an hour and fifteen minutes, the stuffing is removed and the turkey is cooked for another two and a half hours. A gravy is made with the pan scrapings, and it is served over the carved turkey and stuffing. The American turkey has become a sumptuous feast bird in an adopted country that has some of the pickiest eaters in the world!

How Paprika Conquered Hungary

As impressive as the turkey's infiltration was into Europe, particularly France, it stopped there for the most part. The turkey in the Old World after Europe has some significant production in Israel, in ninth place in world production, and in tenth place is Hungary, which has one-sixth the production of France and only 3.5 percent of that of the United States. But those turkeys, when used in a stew (*gulyás*, or goulash), usually are paired with paprika, which of course comes from another New World crop, chile peppers. And paprika, in the words of Zoltán Halász, author of *Hungarian Paprika Through the Ages* (1963), "found its second and, at the same time, true home in Hungary." He adds: "It was in this country that such a high level and veritable cult of the growing, the processing and the use of paprika has been achieved, the like of which cannot be found anywhere else."

Since Columbus was working for the Spanish royalty and brought back chile peppers to Spain on his second voyage in 1493, there is little doubt that Spain was the first point of their entry into Europe. But their spread throughout Europe was not only the result of the international trading of the empire of Charles V but also of the expansion of the Ottoman Empire in the eastern Mediterranean. In the sixteenth century, the empire included Bulgaria, a county called "the gardeners of Europe," according to Hungarian food expert George Lang. The Turks were in possession of chile peppers, or paprika in the parlance, and they taught the Bulgarians to grow the plants. Many Bulgarians emigrated to Hungary, fleeing the Turks but also looking for better land and climate. They found it and began growing paprika, but the common belief that the Turks introduced paprika directly into Hungary is not true. "There is ample evidence that the Bulgarians brought paprika to Hungary and started its cultivation," writes Lang in *Cuisine of Hungary* (1971).

"It was at this point that paprika appeared in the history of spices," writes Halász. "Almost unnoticed, it made a modest, but, it could be added, a cheerful and charming entrance. No countries were subjugated for its sake; no brave Indians put to forced labour." But why were chile peppers immediately accepted in Hungary when it took tomatoes three hundred years to enter mainstream Italian cuisine?

I think it's because paprika was originally thought to be "red pepper," just a variant of familiar but expensive black pepper,

Burnett's Hungarian Noble Sweet Paprika. This Unusual Spice Tin Pre-dates World War 1. Sunbelt Archives.

while tomatoes had no reference fruit or vegetable in the Old World and thus remained strange and suspicious to most cooks. The word "paprika" derives from the Hungarian *paparka*, which is a variation on the Bulgarian *piperka*, which in turn was derived from the Latin *piper*, for "pepper."

Tomatoes, however, made an early appearance in Hungarian cuisine. The Turks occupied parts of Hungary for 150 years, and they also appeared to have transferred both tomatoes and maize to the Hungarians via the Bulgarians. The tomato, writes Lang, "became very popular during this time and remained an essential part of the past three centuries of Hungarian cuisine." This is mostly because tomatoes and paprika were immediate paired together in *Lescó*, an essential condiment that can stand on its own as an appetizer or be used as the main flavoring ingredient of soups and stews. It is made by cooking onions in lard and then adding slices of Italian frying or banana peppers, followed by fresh tomatoes, sugar, salt, and paprika.

The most likely scenario for the introduction of paprika into Bulgaria and Hungary holds that the Turks first became aware of chile peppers when they besieged the Portuguese colony of Diu, near Calicut, India, in 1538. This theory suggests that the Turks learned of chile peppers during that battle and then transported them along the trade routes of their vast empire, which stretched from India to Central Europe. According to Leonhard Fuchs, an early German professor of medicine, chiles were cultivated in Germany by 1542, in England by 1548, and in the Balkans by 1569. Fuchs knew that the European chiles had been imported from India, so he called them "Calicut peppers." However, he wrongly assumed that chiles were native to India.

So, sometime between 1538 and 1548, chiles were introduced into Hungary, and the first citizens to accept the fiery pods were the servants and shepherds who had more contact with the Turkish invaders. Zoltán Halász tells the tale: "Hungarian herdsmen started to sprinkle tasty slices of bacon with paprika and season the savoury stews they cooked in cauldrons over an open fire with the red spice. They were followed by the fishermen of the Danube . . . who would render their fish-dishes more palatable with the red spice, and at last the Hungarian peasantry, consuming with great gusto the meat of fattened oxen and pigs or tender poultry which were prepared in paprika-gravy, professed their irrevocable addiction to paprika, which by then had become a characteristically Hungarian condiment."

In 1569, an aristocrat named Margit Szechy listed the foreign seeds she was planting in her garden in Hungary. On the list was *Turkisch rot Pfeffer* (Turkish red pepper) seeds, the first recorded instance of chiles in Hungary. Upon Mrs. Szechy's death and the subsequent division of her estate, her paprika plots were so valuable they were fought over bitterly by her daughters, and the litigation went on for twenty-five years before the Supreme Court awarded title to Mrs. Szechy's youngest daughter.

After the settlement of this dispute, there was no mention of paprika in Hungarian writings for many years, and Halász speculates that time between the turn of the sixteenth and seventeenth centuries was when "the silent revolution in Hungarian cooking" developed, "with paprika conquering the common people first of all." In 1604, a Hungarian dictionary listed the spice for the first time as "Turkish pepper, *piper indicum*," and the word "paprika" didn't make an appearance until 1775, when J. Csapó called it "paprika garden pepper" in his *Herbarium*.

During this time, "townspeople sprinkled their bacon with paprika, made of crudely crushed 'cherry paprika' and added it to a variety of dishes, mixing it with sour cream," notes Lang, who added that the "landed gentry" were slower to adopt the spice but eventually "recognized that not only was paprika cheaper than black pepper, but it stimulated the appetite and had a most delightful character of its own." Also during this time, Hungarian growers developed the hundreds of paprika varieties ranging

Indianischer Pfeffer. Botanical Illustration by Leonhart Fuchs, 1543. Sunbelt Archives.

from "very hot to sugar sweet," with a wide range of colors and textures. And, "somewhere along the line, the Hungarians hit on the holy trinity of lard, onion, and pure ground paprika," and "this simple combination became the base of virtually unlimited taste combinations."

Capsaicin, the chemical that makes chile peppers hot, became a major focal point of the paprika debate that soon ensued. At the end of the eighteenth century, a visiting nobleman named Count Hoffmanseg tasted paprika for the first time in a cabbage stuffing and wrote to his sister, "It stings terribly, but not for long, and then pleasantly warms the stomach!" On the other side of the debate was, of course, the Catholic Church, with the ultra-conservative Capuchin priest Ubaldis writing around the same time about Hungarian sins: "The spice of their food is some sort of red beast called paprika," he railed. "It certainly bites like the devil."

Lang notes that the nobility was the very last part of Hungarian citizenry that adopted paprika, "probably because it did not stem from aristocratic tradition." But even that refined segment of the population would eventually succumb to the conquering spice. The first time paprika turned up in a cookbook recipe was 1817, when F. G. Zenker, chef of Prince Schwarzenberg, published his *Theoretical and Practical Compendium of Culinary Arts*, which was printed in Vienna. He listed paprika as an ingredient in Chicken Fricassee in Indian Style. This was followed in 1829 with the appearance of two classic Hungarian dishes in István Czifrai's (or Czifray's) cookbook, apparently titled, simply, *The Cookbook of the Master Chef István Czifray.* The first was *halász-hal,* or fisherman's soup, mentioned above, and the second marked the first appearance in print of *paprikás csirke,* or chicken paprikash, perhaps the most famous Hungarian dish in the world.

It wasn't until 1844 that this dish appeared on the menu of the National Casino, the rather exclusive club of the House of Lords, but it soon became the favorite dish of Queen Elizabeth, the consort of Franz Josef I. "A queen couldn't be wrong!" proclaims Lang, "Paprika's victory was now complete." This triumph was followed by another in 1879, when the famous French chef Escoffier bought paprika during his visit to Szeged and on his return to France, introduced it into the *grande cuisine* in the form of *Gulyas Hongrois* (Hungarian Goulash) and *Poulet au Paprika*

(Paprika Chicken), two of the most typical paprika-laden Hungarian dishes.

Around this same time, chile peppers, known as *peperoncini*, and tomatoes, known as *pomodori*, were just becoming accepted into Italian cuisine, an adoption that would forever change that country's cuisine. In 1881, bowls of chiles are commonplace in Giovanni Verga's realistic novel, *I malavoglia* (rough translation: *Me, Reluctantly*); in 1889, Pizza Margherita with tomatoes was named for King Umberto's wife, Queen Margherita; and in 1891 the first all-Italian cookbook, *La scienza in cucina e l'arte di mangiar bene* (*The Science of Cooking and the Art of Eating Well*) by Pellegrino Artusi included many tomato recipes. The story of tomatoes in Italy is told in Part 4.

Types of Hungarian Paprikas

Note: In Hungary, paprika has a great variation and depth of flavor, having not only distinct pod types but also specific grades of the powders made from these pod types. The hottest paprikas are not the bright red ones but rather the palest red and light brown ones.

Special Quality (*Különleges*): The mildest and brightest red of all Hungarian paprikas, with excellent aroma.

Delicate (*Csípmentes Csemege*): Ranging from light to dark red, a mild paprika with a rich flavor.

Exquisite Delicate (*Csemegepaprika*): Similar to Delicate, but more pungent.

Pungent Exquisite Delicae (*Csípös Csemege, Pikant*): A yet more pungent Delicate.

Rose (*Rózsa*): Pale red with a strong aroma and mild pungency.

Noble Sweet (*Édesnemes*): The most commonly exported paprika; bright red and slightly pungent.

Half-Sweet (*Félédes*): A blend of mild and pungent paprikas; medium pungency.

Hot (*Erös*): Light brown, this is the hottest of all the paprikas.

Szgedi Paprika Pods Drying. Photograph by Varadi Zsolt, 2005. Sunbelt Archives.

Today, the great pepper-growing areas around Kalocsa and Szeged have just the right combination of soil characteristics, temperature, rainfall, and sunshine required to cultivate the numerous varieties of paprika successfully. In March, the pepper seeds are put in water to germinate, then transferred to greenhouse beds. Seven weeks later, in May, the small pepper shrubs are replanted in the open fields. Harvesting starts at the end of the first week in September and lasts for about a month, depending on weather conditions. By harvesttime, the mature plants will have grown to a height of sixteen to twenty-four inches. And the pepper pods—three to five inches long and about one to one and a half inches wide—will have ripened from green or yellow to bright red.

In Kalocsa, the annual harvest is celebrated with a paprika festival in September. Known as the Kalocsa Paprika Days, it features an exhibition of food products and agricultural machinery, a professional conference on the topic of paprika, various sports events, a Paprika Cup international chess tournament, and a fish soup cooking contest. But the highlight of all this is the Paprika Harvest Parade, complete with local bands and colorful folk-dancing groups, followed that same night by a Paprika Harvest Ball.

With regards to paprika, the Catholic Church seems to have reversed its original opinion of the "devilish" aspects of paprika. "It isn't surprising how many religious festivals are connected with phases of its cultivation," Lang notes, "man sorely felt the need for divine help." For example, the seeds are placed in water for germination precisely on Saint Gregory's Day in early March, and the harvest begins on September 8, the feast day of the Nativity of the Holy Virgin, which in reality is a combination of a medieval festival and a "vast block party."

So how do those tons of newly picked peppers get turned into the condiment known as paprika, in all of its many forms? Before the Industrial Revolution, farmers used to string all their ripe peppers by hand and hang them up in a protected place to dry. After a certain period of time, the drying process was completed in large earthenware ovens. The peppers were then crushed underfoot and finally pounded into a powder by means of a *kulu*, a huge mortar with a large pestle driven by human power. Water mills later replaced the *kulu* for grinding paprika, and by the late 1800s steam engines were being used for this task.

But until the mid-1800s it was difficult to control the pungency of the paprika produced. The capsaicin, which gives paprika its spicy flavor, is found in the pod's veins and seeds, which were removed by hand before the crushed dried peppers were ground into a powder. This was a time-consuming and inexact process, which yielded paprikas in taste from rather mild to fairly hot. The results were unpredictable. In 1859, the Palfy brothers of Szeged invented a machine for removing the veins and seeds, then grinding the dried pods into a quality-controlled powder. The millmaster could now determine exactly how much capsaicin was to be removed and how much should be retained. The Palfys' technique continued to be used in Hungarian factories for almost a century—until the fairly recent introduction of modern automatic machines that wash, dry, crush, sort, and grind the peppers in a continuous process.

The Palfys' invention made possible the large-scale commercial production of very mild ("Noble Sweet") paprika, which had a much bigger export market than the hotter-tasting varieties. As the industry expanded to meet both local and foreign demand for this mild (but still richly flavored) paprika, the growers saw the advantage of cultivating a spice pepper that did not need to have its veins and seeds removed.

Ferenc Horvath of Kalocsa developed the first variety of Hungarian pepper that was "sweet" throughout—meaning that its veins and seeds contained very little capsaicin indeed. This kind of pepper is now favored by growers in the regions of Kalocsa and Szeged. It can be used alone, ground to produce a mild but flavorful paprika powder—or in combination with other, hotter peppers to produce some of the standard varieties of paprika marketed by the Hungarians. But with all this emphasis on the demand-and-supply of *mild* paprika during the past one hundred years, one is tempted to speculate that Hungarian food *before* Horvath and the Palfys must have been much hotter than it is today.

In the Hungarian countryside, paprika peppers are threaded onto strings and are hung from the walls, porches, and eaves of farmhouses, much like the chile ristras in the American Southwest. Today Hungary produces both pungent and sweet paprikas, but originally all Hungarian paprika was aromatic and quite hot. It was evidently too hot for some tastes, for by the turn of this century other countries were requesting that Hungary develop a non-pungent variety. By accident, farmers produced a sweet variety in their fields when they planted milder "eating" paprika with hotter "seasoning" paprika in proximity, and insects cross-pollinated the two. The resulting hybrid reduced the pungency of the paprika pods and probably led to the non-pungent varieties now grown in Spain.

Food authority Craig Claiborne has noted, "The innocuous powder which most merchants pass on to their customers as paprika has slightly more character than crayon or chalk. Any paprika worthy of its name has an exquisite taste and varies in strength from decidedly hot to pleasantly mild but with a pronounced flavor." This is why for cooking, Hungarian paprika should be favored over that produced in the United States or Spain.

Paprika has exerted a great influence on the culture of the people of Central Europe. Hungarians believe that the passion of a woman is reflected in her capacity to consume the fiery, paprika-spiced food, and bad moods are often blamed on paprika considered too pungent. Paprika also has its own very popular folkloric figure, Paprika Jancsi. Often represented as a puppet, Paprika Jancsi has the shape of a red chile, complete with a large chile hat and a pod-shaped nose. He is the prototype of the folk hero, being at once valiant, generous, knowledgeable, humorous, and ingenious. He is often called the Hungarian Sancho Panza—an appropriate personification of the pungent paprika pod so loved by people of the region of the Danube.

For a country of just ten million people, Hungary has some impressive agricultural production. Although it does not rank in the top twenty countries for tomatoes or potatoes, it is the number twelve country in the world for maize production, number twenty for green chile peppers (producing about 18 percent of what the U.S. grows), and it's nineteenth in world dry chile pepper production, which is a result of all that growing, drying, and grinding of paprika.

The Peperoncino-Eating Contest: A Burned-Out Theater of the Absurd

It took a long time for chile peppers to have any impact on Italian cuisine, despite the fact that they first appeared there in 1526, which indicates that they were transferred about the same time as tomatoes were, which makes sense because of Spain's control over Naples at the time. Antonio Latini briefly mentioned them as an ingredient in some sauces, and a century later Vincenzo Corrado called peppers a "vulgar, rustic food." It wasn't until the nineteenth century that pickled peppers were mentioned; however, in the twentieth century chile peppers called peperoncini were grown extensively in the regions of Calabria and Senise, where they have gradually dominated the local cuisine.

Since Columbus was responsible for the introduction of chile peppers into Europe, it was only fitting that the first Peperoncino Festival was held in 1992, five hundred years after he found them in the New World. Organized by the Accademia Italiana del Peperoncino, or the Italian Pepper Academy, and its leader, Enzo Monaco, the festival started out small but in recent years has drawn tens of thousands of visitors to the small town of Diamante in Calabria, the "toe" of the "boot" that is Italy. The festival is held for four days surrounding the first weekend in September on the *Lungomare*, the promenade on Diamante's seaside. The Italian and other European "chileheads" are drawn by a unique blend of a chile vendor market, music, movies, satire, art, folklore, and samplings from local restaurants. More than a hundred vendors have booths offering up everything imaginable related to the beloved *peperoncini,* including the following:

—*Salsiccia*, a lean pork sausage with fennel seed and *peperoncini*.

—*La Bomba*, a sort of spiced-up sangria.

— A Calabrian peperoncino chocolate liquor called *Crema di cacao al peperoncino.*

— Pungent peperoncino pasta products.

—*Grappa al Peperoncino di Calabria*, the famous Italian grape brandy in a kicked-up version with chiles floating in the bottle.

—*Olio Santo* ("holy oil"), bright red chile-infused olive oil in decorative bottles

—*Alici al peperoncino*, a Calabrian specialty, freshly hatched sardines densely packed with peperoncini and some salt.

— A plethora of sweet heat products, including *Baci di Casanova*, dark chocolates with a creamy-smooth chile-spiced center; *Confettura di peperoncino al cioccolato*, a spicy chile-chocolate spread; *Crostata piccante*, a short pastry tart with a spicy-sweet icing; *Cannoli al peperoncino*, crunchy pastry pipes filled with vanilla creme, spiced up with plenty of peperoncino bits; and *Dolce della nonna al peperoncino*, Grandma's sponge cake with a kick.

—*Vinagra*, a red wine infused with chiles.

The Accademia Italiana del Peperoncino was predicting an attendance of 150,000 or five days for the Peperoncino Festival the year I visited it as the guest of honor, in 2010. Being a show producer, I was skeptical of the estimate, but after witnessing the crowds myself, I was convinced that the projection was not exaggerated. Of course, peperoncinos were just an excuse for the Italians to party, and there were many different foods being served, but that said, the festival focused on chiles to the point of madness usually found only at the National Fiery Foods & Barbecue Show held annually in Albuquerque. So of course they had to have a chile-eating contest, and I had to be a judge of it.

The idea that ten victims would attempt the torture of eating nearly the weight of a chihuahua of hot chiles at one sitting in front of a cheering crowd of two thousand peperoncino-heads may seem strange to Americans, but just consider the extreme eating contests we have in the U.S. Stuffing down dozens and dozens of hot dogs or funnel cakes while attempting to avoid vomiting is great fun for everyone, right?

Well, I had been drafted, protesting, into serving as one of the head judges, and my job was, first, to avoid laughing while judging

and, second, to make sure the contestants were not stuffing the chopped chiles into their pockets and shoes. Third, I had to count the number of finished plastic plates in front of them and multiply them by 50 grams to determine total weight—all while Queen's "We are the Champions" blared from the speakers at top volume. And without even a *birra* to help me through it.

The champion from 2009, Anna Greco, was in the number one position and was determined, it seemed, to surpass her own record of 750 grams. She got off to a great start, wolfing down with a spoon what seemed to be finely chopped serranos while her fans chanted "Anna, Anna, Anna" to the beat of the Queen song. Her competition was not much, and they began to drop like burned-out flies. One ate 50 grams and then ran from the stage, the wimp. Two more soon gave up with embarrassed looks as if they had farted during confession. Anna hung in there, plowing through the peperoncinos, but hey—she outweighed most of the men. Finally, after fifteen minutes or so, everyone gave up except for Anna, who was now holding her stomach, eleven and a half plates of hot stuff devoured, and slowing way down, her face red and contorted with pain. Was that froth on her mouth?

All eyes were on Anna, and all the TV cameras too. Would she break the record? Would she get a medal from the Italian prime minister? But then, in a shocking turnaround, Anna clutched a napkin to her lips, staggered to her feet, and left the table bending over. Anna, it seemed, had lost her peperoncini. Would she be disqualified? Would she return to the table, now having more room in her stomach? To the "Anna, Anna, Anna" chants, she

Anna Greco, Left, Wins the Chile Eating Contest at the 2010 Peperoncino Festival in Diamante, Italy. Photograph by Dave DeWitt.

did return, could not continue, but was crowned the champion with a lousy 640 grams, about 1.4 pounds. I wanted my money back.

Suddenly, I remembered the Italian Party Principle: The length of time it takes for a party to break up is directly proportional to the number of Italians there. Once my friend Marco took me to a dinner party where it took the twenty guests about an hour to devour the five courses, but just to say all the goodbyes took another forty-five minutes! I looked around and calculated thirty-five people on stage and two thousand in the audience. We would be there until the Christmas presents were opened! In the confusion, I snuck to the back of the stage, down the small steps, and out to the street—*Ciao,* baby, bye bye! I found the nearest bar and, to hell with the *birra,* I was soon sipping a *whiskey*—that's Italian for scotch. A reliable witness told me the next day that a half hour later, the on-stage host, Gianni Pellegrino, was still asking into the mike, "Mr. DeVitt, Mr. DeVitt, where are you?"

Chile peppers had conquered yet another European country.

PART 3

EXOTIC, STRONG, AND OFTEN INTOXICATING: NEW DRINKS AND FLAVORINGS

Discussing the War in a Paris Café. Drawing by Frederick Barnard in the Illustrated London News, *September 17, 1870. Sunbelt Archives.*

Saccharum officinarum L.

Sugarcane,
Saccharum
officinarum L.
Botanical Illustration
by Franz Eugen
Köhler, 1897.
Sunbelt Archives.

In this part, I tell the stories of two adopted American crops, sugarcane and coffee, which were re-exported to such an extent that they changed world history—and food history—forever. I call them adopted crops because they had Old World origins but needed just the right conditions to become international commodities, and those conditions were found in the Americas.

I'm also including the American flavorings chocolate and vanilla, which were often combined with sugar in chocolate cafés and coffeehouses in Europe. And the story of sugar is also the story of rum, the first distilled alcoholic beverage of the Americas, the "kill-devil" that became both the "demon rum" that was proudly produced by the distillery towns of Massachusetts, and the original "rumbullion" that evolved into the beloved "grog" of the British Navy.

Sugar's Possible Origins

During the fifteenth century, per capita sugar consumption in Europe was one teaspoon per year. Today's consumption is 87 pounds per year, except for in the U.K., where it is an astonishing 111 pounds—nearly one-third of a pound *per day*. The production and commerce involving this sweet commodity, along with its seemingly addictive properties for Europeans, resulted in the trading of the most evil commodity of all: human slaves. As Charles Schumann writes in *Tropical Bar Book*, "The history of slavery is largely dependent on the late eighteenth-century craving for sugar and rum." But the craving began earlier than that and is quite complex.

The history of sugar is intertwined with the histories of tea, chocolate, coffee, and even tobacco. As far as historian Werner Sobart is concerned, "these commodities are outstanding factors

Vasco da Gama. Painting by António Manuel da Fonseca, 1838. Sunbelt Archives.

in the development of capitalism." It was the more bitter commodities that were the most significant influence on the rapid development of the sugar trade, and C. Anne Wilson, author of *Food and Drink in Britain*, notes that "[t]he biggest single influence upon sugar usage was the introduction of coffee, chocolate, and tea, each with a somewhat bitter natural flavour." That said, not all of the history is so straightforward. In fact, the ubiquitous sugar of today has a rather mysterious early history, as Waverly Root points out. "From the beginning, sugar has played a game of hide and seek with history," he writes. "Now you see it, now you don't. Few foods have fuzzier histories."

That fuzziness is directly related to the fact that it is a very ancient crop, and typical of long-domesticated grasses and grains, it has no wild form now and is totally dependent upon human cultivation of it to reproduce. Its different species were domesticated and grown in ancient times in many regions from India to Indonesia. Arab traders carried it to Europe and the Mediterranean, where it was a rare and expensive spice. Honey was the common sweetener, and much less expensive, but nobility quickly adopted it as a luxury that set them apart from the mere honey-eating commoners. The Venetians, the primary spice traders of the time, had a monopoly on sugarcane until Vasco da Gama reached India in 1498; after that Lisbon became the sugar capital of Europe and the trade was expanding westward to the Spanish and Portuguese Atlantic archipelagos. At the time, the nobility and court historians had no idea that sugarcane from the New World, in the words of food historian Peter Macinnis, was "a crop that was destined to change much of the world."

And there were some forward-thinking adventurers who had a hunch about the future of sugarcane as a crop and made it happen.

Columbus and Cane

In 1424, Henry the Navigator brought sugarcane from Sicily to Madeira Island along with the first Portuguese colonists, thus triggering the western expansion of this precious cargo. At first the colonists raised wheat, but that crop did not produce enough grain, so Henry, as principal benefactor of the islands, began to plant other commercial crops, including sugarcane. The subsequent production of "sweet salt," as sugar was called in Europe, turned it into a popular spice among the wealthy and created a major industry. By 1480, Belgium had about seventy ships transporting the cane to Antwerp, and the sugar capital of Europe switched once again. By the 1490s Madeira had overtaken Cyprus as the major producer of sugar for Europe, and according to Macinnis, Columbus's mother was growing it there in 1480.

It was only natural that the Portuguese, along with the Spanish, should spread sugarcane to the Cape Verde Islands and the Canary Islands in the last decade of the fifteenth century. In August of 1492, Christopher Columbus stopped at La Gomera in the Canary Islands for wine and water, intending to stay only four days. But he became romantically involved with the governor of the island, Beatriz de Bobadilla y Ossorio, and ended up staying a month. When he finally sailed, she gave him cuttings of sugarcane, which he took to Hispaniola and planted, thus expanding sugarcane's cultivation to the New World, or so the story goes. But it's probably true.

Columbus reported that the cane "germinated in seven days" and "the small quantity we planted has succeeded very well." The Spanish quickly established plantations on Hispaniola by 1506, followed by Cuba in 1518 and Mexico in 1524. In Mexico, it was none other than Cortés who was the first sugar baron, planting his large holdings in Cuernavaca with cane and building mills to process it. At first it appeared that the Spanish would dominate sugar production in the New World, but that was not to be for two reasons. The first reason was that the Spanish were distracted by even more precious cargoes, namely gold and silver, which could produce riches much faster than cane. And as the Spanish became more interested in gold and silver, the Spanish American sugar industry in the Caribbean stagnated, and the Spanish Caribbean islands served mostly as way stations on the trade routes for those precious metals from Peru and Mexico, reflecting, as Mintz put it, "Spain's unproductive, tribute-taking, labor-squandering role in the Americas."

The second reason the Spanish could not dominate Caribbean sugar production was competition—they were completely upstaged by the French, Portuguese, and British planters—and their slaves.

When Sweetness Sours: Sugar and Slavery

The European "invasion" of the Americas decimated the native populations through war and enslavement, but mostly it was disease that caused the mass deaths. First it was swine flu and smallpox, and after that, in the words of Charles C. Mann, author of *1493*, "Following . . . came the rest, a pathological cavalcade. . . . Throughout the sixteenth and seventeenth centuries novel microorganisms spread across the Americas, ricocheting from victim to victim, killing three-quarters or more of the people in the hemisphere."

One thing the Europeans were *not* going to do was the back-breaking labor of working in the cane fields, but what was left of the native population was not nearly enough to meet the ever-

growing demand for sugar. And besides, the planters looked down their noses at the Indian slaves as field workers as weak and unmotivated. As Gad J. Heuman and James Walvin noted in *The Slavery Reader*, "In Brazil, the enslavement of native people . . . never proved satisfactory, especially for work in the sugar industry. Indians died, drifted away or simply failed to work as the Portuguese settlers required. But both the Spaniards and the Portuguese knew that other peoples—Africans—had already proved their worth as slaves in the sugar industry of the Atlantic islands."

Africans were the obvious choice for slaves because they were adapted to warm climates and the hard work of farming, and the Europeans could at least partially trade for them. Since this book is about the spread of American crops around the world and not about the history of slavery, I'm not going to detail the horrendous conditions and cruelty the slaves endured but rather focus on the results of their tragic labor, which was remarkable in many ways. Macinnis put it this way: "Without sugar, there might only have been a minor slave trade; with sugar, the slave trade drove European commerce and development." Sidney W. Mintz, author of *Sweetness and Power*, adds: "Slaves were a 'false commodity' because a human being is not an object, even when treated as one. In this instance, millions of humans were treated as commodities."

Slaves Processing Sugarcane. Engraving by Theodor de Bry, 1595. Sunbelt Archives.

As the development of sugar plantations grew after the middle of the sixteenth century, the demand for slaves increased nearly exponentially. Probably "only" one million African slaves landed in the Americas during the sixteenth century, but in the eighteenth century the number was seven times that figure, including the slaves imported for other crops such as maize, tobacco, and cotton. But in reality, those crops were of minor financial importance considering the vast profits generated by sugar. As early as 1700, the value of sugar reaching England and Wales was double that of tobacco. After that, during the next 110 years, Barbados received 252,500 slaves and Jamaica received 662,400. Such a large number of workers forever altered the racial balance of these two islands, and they followed the same pattern as Santo Domingo, which as early as 1530 to 1547 had a ten-to-one slave-to-Spanish population of 3,000 slaves and 327 Spaniards.

As the number of slaves increased, Barbados was cleared of native vegetation and other crops and saved just for planting sugarcane, and thus neither the planters nor the slaves could raise food for themselves. This happened on the other sugar islands as well. "Brazil and the West Indies were perhaps the first societies in world history to be dependent on imports for *all* food beyond the barest necessities," wrote Reay Tannahill in *Food in History*. With perhaps 95 percent of Barbados devoted to growing sugarcane, Britain had to constantly supply salt pork and beef, bacon, and salt cod—in 1783 alone it sent 16,576 tons of salted meat to its West Indian colonies.

The complicated trade patterns involving these food shipments and the interplay of Britain, the American colonies, Africa, and the West Indies led to descriptions of the processes at work that have been oversimplified by historians as "Triangular Trade." Mintz described two triangles of trade. The first linked Britain to Africa and to the New World: "Finished goods were sold to Africa, African slaves to the Americas, and American tropical commodities (especially sugar) to the mother country." That sugar helped to provide the food necessary to keep alive the slaves producing it. The second triangle had rum made in New England shipped to Africa to buy slaves for the West Indies, which then produced the molasses that was shipped to New England to make the rum.

These triangular trading scenarios are great in general theory, but in reality they are much more complex. The triangle involving New England was a piecemeal operation, and no New England traders are known to have completed a full sequential circuit of the triangle. Historian Clifford Shipton spent years studying New England shipping records, and he failed to find a single instance of a ship completing the full triangle as described above. And later, after slaves and rum were added to the trade mix, the trading of the colonies was further diversified—or even became haphazard. For example, some of the colonies sent ships loaded with rum directly to Africa to buy slaves with it, and that was not a triangle at all. However historians wish to describe the trade today, rum, that uniquely American liquor, soon became a major focus of sugar's increasing importance in world trade.

Rumbullion: The Value-Added American Liquor

The story of rum begins and ends with molasses. While rum can be made from various by-products of sugar manufacture like cane juice, cane syrup, and skimmings, molasses is the only one that can be stored and is easily transported aboard ship without preservatives. Hence molasses became a commodity unto itself; it was the result of the third boiling of the sugar syrup and was specifically called "blackstrap molasses." In other words, the sugar for further refinement had been removed twice from the boiled syrup. The first boiling yielded light molasses, the second yielded dark molasses, yet even after the third boiling, the now-surplus blackstrap molasses still contained 52 percent fermentable sugars—enough to be distilled into the liquor called rum, the third incarnation of sugarcane and the second value-added product derived from it.

The origin of the word "rum" has historians doing shots of it while trying to figure out which of the three best scenarios is correct. It was called "kill-devil," which evolved into "rumbullion" (which meant a riot or an alcohol-induced rebellion) just after Richard Ligon's time in Barbados (see below), so it's completely logical to think that rum is just a shortened version of that term. But there are two other possibilities. Since there was a Spice Islands–sugarcane link to rum, it's possible that the word came from the Malay word *brum*, which was the term for liquor made from sugar. Another possibility is that it's an abbreviation of the botanical term in Latin for sugar, *Saccharum officinarum*, which

The Master Heads the Cask of Sugar. Illustration by E. Wallis, 1823. Sunbelt Archives.

has two "rums" in it and translates as medicinal sugar. The latter is an interesting idea, but I doubt that many English vernacular words for beverages came directly from Latin botanical terms. The rum as *brum* scenario has some validity, but considering the vast spread of the British Empire, the rumbullion theory makes the most sense to me.

Although most West Indies planters—and even their slaves—had the knowledge and where-withal to make rum, the first rum to become a brand was Mount Gay, made in Barbados starting in 1663. But before it was a brand, it was commonly distilled in Barbados, and the planters loved to drink it despite the opposition. An early history, "Briefe Discription of the ilande of Barbados" (1650), calls it "a hott, hellish and terrible liquor." Ligon, who was living in Barbados at this time, and later published *A True and Exact History of the Island of Barbados* (1657), named the liquor "kill-devil" and described it as "infinitely strong, but not very pleasant to taste," which, despite the flavor, caused the planters to "lay them asleep on the ground." That was his euphemism for passing out, and Ligon noted, humorously, that the ground was "an unwholesome lodging." His warnings, of course, discouraged no one from drinking it, and his observation recalls a Jamaican saying, "God caused men to raise themselves up onto their feet; rum sees to it that they fall over again."

And that was the norm in Barbados. "All visitors remarked on the planters' heavy drinking," writes Karen Ordahl Kupperman in her introduction to a new edition of Ligon's book, "and how insulted the inhabitants were if anyone refused their offer of hospitality, calling it 'incivility.'" Macinnis puts it a little differently: "A major improvement in the lot of the planters came when rum became part of the sugar industry. It made marginal operations profitable, loss-making plantations became profitable, and planters still losing money found a new comfort."

Rum had other uses, too. It was a form of social control over slaves, a bribe for good behavior like catching rats in the cane

Drinking Rum Milk Punch. Artist Unknown. Sunbelt Archives.

fields or other odious chores. Each slave was given about three gallons a year, but some particularly talented slaves could earn up to thirteen gallons annually, and they were permitted to drink it or barter it for additional food and other treats. It was also—as was sugar—considered to be a medicine and was routinely issued to slaves as a cure for various aliments.

Rum was also a signature value-added product in Jamaica. "Jamaican rum had more character and visibility than did the island's sugar," writes B. W. Higman in *Jamaican Food*. "Highly refined sugars are difficult to tell apart once they approach pure sucrose. Rum, on the other hand, is made distinctive by its peculiarity of fermentation and additives." But, of course, even more distinctions could be made as time went on and the distillers learned about aging the rum. In the early days, rum was pretty raw and was drunk strictly for its intoxicating properties rather than for its sipping flavors.

Rum Begets Wards

While visiting the Mount Gay Visitor Center in Bridgetown, Barbados, in 1996, I learned an amusing story of the first rum brand that concerned Aubrey Ward, who bought the operation in the early 1900s. His hobby was fathering children by his women workers, somewhere between sixty and a hundred kids. Blame it on the availability of rumbullion, an early term for rum. The women were elevated to the lofty position of "child mother," and each was given a brick house to live in. No wonder there are plenty of Wards in Barbados today.

Cane Workers in the Fields of a Jamaican Plantation After Emancipation, Mid-nineteenth Century. Sunbelt Archives.

Its power to intoxicate quickly is why the Africans traded slaves for it (and preferred it to French brandy after 1721) instead of the preferred barter, cloth. African slavers valued the distilled spirits because they were much stronger than their beers and palm wines, and possessing and drinking brandy, and then rum, gave them status. Slave buyers presented large quantities of rum, one of several bribes called *dashee*, as a "gift" before negotiations began with the slavers, even if they were mainly trading textiles. At least three-quarters of the slaves were bought with English cloth, with the remaining barter being rum, iron, cowrie shells, and firearms. This trade in rum for slaves was even more disconcerting when we realize that the traders were drinking it as they were delivering it! "Rum became the lubricant of slavery," wrote rum historian Charles Coulombe.

Because rum, unlike beer and wine, did not go bad at sea, it was actually preferred aboard the ships of traders, pirates,

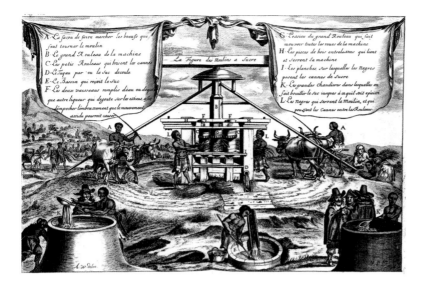

and eventually the Royal Navy and the navies of other nations because it was one of the few creature comforts readily available at sea. "Whatever the flag he served, every sailor could count on his daily ration of rum," writes Schumann, and this presented trouble for the Royal Navy because the daily gallon of beer was replaced by a half-pint of rum and there were more incidences of drunkenness and discipline problems. Admiral Edward Vernon ordered the half-pint of rum to be diluted with a quart of sugar and lime juice, resulting in a cocktail called "grog," which was named after the coarse fabric the admiral wore, grogham. So, while sailors were now more likely to fall overboard, the lime juice helped to prevent scurvy, which of course was the primary cause of death in the navy. And it also caused the sailors to be nicknamed "limeys," which irritated them to no end.

It's nearly impossible to write about rum without mentioning pirates because they are famously linked to the liquor, especially these days with Captain Morgan Rum being the second most popular in the world. And amazingly enough, pirates were better treated aboard ship than sailors in the Royal Navy. Rich English, writing in *Modern Drunkard Magazine*, observes: "Surviving records from the High Court of the Admiralty (Britain) are stuffed full of brutal acts dispensed by captains on crewmen. Flogging was an everyday event on British ships . . . and when sailors weren't being whipped, they were confined in shipboard crawlspaces ("brigs"), lashed to masts to bake in the sun, dangled over the gunwales by their ankles, and deprived of their rum." And the

Sugar Mill Driven by Oxen. Engraving by Charles de Rochefort, 1667. Sunbelt Archives.

A Design for a
Pastillage (Sugar
Paste) Pièce Montée
in the Form of a Putto
in a Chariot Being
Drawn by a Hunting
Poodle. Watercolor,
Artist Unknown,
1820s. Sunbelt
Archives.

last was the principal cause of mutinies—the captains withheld rum from the men while they indulged in French brandy.

Pirates, on the other hand, received better pay than the sailors and could drink whenever they wanted. English writes, "Pirates drank while eating, they drank while sailing, they drank before, during, and after fighting, making them the first great multi-taskers. People molested by pirates routinely complained that their oppressors smelled of two things: tar and rum. While rum was the most popular beverage, these guys weren't picky. You name it, they drank it." Henry Morgan, one of the most famous pirates, was also one of the biggest drinkers, able to consume six pints of rum per night without showing any obvious signs of being drunk.

Coulombe, the author of *Rum: The Epic Story of the Drink That Conquered the World*, described the pirates's behavior as "drunken schizophrenia." He wrote: "One moment, the pirates are courteous to their captives, the next brutal, and vice versa. Almost always, the catalyst was the rum bottle." In fact, such rum-fueled behavior led to the demise of one of the most famous pirates of all, Blackbeard. In 1718, a drunken beach-party barbecue with another famous pirate of the day, Charles Vane, led to an informant telling Lt. Governor Alexander Spotswood of Virginia about the festivities, and he sent two sloops to Okracoke Island, off the coast of North Carolina, when they cornered Blackbeard. The pirate, drunk as usual, decided to fight. During the battle, one of the Virginia seamen nearly severed Blackbeard's head from his body with a cutlass, and that was the end of him. A later investigation shows that at least the rum made him fight well: He had five pistol balls in his body and twenty cutlass wounds on his body.

Far away from the Royal Navy at sail and the pirates, rum was taking England by storm. "'Kill-devil had invaded almost all areas of English social life," writes Matthew Parker, author of *The Sugar Barons*. "From 2,000 gallons a year in 1700, by 1773 rum imports into England and Wales had risen to two million gallons, further swelling the coffers of the sugar barons." Additionally in England, sugar and other luxuries like chocolate, coffee, tea, and tobacco were shaping a "consumer mentality" among common people that Parker says was making them "more pliant and willing to accept factory discipline in order to afford their luxury stimulants."

A Mill Yard. Painting by William Clark, 1833. Sunbelt Archives.

Queen Elizabeth's Teeth and the Sugar Poet

And these luxury stimulants were the result of the English drive for profits. "England fought the most, conquered the most colonies, and went furthest in creating a plantation system," writes Mintz. It completely drove Spain and Portugal out of the European sugar trade and reached a virtual stalemate with France that settled into a situation where French colonies supplied sugar only to France, and English colonies only to England. Neither country needed the other, and English sugar imports skyrocketed in less than a hundred years. From 1660 to 1753, sugar imports went from a thousand hogsheads to a hundred and ten thousand hogsheads, with a hogshead barrel equaling about 145 U.S. gallons.

The popularity of sugar caused political changes as well as social ones. "By the 1670s sugar was a trading commodity of such importance that the Dutch yielded New York to England in exchange for the sugar lands of Surinam, while in 1763 France abandoned the whole of Canada to the British for the sake of Guadeloupe," writes Tannahill. After 1660, sugar imports totaled more than all other imports (including tobacco) combined, and by 1750, "the poorest English farm laborer's wife took sugar in her tea," according to Mintz. By 1800, British sugar consumption had increased 2,500 percent in 150 years, a record that no other foodstuff in history could match. Mintz notes that like tea, "sugar came to define English 'character.'"

One of features of the English sugar-eating character was bad teeth, the result of way too much sugar combined with little or no dental hygiene. When the German attorney Paul Hentzner visited England in 1598, he met Queen Elizabeth when she was sixty-five years old and described her as "very majestic; her face oblong, fair, but wrinkled; her eyes small . . . her lips narrow, and her teeth black." There were no toothbrushes in those days, and her only dental tools were Holland tooth-cloths, edged with black and silver. She suffered from toothaches and was lisping because her teeth were falling out one by one, as she was rightly terrified by the extraction techniques of the day. The stories spread that she had wooden teeth, but that's a myth. False teeth would not be invented for another century, so the queen used plugs of rolled cloth to fill in the gaps between her blackened teeth. The plugs probably resembled wood, thus giving rise to the myth.

Sugar's rise to glory inspired poetry—of a sort. In 1764, an English doctor named James Grainger living in St. Kitts in the Caribbean published a book in London called *The Sugar-Cane: A Poem in Four Books* that was penned in the style of Virgil's *Georgics,* that paean to agricultural practices. The book was a blank verse description of all aspects of sugarcane cultivation, and true to *Georgics* style, Grainger could not call a spade a spade and made it vaguely sexual in today's vernacular.

Metallic Blade, wedded to ligneous Rod
Wherewith the rustic Swain upturns the sod.

As might be imagined, the wags of the time were highly amused by this poem and ridiculed Grainger in print. Dr. Johnson had a great time recounting how "all the assembled wits burst into a laugh, when, after much blank-verse pomp, the poet began a new paragraph thus: 'Now, Muse, let's sing of rats.'" According to Boswell, Dr. Johnson also commented: "What could he make of a sugar-cane? He might as well write the 'Parsley-bed, a Poem,' or 'The Cabbage-Garden, a Poem.'"

The critics missed the fact that hidden within all of Grainger's tortured poetry was a serious and important guidebook to sugar production. Thomas W. Krise, in an article about Grainger, noted, "The effect of reading the complete poem with all its footnotes is to take a sort of grand tour of the West Indies while the islands were at the height of a sugar-and-slavery system that produced more wealth for Great Britain than all the North American colonies combined." But the people of the time laughed at Grainger, book sales were poor, and he never realized his dream to make enough money off of it to retire "home to England," where sugar was more popular than he ever imagined.

The "White Spice" In British Cookery

From early on, cooks in England preferred their sugar to be as white as possible. By the 1540s, London had its own sugar refineries to remove impurities. In them, the brownish sugar was boiled with a lye of ashes, then clarified with egg whites, and finally covered with wet clay from which water dripped though the sugar, displacing any molasses left in it. The dried clay was cracked off, leaving loaves of pure sugar weighing up to fourteen pounds. Soon there were fifty refineries processing the ever-increasing shiploads of raw sugar.

In the 1570s, sugar was sold by spice shops even as it was beginning to replace the Medieval and Renaissance spices in cooking. At first sugar, the "white spice," was combined with other spices such as ginger, saffron, pepper, and salt, and such combinations were sprinkled over roasted meats and dishes like "stewed trouts cooked with wine." These sugary entrées offended later British food historians like William Mead, who whined: "Everyone is aware that nothing is more sickening than an oyster sprinkled with sugar. Yet we have more than one old receipt recommending such a combination."

But there were far more practical uses for sugar than frosting oysters, and C. Anne Wilson observes: "It is hardly surprising . . . that the department of cookery which took up the most sugar

---

To make little fine Cakes.

ONE pound of butter beaten to cream, a pound and a quarter of flour, a pound of fine sugar beat fine, a pound of currants clean washed and picked, fix eggs, two whites left out; beat them fine, mix the flour, sugar, and eggs by degrees into the batter, beat it all well with both hands; either make into little cakes, or bake it in one.

A Surinam Planter with Slave Pouring Rum. Illustration from The Narrative of a Five Years Expedition against the Revolted Negroes of Surinam, *by John Gabriel Stedman, 1796. Sunbelt Archives.*

was that of preserving and candying." This makes a lot of sense, because sugar has for millennia been the primary preservative of fruits of all kinds and in many forms. Wilson quotes a sixteenth-century description of this use of sugar at a banquet: "jellies of all colours . . . conserves of old fruits . . . marmalades . . . and sundry outlandish confections, altogether sweetened with sugar." It should be noted that preserving fruit in sugar did not pass down to commoners as fast as sugared tea, and it took until the nineteenth century for the transformation of these treats to become manufactured preserves such as those made by Crosse & Blackwell.

Two factors delayed this transformation: the traditional British resistance to fruit, and a safe preservation medium that was inexpensive. When these two variables aligned, as they finally did after the price of sugar fell sharply during the free-trade movement, then a rare substance would be transformed into a common one and an expensive treat into a cheap food. While this was happening over centuries with sugar-based manufactured foods, sugar was inexorably playing a larger role in home cooking, and the sweetened meats transitioned into sweet sauces, dessert wines, as well as pies, cakes, and many types of homemade breads and tarts.

The ever-increasing popularity of sugar in home cookery was exemplified in one of the most famous and influential cookbooks of all time, *The Art of Cookery Made Plain and Easy,* by Hannah Glasse, published in 1747. Sugar is a standard ingredient in the kitchen, mentioned more than one hundred times, and is used in large amounts as in the accompanying recipe for "little fine Cakes."

Soon after Glasse's cookbook was published, sugar became as ubiquitous as flour in the English diet, appearing in elaborate complex carbohydrates such as pastries, hasty puddings, jam-smeared breads, buns, tarts, biscuits, and candy. Hot beverages like tea, coffee, and chocolate always were served with copious

amounts of sugar—so much that Mintz commented: "By no later than 1800, sugar had become a necessity—albeit a costly and rare one—in the diet of every English person; by 1900, it was supplying nearly one-fifth of the calories of the English diet." During most of this time, sugar was still supplied by slave labor, although this would change rapidly as the eighteenth century became the nineteenth.

Hoeing a Cane-Piece. Painting by William Clark, 1833. Sunbelt Archives.

In 1772, Lord Chief Justice Mansfield declared that a slave entering Britain would be free because "the status of slavery is so odious that nothing can be suffered to support it but positive law." The emancipation movement gained momentum when British-controlled India began producing sugar without slaves in competition with the West Indies, and this gave the East India Company the self-serving opportunity to attack slavery. In 1792, the company claimed that the cost of a sugar slave's life was 450 pounds of sugar and in supposed moral outrage said that "a family that uses five pounds of sugar a week will kill a slave every twenty-one months." And to obscure the fact that Indian sugar was twice as expensive as Caribbean sugar, the East India Company distributed sugar bowls imprinted with the message "EAST INDIA SUGAR NOT MADE BY SLAVES."

Slavery in the British Empire was officially abolished in 1833 and revised to eliminate the sham of a twelve-year "apprenticeship" in 1837, but the anti-slavery movement still had to deal with the likes of Thomas Carlyle, who published a pamphlet in 1849 obnoxiously titled *Occasional Discourse on the Nigger Question*, in which he supported the "less fortunate

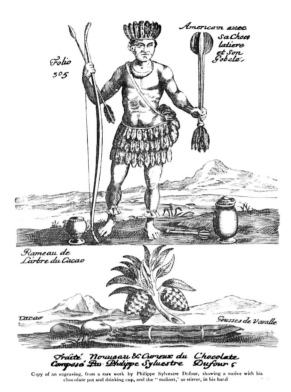

Copy of an engraving, from a rare work by Philippe Sylvestre Dufour, showing a native with his chocolate pot and drinking cup, and the "molinet," or stirrer, in his hand.

Native with a Chocolate Cup and Stirrer. Illustration from A Treatise on the New and Curious of Coffee, Tea and Chocolate, *by Philippe Sylvestre Dufour, 1685. Sunbelt Archives.*

white man of those tropical localities" and railed against ungrateful blacks who were freed but would not help feed the whites or help them make sugar. He suggested, absurdly, that the black man not be allowed to grow his pumpkins (that era's racist equivalent to the watermelon of later caricatures) "till you agree to do the State [think "planters"] so many days of service."

More rational men, like the poet Matthew Arnold, called Carlyle a "moral desperado," and fortunately only a few people agreed with Carlyle's racist rantings. Slavery was officially dead, and the sugar industry in the West Indies declined because of the Indian sugar competition, the entrance of the sugar beet into the sugar-making industry, and the rise of new technology for sugar making. But its triumph in England, Europe, and the rest of the world was complete; in 1970, 9 percent of all food calories were in the form of sucrose, and countries like Iceland, Ireland, the Netherlands, Denmark, and parts of England were consuming slightly more than 120 pounds of sucrose a year, or about a third of a pound per day.

Even some food historians don't comprehend the meaning and consequences of sugar's rise and spread around the world. Peter Macinnis, for example, ends *Bittersweet* by observing that although sugar caused the deaths of millions of humans and the "destruction of soil and whole environments," on the "plus side," it has "provided us with many taste delights, and had a beneficial effect on the economies of many nations." This is like saying, "As bad as dropping the atomic bombs on Hiroshima and Nagasaki were, the technology that caused hundreds of thousands of innocent people to die led to great advances in nuclear science and made possible cheaper forms of electricity so that people could enjoy their television programs without worry."

I think Henry Hobhouse, author of *Seeds of Change*, sums it up best: "Sugar, then, is the most notable addiction in history that killed not only the consumer but the producer too. Every ton represented a life. Every teaspoonful represented six days of a slave's life. Put that way, would anyone in eighteenth-century England have touched sugar? But, of course, few people in the eighteenth century did put the problem quite like that."

The Ultimate Flavors: Chocolate and Vanilla

In 1921, archaeologist Neil M. Judd began excavating the massive, eight-hundred-room Pueblo Bonito complex at Chaco Canyon in northwest New Mexico. By the time he completed the task in 1924, he had uncovered a cache of 111 tall, cylinder jars of a type that was unknown in the Southwest. Decades later, the mysterious jars intrigued University of New Mexico archaeologist Patricia Crown, who thought they looked like some Maya jars she had seen, so she consulted with Dorie Reents-Budet, a Maya ceramics specialist at the Smithsonian Institution, who confirmed that glyphs on the vessels indicated that they were used to drink cacao beverages, which was unheard of north of the Mexican border.

Crown's next step was to team up with analytical chemist W. Jeffrey Hurst of the Hershey Center for Health and Nutrition. She sent him potsherds of similar jars she found in the trash mounds beside Pueblo Bonito, and Hurst ground them up, tested them, and discovered the presence of theobromine, a marker chemical for chocolate. And the fact that this chemical had penetrated the unglazed jars was a definite indication that liquid chocolate was absorbed into the jars. The Anasazi inhabitants of Chaco Canyon around AD 1000 were drinking chocolate that was 1,200 miles north of its nearest natural source. This discovery was just one of chocolate's many long journeys away from its home in central Mexico.

Ancestral Pueblo Jars Like These Were Used to Drink Cacao Beverages. AD 900–1130. Pueblo Bonito, Chaco Canyon, New Mexico. National Museum of the American Indian.

Chocolate for Turquoise?

By studying ancient North American trade routes, a theory can be advanced about how chocolate arrived in Chaco Canyon. From the time of the height of the Maya civilization (the first century AD) until the Aztecs were conquered by the Spanish (c. 1500), long-distance traders called *pochteca* traveled far and wide from southern Mexico. The *pochteca* were a hereditary class, similar to a guild, and had their own rites, insignia, and gods. They were also foreign agents of expansionist empires, beginning with the Maya and ending with the Aztecs.

The *pochteca* established what anthropologists call a "down-the-line" trading system that connected the Mexican civilizations with what is now the American Southwest. In this system, the Mayas or the later Toltecs, for example, would not have a great amount of direct trade with the Anasazi, but rather the commerce, directed by the *pochteca*, would proceed "down the line" from one culture to another, or in the case of chocolate at Chaco, "up the line." That said, a 1,200-mile trading journey could have been accomplished on foot in a month or two if there were a pressing need for the Mexicans—like turquoise.

The connection between the Southwest civilizations and the Mexicans was through Paquimé or Casas Grandes in Chihuahua, which was another major pre-Columbian settlement. From about AD 900, regular trade routes were established between Casas Grandes and the ancestors of the Rio Grande pueblos, the Anasazi, and also the Hohokam people of Arizona and northern Sonora. The people of the Southwest traded turquoise and salt for copper bells, seashells, parrots, macaws, cotton, and presumably at some point in time chocolate pods or seeds. This hypothetical scenario does not assume that the Anasazi attempted to grow chocolate in the Southwest (impossible for that tropical plant) but that they had been supplied cacao by the *pochteca* associates and taught how to make a chocolate drink.

Archaeologist Dorothy Washburn of the University of Pennsylvania in Philadelphia believes that this trade extended to about 1400 and that everyone from low-ranking farmers to the elite was drinking chocolate, so she thinks "active trading for cacao must have occurred with Mesoamerican states." Other researchers working on the turquoise end of the exchange have matched the chemical signature of turquoise from mines in New Mexico to that of turquoise found at several Mesoamerican sites, including the Maya site of Chichen Itza. Washburn believes that turquoise mines in the U.S. Southwest, but not Mexico or Central America, had the highest-quality stones needed for use as mosaic tiles in Mesoamerican designs. And on breaks from their turquoise tileworks, the Aztec tilers were drinking chocolate.

Aztec Origins, New Spanish Drinks

An evergreen tree that produces the "food of the gods" in capsules on its stem and an orchid on a vine 350 feet long with pods that are the second most costly spice in the world—chocolate and vanilla couldn't be more different, yet their flavors are often combined in sweet foods. For that delightful combination, we owe a debt of gratitude to the Aztecs, who were the first foodies ever to experiment with that striking combination.

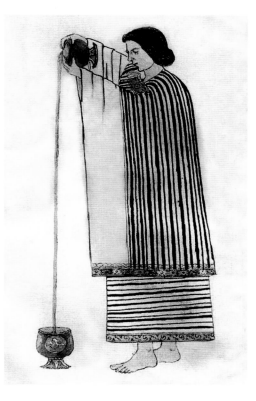

Mujer Vertiendo Chocolate (Woman Pouring Chocolate). From the Codex Tudela, c. 1553. Sunbelt Archives.

But their savory synthesis was not a sweet dessert but rather a spicy and sharp after-dinner drink.

Bernardino de Sahagún, the Spanish chronicler of the Aztecs introduced in Part 1, was the first person to write about the combination, and historians are still trying to decipher what he meant when he described the chocolate drink with vanilla that was served to the Aztec emperor Montezuma: "chocolate . . . flavored with green vanilla." Food historians Sophie and Michael Coe commented, "The vanilla would have been dried and ground," but it's not that simple. Vanilla must be fermented or cured to achieve the flavor we know and love today, so we don't really know what that vanilla tasted like.

The cacao beans were not only used to make these flavored drinks, they were also the principal currency in the markets. A turkey hen sold for a hundred beans, an avocado for three, and a large tomato was worth three beans, as was a single tamale. A large *axolotl* (an Aztec delicacy—a salamander) could be purchased wiggling for four cacao beans. And where there's currency, there's counterfeiting, and Sahagún's informants told him several ways this was done, but the best was to make fake seeds using amaranth dough covered with broken avocado pits and shaped like the beans and mixed in with them.

In the Aztec world, both cacao and vanilla were tributes paid to the court of the reigning emperor by settlements or outliers of Tenochtitlán, along with just about any crop or foodstuff that can be imagined. These tributes, which also included gold, quetzal feathers, balls of rubber, jade, and clothing, were the basis of the incredible wealth of Montezuma and other emperors. Vanilla was one of the main flavorings of chocolate, along with various "flowers," honey, and ground *achiote* (annatto) seeds, which colored the drink blood red. This color ties into cacao bean symbolism, as it was a representation of the human heart torn out during sacrifices, probably because both were repositories of precious liquids, and the more that chocolate resembled blood, the more significant the symbolism.

After an initial resistance that lasted more than fifty years, with comments including "a drink for pigs," the conquering Spanish eventually adopted chocolate with a passion, making it in chocolate pots by dissolving the powder from the crushed pods and flavoring the mix with sugar, cinnamon, and vanilla. This happened mostly because mixed-race wives of the second-generation Spaniards, called creoles in the day, loved chocolate drinks so much that they refused to sit through Sunday mass without their cups of it, which prompted a clerical ruling: Chocolate was a liquid, not a food, and thus could be consumed during fasting times. This ruling, of course, ensured that the churches were full of women. José de Acosta, the Jesuit who wrote *Natural and Moral History of the Indies*, wrote that "Spanish women are addicted to black chocolate." The powder used for these church drinks was made into wafers by the Aztecs to create "instant chocolate" during military campaigns, and the Spanish seized on this idea as a handy way to store and ship dried chocolate to Spain, in addition to the dried beans themselves. Already, chocolate had two forms. It would have many more in just a few centuries.

A New "Medicine" for Spain

Contrary to popular belief, Cortés did not introduce chocolate to Spain in 1528 when he put on a dog and pony show at the court

of Charles V, the Holy Roman Emperor. Cortés's show included ball players bouncing their strange rubber balls, albino Aztecs, jaguars, an armadillo, feather fans, and obsidian mirrors, but no cacao. That would have to wait until 1544, when Dominican friars took Kekchi Mayas to visit Prince Philip and brought with them chiles, beans, maize, and receptacles of beaten chocolate, which marks chocolate's first appearance in the Old World. It wasn't until 1585 that the first shipment of cacao beans reached Seville from Veracruz. I think vanilla was also introduced to Spain during this 1544 show-and-tell of the foods of New Spain mostly because the court of Charles V was soon flavoring chocolate drinks with vanilla.

After its introduction into Spain, chocolate was a drug or medicine, much like sugar had been early on in Europe, when it was sold in spice shops along with other "medicines." Cacao, now called chocolate, fit neatly into the humoral system of medicine prevalent at the time, and as the Coes point out, it "traveled in Europe from one court to another, from noble house to noble house, monastery to monastery." But its spread had more to do with its flavor, filling nature, and its stimulating properties because of the caffeine it contained than it did with its purported medicinal qualities. The Coes use the analogy of Coca-Cola, which began as

Still Life with an Ebony Chest. Note the Chocolate-Drinking Utensils on the Left. Painting by Antonio de Pereda y Salgado, 1652. Sunbelt Archives.

a patent medicine (also with caffeine) and eventually became the most popular bottled drink in the world. It also contains caffeine, as does coffee, the next European stimulant to be the star of the show.

Historian Marcy Norton notes that "the common view that coffee consumption led to chocolate consumption in Europe is backward. Rather, it seems, chocolate helped pave the way for coffee by creating a craving among consumers for dark, bitter, sweetened hot stimulant drinks." In this way it was chocolate that first increased the demand for sugar, not coffee. Chocolate had a significant presence in Spain by the 1590s and had spread northward by the 1620s, but coffee did not gain significant acceptance in England and the rest of Europe until the 1650s.

Between 1544, when chocolate first arrived, and 1556, when Charles V abdicated the throne of Spain, he "is credited with achieving the happy admixture of chocolate and sugar, a confection that yielded a drink not only palatable but delicious to Europeans," according to Bennett Weinberg and Bonnie Bealer, writing in *The World of Caffeine*. And the Spaniards made their chocolate strong and thick, which made it a powerful stimulant due to the concentration of caffeine and theobromine. While many historians believe that Europeans transformed chocolate from a primitive, peppery drink to an elegant drink to be served at court, Norton accuses them of failing to "explain how chocolate got a foothold among European consumers in the Americas and then Europe." She states that the "transmission of taste" of chocolate did not come from the top of society to the commoners, but "instead it flowed in the opposite direction: from the colonized to the colonizer, from the 'barbarian' to the 'civilized,' from the degenerate 'creole' to the metropolitan Spaniard, from gentry to royalty." This is precisely what happened in northern Italy with maize turning into polenta "cults" (see Part 2), but this time the commoners were from the New World, not the Old, and chocolate was a stimulant and a curiosity, not a basic food. She concludes that "the European taste for chocolate emerged as a contingent accident of empire."

And this accident enabled the Spanish, who had "discovered" chocolate, to keep it a secret for just a few decades, but during this time, the Spanish clergy learned how to fashion hard chocolate using Aztec techniques, while English and Dutch privateers, when intercepting Spanish ships for precious cargo like gold and silver, were dumping the cacao overboard because they had no idea that it was a valuable luxury trade item. But in Spain, the center of European society and fashion, the secret of chocolate would soon suffer the same fate as the Chinese secret of tea and the Islamic secret of coffee. Travelers from all over Europe came to Madrid for business and were served chocolate, while Spanish monks were busy showing off their chocolate to visiting brothers, who took it back to their own countries. Chocolate would soon become, after wine, the most popular drink in all of Europe.

Italy's Perfumed Chocolate

Italy was next for chocolate the conqueror, and we must remember what the "country" was like in the mid-seventeenth century. In the first place, it wasn't a country at all until unification in 1870 but rather a combination of still-independent city-states and territories of other countries, particularly Spain, which controlled all of southern Italy. Various states in the north were controlled by France and Austria off and on, and many armies were doing battle in the ever-shuffling effort to control them. Even the pope had his own army, and didn't hesitate to use it, ruling like a king most of the middle portion of Italy from Rome. Each of the states had royal or noble houses, and intermarriage with other noble houses was the preferred way to form political and military alliances. Often, when women from one state moved to another for a marriage of convenience, they carried their favorite personal items with them, and those were often culinary in nature.

But the introduction of chocolate into Italy was the result of four men who were inadvertently collaborating with each other, Francesco d'Antonio Carletti, Paolo Zacchia, Cosimo III (the de' Medici from Florence), and his physician, Francesco Redi, who was also a philologist and poet. Here's how it worked: Carletti was a business world traveler who left Florence in 1591 seeking his fortune and found himself on the west coast of El Salvador in 1600, where he studied the vast cacao plantations and wrote a report on them. He returned to Florence in 1606 with chocolate and presented his report to Ferdinando I de' Medici, who apparently kept it in his state files, where it was eventually consulted by Francesco Redi some time before 1666 and who served under three successive de' Medici rulers of Florence.

Meanwhile, in 1664, a Roman physician Paolo Zacchia praised chocolate in his book with the odd title *Of Hypochondriacal*

Sicknesses as a good drug that comforts the stomach and aids digestion when taken in the morning. Based on his comments, we can see that chocolate was a novelty at that time in much of Italy, except for the southern Spanish territories, where chocolate drinks were already popular. But it would not remain a novelty for long, because it would soon be disseminated to northern Italy by the Jesuit priests, who numbered about sixteen thousand at the time both in Europe and the Americas. They had eagerly embraced chocolate drinking, and their lucrative trade in it through their colleagues in New Spain was, of course, "for the great glory of God."

In Florence, Redi was tending to his third de' Medici ruler, Cosimo III, a glutton who, in the words of historian Sir Harold Acton, "regardless of calamities . . . spared no expense to summon the rarest and most precious condiments from all sections of the globe to his table." Christopher Hibbert, another historian specializing in the House of Medici, added, "He himself consumed gargantuan platefuls of the richest delicacies, becoming fatter than ever with a complexion not so much ruddy as inflamed." Redi took charge and placed Cosimo on a strict diet, and the ruler lived on until he was eighty, enjoying chocolate drinks that had been introduced into Florence in 1668. This seemingly contradicts Carletti's 1606 introduction of chocolate, but what probably happened was that Carletti's chocolate was in such small amounts that it was used up in no time, and there was no other source of it until the late 1660s.

Redi was a busy man, writing a dithyramb (a poem of exaltation) in which Bacchus, the god of wine, denounces chocolate, tea, and coffee as "not medicines made for me" and would sooner "take to poison." This is Bacchus speaking through Redi, who actually loved chocolate and devised a secret recipe for what the Coes called "the most Baroque of all chocolate drinks," Jasmine Chocolate, which became the specialty of Cosimo's court. "Baroque" in this sense means excessive ornamentation or complexity, and the addition of fresh jasmine flowers, ambergris, and vanilla—all perfume ingredients—was what pushed this recipe over the top. Redi bragged about it in glowing terms: "The very genteel odor of jasmine, which, together with cinnamon . . . and vanilla, has a prodigious effect upon such as delight themselves by taking chocolate." Redi died in 1697, and his secret recipe was later uncovered by naturalist Antonio Vallisneri, which shows that as the eighteenth century approached, vanilla was still used primarily to flavor chocolate. But that would soon change when both commodities entered France.

The Chocolate Seduction of France

When the Spanish princess Maria Theresa (also known as Marie Thérèse) was betrothed to Louis XIV of France in 1660, she gave her fiancé an engagement gift of chocolate, packaged in an elegantly ornate chest. He was not impressed. When she moved to Versailles, she brought her precious cacao beans with her, as well as her chocolate-loving ladies-in-waiting and a crew of retainers just to make it for her. Hot chocolate was served at the wedding reception to the cream of European society, and it was a huge hit. Theresa was quoted as saying, "Chocolate and the King are my only passions," but courtiers noted that she put chocolate first in that comment. Louis initially resisted the chocolate, but his court loved it so much that he gave in and eventually came to love it nearly as much as he loved his mistress. It is said that his personal recipe included an egg yolk to guarantee a rich, thick concoction.

But is this story of chocolate history in France true? It is taken from *Memoirs*, by the Duchess of Montpensier, a courtier who attended the wedding and who wrote that two ladies-in-waiting for Maria, Molina (so named from the *molinillo*, the special chocolate-stirring stick of New Spain) and La Philippa, prepared her chocolate in the Spanish style and she drank it in secrecy, but everyone at court knew about it. This tale was contradicted by Pierre Jean-Baptiste Legrand d'Aussy, who published a history of French social customs in 1782. He wrote that Maria could not have been responsible for popularizing chocolate in France because her consumption of it was in complete secrecy.

His protestation was countered by the memoirs of a person intimately related to the story, the Marquise de Montespan, who was Maria's maid of honor and subsequently Louis's mistress, who told of how Molina helped Maria popularize the chocolate beverage: "The Señora Molina, well furnished with silver kitchen utensils, had sort of a private kitchen or scullery reserved for her own use, and there it is that the manufacture takes place of clove-scented chocolate, brown soups and gravies, stews redolent with garlic, capsicums, and nutmeg, and all that nauseous pastry in

The Penthievre Family or the Cup of Chocolate. Painting by Jean Baptiste Charpentier, 1768. Sunbelt Archives.

which the young Infanta revels." Certainly her chocolate spread to the rest of the court and then into general French high society.

And the "secrecy" of her chocolate is really just privacy, because Maria loved her food in the style of New Spain as transferred to Spain, with all its spices—plus garlic—and was probably just trying to keep her "low class" meals private. The chocolate she drank, along with those "nauseous pastries," caused her to have the same problems as Queen Elizabeth I. The pastries were undoubtedly sugar-laden and probably were flavored with vanilla imported from Spain, which contributed to her declining beauty. Maria's sister-in-law, Elizabeth-Charlotte, Duchesse d'Orleans, described her appearance: "Her teeth were very ugly, being black and broken. It was said that this proceeded from her being in the constant habit of taking chocolate; she also frequently ate garlic." No wonder Louis had a mistress.

Chocolate was making gains in popularity in Versailles and other centers of elite circles during the mid- to late 1600s, but it was still quite expensive, difficult to prepare, and usually not available to the small middle class. Except, that is for Bayonne and the French Basque country, where the "Portuguese Jews," as they were called, imported cacao from Cadiz and turned it into a paste that they sold to anyone with the money to buy it. They were opposed because of religious intolerance by the non-Jewish chocolate makers, who formed a guild to exclude them from making it because they were not part of the guild, but in this particular case their effort failed when the French parliament dissolved the guild—a rare victory for Jews of that age.

Louis XIV was forced to end his three-times-a-week "chocolate receptions" in 1693 because of financial difficulties, but by 1686–87 chocolate mania had spread to Paris, where a directory of the time listed three artisan chocolate makers who fashioned chocolates of all kind and sold them from their workshops. Other artisans were creating the special chocolate cups and pots, some of which were quite elaborate and made of precious metals, like a silver chocolate set with golden flowers. A café called Le Procope opened and began to sell chocolate ice cream, which had the chocolate flavor but not the same amount of the stimulant, thus cutting the cost of tasting it and making it available to the lower classes. That café is still open today. By 1692, winemakers were complaining that these new beverages, namely chocolate, tea, and coffee, were cutting into their profits, which just shows how entrenched the new drinks had become, not only in France but England, Holland, Germany, and Austria, too.

In 1657, a Frenchman opened a shop named Coffee Mill and Tobacco Roll in London, which actually specialized in chocolate bars that could be melted to make drinks or use in desserts and treats. These bars were worth one-half to three-quarters of their weight in gold, largely because of the extremely high duties on importing it, which, of course, led to the smuggling of cacao, probably from Venezuela to the "smuggler's coast" of Cornwall. The English invented milk chocolate in about 1700 (some say 1730), which was another way of diluting the chocolate to make it less expensive. Unlike in France and Spain, where chocolate was initially available only to the aristocracy, in England and Holland, chocolate was sold to the public from shops almost from the start of its popularity. Still, only the prosperous could afford it. Wolfgang Schivelbusch in *Tastes of Paradise* (1993) makes a distinction between the coffee houses and chocolate parlors in late seventeenth-century London. The former were "bourgeois and puritanical," while the latter were "thoroughly anti-puritanical, perhaps even bordello-like places," which would certainly tie in to chocolate's ongoing reputation as an aphrodisiac.

The chocolate parlors in London had turned into gambling clubs by 1675, and King Charles II decreed that they be suppressed, so in 1702, only five survived, including one of the orig-

How To Make Chocolate, by Hannah Glasse, 1756

TAKE six pounds of cocoa-nuts, one pound of aniseeds, four ounces of long pepper, one of cinnamon, a quarter of pound of almonds, one pound of pistachios, as much achiote as will make it the colour of brick; three grains of musk, and as much ambergrease, six pounds of loaf sugar, one ounce of nutmegs, dry and beat them, and force them through a fine sieve: your almonds must be beat to a paste, and mixed with the other in-

gredients; then dip your sugar in orange-flower, or rose-water, and put it in a skillet, on a very gentle charcoal-fire; then put in the spice, and strew it well together; then the musk and ambergrease; then put in the cocoa-nuts last of all; then achiote, wetting it with the water the sugar was dipt in; stew all these very well together over a hotter fire than before; then take it up, and put it into boxes, or what form you like, and set it to dry in a warm place. The pistachios and almonds must be a little beat in a mortar, then ground upon a stone.

La Belle Chocolatiere. Painting by Jean-Etienne Liotard, 1745. Sunbelt Archives.

inal ones, the Cocoa Tree. But chocolate was still served by the coffee houses for about twelve pence a quart, or twice that of coffee or tea. Later, the gambling ceased and both the chocolate parlors and the coffee houses became political clubs, with the Tories meeting at the Cocoa Tree while the Whigs downed their chocolate at the St. James Coffee House. These anticipated the rise of taverns in the American colonies, which became the centers of political revolution against England.

Hannah Glasse's famous cookbook, *Art of Cookery*, was published in 1756 in London, and it contained recipes not only for chocolate and vanilla but also for ice cream. She has two recipes for making chocolate, including one with "vanelas," referring to vanilla pods. Noted food historian Karen Hess, who wrote the historical notes for the 1998 American edition of the book, observes that the recipe "has hardly changed from early Spanish sources" and comments: "It does show . . . that the use of chocolate had reached home use among fairly ordinary people in England." Ordinary people who had money, that is.

Chocolate arrived in Hanover, Germany, by 1690, and in 1711, Charles VI became Holy Roman Emperor and transferred his Spanish court, along with its chocolate, to Vienna, Austria, which began the chocolate surge that would soon engulf the rest of Europe, including the notable later chocolate centers of Holland, Germany, and Switzerland. Unlike other monarchs of the time, Charles kept the chocolate tariffs low, and as a beverage chocolate became so popular that it was considered a national drink. A pastel on parchment, "La Belle Chocolatière" (1743), by Jean-Étienne Liotarda, a Swiss artist working in Austria, shows the artist's chocolate-serving maid carrying a tray with a porcelain chocolate mug and a glass of water. This is the first known example of chocolate featured in the visual arts in Europe outside of Spain, and it was later was used in advertising for the American Baker's Chocolate Company (1862) and served as inspiration for the commercial illustration of the "nurse" that appeared on Droste's cocoa tins (1900).

By the turn of the nineteenth century, chocolate was entrenched in Europe, with prices dropping as supplies increased, and it was slowly entering the growing middle-class society. But for this uniquely American foodstuff to achieve its evolution from a luxury indulgence to an industrial product, chocolate needed one last transformation.

Cacao Becomes Cocoa

In the 1854 translation of the French edition of *The Physiology of Taste* (1825), the great gourmand Jean-Anthelme Brillat-Savarin was quite positive about adding vanilla to chocolate. "Sugar is the integral part, for without sugar the compound is cocoa and chocolate," he wrote. "To sugar, cinnamon and cocoa is joined the delicious aroma of vanilla, and thus is obtained the *ne plus ultra* to which this preparation can be carried." The definition of "cocoa" used by Brillat-Savarin was about to change radically, because what he was talking about still contained all the butterfat that chocolate possessed at the time. But three years after his death, the Dutch chemist Coenraad J. van Houten patented a press that removed most of the fat from chocolate, which accounts for more than half the weight of the roasted and ground cacao beans. Two products were the result of this process: a hard cacao cake that was ground into the new cocoa powder, and the cacao butter, which has a mild chocolate aroma and flavor. The cocoa powder (carefully blended with some amounts of cocoa butter) became the basis for the chocolate bars and cakes so familiar to us today, while cocoa butter itself is used in the commercial production of white chocolate, milk chocolate, and chocolate drinks like hot chocolate.

Food chemistry expert Harold McGee explains that Van Houten's technique "became the key to the development of modern chocolate candy. This was cocoa butter that could be *added* to a paste of ordinary ground cocoa beans and sugars to provide a rich, melting matrix for the dry particles."

Before this invention, bakers had not been able to make delicate chocolate cakes and pastries because of the natural bitterness and graininess of cacao. But Van Houten's process changed all that, and now Viennese bakers could invent, in 1832, the famous Sacher torte by using a mixture of cocoa powder and cocoa butter. Schivelbusch notes: "This process put an end to the Spanish tradition of chocolate drinking in which solid and liquid chocolate were identical" and commented that it was "an irony of history" that two "arch-Protestant" countries (Holland and Austria) ended the Spanish Catholic chocolate tradition. Schivelbusch, a German citizen, takes delight in the fact that "the former status drink of the *ancien régime* had sunk to the world of women and children," and he echoes the sentiments of Marcy Norton earlier that chocolate flowed from the commoner to the elite when he

writes, "Bourgeois society, as the historical victor over the old society, made a mockery of the status symbols once so important to the aristocracy."

Chocolate technology evolved quickly after Van Houten's process became widely used. The first commercial solid eating chocolate was made in England by Fry and Sons in 1847. Their main competition was a company owned by John and Benjamin Cadbury, which began chocolate production two years later. Through advertising and the press, the two companies battled for thirty years over who had the "purest" (read: unadulterated) chocolate until Cadbury finally won. The two companies merged in 1918. In 1867, Henri Nestlé invented powdered milk in Switzerland, and later he partnered with Daniel Peter to invent the first commer-

Chocolate, Theobroma cacao. *Botanical Illustration from Flora de Filipinas, by Franciso Manuel Blanco, c. 1880. Sunbelt Archives.*

cial milk chocolate, which of course eventually became the best-selling chocolate concoction. In the thirty years between 1849 and 1879, chocolate companies owned by Domingo Ghirardelli, Milton Hershey, Henri Nestlé, and Rodolphe Lindt all established the first chocolate "empires," which resulted in British chocolate consumption quadrupling between 1880 and 1902.

The Coes wrote that "Baroque Europe was always chocolate's real conquest," noting that chocolate never caught on in India, Southeast Asia, and the Far East, with the exception of the Philippines. Look for a surprising reversal of that supposition in Part 7. Weinberg and Bealer agree with the Coes about Asia and wrote that chocolate appreciation is "still developing in Africa," probably because the Ivory Coast, Ghana, Nigeria, Cameroon, and Togo grow about half the world's production of cacao, some of which filters down the pipeline to chocolate makers and home bakers.

In 2008, the International Cocoa Organization, the European Union Association of the Chocolate, the Biscuit and Confectionery Industries, and the International Confectionery Association released their list of the countries with the highest per capita chocolate consumption. Germany was at the top of the list with 25.1 pounds per year, with Switzerland in second place with 23.7 pounds per year.

Because Germany finished first, I had to call my good friend and food expert Harald Zoschke, who lives with his wife on the shores of the Bodensee in Kressbronn and ask him what was going on.

"Chocolate is certainly one of the most precious gifts from the New World to the Old World," he told me. "Two notable nineteenth-century inventions led to the chocolate bar that we enjoy so much today: Englishman John Cadbury developed an emulsification process to produce solid chocolate, and Swiss chocolate maker Theodore Lindt introduced conching of the cocoa mass, creating a much smoother texture of the finished product. Here in Europe, we're lucky to have various countries that developed a high 'chocolate culture.' Switzerland is one of them, and since this is also milk and cheese country, no wonder they're also famous for their milk chocolate. Fine chocolate comes also from Belgium and my home country of Germany, but for my personal taste, the best European chocolate is made in Italy and in France. All Europeans love chocolate, but the Swiss and Germans are leading the pack by consuming more than eleven kilograms per year. The British come close, followed by Scandinavians.

"When it comes to chocolate bars, there are two totally different trends—inexpensive mass products in the one to two Euros per 100-gram bar range are piling up in supermarkets. The consumer doesn't know (and doesn't care) which cocoa varieties are used, or actual cocoa mass percentage. This kind of chocolate is also featured in unbelievable amounts of seasonal hollow chocolate figures like Santas and Easter bunnies. The other trend for the past ten years, still on the rise, is high-end chocolate with price tags from four to fifteen Euros per 100-gram bar. Connoisseurs of these products care for the cocoa varieties used, cocoa mass percentage (**70%** and up is preferred) and plantation location. Especially in larger cities, specialty chocolate stores are popping up, and I'm glad that we have at least three of them in Munich. I don't smoke, so I don't feel guilty shopping for my favorite high-end brands like Amedei, Valrhona and Bonnat every other month or so at the Bavarian capital. About ten years ago, people smiled at me when I enjoyed a piece of 75% Criollo chocolate with a glass of fine Merlot or Amarone. Today there are even books about pairing wine and chocolate. That's not amazing, as both contain hundreds of flavor components, and many harmonize quite well.

"A smaller but increasing trend we're seeing over here is 'fair trade' chocolate. With lots of pressure by large trade corporations, working conditions in cocoa-producing countries are often disastrous, including child labor. As with coffee, organizations working directly with the producers are trying to help, and the resulting chocolate, mostly of good quality, is offered at competitive prices. The German city of Cologne is home to a unique chocolate museum that no chocolate lover should miss when visiting."

Chocolate vs. Vanilla

To complete the story of chocolate and vanilla for this brief tale of two American flavorings, I must attempt to answer the question "Which is the more preferred flavor?" The answer depends on who you ask, what type of treat you are speaking of, and what the exact question is. For example, the National Confectioners'

Association website says: "A recent survey revealed that 52% of U.S. adults said they like chocolate best. The second favorite flavor was a tie (at 12% each) between berry flavors and vanilla." Meanwhile, the International Ice Cream Association (Washington, D.C.) says America's favorite ice cream flavor is vanilla (29%), with chocolate a distant second (8.9%).

Focusing just on ice cream consumption figures, the NPD Group's National Eating Trends In-Home Database indicates that the top five individual flavors in terms of share of segment in the United States are vanilla (27.8%), chocolate (14.3%), strawberry (3.3%), chocolate chip (3.3%), and butter pecan (2.8%). Internationally, regardless of whether ice cream is full fat, premium, or economy, the world's favorite flavor is still vanilla. In the U.S., by far the world's largest market with per capita consumption almost six and a half times the world average, nearly 30% of volume sales are vanilla. According to Euromonitor, this figure is even higher across other key markets in this US$45 billion industry. Vanilla represents 55% of volume sales in the U.K., while in Japan, ranked as the tenth biggest spender on ice cream globally, the figure is nearly 40%. Canada, Germany, France, and Italy, all among the top ten markets for ice cream, prefer vanilla. In fact, only three of the top ten ice-cream-loving countries prefer something

Synthetic Vanilla

Synthetic vanillin accounts for more than 90 percent of the U.S. vanilla flavoring market and about 50 percent of the French market (the lowest national share). One ounce of artificially produced vanillin has roughly the same flavoring power as a gallon of natural vanilla extract. Synthetic vanillin costs one-hundredth the price of the natural product and not only substitutes for vanilla but also supplements adulterated vanilla extracts. Despite the strong competition from synthetic vanilla, a number of factors have strengthened the demand for vanilla beans during the past decade: increased health awareness and preference for natural products; escalating consumer demand for processed foods, which use new flavors and spices; and an explosion in popularity of gourmet ice creams, which tend to use pure natural flavors exclusively. —From the website of Agriculture of Papua New Guinea, a producer of natural vanilla.

different, with Australia and Brazil favoring chocolate, while in Russia the preference is for *plombir*, a high-fat buttercream.

So it would appear that within the huge ice cream market, vanilla is preferred, probably because it is more versatile than chocolate and more suitable for various toppings and sauces that work well with vanilla's rather "plain vanilla" flavor. But generally speaking, considering everything that contains either chocolate or vanilla, there's no doubt in my mind that, with the exception of the world of ice cream, and considering natural rather than synthetic flavors, chocolate is by far the more popular of that two. How did I reach that conclusion? I just examined the 2009 FAO statistics for the total world value of vanilla versus chocolate crops in International Dollars. The vanilla crop was worth $164.7 million, while the chocolate crop was valued at $4.2 billion. I rest my case.

Vanilla planifolia. *Botanical Illustration by Franz Eugen Köhler, 1897. Sunbelt Archives.*

American Coffee, Featuring the Return of Slavery

The tale of coffee as an adopted American crop begins with a purloined plant and an egotistical smuggler—at least so the legend goes. As with much of history—and food history is no exception—we rely mostly on what the published documents reveal, knowing in advance to maintain some degree of skepticism, even if it is a damned good story, like the one of Gabriel-Mathieu de Clieu, the French naval officer turned smuggler.

The date was 1723 and the setting was the island of Martinique in the Caribbean, then a French colony and now a department of France. Gabriel-Mathieu de Clieu was stationed there in the navy but needed to return to France because of undetermined "personal affairs." During the trip, as coffee historian William Ukers puts it, "he conceived the idea of utilizing the return

Coffee. Painting by Rev. John Lindsay, 1770. Sunbelt Archives.

voyage [to Martinique] to introduce coffee cultivation." History does not record why or how he conceived this notion, but from all accounts he was a very determined man.

In Paris, he discovered that coffee plants were being cultivated in the royal botanical garden, called Jardin Royal des Plantes, of Louis XV, who loved coffee as much as his predecessor loved chocolate. The conservator of the garden, Bernard de Jussieu, took his job very seriously and would not allow any cuttings to be taken and would not share the seeds. But the story goes that the clever de Clieu knew a way to circumvent him, and with the help of a woman variously described as "an aristocratic young lady" and "a lady of quality," he managed to convince the royal physician, one M. de Chirac, to intervene. So de Chirac either used his mandate of being able to use any plant in the garden for medical purposes or he "purloined" two coffee seedlings and sent them to de Clieu.

De Clieu and the coffee plant (apparently one died in transit) boarded the aptly named *Le Dromadaire* (camels had transported coffee in North Africa) with his plant in a glass-lined box very similar to a Wardian Case, a portable terrarium that would not be invented for 106 years. As de Clieu describes the journey back to Martinique, "Water was lacking to such an extent, that for more than a month I was obliged to share the scanty ration of it assigned to me with this my coffee plant upon which my happiest hopes were founded and which was the source of my delight." He also protected the plant from a would-be thief that several historians speculate was a Dutch espionage agent, and he and the plant arrived safely in Martinique, where he planted it. The tree "multiplied with extraordinary rapidity and success," he writes, and was soon able to send plants to Santo Domingo, Guadeloupe, and other nearby islands.

The success of the new coffee plantation was described by Ukers: "The first harvest was very abundant; with the second it was possible to extend the cultivation prodigiously, but what favored multiplication, most singularly, was the fact that two years afterward all the cocoa trees of the country, which were the resource and occupation of the people, were uprooted and totally destroyed by horrible tempests accompanied by an inundation which submerged all the land where these trees were planted, land which was at once made into coffee plantations by the natives."

The Sultana Being Served Coffee by a Slave. Painting by Charles Andre van Loo, 1747.

Historian Anthony Wild points out that regardless of de Clieu's success, coffee was already growing in the Western Hemisphere: in the French colony of Saint-Domingue since 1715 and in the Dutch colony of Surinam since 1718. Nevertheless, ten years after de Clieu's importation, there were tens of thousands of coffee trees growing on Martinique and sixty thousand slaves to take care of them.

Another romantic and far less believable account, this time about the smuggling of coffee from Surinam to Brazil, which supposedly launched the Brazilian plantations, has a Brazilian envoy, Lt. Colonel Francisco de Melo Palheta settling a border dispute between French Guiana and Dutch Guiana. While working as an arbitrator in French Guiana, Palheta had a passionate affair with the wife of the French governor, and upon his departure from the country, she gave him a bouquet in which was hidden either a cutting of a coffee tree or a branch with ripe berries, depending on the source you read. This is fanciful stuff that Wild dismisses as "coffee mythology" with the "addition of sex . . . typically Brazilian," and he drily notes, "more prosaically, coffee was in fact introduced to Brazil in 1774 by a Franciscan friar."

The Great Soberer

Before coffee was transferred to the New World, it had spread through the Middle East and Near East after some unknown brewer decided that making wine out of its freshly picked berries was counter-productive and switched to drying and roasting the fruits to produce coffee beans, which were then ground and added to hot water. Muslim pilgrims spread coffee after major cultivation off coffee trees began in Yemen at the end of the fifteenth century. Some historians speculate that the popularity of coffee in Muslim countries was the result of not only finding a beverage to replace forbidden wine in religious ceremonies but also because coffee was a stimulant that could prolong the hours of prayer.

Coffee House in Palestine. Photograph by B. L. Singley, 1900. Sunbelt Archives.

Coffee, via Venetian merchants, landed at the Vatican in 1600, when Pope Clement VIII was prevailed upon to pass judgment on this new beverage arriving from the east. Conservative Catholics (and some wine merchants) believed that the devil had prevailed upon the infidel Muslims to sell coffee to the West to replace wine. Of course, the curious pope had to taste this aromatic black beverage, and his response was quite positive: "Why, this Satan's drink is so delicious," he reputedly said, "that it would be a pity to let the infidels have exclusive use of it." He "baptized" coffee as suitable for Christian use.

After that, the exact date of coffee's mass arrival in Western Europe has long been debated. Many online sources state that Venice received its first major coffee shipment in 1615, but that seems early to me and I have not been able to corroborate it. Most books on the subject indicate that a better date is around the end of the seventeenth century (some say 1670), and we know for certain that a coffeehouse opened in Venice in 1683.

Its later popularity in Paris was boosted by exotic parties given by the Turkish ambassador there in 1688–89, as described by Isaac D'Israeli in his *Curiosities of Literature* (1817) in one

*Morning Coffee, by
Francois Boucher,
1734. Sunbelt
Archives.*

of the finest run-on sentences ever penned in food history: "On bended knees, the black slaves of the Ambassador, arrayed in the most gorgeous Oriental costumes served the choicest Mocha coffee in tiny cups of egg-shell porcelain, hot, strong and fragrant, poured out in saucers of gold and silver, placed on embroidered silk doylies [sic] fringed with gold bullion, to the grand dames who fluttered their fans with many grimaces bending their piquant faces—be-rouged, be-powdered and be-patched—over the new and steaming beverage."

The first coffeehouse in London opened in 1652, in Vienna in 1685, and the café Le Procope (mentioned above) first served coffee along with chocolate ice cream in Paris in 1689. The ever-growing popularity of coffee was described by the French historian Jules Michelet as "the auspicious revolution of the times, the great event which created new customs, and even modified human temperament." The coffeehouses of Europe soon became, in the words of coffee historian Mark Pendergrast, "egalitarian meeting places," and Margaret Visser, author of *Much Depends on Dinner*, noted that "men and women could, without impropriety, consort as they had never done before. They could meet in public places and talk."

But that was not always the case, as women were excluded from the early coffeehouses in 1674 and responded by publishing a broadside entitled *The Women's Petition Against Coffee*, written in support of "several Thousands of Buxome Good-Women, Languishing in Extremity of Want." The risqué text accused men who drink this "boiled soot" of losing their "Old English Vigour" because they would "trifle away their time, scald their Chops, and spend their money, all for a little base, black, thick, nasty, bitter, stinking nauseous Puddlewater." One racy sentence indicated the condition of men coming home from a coffeehouse: "They come from it with nothing *moist* but their snotty noses, nothing *stiffe* but their Joints, nor *standing* but their Ears." Some outraged men of London responded the same year with *The Men's Answer to the Women's Petition Against Coffee* and stated bluntly that coffee did not cause impotence. On the contrary, they wrote, it promoted "vigorous erections" and "full ejaculations" and they quoted in their defense the physician William Harvey, who advocated coffee as a lubricant to the body's natural functions.

This was the "first wave" of coffee to wash over Europe, but why was it so popular, considering all the controversies over it and the fact that it was competing against chocolate and tea? Shivelbusch comments that coffee was regarded during those times as "the great soberer" and theorizes that "the coffee drinker's good sense and business efficiency were contrasted with the alcohol drinker's inebriation, incompetence, and laziness." It was also viewed as an "*instant* soberer," as Philippe Sylvestre Dufour, author of *Traitez Nouveaux & Curieux du Café, du Thé et du Chocolate,* reported on his application of it in 1671: "Coffee sobers you up instantaneously, or in any event it sobers up those who are

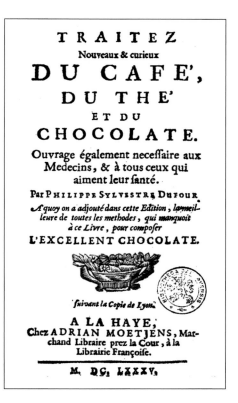

Cover of A Treatise on the New and Curious of Coffee, Tea and Chocolate, *by Philippe Sylvestre Dufour, 1685. Sunbelt Archives.*

Coffee Smuggler Gabriel de Clieu Waters His Precious Coffee Plant. Artist Unkown. Sunbelt Archives.

not fully intoxicated. One of my friends who had too much wine sat down at the gaming table one evening after dinner. He was losing considerable sums, because . . . he was confusing hearts with diamonds. I took him aside and had him drink a cup of coffee, whereupon he returned to the game with a completely sober head and clear eye."

Now, sober but addicted to caffeine—at least psychologically—the coffeehead Europeans wanted more of it at lower prices, and the colonies of the New World were more than happy to supply their need.

The Second Wave of Coffee

Around the time that de Clieu was cultivating his first coffee trees in Martinique, the Dutch East India Company (VOC) was supplying most of the European market with coffee beans from their plantations in Java and also from Mocha, Yemen, where it was originally grown. Total British coffee imports from the West Indies were a meager 270 pounds in 1750, but by 1775 that had grown to 60,000 pounds, and by 1884, total coffee imports into England were 109 million pounds, most of that coming from its Caribbean colonies. Such a monumental increase in coffee production would not have been possible without slave labor.

Slavery expert David Brion Davis, author of *Inhuman Bondage,* puts it this way: "As the British and then French Caribbean began producing sugar, molasses, rum, and coffee for an international mass market, the West Indies became the true economic center of the New World. . . . Along with all the other foods containing sucrose, slave-grown sugar in one's tea was a necessity that virtually every English person took for granted." Stewart Lee Allen, author of *The Devil's Cup*, writes that it is ironic that "Africans arrived in the New World and found themselves enslaved in the harvesting of a plant stolen from Africa just as they had

been." It was a reprise of the sugar slavery days, but with a new crop that fit in perfectly with sugar production.

Mark Pendergrast in *Uncommon Grounds* quotes an unnamed French traveler of the late eighteenth century who neatly summed up the link between coffee and sugar: "I do not know if coffee and sugar are essential to the happiness of Europe," he wrote, "but I know well that these two products have accounted for the unhappiness of two great regions of the world: America [i.e., the Caribbean] has been depopulated as to have land on which to plant them; Africa has been depopulated so as to have the people to cultivate them."

But the tide was slowly turning against slavery. The Society for the Abolition of the Slave Trade was a British abolitionist

The Blue Bottles. An Old Viennese Coffee House Scene. Painter Unknown, c. 1900. Sunbelt Archives.

group formed in 1787. It published William Cowper's anti-slavery poem "Pity for Poor Africans" with a subtitle "A Subject for Conversation at the Tea Table." This poem was distributed to thousands of middle-class housewives, who, the abolitionists believed, controlled the purchase of slave-grown products like coffee and sugar. Here is a well-known quotation from the poem, and remember that it is highly ironic:

> I pity them greatly, but I must be mum,
> For how could we do without sugar and rum?
> Especially sugar, so needful we see?
> What, give up our desserts, our coffee, and tea!

Cowper was part of the coffeehouse scene in the later eighteenth century. Historian William Trego Webb, who edited a selection of Cowper's letters in 1895, commented: "In the eighteenth century the London coffee-house took the place of the modern club, and formed a meeting-place for men of similar tastes and occupations. Thus the politicians of Addison's time gathered at Will's coffee-house, and the wits at Button's; Child's was much frequented by the clergy; besides which there were St. James's coffee-house and the Rose." Dick's Coffee-House on Fleet Street was Cowper's favorite place to socialize with other poets, although he probably hung out at the St. James too, where Swift and Goldsmith once conversed and got sober and caffeinated with other writers.

If the coffeehouses had one outstanding achievement, it was the invention of the famous insurance company Lloyd's of London. Edward Lloyd opened his coffeehouse in London in the late 1680s, and it soon turned into a meetinghouse for ship captains, shipowners, and merchants who wanted to hear about the latest news in maritime circles, and Lloyd began to publish a newsletter that collected all of the information gleaned from his customers. Then he rented booths inside his coffeehouse to underwriters who insured the ships, and finally, in 1771, a group of seventy-nine of these agents established the Society of Lloyd's, which survives today as one of the largest insurance companies in the world. A similar situation led coffeehouses to be transformed into the London Stock Exchange as well. Tom Standage writes in *A History of the World in 6 Glasses* that "London's coffeehouses were the crucibles of the scientific and financial revolutions that shaped the modern world."

Goethe and the Discovery of Caffeine

Most people know that Johann Wolfgang von Goethe wrote *Faust* and is considered to be one of the greatest poets ever, but few realize that he was a polymath with interests beyond literature. He was also a biologist and theoretical physicist who wrote *Metamorphosis of Plants* and *Theory of Colours,* and, at the time of his death, had the largest collection of minerals in Europe, all 17,800 of them. During his Italian grand tour of 1786–88, he frequented Café Greco in Rome and Café Florian in Venice and, while drinking coffee much stronger than in his native Germany, became convinced that it contained a harmful drug that could be dangerous if one drank too much of the stimulant.

Coffee, Coffea arabica L. *Botanical Illustration by Franz Eugen Köhler, 1897. Sunbelt Archives.*

Goethe was friendly with the famous chemist Johann Wolfgang Döbereiner, who told him about a promising young student of his, Friedlieb Ferdinand Runge, who was researching plant chemistry, a subject that Goethe loved and wrote about. Döbereiner told Goethe that Runge had extracted a compound from deadly nightshade that would dilate his cat's eyes. Interested, Goethe had Döbereiner set up a meeting with Runge to demonstrate this feat. In a borrowed formal frock coat, the twenty-five-year-old Runge carried his cat to Goethe's house in Weimar on foot and with a vial of nightshade extract in his pocket. Goethe was seventy at the time and Europe's first literary celebrity, so Runge was understandably nervous about meeting him.

At Goethe's house, Runge dilated the cat's eyes and the great man was very impressed. Goethe gave Runge a box of rare Arabian coffee beans and suggested that he analyze them for the source of their stimulating properties. Momentarily excited by the gift, Runge prepared to leave the house without his cat.

"You are forgetting your *famulus*," Goethe told him, using the Latin term for "servant" and meaning the magical animal companions of the ancient alchemists. Runge retrieved his cat and left with the box of beans. Within a few months, he had

Johann Wolfgang von Goethe at Age 79. Painting by Joseph Karl Stieler, 1828. Sunbelt Archives.

successfully extracted and purified caffeine and later wrote that Goethe was correct in saying that there was value in studying coffee.

Inspired by his meeting with Goethe, Runge went on to earn a doctorate from the University of Berlin; then became the first chemist to isolate quinine from the bark of the *chinchona* tree (often attributed to Pelletier and Bienaimé); developed the first synthetic dye, aniline blue, from coal tar; and, some say, invented paper chromatography, a primary tool for the analysis of the components of chemical compounds. Later researchers extracted caffeine from other plants, including tea, maté, and cola nuts, and in 1869 the London *Daily News* reported that "a piece of kaffeine, of the size of a breakfast plate, [was] produced from 120 pounds of coffee."

The Decline of Coffee in England

Much is made over the dates for the end of the slave trade and the attribution of it to legislation like the American prohibition of it in 1808 and the British emancipation of eight hundred thousand Caribbean slaves in 1833, but in reality, the end of the slave trade came about for far more prosaic reasons: By 1800, slaves in most areas, including the United States, had high fertility rates and relatively low death rates, which meant that the slave owners did not need to buy any more slaves from Africa because they were literally breeding their own. Slavery was still reprehensible, and this was not total freedom for the slaves, but it was a start. It also was the beginning of the end of the vast profits from slave-grown sugar and coffee.

In England, tea from China began to replace coffee as the preferred beverage. Schivelbusch calls this transformation an "unexplained phenomenon" and "an unsolved problem," but I disagree. Yes, there were many independent factors contributing to this switch in preferred caffeine delivery systems, but as usual, the answer begins and ends with one thing: money. In the first place, unlike the scenario with sugar, England had no coffee-producing colonies. France controlled Martinique and most of the coffee production in the Caribbean, the Portuguese had Brazil's enormous coffee industry, and the Dutch controlled Indonesian production. Allen sums it up: "This meant that every cup of java downed by British subjects put money in the pockets of European competitors."

England didn't possess any tea-producing colonies either, but they owned the opium-producing poppy farms of northern India. Opium was useless to the British but treasured by the Chinese, who would trade it for tea. By 1750, the Chinese tea was half the price of coffee and had a larger margin of profit. And the tea trade was a monopoly controlled by the extremely powerful East India Company, while coffee producers were independent entrepreneurs. As Schivelbusch points out, the winner of the coffee versus tea competition was never in doubt, and the "East India Company's strength was surely an essential factor in establishing tea on the English market and ultimately fixing it firmly in English taste to this day."

The price of tea on the English market, because of demand, increased faster than the price of coffee until it eventually surpassed it, but tea was still cheaper to use because an infusion required only about a third or fourth the quantity needed to make coffee. Tea could also be used twice or three times while coffee grounds could not, and yes, the tea was weaker, but it still had plenty of caffeine. So tea imports into England by the East India Company from 1650 to 1700 were 181,545 pounds total but in the next fifty years totaled 40 million pounds, a two-hundred-fold increase. Even more telling are the relative values of coffee and tea imports into England. In 1700, the value of imported coffee was £36,000 (about $6 million today) and tea was £14,000 (about $2.3 million). By 1750, tea was leading coffee £484,000 ($8.3 billion) to £75,000 ($1.3 billion) and by 1790, tea was totally dominant, at £1,777,000 ($23 billion) to £390,000 ($1.2 billion).

Coffee's decline was further exacerbated by a switch in consumption patterns from coffeehouses to the home. That took quite a while to happen—a half-century in England and a full century in Germany, but eventually coffee became a breakfast and afternoon drink until it was eclipsed by tea. Part of the process began in 1732, when Vauxhall Gardens was turned into England's first tea garden, complete with "outdoor walks lit by thousands of lamps, bandstands, performers, dancing, fireworks, and food and drink including, of course, coffee, tea, and chocolate," as Weinberg and Bealer describe it. Women were more welcome in the tea gardens than the coffeehouses and felt more comfortable there. More tea gardens and tea shops and teahouses opened as coffeehouses lost customers.

England turned to tea so much that now three-quarters of all the caffeine produced comes from tea, and today the formerly largest consumer of coffee ranks forty-fourth in per capita coffee consumption. Italy, Germany, and France are respectively ranked in eleventh, fifteenth, and seventeenth places, while the U.S. is in twenty-fifth place. The largest per capita consumer of coffee is Finland, where each caffeine-hungry consumer drinks 26.4 pounds of it per year!

And if we examine the top ten coffee-producing countries for 2009, we see that none of these countries are in the Caribbean. Brazil is by far the number one producer, but Vietnam is in second place, followed by Colombia, Indonesia, India, and Ethiopia. The final four of the top ten are in the Americas: Peru, Guatemala, Mexico, and Honduras. The patterns of coffee production have completely changed during the last two centuries, and although the coffee production of the Americas is still quite significant, it does not have the near-complete dominance it once did. That said, New World coffee had a profound impact on Europe, and the top twelve per-capita coffee consuming countries are all in Europe. Brazil, the largest producer, is number thirteen in consumption.

PART 4

VENEROUS ROOTS, POISONOUS LOVE APPLES, AND THE KING OF FRUITS

The "Venerous Roots" Invade Europe. Artist unknown. Sunbelt Archives.

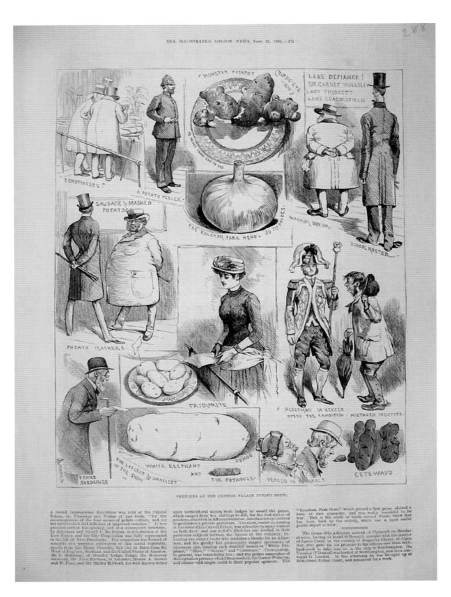

Cartoon Report on the Crystal Palace Potato Show in London. Illustrated London News, *September 22, 1883. Sunbelt Archives.*

NEW WORLD FOODS LIKE MAIZE AND TURKEYS
WERE READILY ACCEPTED IN EUROPE BECAUSE THEY RESEM-
BLED FOODS ALREADY BEING EATEN—OTHER GRAIN CROPS
AND LARGE BARNYARD BIRDS LIKE THE PEACOCK. BUT PEOPLE
WERE IMMEDIATELY SUSPICIOUS OF POTATOES AND TOMATOES
BECAUSE FIRST, THEY WERE NIGHTSHADES IN THE SOLANACEAE
FAMILY, MANY OF WHICH WERE KNOWN TO BE POISONOUS, AND
SECOND, THE HERBALIST JOHN GERARD IN HIS *HERBALL* OF
1633 WARNED AGAINST ONE OF THEIR CLOSE RELATIVES, THE
INNOCENT AND HARMLESS EGGPLANT, THE FRUITS OF WHICH HE
CALLED "MADDE APPLES" AND COMPARED THEM TO "VENOMOUS
AND DEADLY" MUSHROOMS "WHICH BEING IN THE HANDLING OF
AN UNSKILLED COOK MAY PROCURE UNTIMELY DEATH."

As for the tomato, Gerard wrote that it had a "rank and stinking savor," which could mean only one thing to a herbalist of the
time: A bad-smelling plant means a poisonous fruit. As a food,
"they yield very little nourishment to the body, and the same
naught and corrupt." In fact, tomato leaves and stems are toxic,
which did not bode well for the acceptance of the fruit in cuisine.

He is gentler with the potato, comparing it favorably to the
sweet potato, but not everyone agreed with him about the tubers, which were a new food substance, different from roots like
carrots, parsnips, and turnips. Nightshade expert Charles Heiser
writes that "some people actually thought that potatoes caused
diseases, leprosy and scrofula among them." However, the potato is toxic too, containing solanine, especially in its green form,
which is a poison. The potatoes that first reached Europe had far
more of it than ours of today.

With reputations like those it's no wonder it took hundreds
of years for these two plants to be accepted. But they were to
be much more than just accepted—potatoes would eventually
become the world's fourth largest food crop, after maize, wheat,
and rice. Tomatoes would forever change the cuisine of an entire country and would become the main flavoring of one of the
world's favorite dishes. And not to forget the fruits, the English

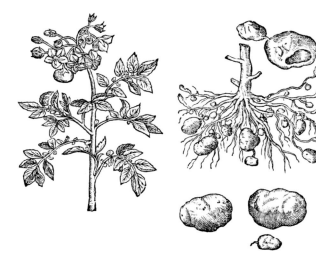

Potato. Engraving from Clusius, Rariorum Plantarum Historia, L. IIII, p. lxxix, *1601. Sunbelt Archives.*

mania for pineapples was unprecedented for any uniquely New World crop and produced images of pineapples as symbols of luxury, wealth, status, power, faith, and perhaps hospitality.

The Spud Migration East

As with many of the New World plants, the potato's journey from Peru to Europe is difficult to track accurately, and historians have spent countless hours trying to determine who actually brought the first potatoes to Europe in what year, and were frustrated by the confusion between *patatas,* potatoes, and *batatas,* sweet potatoes. Some facts were known, namely that the first Spanish reference to them appeared in Colombia in 1537 and the first published mention of them was in 1552 by López de Gómara. But there was a time gap between these accounts and the first mentions in European literature, like those of the herbalist Clusius in 1588. Gradually, researchers J. G. Hawkes and J. Francisco-Ortega were able to close that gap significantly after they read about market archives from the Hospital de La Sangre (imagine naming a facility the "Hospital of the Blood," which of course refers to the blood of Christ) in Seville, which indicates they were being grown in the area around 1570. But who brought them there originally?

Since several other researchers had suggested that New World plants probably arrived in the Canary Islands before Spain, Hawkes and Francisco-Ortega turned their attention there. In the records of a notary public named Lorenzo Palenzuela dated November 28, 1567, they found a bill of lading for a shipment of three barrels of mixed potatoes, oranges, and green lemons from Juan de Molina of Las Palmas de Gran Canaria to his brother, Luis de Quesada, who lived in Antwerp, Belgium. Another bill of lading shows a shipment of potatoes and brandy to Rouen, France. The researchers concluded that these records "indicate quite clearly that potatoes were being grown there and shipped to ports in continental Europe." They theorize that the potatoes were introduced into the Canary Islands in 1652, only ten years after de Gómara wrote about them. Thus no single adventurer introduced them to Europe—it resulted from the prosaic, routine trade in foodstuffs.

As the potato arrived in the various ports of Europe, reactions to it varied quite a bit. In England people thought it was an aphrodisiac, like William Harrison, who called it a "venerous root" in his *Description of England* (1577). And the playwright John Fletcher wrote in 1637:

> A Banquet!—Well! Potatoes and eringoes
> And, I take it, cantharides! Excellent!
> A priapism follows; and as I'll handle it
> It shall, old lecherous goat in authority.

In another one of his plays, *The Loyal Servant*, come the lines:

> Will your Lordship please taste a fine potato?
> 'Twill advance your withered state.
> Fill your Honor full of noble itches.

Despite this reputation, English gardeners didn't much like it, with Phillip Miller, former chief gardener at the Chelsea Physic Garden, describing it as "despised by the rich and deemed only proper food for the meaner sort of persons" in the 1754 edition of his book *The Gardener's Dictionary*. Even the *Encyclopedia Brittanica* was critical of the potato, calling it in its first edition a "demoralising esculent." Translated, that means a corrupting food.

The French didn't see anything erotic about it because they were too busy dismissing it out of hand. "The potato is rightly held responsible for flatulence," wrote the scholar Denis Diderout in his eighteenth-century *Encyclopedie*. "But what is flatulence to the vigorous organs of peasants and workers?" The French naturalist Raoul Combes called it "the worst of all vegetables in the general opinion" and eaten only by "the people, which is the most numerous part of humanity." Combes was referring again to the commoners, and he was echoed by Legrand d'Aussy, the historian who wrote: "The pasty taste, the natural insipidity, the unhealthy quality of the food, which is flatulent and indigestible, has caused it to be rejected by refined households and returned to the people, whose coarse palates and stronger stomachs are satisfied with anything capable of appeasing hunger." Ouch.

The Italians considered potatoes to be a curiosity, and they were cultivated in the gardens of the wealthy as an ornamental plant before they became a field crop. They called them "small truffles," hence the name *tartufoli,* but that name was dropped for the Spanish-derived *patate.* Waverly Root commented in *The Food of Italy*: "Even today, the Italians have not really taken the potato to their bosoms."

John Reader, in his book *Potato*, notes that the potato first appeared in Europe when poverty was rampant. In Bergamo, Italy, 40 percent of the population were registered as paupers in 1575, and in 1630 Madrid had the same percentage of the poor. "The potato arrived in Europe and established itself as a staple food just as economic developments were pushing the price of wheat beyond the means of many households," he writes, and despite all the negativity associated with its arrival, "the potato's contribution was huge and incontestable." It took quite a while—250 years—for its value to be totally ascertained, but Reader notes that "it is hard to imagine where Europe would have been without the potato."

It wasn't until the eighteenth century that the potato left the garden and became a regular field crop, even though the beginning of this trend started in Belgium in 1642 with "almost all the inhabitants of the parish [in Tielt]" growing them "each for his own consumption and convenience." Potatoes were an established field crop in Belgium from 1740 on. It was necessity, not the love of the bland potato's flavor, that caused this change, and since potatoes yield up to four times the calories than grain from the same-sized field, about an acre of potatoes and the milk from one cow "was enough to feed a whole family for a year," according to Reader.

Wars were another reason that the poor turned to potatoes. The Thirty Years' War (1618–48) was the last war fought in northern Europe before potatoes "became widespread enough . . . to cushion rural starvation," writes historian William H. McNeill is his paper "How the Potato Changed the World's History." The potato not only could feed the poor but was somewhat of a surreptitious crop because its yields were hidden in the ground while foraging soldiers were seizing grain harvests from their barns to

Serpillum citratum. Papas Peruanorum. Thymus vulgatis.

feed the army. While the grain was easy to seize and transport, the soldiers did not have the time to laboriously dig the tubers from the ground one by one.

In England, potatoes slowly became a specialty food, and they were used occasionally boiled and mashed. They did not become a field crop there until 1780, and during the reign of George III (1760–1829), Root writes, "they were so despised . . . that Thomas Coke had to carry out seven years of patient experiments with them before it was agreed, grudgingly, that they made a good enough winter food—for cattle."

It was a far different story in Ireland, where the potato saved the country from famine and then doomed it because of its monoculture.

Papas Peruanorum. (Peruvian Potatoes). Botanical Illustration by Basilius Bessler from Hortus Eystettensis, *c. 1616. Sunbelt Archives.*

Ireland's "Lazy Roots" Rot

The story of how potatoes arrived in Ireland reads like fiction with a cast of famous characters, and I was skeptical when I first read it, certain that my leg was being pulled because the story has been told so many times that dozens if not hundreds of secondary sources include it, obscuring its origin. In summary, the story goes like this: Sir Francis Drake, the English privateer, brought potatoes from the Caribbean, Virginia, or the Canary Islands to London in 1586. He instructed his associate, Thomas Hariot, to give some samples of the potatoes to both John Gerard (who never mentioned the exchange in his *Herball*) and Sir Walter Raleigh. You read earlier what Gerard thought of potatoes, but apparently Raleigh saw some value in them, and somewhere between 1586 and 1589, his gardener planted the first potatoes in Ireland in lazy beds on his estate at Myrtle Grove, Youghal, near Cork.

To corroborate the tale, I started researching the main characters through word searches in Google Books, and immediately discrepancies appeared. The major biographies of Sir Francis Drake do not mention potatoes, which is not really surprising because few biographies or histories have much to say about foodstuffs. Sir Sidney Lee, writing in *The Dictionary of National Biography* in 1896, commented: "The assertion that . . . Sir Francis Drake introduced the potato long before Raleigh initiated colonial enterprise appears to be erroneous. It seems that [he] brought over in 1565 some specimens of the sweet potato . . . which only distantly resembles the common potato." Since they were often confused, and the Peruvian potato only reached Virginia in later years, Lee's statement is probably correct.

Then I noticed that many historians used weasel words when attributing the appearance of the potato in England to Sir Francis Drake and in Ireland to Sir Walter Raleigh. A source in 1867 writes: "In Drake's ship was *most probably* brought home our potato," and Waverly Root comments: "*If* Sir Walter Raleigh was *really* growing potatoes in Ireland...." (emphasis mine). My attempts at corroboration were going nowhere fast, and the story had all the earmarks of legend because the writers were repeating and speculating upon secondary sources and not one primary source, like Drake's or Raleigh's autobiographies mentioning the potato was cited—and neither man wrote one. I must conclude that like the yarn about Raleigh's potatoes that were given to Queen Elizabeth I and her cooks serving her the green tops of the plant instead of the tubers, the entire Drake story recounted above is just wishful thinking.

But we do know that sometime around the dawn of the seventeenth century, Irish peasants were growing the "lazy root," as the English snidely called it. But why was it called that? Many sources speculate that it's because the potato's cultivation required little effort, like *The Independent* in 1917 with this observation: "Requiring no capital and no machinery, little skill in the husbandman for the raising of it and little skill in the housewife for the cooking of it, the potato became too popular with the poor." This comment may be true to a certain extent, but the real reason the potato is "lazy" is that originally it was grown in a lazy bed, a raised planting ridge

Sir Francis Drake. Engraving by Jodicus Hondius, 1583. Sunbelt Archives.

four to nine feet wide and separated from other beds by trenches. It was lazy because essentially after the bed was fashioned and the potato eyes planted, it required very little maintenance, and because of that, critics said it was sloppy husbandry and that it mocked honest labor. As Larry Zuckerman notes in his potato book, "the phrase *lazy bed* came to evoke that most terrible Victorian sin, indolence." And when the Irish planters used the same cultivation technique, they were ridiculed by the British for their "lazy roots," a doubly racist insult that criticized their essential food and their humble heritage at the same time.

And the biggest racist of all, soon on an anti-potato crusade, was William Cobbett, who became England's most popular journalist despite starting as an illiterate commoner. Like a lot of popular rabble-rousers over the centuries, Cobbett seemingly hated everything, and in the words of Stewart Lee Allen, his pet peeves were "Shakespeare, paper money, tea and above all, that damned Irish potato," which was the "root" of "slovenliness, filth, misery, and slavery." His voice was his newspaper, *The Political Register,* described by a member of Parliament as "two-penny trash." Instead of being insulted by this, Cobbett renamed the paper *Cobbett's Two-Penny Trash*, and its circulation increased.

Engraving of a Starving Irish Family During the Potato Famine. Artist Unknown. Sunbelt Archives.

Cobbett believed that wheat bread was the natural food of man and that the "pig food" potatoes transformed the Irish into doglike creatures that did nothing but sleep and fornicate. So he urged his readers to overthrow the government unless the "depraved food" was banned. Protesting mobs with potatoes impaled on sticks like small whales on large harpoons picketed Parliament. Cobbett was jailed for treason but continued to run his paper from his cell. After his jail term expired, Cobbett was elected to Parliament.

What was really happening behind the scenes of Cobbett's racist rants was that the potato was giving Irish peasants something they had never achieved before: a measure of freedom from the British land barons who controlled Ireland. Just growing potatoes gave them a much better standard of living. And because of this, the nobility was quite worried, as noted in the respected *Edinburgh Review* in 1822 in an editorial so insulting that it could have been written by Cobbett: "So long as Ireland was only occupied by a million . . . starving wretches, it was relatively easy to hold them in servitude. But thanks to the Potato and the Cottage System, Ireland contains at this moment nearly *seven* millions of inhabitants," the paper complained, which meant that they could not be controlled by physical repression. The "cottage system" was the old Irish method of raising crops, sometime communally, in small plots while producing their own food independent of the Industrial Revolution. The term evolved into "cottage industry," which is viewed favorably these days, but back then the British despised the system because it gave the peasants self-control when they should have been properly working in factories and making the owners wealthy.

By 1815, Ireland's population had swelled to 4.7 million, and for 3.3 million of them—more than 70 percent—potatoes were all they had to eat. Cecil Woodham-Smith, author of *The Great Hunger*, reported that in the during the next thirty years, more than a hundred commissions and special committees reported on the state of Ireland, and all of them predicted disaster based on over-population, lack of food, unemployment, and terrible living conditions. As it turns out, they were right, but the cause of the disaster was not the potato but rather a fungus, *Phytophthora infestans*.

In September of 1845, farmers watched with dismay as their crops withered and died and the potatoes in the ground and already harvested turned black and disintegrated into repulsive, stinking messes. The predicted harvest of fifteen million tons of potatoes was devastated by the blight, and the Great Famine began. The fungus struck again the three following years until potato farming nearly ceased. At least a million people died of starvation, and between one and six million people emigrated (depending on the source and time frame). Ireland's population was cut roughly in half.

I don't have the space here to detail the devastation and all of its consequences, but this was an important lesson for later farmers on the dangers of monoculture, or the planting of identical crops over wide areas. The potatoes were clones, identical duplicates of each other from the "eye" potatoes, and they had no resistance to the fungus. The "Understanding Evolution" section of the University of California at Berkeley's website explains: "Although the famine ultimately had many causes, the disaster would likely not have been so terrible had more genetically variable potatoes been planted. Some potatoes would have carried the right genes to make it through the epidemic, and more of the resistant varieties could have been planted in the years following the first epidemic. Later, scientists identified resistance genes in a potato from South America, where farmers have preserved the genetic variation of potatoes by growing many cultivated varieties alongside the potato's wild cousins." Yet despite the blight, monoculture is the rule, not the exception, in modern agriculture. In the U.S., all the major crops are monoculture: maize, wheat, cotton, and soybeans, and there were severe losses of maize in 1970 and grapes in the 1980s from monoculture farming.

In 2009, total potato production in Ireland was 361,000 metric tons, which doesn't even place it in the top twenty potato-growing countries. In fact, that's only 5 percent of the total production in what's become, surprisingly, a potato-loving country: France, now the world's sixth-largest potato producer.

Les Pommes de Terre de Paris

The initial resistance to potatoes in other countries was the fear of poisoning, but in France the tuber was simply ignored because of matters of flavor and fame. To the gourmands of the day, potatoes were an inelegant, bland peasant food that no chef had yet elevated to haute cuisine. To more ordinary people, there was no positive buzz about potatoes in the streets and on the farms, so why bother with them?

Considering flavor issue first, in his *Physiologie du goût*, published in 1825, the famous gourmand and author Jean Anthelme Brillat-Savarin has an amusing collection of imagined discussions at dinners with corpulent (his term) people about certain foods they love, like bread, rice, beans, pastries, and, of course, potatoes:

> *A Very Stout Person*: Will you oblige me, sir, by passing the potatoes in front of you; at the rate they are going, I am afraid of not being in time.
> *Myself*: There, sir, they are within your reach.
> *S. P.*: But you will surely help yourself to some? There's enough for both, and those who come after must do as they may.
> *M.*: I never take any. I think nothing of the potato unless as a stop-gap in times of great scarcity. It is, to my taste, most insipid.
> *S. P.*: Gastronomic heresy! There is nothing better than the potato. I eat them done in all the different ways, and should they appear in the second course, whether *à la*

lyonnaise or *au soufflé*, I hereby enter a protest for the preservation of my rights.

Brillat-Savarin found potatoes so insipid that once on a trip to the countryside, he stopped at an inn in the village of Mont-sous-Vaudrey, where he rejoiced when he saw that one of the meals being served included "royal quails" being turned on a spit, and a roasting *leveret*, or young hare, with an aroma "unknown to men in town, the perfume of which would fill a church." He continues, "To my grievous disappointment I found that what I saw was for some gentlemen of the law who had been engaged near the village as legal experts. For me there was nothing but potato soup, and the beef which had been boiled in it, with some shoulder of mutton and haricots. That tempting bill of fare which I had fondly imagined to myself only made me feel more desolate, and I was again overwhelmed with my misfortunes."

He charmed his way into joining the lawyers' meal and then revealed why he desperately wanted to avoid potato soup: "And what a dinner we made! I remember particularly a chicken *fric-assee,* richly dowered with truffles, sufficient to have renewed the youth of Tithonus [an immortal who continued aging]. The dessert consisted of vanilla cream, some choice cheese, and fruit; and we moistened the whole, first with a light pink-coloured wine, then with some hermitage, and afterwards with some soft and generous wine of a straw-colour."

Our culinary hero was no longer feeling quite so desolate, but the question remains: What was in those potato soups, anyway? It's really what *wasn't* in them that matters. I tracked down a recipe of the era for *potage purée de pommes de terre*, or purée of potato soup, and it's, well, insipid. Only small amounts of mild flavorings like butter, leeks, and sometimes chervil are in it, so it's very unspectacular. The potato favorite of the Stout Person, *pommes de terre à la lyonnaise* is simply potato slices sautéed in a little butter with a few tablespoons of fried onions and no herbs or spices added. Considering what he was accustomed to eating, it's no wonder that Brillat-Savarin hated potatoes—but amazingly enough, the *lyonnaise* recipe still exists, unchanged, in my 1966 edition of *Larousse Gastronomique*.

What the potato needed in France was a celebrity chef—but what it got was a celebrity pharmacist.

Parmentier: From Prisoner to Potatohead

In 1762, the foremost potato promoter who ever lived was confined in a Prussian prisoner-of-war camp in Westphalia, pondering potatoes, because that's all he had to eat. This was the fifth time he had been captured, as if he had been targeted by the enemy because he was a talented medic and they needed his help as casualties from both sides of the Seven Years' War flooded into the camp. Despite living on potatoes—and some say gin, too, as a reward for his work—Antoine-Augustin Parmentier had a positive outlook and, after being strip-searched by the guards, joked that they were the best *valets de chambre* he had ever met.

Parmentier was born in 1727 and became an apothecary and then a pharmacist and, after joining the French army, held the rank of assistant apothecary or chief pharmacist and health officer, depending on which source you believe. Upon his release, he marveled at the fact that not only did he survive on just potatoes, he was in remarkably good health. He decided then and there that his mission in life would be to study and promote potatoes, which was a very radical move considering the fact that potato cultivation had been banned in France for decades.

In 1748, the Besançon parliament had declared the potato responsible for leprosy and had forbidden its cultivation. Parmentier and a number of other forward-thinking men ranging from professors to priests thought that banning a valuable food during France's increasingly severe economic situation was nonsense, so after Parmentier returned to Paris, he decided to learn all he could and find a sponsor for his quest. The Bishop of Castres—far away from the capital—was enlisted to help, and he declared potatoes to be "miraculous" and instructed his priests to encourage people to plant potatoes and eat them. This experiment, and one involving the parish priest of Saint-Roch in Paris who served potato soup to his flock, proved not to be enough. But Parmentier had an idea.

Cover of Parmentier's Journal Examen Chymique Des Pommes de Terre *(The Chemical Examination of Potatoes), 1773. Sunbelt Archives.*

The Académie of Besançon conducted a competition for "a study of alimentary substances which may alleviate the disaster of famine," and Parmentier decided to enter the contest on behalf of his beloved tuber. He won the contest in 1770 with a paper entitled "Inquiry into Nourishing Vegetables That in Times of Necessity Could Be Substituted for Ordinary Food," which, of course, starred the potato with an argument that potato starch made good bread, even though the bread was so dense it was almost inedible because potatoes lack gluten. But his win was his first success at promoting potatoes because the *parlement* decided not to enforce the potato ban.

By this time Parmentier was a pharmacist at the Hôtel des Invalides, a prominent hospital, and he was on good terms with the medical faculty and soon attracted the

Le centenaire d'un bienfaiteur de l'humanité

Parmentier on the Cover of Le Petit Journal, *December 14, 1913. Sunbelt Archives.*

attention of Louis XVI and Marie Antoinette. The king, intrigued by his potato theories, made fifty acres of land at the Plaine des Sablons in Neuilly, just outside the capital, available for Parmentier's potato experiments. Although it sounds like legend, all the accounts I could find agree that Parmentier pulled off a publicity stunt at the field that launched the potato into fame in France by elevating it in the public's estimation. He had the king post armed guards around the field day and night, which, as food historian Maguelonne Toussaint-Samat notes, "naturally attracted intrigued spectators every Sunday." The attitude of the visitors "was that if the King sent his army to guard a plant previously considered fit for only animal fodder it could not be so bad after all."

Louis XVI visited the field and Parmentier gave him purple potato flowers, which the king wore in his hat—or buttonhole—and the queen wore them in her hair during a court ball, attracting

Statue of Parmentier
Giving Potatoes to the
People, Montdidier
(Somme, France).
Photograph by
Marc Roussel, 2008.
Sunbelt Archives.

even more attention and causing a fashion for wearing them at
court. Soon, potato flowers were patterns on the fine china made
by Moustiers and Marseilles. Then the guards were removed
from the field and, of course at night peasants came and stole
the potatoes, which Parmentier had planned for all along. He was
delighted, saying, "There can scarcely be any remaining prejudice
against my poor potatoes, else they would not be stolen."

Farmers descended upon the field seeking seed potatoes,
which Parmentier gladly supplied, and soon a serious proposi-
tion was made to change the name from *pomme de terre* to *par-
mentiere*. That idea was never made official, but in a few years'
time so many potatoes were planted in France that it was, as
The Independent noted, "for a time . . . the foremost producer
of this crop on the continent." As John Reader reports, "Eating
potatoes became routine. They could be bought on the streets
of Paris, either raw or roasted like chestnuts, and soup kitchens
supplied the needy with potato soup." Outside of Paris, particularly in northern France, potato-growing surged, and the harvest
between 1815 and 1840 more than quintupled.

Parmentier continued his promotion with all-potato dinners, where every dish "of which consisted of the potato disguised in some variety of form, and even the liquids used at table were extracted from it," and he invited notables to attend, which they did, including Benjamin Franklin, Antoine Lavoisier ("the father of modern chemistry"), and probably Thomas Jefferson, who replaced Franklin as U.S. commissioner. I speculate that was the case because a copy of Parmentier's prize-winning potato essay ended up in Jefferson's library at Monticello. Jefferson is also credited with introducing the french-fried potato to America, but that's a myth—there are only scant mentions of the vegetable in his papers, and most of those relate to the Irish dependence on potatoes.

The king told Parmentier that "France will thank you some day for having found bread for the poor," which France has done many times over. Louis, of course, met his fate at the guillotine during the Revolution, but Parmentier remained a potato hero, even though he later wrote books on bread and chestnuts. In 1780, his *Traité de la châtaigne* (*Treatise on the Chestnut*) was published and the Paris Commune declared that potatoes were republication and compulsory. That was followed in 1789 by his potato masterpiece, *Traité sur la culture et les usages des pommes de terre*, or *Treatise on the Culture and Customs of Potatoes*. In 1793, the first all-potato cookbook, *La cuisine républicaine,* was published and another first for the book was that it was the first French cookbook written by a woman, a Mme. Méridiot.

Parmentier was among the first members of the Légion d'Honneur that Napoleon created in 1802, and the emperor named him to head up the French health service. Today he is a national hero in France, especially among foodies. There are statues of Parmentier in Neuilly, where he had the large field, and in Paris at a Metro station named after him. In Neuilly, he is peeling a potato; in Paris, he is presenting one to a peasant who has a dubious expression on his face. Streets were named after him, and he was on the cover of *Le Petit Journal* for the hundredth anniversary of his death, on December 14, 1913.

Even his recipes live on, like *hachis Parmentier,* a dish made with mashed baked potatoes, combined with diced meat and *sauce lyonnaise* that was originally served in potato skins. It later evolved in England to the dish known as shepherd's pie.

But as Touissaint-Samat points out, the potato "became really popular once it got together with frying oil." The french fry was thus invented, later to become the most popular cooked potato form. Alexandre Dumas, "a gastronome of distinction," ignored all other ways of cooking the potato and wrote only about *maître d'hôtel* potatoes fried in butter.

Perhaps the ultimate form of fried spuds, soufflé potatoes, were invented by accident on August 26, 1837. On that date, King Louis Philippe and Queen Amélie were on board the first train to take the new railway between Paris and Saint-Germain, where a banquet was to be served for them when they arrived. But the train was late, and the chef preparing the grand meal was thrown off on his timing of the roast fillet of beef with fried potatoes. He fried the potatoes expecting the imminent arrival of the royal couple, but when they didn't show up, he removed the potatoes from the oil and they shriveled up and looked pathetic. As the train pulled into the station, he put them back into the hot oil, and the potatoes "puffed up into golden bubbles" and were regarded as a triumph of the kitchen art.

But while potatoes were saving the French from starvation and offering French chefs new opportunities for recipe creation, in other parts of Europe potatoes were becoming the seeds of conflict.

Tubers of War

In his essay "How the Potato Changed the World's History," William McNeill writes: "It is certain that without potatoes, Germany could not have become the leading industrial and military power of Europe after 1848, and no less certain that Russia could not have loomed so threateningly on Germany's eastern border after 1891." Here's how that happened.

Between 1750 and 1850 the population of Europe nearly doubled, going from an estimated 140 million to 266 million. Historian William Langer attributes that increase to the introduction and spread of two New World crops, maize and potatoes, because they "were well-adapted to European conditions" and were "easy to cultivate even with hand tools [and] were exceedingly productive and highly nutritious." Potatoes were particularly useful for northern European peasants because they took only a little more than half the time to mature than maize and other grains, about four months, and they produced at least three times the food value as grain. The potato could grow on fallow land in very small plots and thus, as we have seen in Ireland, perfect for peasants to grow. "Historically, it has been described as the only significant addition to the peasant's food in two centuries," Langer writes, and then he goes on to quote other praise such as "the greatest blessing that the soil produces" and "the miracle of agriculture."

The timing of the potato was perfect because of the frequency of famines in Europe. France, for example, had forty national famines between 1500 and 1800 and England had seventeen, but even these didn't count the hundreds of local famines. Potatoes, planted on land at rest between grain cycles, effectively doubled Europe's food supply and became a staple food. Historian Charles C. Mann writes, "Routine famine almost disappeared in potato country, a 2,000-mile band that stretched from Ireland to Russia's Ural Mountains in the east. At long last, the continent could produce its own dinner."

But that didn't mean that people embraced the potato gastronomically. The Prussians, living in the most powerful state that would later become the German Empire, resisted planting and eating them until Fredrick the Great intimidated them. In 1744, he ordered his government to issue free seed potatoes to farmers, along with instructions on how to grow them. When potato-haters protested that the tubers had no taste and "not even dogs would eat them," Frederick threatened to have his soldiers cut the ears and noses off of everyone who refused to eat them. He never enforced that edict, but soldiers were enlisted to show the people how to cook them. Consequently, when Prussia was invaded by France, Austria, and Russia during the Seven Years' War, their soldiers and citizens—and even prisoners-of-war like Parmentier, survived on potatoes. One online source theorizes: "This resilience helped Prussia grow into the German State of the 20th Century and perhaps the memory of such seemingly superhuman fortitude of Prussians led to the arrogance of the Kaiser that set off World War I. Not perhaps a particularly auspicious moment in the history of the potato then."

The invading countries began to grow potatoes as well, and historian Chris Vandenbroeke stated that "the diffusion of pota-to-growing meant that for the first time in the history of Western Europe, a definitive solution had been found to the food prob-

Maine Potato Week Poster, 1918. Sunbelt Archives.

lem." And by 1800, the crop "had become an indispensable part of the diet from the Alps to the steppes of Russia," according to Reader. He concludes that "the potato was an integral part of developments that established the foundations of the modern economic and political order." And that "order" included many wars in which the potato played a major role in not only supply lines for the armies but also, as we have seen, they were a boon to peasant farmers whose grain had been seized.

When the Habsburg monarchy in Prussia wanted take over the Duchy of Bavaria in 1778, it was opposed by a Saxon-Prussian alliance, and the resulting War of the Bavarian Succession pitted Prussia against Austria. The war was also called the *Kartoffelkrieg* (Potato War); actually, there was no real war with battles except for some skirmishes, but several thousand soldiers starved when they ran out of potatoes to forage, hence the war's nickname. It is estimated that twenty thousand civilians on both sides also suffered and died.

Russia was the last major country to adopt potatoes as its basic crop even though they were unknown in St. Petersburg until about 1800. But a few years before her death in 1796, Catherine the Great believed that potatoes were an effective antidote to typhus (they aren't, of course), so she ordered that potatoes be promoted by her government agricultural bureaus. That resulted in potatoes being grown extensively in western Russia and the Ukraine, but in central Russia there was still suspicion about them and opposition to them. As Kenneth Kiple and Kriemhild Ornelas point out: "'Old Believers' continued to reject potatoes as 'Devil's apples' or 'forbidden fruit of Eden,' so that as late as 1840, potatoes were still resisted. When, in that year, the government ordered peasants to grow potatoes on common land, they responded with 'potato riots' that continued through 1843, when the coercive policy ceased. But, in the next half-century, the potato's obvious superiority to most grain crops and other tubers encouraged its wider growth, first as a garden vegetable and then, as it became a dietary staple, as a field crop."

That happened in Russia despite opposition to them, because after the crop failures of 1738–39, Nicholas I saw his opportunity to promote alternative crops, especially the potato, and instituted new promotional programs. This time it worked, and by 1850 the potato was well established; in 1900 Russia was in second place for European potato production, after Germany. But all that German potato production was not much use for them in World War I. Large supplies of potatoes in storage suffered the same fate as they did in Ireland, for the villainous *Phytophthora infestans* struck in 1916, with disastrous results that finally contributed to Germany's surrender and the end of the war.

The story was quite different in England and the United States, where there were plenty of potatoes and propaganda campaigns to eat them left a legacy in song in a 1918 wartime recipe book:

> Eat potatoes with their starch,
> Help the fighters on the march.
> Each baked potato that you eat,
> Will help fill the ships with wheat.
> Eat potatoes, save the wheat,
> Drive the Kaiser to defeat.

In the 1930s, Russia took over as the leading producer and also became the world's largest exporter. That said, Germany was still potato-ready for World War II—and so was Russia. As Kiple and Ornelas put it, "[P]otatoes played significant nutritional roles during ordinary times and assumed extraordinary nutritional roles in war years." The first "potato war" of the eighteenth century was a flop, but the second was the real thing.

Based on the experiences of World War I, the European leaders realized that the potato was just as valuable as wheat as a wartime food, but it came with its own set of problems beyond blight. There was a higher cost of production, a limited storage life, and a degree of speculation involving prices during the fluctuations between shortages and surpluses. These realizations are reflected in the rations of the various armies during the early stages of the war. Rommel's men in North Africa were eating sardines in oil and "bulky tinned sausages" as well as foods provided by allied Italy, like cheese, coffee beans, and other preserved meats. Neither the German nor the Italian armies liked these rations, and since they were stamped with the initials A.M., the Germans and Italians called them either *Alter Mann* ("old man," for Mussolini) or *Arabio Morte* ("dead Arab").

Meanwhile, the British army had much tastier rations, including corned beef, white bread, jam, tea, hard tack biscuits, and tinned fruit. Timothy Dowling, in his book of personal revelations of soldiers at the front, wrote that "[w]henever a British supply dump was raided, there was always much rejoicing as the Germans" could indulge in the above, or in the luxuries they sometimes found: beer, cigarettes, and "tinned South African pineapples for dessert." Potatoes are mentioned only once in this particular German soldier's revelations, and that's when they occasionally found cans of Irish potatoes.

The German supply line between Berlin and Moscow was a thousand miles long, which was much too far for the Third Reich to adequately supply food to its fast-moving troops in Russia, so the German army was forced to do exactly what armies were doing hundreds—if not thousands—of years before: foraging, which is a cleaned-up verb for stealing food at gunpoint wherever they could find it. And the Russian leaders knew they had to do something—plant, plant, plant potatoes.

According to Walter Moss, author of a history of Russia since 1885, "The drive to get people to grow potatoes bordered on the deification of the tuber." Russian leader Mikhail Kalinin said in a speech in 1942, "It is unnecessary to prove the importance of the potato in the national diet." And a month later, he advised, "If you wish to take part in the victory over the German fascist invaders, then you must plant as many potatoes as possible." Moss concludes that "[p]otatoes were called upon to substitute for virtually every category of food."

A wartime magazine call *Rabotnitsa* (*The Woman Worker*) published recipes that "were variations on the perpetual theme of 100 ways to eat potatoes and cabbage." And Moss notes that since all the potatoes now went for human consumption, "animals were fed military garbage . . . weeds, vegetable leaves, corn cobs, or scraps from beet production." But that was not enough because

The Seeds of Victory
Insure *the* Fruits of Peace

For Free Book Write to
NATIONAL WAR GARDEN COMMISSION
WASHINGTON, D.C.

Charles Lathrop Pack *Pres.*   Percival S. Ridsdale *Sec'y.*

German troops were seizing "all the grain, potatoes, livestock, and poultry of the village inhabitants," said one peasant. It got to the point that "[t]he Jews bought food with money, clothes and gold from the peasants," wrote a reporter in *Izvestia*, "Not even everybody had potatoes. We made soup from potato skins."

The German prisoners of war survived on potatoes, even if they had to steal them. In his book, *Prisoners of Nazis*, Harry Spiller quotes American prisoner of war Private First Class Melvin W. Zerkel: "One spring day we saw some German farmers planting potatoes in a field near the tracks. We told the guards we needed a nature call and slipped into the field, where we dug up potato sets and ate them. Another time, we were sent to a nearby castle to clean it out before the Russian army arrived. We took

National War Garden Commission Poster. By Maginel Wright Enright Barney, a Children's Book Illustrator from the First Half of the Twentieth Century, Who Was the Sister of Frank Lloyd Wright, c. 1919. Sunbelt Archives.

out the furniture and the paintings and were then sent into the cellar. While in the cellar, we filled our pant legs and coats with potatoes we found."

When the potatoes ran out in Leningrad, the "[e]xtreme hunger . . . led people to eat all kinds of things not normally consumed," writes William Moskoff in *The Bread of Affliction*, "including acorns, tree bark, grass, wallpaper paste, dogs, cats, and mice. Even isolated cases of cannibalism occurred." More than one million people died of starvation in Leningrad, and the total number of Russian civilian starvation deaths is estimated at four million. Total German civilian deaths were between one and three million people, but determining the number who starved is very difficult, but surely at least a third of them died from the lack of food. This does not count soldiers in POW camps or Jews in concentration camps. Even potatoes could not save everyone.

One of the Soviet republics, Belarus, lost 25 percent of its civilian population, a total 1.67 million people. Today, Belarus has the highest per-capita potato consumption in the world—400 pounds of potatoes per person per year, as compared with 150 for the U.S. The effects of the war still linger, as reflected by potato-eating statistics like that, but there were no wars associated with the introduction of the next nightshade in Europe, the love apple.

Naples, the Birthplace of the Italian Tomato

"Tomato sauce," writes John Dickie in *Delizia!*, "is now more recognizably Italian than the tricolor or the Leaning Tower of Pisa. It is the lifeblood of Italian food—some would even say of the Italians themselves. It is a national religion: its Holy Trinity is Fresh, Tinned and Concentrate; and its Jerusalem is Naples." The entire story of tomatoes in Italy begins in Naples, but when they first arrived there, Naples was not a part of Italy—it belonged to Spain as part of what they called Kingdom of Naples.

When the Italian *scalco* (steward) Antonio Latini took over management of the kitchen at the villa of Esteban Carillo y Salcedo, the regent to the Spanish viceroy of the kingdom in the late 1600s, he was not afraid to experiment with the new ingredients available to him: turkeys, chocolate, chile peppers, maize, and tomatoes. In three of his recipes of note that were published in *Lo scalco alla moderna* (*The Modern Kitchen Steward,* 1696), tomatoes appeared for the first time in European

Pomi doro sonno buoni da Mangiare come le meli insieme 1136. se ritrovano di doi sorte luna rossa e laltri gialli e se rasembrano oro.

culinary literature. And in one of them, *Salsa di pomodoro alla spagnola* (Spanish-style Tomato Sauce), chiles appear for the first time, too. This is a condiment to accompany boiled foods and calls for charred tomatoes, onions, and chiles mixed with a little salt, oil, and vinegar. The recipe is identical to the way fresh salsa is made today in the Mexican state of Chihuahua. The same recipe appearing in two Spanish colonies 5,500 miles apart is a testament to the breadth of Spain's empire.

Pomi d' Oro. Botantical Illustration from the Erbario Miniato *of Federico Cesi, c. 1620. Sunbelt Archives.*

Just sixty-three years before Latini's book, nightshade-hating John Gerard had labeled tomato plants as stinky and the fruits "of the highest degree of coldness," but apparently the Spanish—and now the Italians—weren't buying this. After three hundred years of being either ignored or denigrated all over Europe with descriptions and insults very similar to those of potatoes, tomatoes were included in a cookbook that represented what Italian food expert David Gentilcore describes as "the culmination of Italian court cooking before the triumph of French cuisine in the eighteenth century."

Dickie is not as impressed as Gentilcore was about Latini's tomato recipes. He writes, "Antonio Latini was as oblivious to its potential as the rest of his contemporaries. He suggests perfunctorily that it makes 'a very tasty sauce for boiled meat, or other things,' and never mentions it again." But the recipes were

Tomatoes. Botanical Illustration from the Ernst Benary Seed Growers Catalog, Erfurt, Hannover-Muenden, Germany, 1879. Sunbelt Archives.

a start for the tomato's eventual takeover of Italian cuisine in most of those regions that were not yet united as a country called Italy.

An unpublished manuscript of a recipe collection known as the *Levitico* by Francesco Gaudentio in Rome in 1705 concerns the foods consumed by Jesuits on feast and fast days, and Gaudentio's tomato recipe shows how the use of the fruit was slowly spreading north. The tomatoes were "cultivated in gardens," and he suggests chopping them up and sautéing them in oil along with eggplants or squash. It would take a while for tomatoes to move from the garden to the field and become a farmer's crop. Since no Italian cookbooks were published between 1694 and 1773, and no Spanish ones from 1611 to 1745, we can only theorize how they spread to more northerly parts of Europe. I assume they just moved slowly from garden to garden and kitchen to kitchen.

The next time tomatoes appear in a cookbook is 1773 in Vincenzo Corrado's *Il Cuoco galante, The Gallant Cook*. Corrado was a Celestine Benedictine monk who had traveled all over Italy between 1758 and 1760 visiting other Benedictine orders, and so his recipes represent ways to cook tomatoes from different regions. The recipes include tomatoes stuffed with pulped veal, or with rice and then simmered in milk, butter, sugar, and cinnamon. He also advises mincing tomatoes and mixing them with butter, eggs, and ricotta to make croquettes for frying. There is one tomato sauce in his book, a simple one made with vinegar, garlic, and rue

Vincenzo Corrado, 1773. Artist Unknown. Sunbelt Archives.

to accompany mutton. Because of the pungent rue, Dickie writes sarcastically, "Clearly, it was not considered gallant for a Neapolitan cook to prepare tomato dishes that actually tasted of tomato." Maybe so, but Gentilcore suggests that these recipes indicate that tomatoes were blended with local ingredients and thus "were being acculturated."

Religious orders continued Corrado's tomato experimen-tation. The Celestine nuns of Trani loved their *brodetto al pomodoro*, tomato soup, while the nuns in Catania in Sicily were snacking on *mortaretto*, a pastry filled with tomatoes and herbs. The fact that all of these orders inventing new recipes with tomatoes were Benedictines like Corrado suggests that his book was being circulated though religious exchanges among the convents and monasteries in southern Italy.

Pomidori alla Napolitana, by Vincenzo Corrado

Peel the skin off the tomatoes and cut them in half. Remove the seeds and place the halves on a sheet of paper greased with oil in a baking tray. Fill the halves with anchovies, parsley, oregano, and garlic. Then cover them with bread crumbs, bake them in the oven, and serve them.

Interestingly, Corrado wrote another book, called *Treatise on Potatoes* (1798), in which he praised the tubers as "an excellent food for the poor because they are very nourishing and very cheap." He was, of course, too far-thinking, and no one paid much attention to his elegant potato recipes like serving them in a sauce of toasted almonds and caviar. Dickie says "this was avant-garde cookery, far ahead of its time—and in some ways still ahead of ours."

On the island of Sardinia, by this time a Piedmontese possession, cooks were exploring new tomato recipes that included their preservation. One from the mid-eighteenth century was a relish in the Spanish style and called for tomatoes "less than ripe" to be mixed with sour grapes, chiles, and vinegar. The other taught people how to preserve them by drying them in the sun: "Gather the ripe and round whole tomatoes before it rains, cut them down the middle, put a little salt on each half, and [when] dried, bottle them to be used throughout the year." This is perhaps the earliest reference to sun-dried tomatoes that are so popular today.

But so far in the history of the Italian tomato, no cook had invented the classic tomato sauce that would be the hallmark of Italian food to the rest of the world.

Tomatoes Meet Pasta and Pizza

Food historian Silvano Serventi, one of the authors of *Pasta: The Story of a Universal Food*, wrote in that book: "The meeting between tomato and pasta was inevitable, or to use the words of Jeanne Carola Francesconi, 'fatal, like the destiny of two lovers born one for the other.'" But the courtship of pasta and tomatoes was quite slow to develop, and what now seems to us to be the natural and inevitable combination of flavors went down some blind alleys. Alexandre-Balthazar-Laurent Grimot de la Reynière, the French author of *L'Almanach des gourmands,* written in 1807, noted that the same tomatoes used in soups could replace the purées and cheeses usually mixed with vermicelli before serving, but he did not create a recipe for a tomato sauce.

The next step took place in Naples around 1837, when Ippolito Cavalcanti published his guide to "home cooking," *Cucina teorico-pratica (The Theoretical and Practical Kitchen).* In it he wrote that the secret of a successful dish of baked vermicelli with tomatoes was first to make the tomato sauce dense. But he didn't give a recipe for the sauce because "everyone knows how to make it," whether from fresh, preserved, or sun-dried tomatoes.

Tomato sauce recipes started appearing in regional Italian cookbooks toward the end of the nineteenth century, including *La vera cuciniera genovese facile ed economica* (*Real Cooking Easily and Economically in Genoa*), by Ratta and Ratta in 1863, and that same year in *Cuoco milanese* (*The Cook of Milan*) and later, in 1890, in *La vera cucina lombarda* (*The Real Kitchen of Lombardy*). So sauces were all over Italy now, ranging from Naples in the south to Milan in the north. But the master cook who put tomato sauce on the map of the world was the Florentine Pellegrino Artusi.

It was Artusi who broke free from regional cookbooks to produce the first truly pan-Italian cookbook in 1891, some thirty years after the unification of Italy. This great cookbook with the clumsy title *La scienza in cucina e l'arte di mangiar bene* (*The Science of the Kitchen and the Art of Eating Well*) included recipes from Tuscany, Emilia-Romagna, and other regions and featured recipes mixing "high and low cuisines," as Gentilcore puts it. His *salsa di pomodoro* is made by mixing together chopped onion, garlic, and celery seasoned with basil and parsley and then adding seven or eight mashed tomatoes and cooking everything together in olive oil. When the sauce has cooked down to the consistency of "runny cream," it is taken off the heat and passed through a sieve. Artusi suggests using it over boiled meat, with cheese and butter over pasta, and even served over polenta. He also provided a recipe for *maccheroni alla napolitano,* Neopolitan-style macaroni, a meat sauce and pasta dish that crossed the seas and became a "classic of Italian-American cooking." My mother, who was not Italian at all, regularly made this dish for the family in the 1950s, cooking the meat sauce for hours until its aroma filled every room in the house. After rare-roasted prime rib of beef, it was my brother's and my favorite food when served over—what else?—spaghetti.

Like Cavalcanti, Mom didn't need a recipe for her sauce, but I did discover one in her recipe-card file box from 1955 for "Lazy Day Spaghetti," the quick version of her lengthy spaghetti sauce creation, and it shows that the basic ingredients used in both were ground beef, onion, bell pepper, garlic, a lot of salt, and canned tomato sauce. In the longer recipe I remember she used tomato paste as well. She always skimmed the fat from the beef off the top of the sauce as it cooked, and I think we ate spaghetti about once every week or two. But we never had pizza because it was "too much trouble" to make from scratch.

Waverly Root notes that "the Pompeiians also ate pizza, but it was pizza without tomatoes, for 1,500 years had to lapse before the first tomato would be seen in Europe." Professor Carlo Mangoni of the University of Naples puts the date for the joining of tomatoes and bread at approximately 1760. Some of these early pizzas, as Dickie tells it, were definitely different: "It should not come as too much of a surprise that early in its history, in the late 1800s, pizza was disgusting." This is because, as Rosario Buonassisi writes in his book *Pizza*, "In various parts of Europe as late as the end of the eighteenth century, when salt was such a luxury, the poorer classes used to salt their food with a mixture of salt and ashes from a wood fire, or when poverty was extreme, with ashes alone."

Such practices probably led to many of the unfavorable descriptions of pizza by travelers to Naples. Carlo Collodi, famous author of Pinocchio stories, traveled to Naples and in his book of 1876, *Il viaggio per l'Italia di Giannettino* (*Giannettino's Trip Through Italy*), has a very unflattering description of pizza: "The blackened aspect of the toasted crust, the whitish sheen of garlic and anchovy, the greenish-yellow tint of the oil and fired herbs, and those red bits of tomato here and there give pizza the appearance of complicated filth that matches the dirt of the vendor."

Other the other hand, pizzas were cheaper to make and buy than macaroni, and Alexandre Dumas, author of *The Three Musketeers*, has a more flattering description of pizzas in the 1830s: "There are pizzas with oil, pizzas with different kinds of lard, pizzas with cheese, pizzas with tomatoes, and pizzas with little fish." Those "little fish" are probably anchovies, still a pizza topping today, and don't let the comment about lard disturb you. Italians prize their *lardo,* which is cured and flavored back fat, while *strutto* is the run-of-the-mill, ordinary kidney variety or leaf lard. I was fortunate enough to taste three different cured *lardos* at a brunch at a chile-pepper research facility outside of Parma, and they were delicious.

Toward the end of the nineteenth century, tomatoes were so important to pizza-making around Naples that early tomato breeders developed a tomato that was an "extraordinary cropper" and a trailing variety about the size of a hen's egg that was easier to grow than other types because it did not require staking. This was the "King Humbert" variety, named for the King of Italy at the time, Umberto I, and it finally met the high demand for tomatoes in Naples. This tomato was nearly lost in the transition to newer varieties and in the words of David Gentilcore "is now a rarity eagerly sought by Italian collectors of 'heirloom' seeds." Ironically in the world of food history, Umberto I is mostly forgotten, but his wife, Margherita, remains famous even today.

That's because she has her own pizza, Pizza Margherita, that was invented for her in 1889 by the famous *pizzaioli* Raffaele Esposito. The story goes that the king and queen were visiting Naples that year to see the construction work on

Queen Margherita of Savoy. Photograph by Henri Le Lieure, November 20, 1851. Sunbelt Archives.

modernizing the water and sewage system of Naples. Margherita was tired of the French cuisine at court and wanted a pizza, certainly an understandable craving that we all know today. So she brought in Esposito to man the pizza oven in the palace that had been installed by Ferdinand II, who was King of the Two Sicilies from 1830 to 1859. He made three pizzas for the queen, one with olive oil, one with whitebait (baby anchovies), and one with tomato, mozzarella, and a few torn basil leaves.

Margherita loved the last one, supposedly because the colors echoed the flag of the recently unified Italy, and thus was born an instant culinary tradition that lives on today. Gentilcore points out that this "invented tradition" became famous because local, popular cooking had triumphed over the imported French cuisine of the "vanquished Bourbons" and the "Italianizing" of a Neapolitan specialty with the framework of a unified Italy. Advocates of "southern pride" in Italy, he notes, "would like to see it renamed Pizza Ferdinando for the earlier king who loved pizza and had the oven installed, but that's not going to happen."

Frank Pepe, Founder of the Oldest Pizzeria in the United States, Established in 1925 in New Haven, CT. Photographer Unknown. Sunbelt Archives.

Despite unification, pizza was slow in moving into other regions of Italy. The journalist Matilde Serao, author of *Il ventre di Napoli* (*The Bowels of Naples*, 1884), wrote: "Pizza, when taken away from its Neapolitan environment, seemed out of place; it was indigestible." This was more than just a culinary observation. Pizza, like the tomato before it, was resisted because of fear: It was from Naples, after all, a city that Mark Twain had visited in 1867, writing famously, "See Naples and Die." This was because of cholera caused by Naples's unsanitary water supply.

But soon it was King Umberto to the rescue, with his slogan, "Naples must be disemboweled." During an earlier visit in 1884, he saw to it that tenements were demolished and the water supply fixed, so that when he and Margherita returned in 1889, it was a much safer place. Margherita's approval of what Dickie calls "the poorest dish of the poorest city in Italy" was a political statement: "With pizza, Margherita took her own journey into the bowels of Italy." After that journey, Queen Margherita was the toast of Italy. Fashion magazines ran stories about her; "fawning biographies," as Dickie describes them, were published; and she became a model for Italian womanhood. "She was an exemplar of beauty, elegance, charity, and *hygiene*," he writes, with the emphasis his, "a buzz-word of the era that embraced everything from washing and exercise to medicine and diet."

But Margherita's hygiene was still not enough to make the pizza famous in all of Italy. It would take far longer for the image of cholera-ridden Naples to fade into a distant memory and for pizza to slowly creep into all parts of the country. The word "pizzeria" didn't make it into Italian dictionaries until 1918, and Dickie writes that "[i]t was not until the 1960s and 1970s that most of the rest of Italy found pizza not only digestible, but delicious."

We all know what happened after that. Pizza was brought to the United States by Italian immigrants and took the country by storm, creating variation after variation, like thin-crust pizzas, pan pizzas, and Chicago deep-dish pizzas, much to the horror of Neapolitan pizza-makers, who responded by forming the True Neapolitan Pizza Association in 1984—exactly a hundred years after King Umberto's first visit—which created exact guidelines for the making of Neapolitan pizza. Only two kinds are allowed,

Marinara and Margherita, and they must be made entirely by hand. No mixers or rolling pins are allowed, and the pizzas must be exactly thirty centimeters (twelve inches) in diameter. They must be baked in a wood-fired oven for exactly a minute and a half. No variations from this process are permitted for the pie to be "true Neapolitan." The formerly "instant tradition" is now formally defined, and it only took a century for that to happen.

So, finally, what hath the tomato wrought in Italy? Capatti and Montanari sum it up nicely: "The image of islands and beaches, as exemplary origins of the modern diet, proved to be a successful concept," and thus "the Mediterranean diet" was born. They continue: "This increasingly polluted and almost completely landlocked sea had . . . seen the development of mass tourism, characterized by the season migration of travelers from wealthy countries. Tourists have an interest in food and food festivals. Sun, spaghetti, pizza, and vegetables have by now become part of the myth of good health. Italy is the central focus of this interest because of its diversified cuisine and food industries, which had been living off the Mediterranean myth for centuries."

And now, my focus on the influence of New World plants on the Old World must shift gears from crops that prevented starvation or changed the cuisine of a nation to one that had few economic or culinary effects on Europe, but people still desired it nonetheless: the so-called "king of fruits," the pineapple.

Lust for Plants

Human beings are collectors of every object imaginable, from pig memorabilia to automatic weapons, and there are a number of instances where certain plants triggered a mania to develop for them, sometimes irrational, sometimes not. The first example that comes to mind is the tulip mania that hit what is now the Netherlands in the 1630s, when speculative traders caused bulb prices to skyrocket to obscene prices before the tulip market eventually crashed. A single bulb from a variety known as "Semper Augustus" sold for more than three thousand guilders, about ten times more than the annual salary of a silversmith. According to a pamphlet of the day, that amount of money could have purchased "eight pigs, four oxen, twelve sheep, twenty-four tons of wheat, forty-eight tons of rye, two hogsheads of wine, four barrels of beer, two tons of butter, a thousand pounds of cheese,

Oldest Known Pineapple Illustration. From Gonzalo Fernández de Oviedo y Valdés' Historia General y Natural de las Indias, *1535. Sunbelt Archives.*

a silver drinking cup (as well as clothes, bed and mattress, and a ship)." After the crash in the winter of 1636–37, that same bulb would have been worth thirty guilders, or one one-hundredth of its previous value.

The lust for this particularly beautiful plant was driven by greed, but in recent years new scholarship has shown that very few of the investors were hurt financially because they never paid for what they had bid on—it was a game of futures. If they defaulted on their bid, the Dutch court ruled, they could settle with the seller for 10 percent of the bid price. One historian, Peter Garber, author of *Famous First Bubbles: The Fundamentals of Early Manias*, wrote that the speculation "was no more than a meaningless winter drinking game, played by a plague-ridden population that made use of the vibrant tulip market." Even if this is true, tulip mania produced quite a financial legacy: The total flower bulb export value of the Netherlands in 2005 was $756 million, most of that being tulips.

Other plant manias over the centuries have included tomato mania in the United States that began in the 1830s with "miraculous" tomato pills said to cure "scrofulous diseases" of the glandular system that led to tomatoes becoming the most popular garden crop today. Other "cult" plants with fanatically devoted home horticulturists worshipping them around the world have been roses and orchids, and many books have been written about them, for me most notably *Orchid Fever* (2000) by Eric Hansen. But none of the plant manias have been as eccentric, charming, and amazing as the British-American infatuation with pineapples.

"It Tastes like a Raspberry—No, Make That a Melon."

I clearly remember clearly the first time I ever tasted a mango. I was twelve years old and living in northern Virginia. A friend of my father had brought some mangos back from a trip to Mexico and gave a few ripe ones to him. Dad brought them home from his office at the Pentagon and we had a family tasting. I thought I had died and gone to heaven—it was the best-tasting fruit I'd ever had and is still my favorite. I told some friends at school about it, and the first question out of their mouths was, "Well, what did it taste like?" I was stumped. It tasted like a mango, like an apple tastes like an apple. I think I answered, "Sorta like a ripe peach."

So I completely understand what the Europeans went through in attempting to describe the taste of the pineapple other than "It tastes like a pineapple." One of the first Europeans who tasted it was the Spanish historian Gonzalo de Fernández Oviedo y Valdés, who in 1535 described it as having the flavors of melons, strawberries, and apples, and Père Jacques du Tertre, the French missionary and historian who wrote that "one finds in it the aroma of the peach, the apple, the quince, and the muscat grape." Even priests tried to describe it when in 1634 Father Andrew White tasted one in Barbados and proclaimed its flavor was a cross between wine and strawberries.

After the pineapple arrived in Europe, it was often called "the king of fruits" for two reasons. First, the

BROMELIA ANANAS —Linn.—Blanco.
ANANASSA SATIVA:—Linn.—Miq.
VAR.—ATROVIRIDIS.

Pineapple, Ananas aculeatus. *Botanical Illustration from* Hortus Nitidissimis *by Georg Ehret, 1750.*

"The Best Thing He Ever Tasted..."

"The pineapple moved in the best social circles from the beginning of its European career. Difficult but not impossible to bring fresh from the West Indies in an early sailing ship, it was picked slightly green, and if the ship was favored by wind and the seas, a few pineapples might arrive unrotted. Peter Martyr records King Ferdinand of Spain, who died in 1519, tasting a pineapple. Only one fruit, the one the king ate, arrived in edible condition. He said it was the best thing he had ever tasted. There was not enough left for Peter Martyr to try, but he consoled himself by telling us that in shape and color it was like a pinecone, and that people who had eaten them on their native soil had been amazed by the flavor."
–Sophie Coe

fruit sported a crown of new growth, which is cut off, dried, and then set in moist soil for rooting—a perfect clone of the original. Second, when it was tasted by King Ferdinand of Spain, he said that its flavor "excels all other fruits." Concerning flavor, even a philosopher got into the game: John Locke, who had never tasted one, logically wrote in his *Essay Concerning Human Understanding* (1690) that it was impossible to truly know the flavor from descriptions, "which will still be very different from the true taste of the Fruit itself." In other words, to taste it is to know it.

David Hume said essentially the same thing in his book *A Treatise of Human Nature* (1739), but by that time, the upper class was not only paying extremely high amounts for imported ones but also building "pineries" to grow them in England throughout the year. This was because a large percentage of the pineapples coming into the Port of London were rotten when they got there, further increasing the value of the good ones because of the old supply and demand equation—after all, the cost of the freight had to come out of the value of the ones that were left. And there was one key factor in why the wealthy were building pineries: The pineapples grown in them were superior in flavor and texture to the imported ones—and they were much, much larger. The record weight for pinery-grown pineapples was an astonishing fourteen pounds, twelve ounces—a weight that no imported pineapple could achieve.

Pineapples fit neatly into the national crazes for natural things in England, such as "ferneries," which indicated that collectors were deeply devoted to "pteridomania," or "the madness for collecting and keeping ferns," in the words of Richard Conniff, author of *The Species Seekers* (2011). Other later natural passions in England included a fascination with limpets in the 1830s and later baby alligators.

By the mid-1720s, every self-respecting aristocrat in England wanted to own a pinery and by the 1770s, notes Fran Beauman in her excellent book *The Pineapple: King of Fruits*, "anyone who was anyone around the upper echelons of society grew their own pineapples. Within a phenomenally short space of time, they had acquired a central role within English high society." And it was phenomenally expensive to grow them. Since they took two or three years to reach maturity in pineries, the cost to grow a single pineapple in the 1870s was about £80—that would be about

Opposite: Bizarre Pineapple Illustration from The Nuremberg Hesperides, *by Johann Christoph Volkamer, 1708. Note the Tarantula Eating a Bahama Honeycreeper. Sunbelt Archives.*

Portrait of John Murray, 4th Earl of Dunmore (1730-1809). Painting by Joshua Reynolds, 1765. Sunbelt Archives.

$30,000 today. The fruits were so expensive that many people didn't eat them but rather rented them out as table decorations because, after all, a home-grown pineapple was the ultimate status symbol in England, "the one essential guest to feature at all society parties of the age," says Beauman. She also notes that a single pineapple was "passed on from party to party until it began to rot so much it smelt out the whole household." And the same fascination with this fruit was happening in America.

The Pineapplehead Politician

John Murray, the Fourth Earl of Dunmore, was the most notable pineapple connoisseur in Scotland and England and was also responsible for the complete destruction of the largest city in Virginia, Norfolk, during the Revolutionary War. In Scotland, he sat as a Scottish representative peer in the House of Lords from 1761 to 1774 and from 1776 to 1790. In America, he was the royal governor of the Colony of Virginia from 1771 until his departure to New York in 1776 and had to fight the rebellious colonists. Then, from 1787 to 1796, he served as governor of the Bahamas, which was, ironically, supplying most of the pineapples to the American colonies. Here's how all of this transpired chronologically in both England and America.

In 1730 (some sources say 1750), William Byrd installed stone pineapples on gateposts and a molded pineapple above the main doorway of the main house of his Westover Plantation on the James River near Richmond, and soon other plantations and urban houses followed suit. In England, with pineapples imported from the West Indies becoming more available in markets, the first recipe for using them, "Tart of Ananas, or Pine-Apples," appeared in Richard Bradley's book *The Country Housewife* (1732). Bradley's recipe calls for stewing the pineapple slices in Madeira wine and sugar, then cooling them, coating them with a sugar paste, and then baking them. They were served hot or cold with cream over them. Note the typically excessive amount of sugar that was added to a fruit that was already very sweet.

A year after a pineapple was installed above the doorway of Poynton House in Salem, Massachusetts, in 1750, George Washington was tasting pineapples in Barbados and he liked them a lot, writing in his diary "none pleases my taste as do's the pine." And a year after that, in 1752, the *Virginia Gazette* announced the arrival in Williamsburg port of seven dozen pineapples from New Providence in the Bahamas, and local grocers were selling them at high prices, but the consumer could get a better price by buying them off the dock. By 1768, the typical cargo of pineapples arriving was up to 100 dozen.

The appeal of the fruit spread, and according to Michael Olmert, an expert on Colonial Williamsburg, "[t]he sweetness and unusual appearance of the pineapple and its association with fertility and agriculture made it a sought-after delicacy in colonial America. When it was served to guests, they were naturally flattered at the honor, and thus may have evolved the idea that the pineapple was considered a sign of the highest form of hospitality." Olmert adds that the "pineapple became an essential element in the Christmas decorations of Colonial Williamsburg." In fact, in 2011, the online catalog of the shop at

Front Façade of Dunmore House, Scotland. Photograph by Giann Andrea, June 10, 2010. Sunbelt Archives.

A Wedgwood Pineapple Pitcher, c. 1765. Photographer Unknown. Sunbelt Archives.

Colonial Williamsburg offered eighty-four pineapple-themed accessories and gifts, many hospitality-oriented, including night-lights, door stops, paperweights, crystal coasters, doormats, and salt and pepper sets, to name just a few of them.

Back in Scotland, John Murray installed a hothouse at his Dunmore Park estate in 1761 that was used, among other things, for growing pineapples. The south-facing ground floor had glass windowpanes for light and heat, and additional heating was provided by a furnace that circulated hot air through cavities in the wall between the furnace room and the hothouse. The smoke from the furnace was released into the air through four chimneys that were disguised as Grecian urns.

Around this same time, Josiah Wedgwood (the grandfather of Charles Darwin) was targeting the very people who could afford to grow pineapples with his "Queen's ware," which were sugar dishes, teapots, bowls, and sauce boats with pineapple designs made by his pottery factory. These very expensive accoutrements were designed specifically to complement the pineapple itself by dispensing the sugar, cream, and tea that were part of the pineapple-eating ritual. Wedgwood sold much of his overstock pottery to the American colonies, particularly Williamsburg, and Michael Olmert notes that "In Williamsburg, archaeologists found large shards of Wedgwood pineapple ware similar to the 'green and gold glaze' tea, cream, and sugar set now on display in the DeWitt Wallace Museum of Decorative Arts."

In 1767, William Wrighte's best-selling book in England, *Grotesque Architecture,* featured a garden temple topped with a pineapple, which may have given John Murray an idea for his own estate. This temple, a rather elaborate gazebo (or pagoda, pavilion, or kiosk), probably did not show off the fruit as much as Murray would have liked. The following year, Thomas Jefferson purchased pineapples and oranges, and there is speculation that since Jefferson was very fond of both fruit and puddings his cook at Monticello probably served pineapples as a pudding. In Marie Kimball's *The Thomas Jefferson Cookbook*, pages 41–117 include recipes taken from a manuscript cookbook in the hand of Jefferson's granddaughter, Virginia Randolph Trist (1801–1882). Below is a recipe attributed to a Mrs. Putnam for a Pineapple Pudding that was probably served at Monticello.

A year later, George Washington wrote a letter to Captain Lawrence Sanford of the brig *Swift*, who was his Caribbean food connection. Washington had a very successful fishing operation on the Potomac River, and his slaves would salt down the herring caught in nets in the spring and send them aboard the *Swift* to the West Indies, where Sanford would sell them for him and bring back whatever Washington wanted from the islands. On September 26, 1769, he proposed to Sanford, "Sir: In Return for my Venture of Fish, which are committed to your disposal, I should be obliged to you for bringing me the following Articles first deducting the Freight and Commissions." What he ordered in trade for the salted fish are very revealing considering the previous parts in this book: a hogshead of rum, about thirty-two gallons; a barrel of brown sugar and 200 pounds of refined sugar ("if good and Cheap"); five pounds of green sweetmeats (fruit candy); two or three dozen oranges; one dozen "cocoa nuts" (cacao nuts, that is); and a "a few Pine Apples." Five years later, his pineapple order had increased to three dozen. After 1787, Washington had his own greenhouse, so it's possible that he experimented with growing pineapples, since he was growing lemon, lime, and orange trees, coffee trees, sago palms, and aloes, but so far I've not been able to track down a specific citation to that effect.

Back in England during this time, pineries were more popular than ever; estates like Chatsworth, Sledmere, and Castle Howard cultivated their own pineapples, sometimes hundreds at a time. Richard Weston, author of *Tracts on Practical Agriculture and*

Pineapple Pudding

Peel the pineapple, taking care to get all the specks out, and grate it. Take its weight in sugar and half its weight in butter. Rub the butter and sugar to a cream and stir them into the pineapple. Add 5 well-beaten eggs and one cup of cream. It may be baked with or without the pastry crust.
—Mrs. Putnam.

Gardening (1769), commented: "No garden is now thought to be complete without a stove for raising of pine-apples." The colonists, meanwhile, were not growing pineapples but rather celebrating them in the decorative arts—in 1771, Charles Carter added a three-and-a-half-foot-tall white pineapple finial to the top of the roof at Shirley Plantation near Williamsburg.

Lord Dunmore didn't spend all his time gazing at his pineapples in Scotland, for he was a well-connected government man and was named royal governor of the Province of New York in 1770 and then Virginia in 1771. At first, things between the governor and the Virginians went fine, but as the colonies drifted toward revolution, the situation degenerated quickly. In 1773, he dissolved the Virginia House of Burgesses of the Colonial Assembly because it wanted him to carry its taxation complaints to the king. The following year saw the "Gunpowder Incident," which infuriated the citizens when he attempted to remove all the gunpowder from the magazine at Williamsburg and was confronted by an angry mob. After the incident, he threatened the rebellious Virginians: "I have once fought for the Virginians and by God, I will let them see that I can fight against them."

As the violence increased during the colonial protests, Dunmore fled the Governor's Palace in Williamsburg with his family and took refuge aboard the frigate HMS *Fowey* at Yorktown on June 8, 1775. I seriously doubt that the navy was serving him pineapples aboard ship. The House of Burgesses said abdication of the palace was a resignation, and Dunmore's response was his famous proclamation of November, which was published by the *Virginia Gazette*. In it, Dunmore declared martial law, accused all "patriots" as traitors to the crown, and freed all slaves who would take up arms and join him. You can image the Virginians' response to this: war.

George Washington commented about the situation in December: "I do not think that forcing his lordship on shipboard is sufficient. Nothing less than depriving him of life or liberty will secure peace to Virginia, as motives of resentment actuate his conduct to a degree equal to the total destruction of that colony." Soon after that, at least Washington's desire for depriving Dunmore of his liberty in Virginia was granted—at a very great cost—during the Battle of Great Bridge on December 9, which historian Louis Guy said was "Virginia's Bunker Hill and Dunmore's biggest mistake." The battle took place south of Norfolk in the village of Great Bridge, which was surrounded by the Great Dismal Swamp. Dunmore's troops were completely defeated, and all the British loyalists fled to navy warships in Norfolk, where Dunmore exacted his revenge. On January 1, 1776, Norfolk was destroyed by bombardment and by landing parties that burned every building to the ground in Virginia's largest city, except for one church.

Dunmore fled to New York, then back to Scotland, where he was soon building the world's largest pineapple (at the time) while Washington was signing the Declaration of Independence.

Symbol of Status, Faith, or Hospitality? Or All of Them?

Fran Beauman commented online about the colonists' use of the pineapple in the decorative arts: "All the associations that surrounded an artistic representation of a pineapple in this period were, in fact, inherited wholesale from England, particularly status. On a gatepost, for example, it served to differentiate between the haves and the have-nots." And in England, this pineapple-as-status situation had a long history because of its association with royalty and high society. "The pineapple was an invaluable pawn in the intimate world of politics," Beauman wrote in *The King of Fruits*, "where as much could be achieved at dinner as at a formal committee meeting."

Since money is power, the pineapple symbolized power as well as status. The presence of a pineapple at the dinner table or as decoration "served to emphasize the fruits of British victory overseas," Beauman writes, omitting the fact that Britain lost the American colonies and all of their decorative pineapples. Thus the pineapple was used politically, like when Sir Robert Walpole, the First Lord of the Treasury and a free trade advocate, presented pineapples to his dinner guests as a dramatic example of the benefits of free trade, a gesture much more impressive than showing them sugar crystals or tea leaves. And the pineapple as a gift was much more than mere generosity—it asserted the status, power, and money of the "lord of the manor," especially if his manor included a pinery.

The pineapple was also a symbol of Christianity. As Michael Olmert comments, "Each pineapple plant gives its own life to produce a single fruit, and since 1681, the pineapple has been recognized as a Christian symbol. Around this time, Christopher Wren began using pineapple finials on churches." And this practice probably evolved from Roman times, he speculates, but pinecones on Roman buildings symbolized the "administrative, judicial, and defensive power of the state. . . . Thus the use of pineapples on Wren's great public buildings may mimic the pinecones on Roman buildings, with the added luster of English colonial power.

In 1666, with St. Paul's Cathedral in London in disrepair, the architect Wren submitted a plan for its renovation that was outrageous. The author of a biography of him, Lawrence Weaver, writes: "This design is preserved at All Souls, and shows an inner and outer dome surmounted by a lantern crowned with a huge openwork pineapple 68 feet high, of what Sir Reginald Blomfield justly calls 'a monstrous and horrible design.'" Soon after he presented the design, the cathedral burned to the ground in the Great Fire of London. Wren was appointed chief architect for the rebuilding, and he managed to get two much smaller pineapple on the cathedral—not on the dome but as gilt copper pinials on the tops of the southwest and southeast towers.

"The pineapples at the tops of the towers are symbols of peace and prosperity," tourists to London are informed, but William Hogarth, who was an art critic as well as a painter, printmaker, and satirist, had a different opinion in 1772: "Could a more elegant simple form than this have been found; it is probable that judicious architect, Sir Christopher Wren, would not have chosen the pineapples for the two terminations of the sides of the front of St. Paul's, and perhaps the globe and cross, tho' a finely varied figure, which terminates the dome, would not have had the preference of situation, if a religious motive had not been the occasion."

The pineapple in America is seen as a symbol of hospitality, but the debunkers of that concept are out in full force. Beauman comments that no contemporary references to this idea can be found and credits the "myth" to arising in the 1930s as "historic house museums sought to recreate an idealized colonial past." And an anonymous writer on the website History Myths Debunked states, absurdly, "It is really the pinecone that the colonists were using in their decorative arts (carving on bedposts or using as finials on gateposts, for instance), evoking the classical symbolism that they, educated in the classics, understood very well." It's a bit of a stretch to think our colonial forebears were carving pineapples on their bedposts as welcome-to-my-bed hospitality symbols.

As to the debunkers, a lack of evidence ("no contemporary references") has never proven anything, and regarding pineapples, I extensively researched colonial history for my book *The Founding Foodies* and never once read a primary source who wrote anything about decorating his house with representations of pinecones. I grew up in the South, and what I saw everywhere was pineapple decorations and not a single pinecone. The fact that no one wrote, "I put a pineapple on my house to invite people to visit" is meaningless as evidence. And I don't think the colonists were putting pineapples on their property to say, "I'm richer than you are, and I have more status, too!" Pineapples may not have precisely symbolized hospitality in the eighteenth and nineteenth centuries, but they do now. So if they didn't then, what *did* they mean, and why did Charles Carter put a three-and-a-half-foot-tall white pineapple on the top of the main house at his Shirley Plantation west of Williamsburg? It was hardly a sign signifying pinecones for sale.

The Southwest Clock Tower of Saint Paul's Cathedral in London. Note the Golden Pineapple Atop the Spire. Photograph by Julie Anne Workman, 2010. Sunbelt Archives.

And what was the sign Lord Dunmore was making when he built a fifty-three-foot-high garden folly of a pineapple sculpted from stone atop his pinery? Historian Johanna Lausen-Higgins describes it: "[T]he leaf-like bracts and plump fruitlets give it an incredibly naturalistic look. The structure is completed with a spiny-leafed crown. To anyone familiar with pineapple varieties it is immediately obvious that the cultivar 'Jamaica Queen' must have been used as the model, a variety with fiercely spiny leaves, outward projecting fruitlets and a perfectly egg-shaped outline tapering more towards the top." Was this pineapple an egregious assertion of the Lord's status and power? Most certainly.

Beauman explains: "It is surely Dunmore's experiences in the New World that hold the key to his garden folly. While there, he had been spectacularly unsuccessful in meeting his brief from the King of England to suppress the festering uprising in Virginia—he had proved incapable of asserting his authority over the foreign. . . . . [With the giant pineapple] he sought to translate a foreign, somewhat threatening entity into the familiar cultural setting of his apple orchard, a setting in which he felt able to control it, even dominate it, in a way he had so publicly failed to do in reality. In essence, the Pineapple at Dunmore Park is a spectacular attempt by the master of the house to contextualize the exotic on his own terms."

And maybe Beauman has explained all of the manifestations of pineapple decoration with her phrase "contextualize the exotic."

PART 5

OF *KENKEY*, CHOP, *PIRI-PIRI*, AND THE TESTICLE TREE

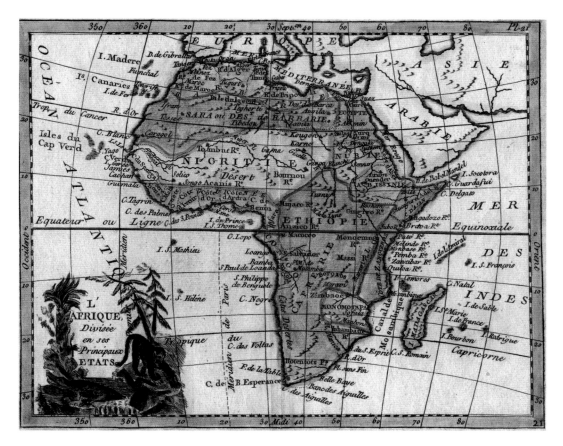

L'Afrique Map of Africa by Joseph De La Porte, 1786. Sunbelt Archives.

Europeans Arriving in Africa. Painting by Nicolas Colibert, 1795. Original in the Musée National des Arts d'Afrique et d'Oceanie. Sunbelt Archives.

I'M SURE ALFRED CROSBY WAS CORRECT WHEN HE WROTE THIS COMMENT ABOUT AFRICA IN 1972: "THE IMPORTANCE OF AMERICAN FOODS IN AFRICA IS MORE OBVIOUS THAN IN ANY OTHER CONTINENT OF THE OLD WORLD, FOR IN NO OTHER CONTINENT, EXCEPT THE AMERICAS THEMSELVES, IS SO GREAT A PROPORTION OF THE POPULATION SO DEPENDENT ON AMERICAN FOODS." BUT A LOT OF THINGS HAVE CHANGED IN FORTY YEARS, AND HIS STATEMENT IS NO LONGER ACCURATE. REPLACE THE WORD "CONTINENT" WITH "COUNTRY" AND CHINA FOR AFRICA, AND YOU WOULD BE CORRECT. I TELL THAT STORY IN PART 7, BUT FOR HUNDREDS OF YEARS AFRICA WAS PRECISELY AS CROSBY DESCRIBED IT—DEPENDENT UPON NEW WORLD FOODS. IN THIS PART, MAIZE RETURNS AGAIN TO FEND OFF FAMINE, BUT ON A MASSIVE SCALE, AFRICANS STRIKE OIL WITH PEANUTS, CHILE PEPPERS CONQUER A CONTINENT RATHER THAN A SINGLE COUNTRY, AND THE FRUIT OF THE TESTICLE TREE, THE AVOCADO, GOES FROM THE GARDEN TO THE GROVE.

Mungo Meets Mealie

In 1795, Mungo Park, a Scottish surgeon and African explorer in search of the mysterious Niger River, was in bad shape. He was attempting to find the Niger and determine its true course. Was it part of the Congo River, and flowed into it, or was it a separate river that flowed into the Atlantic? His expedition was not going well. He had been robbed of all his money and equipment, had just escaped from the Moors after four months of captivity, and was traveling through what is now Senegal and Mali with just his horse and a pocket compass. T. Banks Maclachlan, who wrote a biography of him in 1898, explains: "Once more Mungo Park was free to pursue his mission. But in every other respect his condition was desperate. His health had been impaired by months of hardship. He was utterly destitute; without food or money to buy it. He had neither guide nor interpreter. His horse had become so weak that it was scarcely able to carry him. And finally, and worst of all, the rain season was about to begin. If ever an explorer had good reasons for relinquishing his task and taking the nearest way home, Park was that one."

But he couldn't get home if he wanted to—he was starving to death, and his horse, too. Hungry Mungo was saved by two things: He could understand a little Arabic, and there was plenty of *mealie* around, known to him as corn. Park explains how it happened after he was first refused food in a village:

> Turning from this inhospitable door, I rode slowly out of the town, and perceiving some low scattered huts without the walls, I directed my route towards them; knowing that in Africa, as well as in Europe, hospitality does not always prefer the highest dwellings. At the door of one of these huts, an old motherly-looking woman sat, spinning cotton; I made signs to her that I was hungry, and inquired if she had any victuals with her in the hut. She immediately laid down her distaff, and desired me, in Arabic, to come in. When I had seated myself upon the floor, she set before me a dish of *kouskous*, that had been left the preceding night, of which I made a tolerable meal; and in return for this kindness I gave her one of my pocket handkerchiefs begging at the same time, a little corn for my horse, which she readily brought me.

Food lovers reading this are thinking: What does couscous have to do with corn? It's made with semolina wheat. Yes, and before that, it was made with millet. The tribal woman who helped Mungo didn't have any wheat, as it doesn't grow well in tropical Africa. All she had was corn, or maize, or *mealie*. Park, now in the role of food historian, details the process:

> The corn thus freed from the husk, is returned to the mortar, and beaten into meal; which is dressed variously in different countries; but the most common preparation of it among the nations of the Gambia, is a sort of pudding, which they call *kouskous*. It is made by first moistening the flour with water, and then stirring and shaking it about in a large calabash, or gourd, till it adheres together in small granules, resembling sago.

It is then put into an earthen pot, whose bottom is perforated with a number of small holes; and this pot being placed upon another, the two vessels are luted [joined] together, either with a paste of meal and water, or with cow's dung, and placed upon the fire. In the lower vessel is commonly some animal food and water, the steam or vapour of which ascends through the perforations in the bottom of the upper vessel, and softens, and prepares the *kouskous,* which is very much esteemed throughout all the countries that I visited. I am informed, that the same manner of preparing flour, is very generally used on the Barbary coast, and that the dish so prepared, is there called by the same name. It is therefore probable, that the Negroes borrowed the practice from the Moors.

Portrait of Mungo Park. From Dr. Edward Schauenburg, The Travel in Central Africa by Mungo Park Up on Dr. Barth and Dr. Bird. *Lahr, 1859. Sunbelt Archives.*

Park was correct—the *kouskous* method was passed along to the new grains the same way that polenta evolved in Italy. No matter what corn was called in any of the two thousand African languages, "fully one-third of the world's linguistic heritage," as linguist Maarten Mous puts it, similar corn traditions from growing to cooking were transferred from culture to culture. As maize expert James McCann notes, "Naming the stranger, the new crop, was in each society a process of trying to make the exotic more familiar." Sometimes the name was an attempt to place the origin of the grain, as we saw earlier with it called "Indian wheat" or "Turkish wheat" in Europe. In Africa, the same thing happened; in Ethiopia the Amharic *yabaher mashela* meant "the sorghum of the sea," while on the East African coast, the Swahili term was *muhindi*, "[the grain] of India." And often, the new term was a corruption of a European language spoken by the colonizers— this is how *mealie* in Afrikaans developed from the Portuguese *milho* (maize).

In terms of maize's cultivation, Park, now an agricultural reporter, observes: "The grains which are chiefly cultivated are Indian corn, (*Zea mays*); two kinds of *bolcus spicatus* [rye grass] . . . These, together with rice, are raised in considerable quantities;

besides which the inhabitants, in the vicinity of the towns and villages, have gardens which produce onions, calavances [beans], yams, cassava, ground-nuts [peanuts], pompions [pumpkins], gourds, water melons, and some other esculent plants." This, too, is accurate. In West Africa, where Park was exploring, along the coast maize was intercropped with cassava, as it was in the forest zone; in the savannah zone, it replaced millet and sorghum and was intercropped with peanuts.

Park continues his agricultural description: "I accordingly took up my residence at the Dooty's house, where I staid four days; during which time I amused myself by going to the fields with the family to plant corn. Cultivation is carried on here on a very extensive scale; and, as the natives themselves express it, 'hunger is never known.' In cultivating the soil, the men and women work together." McCann points out that "maize was a crop that promised survival at a time when plans were of necessary short-term, and solutions expedient."

And corn was grown for different purposes in Africa than it was in Europe. First, 95 percent of all of it produced was consumed by humans rather than livestock, and second, instead of it being just a starchy staple, most African farmers grew it first as "an early-maturing vegetable niche crop," as McCann puts it, with a complex cropping system. This gradually evolved from corn as a garden snack to a grain processed for ground meal that was used in cooked food. McCann nails it when he points out that "[m]aize and cassava were the biotic wedge of a human assault on the forest landscape to convert the forest's biomass and energy into usable carbohydrate calories."

Not only did the tribal woman give Park maize, they took care of him, and when they sang an improvised song, Park was moved:

> The rites of hospitality being thus performed towards a stranger in distress, my worthy benefactress (pointing to the mat, and telling me I might sleep there without apprehension) called to the female part of her family, who had stood gazing on me all the while in fixed astonishment, to resume their task of spinning cotton; in which they continued to employ themselves great part of the night. They lightened their labour by songs, one of which was composed extempore; for I was myself the subject of it. It was sung by one of the young women, the rest joining in a sort of chorus. The air was sweet and plaintive, and the words, literally translated, were these:
>> The winds roared, and the rains fell.
>> The poor white man, faint and weary,
>> Came and sat under our tree.
>> He has no mother to bring him milk;
>> No wife to grind his corn.
>> Pity the white man;
>> No mother has he, &c. &c.

> Trifling as this recital may appear to the
> reader, to a person in my situation, the
> circumstance was affecting in the highest
> degree.

The hospitality and all the *kouskous* enabled Park to recover sufficiently to find the Niger River (he was the first European to see it), but he did not have the resources to continue the expedition, so he turned back toward the coast. The mystery was not solved. Eventually, he returned to Scotland, married the daughter of his mentor, and lived the life of a country doctor. But not for long. When the government wanted him to lead another expedition to the Niger River and solve the mystery, he learned Arabic and eventually sailed from Portsmouth on January 31, 1805, headed to Gambia. He again found the Niger and was on a boat moving southeast downstream in the current with what remained of his fellow explorers when hostile natives attacked in several boats and overwhelmed them. Maclachlan describes what happened.

> There could be but one end to it all. A few minutes
> more, and the gallant little band would be speared, or
> prisoners in the hands of their infuriated enemies. Park
> and his men fought to the last moment, till they were
> exhausted with paddling, and the hopelessness of the
> conflict became plain. Then came the climax, dramatic
> and tragic. The four white men tossed their muskets
> into the water. Park took hold of one soldier, Martyn
> seized the other, and together they jumped into the
> rushing waters. They disappeared in an instant, and
> no man saw them rise again, neither was any trace
> of their bodies ever found. The last remnant of this
> unhappy expedition disappeared as completely as if it
> had vanished into space.

Another one of Park's biographers, Richard Thomson, author of *Mungo Park and the Niger* (1890), wrote, "Mungo Park had left one legacy of theory behind him, viz., that the Niger and the Congo were one. What was known of his last voyage in nowise helped to disabuse men of that idea—on the contrary, it obtained more widely than ever." But it would take twenty-five years to the month before new explorers could prove him right or wrong.

In November 1830, an expedition led by Richard Lander floated all the way down the Niger, probably eating maize cakes along the way, and finally arrived at the Gulf of Guinea, gateway to the Atlantic Ocean. The mystery was solved—Mungo Park had been wrong—the Niger was not the Congo River. As a side note, if you like humorous fiction, T. C. Boyle tells the tale of Mungo Park in *Water Music* (1981) in the style of a nineteenth-century picaresque novel. The *Los Angeles Times* called it "a dark and sprawling, ribald, hilarious, language-intoxicated, exotic and original novel." And I liked it a lot.

Flying Under the Cookbook Radar

Today in South Africa, half of all arable land is devoted to growing maize. In Zambia, up to 59 percent of the country's diet is maize. As it always has been since it was introduced, mankind rather than animals consume up to 90 percent of the maize grown in Africa. Maize was such a versatile food that it was eaten in many different forms that ranged from the green maize that was roasted by vendors on street corners to "the base material for both distilling local white-lightning liquor and brewing beer, drinks that African wives in earlier times would have made with millet, barley, and sorghum," in the words of James McCann.

And this was a process that took about four centuries, and it was only until the twentieth century that maize became the staff of life in southern and eastern Africa. As it spread all over these two regions of Africa, closed linked to cassava, it evolved from its role as vegetable snack to that of a cereal staple. The versatility that was maize was also displayed in its agriculture, because the grain filled unoccupied niches in the existing cropping system,

---

Intercropped with Corn

The American foods most commonly intercropped with corn were peanuts (see below) and cassava (manioc). Cassava was the most important of the two because it adapts to poor soils, has propagation by stem cuttings for easy growing, is resistant to drought and locusts, can be left in the ground awaiting harvest for up to *four years*, and has a high yield for a low cost. These attributes are why cassava is second only to maize as a staple in Africa, and why the continent produces more of it than all the rest of the world's countries combined.

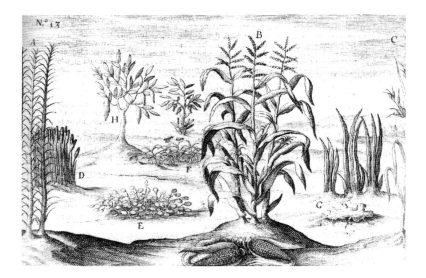

was an "artisanal" rather than an industrial growing operation, and the resulting harvest needed minimal processing. This was all happening in harmony in Africa while in North America and Europe industrial farming operations turned maize into a monoculture.

McCann points out that while maize is the most-produced food crop in Africa, recipes utilizing it are rare in African cookbooks. Since I have authored or coauthored dozens of cookbooks, I can speak from experience when I say that authors of cookbooks try very hard to pick the most appealing recipes for their books, and corn mush is simply not sexy. Also, many of these books are designated as "authentic" or "traditional," and that would eliminate most—if not all—upscale corn recipes. As we have seen in Part 2, ordinary maize can be turned into quite a delicious delicacy as the Italians have done with polenta. Ari Weinzweig of Zingerman's Food Tours writes on their website, "Ironically, in our own times, polenta has been picked up as a darling of good eating . . . and in modern day America, is perceived as a sign of cachet, not poverty. If you want to impress someone, make a pot of polenta."

I checked the recipes in Brigit Legere Binns's cookbook *Polenta: Over 40 Recipes for All Occasions* (1997) and found Polenta Lasagne with Spinach, Zucchini, Herbs, and Fontina; Sage Polenta Gnocchi; Crabmeat Polenta with Lemon and Chive Sauce; and Soft Polenta with White Truffles and Crème Fraiche, among other upscale, "gourmet" recipes. Then I searched a number of African cookbooks and saw no corn recipes that approached these in sophistication, just corn bread, corn in soups and stews, and some puddings and mush. Jessica B. Harris's *The Africa Cookbook* (1998) has *samp* (limed corn, like hominy or posole) in a stew, plus Corn on the Cob, Curried Corn, Grilled Corn, and some other really basic corn recipes.

Even my coauthors and I fell into this maize trap with our *Flavors of Africa Cookbook* (1998), in which we have only two recipes utilizing maize as the main ingredient. One of those, *ikpakpala,* from Nigeria, is Steamed Chile Corn, using fresh corn kernels to make a steamed corn bread, and the other, *akpete* from Ghana, is Sweet-Hot Corn Cakes using cornmeal, flour, and cayenne as the principal ingredients. During our two-week trip to South Africa in 2008, we weren't served a single dish with maize in it, and yet in that country, it's between 32 and 38 percent of the national diet depending on the region.

I decided that I had to dig deeper. I took the polenta trail, and using a combination of printed books from my library, Google Books, Amazon.com, and the Internet, I tracked down some very interesting and surprisingly sophisticated African maize dishes.

From *Kenkey* to *Ablemamu*: The Gold Coast Goes Gourmet

In order to describe the many uses of maize in African cooking, I'm going to jump around a little bit from country to county. Besides the basic green corn recipe, shown in the box, another common use of fresh maize was in soups like *isopho* from the

---

Green Corn, by Emily G. Bradley, 1948

Green corn (young maize) may be eaten as a vegetable or entree. The cobs should be very young and tender. The kernels should burst at once when pressed with a fingernail. Every African garden should, however, have its own patch of sweet-corn grown from imported seed. Leave the last layer of leaves on the cob, but remove the silk. Put into boiling salted water. When tender, drain and remove the leaves. Put sticks or skewers into the ends. Spread with butter, salt, and pepper, and eat slowly in the fingers from left to right. The kernels may also be cut off the cob and stewed in milk, with sugar, pepper, and salt.

AFRICAN WOMEN POUNDING MAIZE.

African Women Pounding Maize. Illustrator Unknown. From James Dabney McCabe, Our Young Folks in Africa, *1882. Sunbelt Archives.*

Xhosa of South Africa, which combines the maize kernels with onion, curry powder, potato, and salt. Another South African maize soup with a wonderful Barney Rubble name is *ugadugadu*, which is made with dried pumpkin and maize meal.

Mealie Bread, another South African specialty, is made with green corn that is boiled, the kernels removed from the cobs and then finely chopped. Sugar, salt, baking powder, milk, and an egg are added to the maize and the mixture is either baked or steamed. After it is done, cooks sometimes drop spoonfuls of it in hot oil and fry it until it is brown, when it becomes *vetkoek* and is served topped with jam or syrup and is served at *braaivleis*, South African barbecues.

Purees sound primitive, but when they combine maize with other vegetables and often chile peppers, they perk up considerably. *Irio* is a specialty of the Kikuyu of Kenya that's a seasoned puree of peas, corn, and potatoes topped with spicy, pan-fried steak fingers as an entrée. The Meru of northern Tanzania make a mash called *managarar*, which is a dry mixture of corn and beans with smoked, nearly ripe bananas. The Swazis of South Africa take the concept and make it wetter with a porridge of maize called *liphalishi* that is not served by itself but rather is mixed with meat and vegetables to make a thick, stew-like concoction. Another, very thin fermented sour porridge from South Africa is a Xhosa favorite, *amarhewu,* which is made with both yellow and white maize meal and was a favorite of former South African president Nelson Mandela. Taking the process in the opposite direction in South Africa, corn dumplings called *ugali* are commonly added to chicken stew.

The evolution of maize is easy to track in the country of Ghana, which I think has the most sophisticated maize cuisine of any of the countries in western, southern, and eastern Africa. Gold Coast was the colonial name of Ghana, and the British controlled this Crown colony until 1957, when it gained independence and changed its name to Ghana, which means "warrior king." In these days of peace a more appropriate name for the country would be "warrior cooks," for their achievements in the transformation of maize, despite the fact that the grain provides only 10 to 16 percent of the average Ghanian diet. But before I get to the transformation, a basic principal of maize cookery should be mentioned here, and I think it is the reason that maize was overlooked by so many African cookbook authors, including myself. As with potatoes, we were probably looking for some spectacular, defining use of maize that would show sophistication. We never found such recipes, so maize was mostly dismissed because, as mentioned, corn mush is not sexy—by itself, that is. As we have seen above, it's the combination of maize with other flavorful and often spicy ingredients that elevates it. Try some Southern cornbread with a little honey and you will instantly taste what I mean.

Fran Osseo-Asare firmly believes that Ghanian cooks have elevated a fermented and steamed corn dough ball called *kenkey* to the same status as polenta. As she explains on her Bitumi Blog, the firm balls of sourdough *kenkey* are often sliced to form, like polenta, a base for more flavorful foods served over it, like Braised Beef over Polenta or Italian Fisherman's Stew over Polenta, recipes I found on the Internet. There are two forms of prepared *kenkey*: *Ga Kenkey* is usually served hot with a red pepper sauce made of ground chile peppers, onions, and tomatoes, or a black pepper sauce locally called *shito,* hopefully pronounced with a long "e." *Fanti Kenkey* is usually served warm with tomato gravy, palaver sauce (see below), or any of a number of stew-like fish, poultry, or meat dishes. In Ghana, guests are often served *fanti kenkey* with red chile pepper sauce and canned sardines or fried fish.

Writing in *The World Is a Kitchen: True Stories of Cooking Your Way Through Culture,* Lydia Polgreen recounts her experience with a *kenkey*-seafood dish that was served to her at the old fish market in Elmina, a coastal city west of Accra. She was invited to join market women for dinner by one of them, Aba Theresa Mensah, and Polgreen watched her prepare the dish. To a bubbling pot of "blood-red" palm oil, Aba Theresa added plum tomatoes stone-ground together with what appeared to be Scotch bonnet chiles, some bits of octopus, red snapper fillets, some peeled prawns, and some salt water from the ocean. Then she bought some prepared *kenkey* from one of the stalls and sliced it onto plates and ladled the stew over it. Polgreen tasted it with her fingers and wrote, "It is called *fanti fanti,* and it is as simple and delicious a fisherman's stew as anything the Mediterranean has produced."

But why was the *kenkey* fermented to make a sourdough bread? African historian Phil Bartle reported that *kenkey* was studied at the Reading University Home Economics and Agricultural Research Station in Weybridge, U.K., and the researchers discovered that the fermentation process added protein to the *kenkey* and that the protein was in a more digestible and available form than the protein of the original corn meal itself. This evaluation appears to be accurate. In *Ferment and Human Nutrition*, Bill Mollison writes that fermentation creates "complete protein from low-protein or unavailable protein foods." And he adds that fermentation makes "undigestible starches far more digestible through enzymatic action." So, the supposedly unsophisticated cooks of Africa knew something that the Renaissance Italians did not; otherwise, the polenta I dined on with delight in Milan would have been sourdough polenta.

The next evolutionary stage for maize was the development of maize flour, a nutritionally rich ingredient that is to Africans what wheat and potato flours are to Europeans and Americans. In Ghana, it is called *ablemanu*, and it is made by heating dried maize in an iron pot until it's brown, then stone-grinding it and finally sifting it. This, of course, is the traditional way of making it, but modern technology has mostly replaced this method; now the process is mechanized, and *ablemanu* is available packaged like wheat flour and sold in markets. It is the most refined version of the grain and was responsible for many excellent bread and dessert recipes, so maybe this is the ultimate "gourmet" use for maize in Africa. There is such a bread recipe in *The Ghana Cookery Book*.

The Ghana Cookery Book was originally published in 1933 as *The Gold Coast Cookery Book* by the British Red Cross Society. When a new edition was published 2007 and edited by David Saffery, not everyone was happy about it. It was reviewed on Amazon.com by Pulo A. Mann, who wrote, "This book is more of a western-type of a book, do not purchase if you're looking for a traditional-type book. It's extremely disappointing." Well, of course it's a western-type book, considering who was originally responsible for its publication. It's valuable because it further reveals the continuing development of African foods once they collided with Western culture and New World crops.

Another review more clearly explains this book: "Providing a fascinating, unique snapshot of West African cuisine during the colonial period, 'The Ghana Cookery Book' features a number of charming period advertisements, and is packed with vintage hints and tips on running a household in tropical Africa." Fran Osseo-Asare comments, "As would be expected, it is basically a 'Western' cookbook, whose (unedited) recipes were contributed by residents in Ghana 'upon whom the sole condition was imposed that all the ingredients of every recipe should be easily obtainable in the Gold Coast.'" Maggie Canvin, writing online for SocioLingoAfrica, comments, "I think *The Ghana Cookery Book* was written to train cooks for expats—not for the expats themselves."

What the book reveals is the evolution of maize flour in Africa as a replacement for wheat flour, certainly because it was readily available and much less expensive. When used in breads like the one below, the fact that it's half maize flour would not matter— the flavor would be virtually the same. And the elegant desserts

---

Miss Spears's *Ablemamu* Baking Powder Bread

Ablemamu is a flour made by the natives from maize corn. The corn is first fried and then pounded into a fine flour. Cook can get it very cheaply from market. A very good baking powder bread can be made from it.

2 cups white flour
2 cups *ablemamu* (maize or corn flour)
¼ cup sugar
1 teaspoon salt
5 teaspoons baking powder

Sift all together and add a tablespoon melted lard or butter, ½ cup milk*. Mix together and bake about 20 minutes in a hot oven.
–Miss Spears, Methodist Girls' High School

*This is not nearly enough milk, so just add milk to the desired texture if you dare to make this 1933 recipe. My baker-wife alerts me that the baking powder amount is very high, too, so take care.

---

in the book, like Banana Meringue Custard, Walnut Blancmange, and Cold Strawberry Soufflé, while certainly western and not African, show the incorporation of large amounts of maize flour to bring maize to its epitome of sophistication in "African" cookery.

Maize or "miele" bread is also very popular in South Africa. The great South African food writer C. Louis Leipoldt commented,

In Darkest Chocolate

It is significant that *The Ghana Cookery Book* has recipes for thirteen chocolate desserts (Chocolate Soufflé included) because today Ghana is the second or third largest producer of cacao in the world (depending on how its production is measured), supplying about 21 percent of all the world's cacao beans.

In 1879, a Ghanaian man named Tetteh Quarshie brought a few cocoa seedlings from Fernando Po in Equatorial Guinea back home to Ghana, which he planted on his farm in the small town of Mampong. The conditions proved ideal for growing cacao (now called cocoa in Ghana), and his crop was exported to England only two years later. This marked the beginning of a revolution in Ghana's national economy, and by 1911 Ghana was the world's largest cacao producer, but by then they called it cocoa. The chocolate farm of Tetteh Quarshie is still in operation, and visitors can see Ghana's first cacao plant, still alive after 133 years!

Other African countries in the top twenty for cacao production are Côte d'Ivoire (1), Nigeria (4), Cameroon (5), Togo (8), Uganda (16), and Sierra Leone (18). Chocolate had little—if any—impact on the cuisines of any of these countries, but their cacao cargo is precious indeed because it makes up a large percentage of their total exports. In Ghana it is about 30 percent. Africa is definitely not a land of chocoholics, and it is said that there are more chocolates on supermarket shelves in Nairobi, Kenya, than there are in Accra, Ghana.

PERSEA GRATISSIMA GAERTN.

"Made from young mieles, it is one of the best dishes I know—even when made from mieles [maize kernels] that are past their best, it is a work of art that deserves to be more widely known... It is a tasty delicacy and can be regarded as one of our genuine Afrikaans dishes, one that tastes as good warm as it does cold." And he added: "Of all our imported vegetables the miele has probably become naturalised the best. We are very much a miele-eating nation." This incredible and profound irony means that a famine-busting American crop has evolved into just another ingredient in modern, upscale cookery and food manufacturing in Africa.

Avocado Fruit Botanical. Illustrator Unknown. From L'Illustration Horticole, Vol. 36, 1889. Sunbelt Archives.

How the Testicle Tree Transformed African Salads

The *Nahuatl* (Aztec) word for avocado, *ahuacatl*, translates as "testicle," an indication of the shape of the fruit, and this genitalia-derived fruit is the perfect foil to chocolate. That important crop did not enter into any of the many cuisines of Africa, but the avocado did. It was readily adopted by African cooks of all heritages for the simple reason that it improved salads, a type of food introduced by the colonists that actually caught on all over Africa. In their book *Cooking the East African Way*, Bertha Montgomery and Constance Nabwire comment on Avocado and Papaya Salad, "This salad is popular in Kenya. Although salads were not served on East African tables until colonial times, they have become more common in modern times."

David Saffery observes that "the contents of earlier West African cookery books, often compiled by the wives of white colonial government servants, basically differ little from British cookery books of the same period." This fact illustrates the desire of the while rulers and settlers to recreate the familiar in a strange new land. This was true for the colonizers from other countries as well. Barlin Ali, in her book *Somali Cuisine*, writes: "Decades of Italian colonial presence in Somalia have left imprints on Somali foods, thereby making pasta a popular dish in southern Somalia."

But the food of the colonizers changed as well, as Will Sellick notes in *The Imperial African Cookbook*: "After 350 years of settlement, British African cookery emerged from a mix of Tudor spices, Indian feasting, Malaysian gastronomy, Victorian gentlemen's club dinners, and Boer survival foods. . . . This unique and, in the final analysis ephemeral[,] cuisine reached its zenith . . . from about 1880 to 1965. Since then, it has largely been abandoned." In South Africa, the country with the largest white population, Sellick notes that colonial cookery is still popular among the elderly and conservative communities, but in the rest of Africa, "British-style cookery is usually regarded at best as an amusing anachronism and at worst as a tangible hangover of colonial rule."

Mayonnaise is a perfect example of that hangover. Jessica Harris, writing in *The Africa Cookbook,* presents her recipe for the same Kenyan Avocado and Papaya Salad and, like Montgomery and Nabwire, has changed the original recipe, replacing the mayonnaise with a vinaigrette dressing. When I tested Avocado and Rock Lobster Salad from South Africa for possible inclusion in this book, I followed a recipe that called for a dressing of mixed mayonnaise and cream. While the result was tasty, I felt that the dressing obscured the rather delicate flavor of the avocado, and my first instinct was to change it precisely as Harris did and substitute a lighter, vinaigrette-style dressing.

Harris writes that "salads are a relatively recent addition to African menus unless they are the traditional small plates of North Africa." Those plates are based mostly on Old World ingredients like cucumbers, eggplants, carrots, radishes, and oranges. Farther south in Africa the development of salads depended on New World ingredients like potatoes, tomatoes, avocados, maize, and even peanuts. For example, two African countries are in the top twenty for potato production, four for tomato production, five for avocado production, six for maize production, and twelve for peanut production.

Commercial avocado-growing in Africa is less than one hundred years old, and it began in the mid-1920s when budded trees from California were planted in South Africa. They adapted well, and the avocado orchards began to expand. From 1961 to 1996, South African production increased more than eleven-fold, and in 2005 the country was the third-largest avocado exporter in the world (after Mexico and Chile), sending eighty-three thousand metric tons or 12.5 percent of the world share to the European Union. Avocados are also a popular crop and food in Rwanda, Kenya, Democratic Republic of the Congo, and Cameroon, and in most of these countries small-scale farmers are also growing them.

Patrick Karanja is such a farmer in the Murang'a district in Central Kenya. He removed more than a hundred coffee trees and is replacing them with avocados. He commented on the benefits of changing crops: "In between my avocado trees I grow sweet potatoes, maize and beans, something that I couldn't do while growing coffee because the coffee trees would drain all the nutrients, so these other food crops wouldn't grow optimally." He sells the fruit to Sunripe, a private horticultural company that exports them to the European Union, and he is benefitting from increased prices, a market that is growing more than 20 percent a year, and the fact that local consumption is rising, now up to more than four pounds per person annually.

And how are Karanja's avocados eaten locally? Probably in salads like the Kenyan one mentioned above. The South African Avocado Association's website has a recipe section for using them, and in the "Salads" section I counted twenty-three recipes including some quite sophisticated ones with other pan-American crops, like Avocado Potato Salad, Avocado and Samp (Hominy) Salad, and Prawn and Avocado Salad with Yellow Pepper Drizzle.

Avocados stuffed with seafood and then dressed are quite popular in South Africa, and the association has recipes serving them with prawns and pomelo, and prawns with a wasabi dressing. Rock lobsters, crayfish, and cooked whitefish are also popular stuffings for avocados, and mayonnaise is commonly used, but sometimes the cooked seafood is chopped and stuffed into an avocado half with the pit removed and seasoned with curry powder.

Other avocado salads include *Avocat Farci*, stuffed avocados from Côte d'Ivoire, which features shrimp and pineapple and a vinaigrette dressing. *Kachumbari*, the African version of Mexican salsa, is a fresh tomato, onion, and chile pepper salad dish to which avocados are now added. Variations of it can be found in Kenya, Tanzania, Rwanda, Uganda, and in central African countries of Malawi and Congo, and it is usually eaten with rice pilaf or the African version of Indian *biryani,* a heavily seasoned dish of rice with various kinds of meats. *Slaai*, a salad from Swaziland, combines cubed avocados with lemon juice, fresh ginger, a little salt, and the ubiquitous chopped peanuts. Once again, New World foods blend seamlessly with those of the Old to improve cuisines that were already pretty good.

With the avocado such a huge success, one would assume that no other fruits of the Americas are as popular now in Africa. One would be wrong.

Bathurst, the Pineapple Capital of South Africa

To celebrate its favorite fruit, some citizens of the town of Bathurst, just inland from the sea on South Africa's east coast, built the Big Pineapple. It's three stories, or fifty-five feet, tall, constructed of steel and concrete with a fiberglass outer skin. Inside is a gift shop with pineapple jams and chutneys, plus local arts and crafts. Okay, it's a tourist trap, but the Big Pineapple has a certain kitschy charm as yet another homage to the King of Fruits.

Locals claim that Jan van Riebeeck first introduced pineapples into the country in 1665, while others claim that the first pineapple plants in South Africa came from Ceylon and were planted in Natal, which is a large pineapple-producing area, but as the Bathurst notes, "the Eastern Cape (especially the Bathurst area) pineries have developed far beyond Natal in the quantity

and quality of fruit produced. The Bathurst area alone delivers over a hundred and thirty-five thousand tons annually to the factory in East London."

This is all very nice, but South Africa is not in the world's top twenty countries in pineapple production; the only African countries to do that in 2009 were Nigeria (8) and Kenya (15). It's just that the South Africans wanted to beat Scotland for the record of the largest pineapple building in the world. And they did. Food legacies tend to travel long distances.

The Big Pineapple, between Port Alfred and Bathurst on the R67 in the Eastern Cape, South Africa. Photo by NJR ZA. Sunbelt Archives.

OF *KENKEY*, CHOP, *PIRI-PIRI*, AND THE TESTICLE TREE   213

Pistaches Isles

Ground-Nut.
Engraving by Jean
Baptiste Labat, 1742.
Sunbelt Archives.

When Senegal Struck Peanut Oil

The peanut farmer Jimmy Carter was seeking the nomination for president at the Democratic Convention in 1976, and some of his supporters—probably not from Georgia—picketed outside the building carrying signs that read MAKE THE PEANUT OUR NATIONAL TREE. Such is the confusion over the lowly legumes that are variously named groundnuts, earth almonds, jack nuts, pinders, manila nuts, pygmy nuts, monkey nuts, and *nguba,* the African word that became the goobers of U.S. southerners.

But sources differ on what language produced the word *nguba.* Waverly Root writes that it's "Gedda," but I've been unable to track down precisely what he means by that. In one citation, Wikipedia states that the language is "West African Kongo" or "kikongo" and in another further confuses the issue by noting, "The name 'Goober' is probably derived from the Gullah (African-Americans living in the low country of South Carolina and Georgia) word *guber* (meaning 'peanut'), which is in turn derived from the KiKongo word *n'guba.*" Cherie Y. Hamilton, in *Cuisines of Portuguese Encounters,* writes that the language is "Kimbundo, a Bantu language of Angola." There's never an African linguist around when you need one, and I will probably never sort this one out, so let's move on and discover why the French economist Léon Say gave the *nguba* this humorous definition: "Peanut, a small nut used to produce olive oil." But actually, it was used to produce soap.

The French soap-making industry was desperate around 1820 because they needed vegetable oil to make the popular blue marble soap of Marseilles, and all of the olive trees in the country had been devastated by frosts, so the manufacturers turned to the peanut, which they could grow in France, but not efficiently. Olive oil was too expensive to import, and palm oil from their African colonies made a yellow soap that no one would buy. It was only natural to think of growing peanuts in the colonies because the peanut had been grown there for centuries, after being introduced to the region by Portuguese traders in the early 1500s, but only for local consumption rather than export.

Gorée and St. Louis, two islands off the coast of Senegal, were targeted for peanut production because their soils were light and sandy and perfect for peanuts. In 1840, France greatly reduced taxes on unpeeled nuts aboard French ships while adding taxes to other oil-producing plants like flax, sesame, and poppy. This action, though it prevented an oil extraction industry in French Africa because tropical oils were more heavily taxed, it guaranteed success for Senegalese and Gambian peanut-growing, and the scene was set for a boom in peanut production. In 1841, about a ton of peanuts was shipped to Marseilles for oil extraction, and that jumped to 205 tons in 1845 and 5,500 tons in 1854. The commerce of Gorée went from about two million francs in 1840 to more than ten million francs in 1859, making peanuts and peanut oil Senegal's top export commodity. By 1880, France was importing fifty-five thousand tons of peanuts from West Africa each year, and the French were cleaner than ever thanks to all that soap. During the explosion of peanut oil in France for soap-making, the oil was also competing with olive oil for home kitchen use, and, of course, some unscrupulous sellers were adulterating olive oil with it, to "stretch" the olive oil and increase profits. Léon Say was proved correct in his ironic comment about peanuts being used to make olive oil. And beyond making soap and pleasing French housewives, peanuts were infiltrating African foodways.

Captain Conneau, the Slave-Trading Food Historian

I am no longer surprised by what strange paths searches in Google Books will send a researcher down. I was searching by doing permutations and combinations of the words "peanut," "Africa," and "stew" during the years 1750 to 1920. I found some good information, but what I was really looking for was another Mungo Park, some British or European adventurer in Africa who liked what he was eating. Finally it occurred to me that "peanut," an American term that came from "goober pea," was a slave expression derived from the African *n'guba* and the fact the foliage resembled garden pea leaves. Elsewhere, they were known as a groundnut, so I searched for that term and a hyphenated

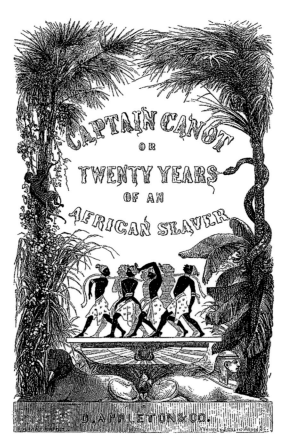

Front Cover of
Captain Canot; or
Twenty Years of an
African Slaver, *D.
Appleton & Co., 1854.
Illustrator Unknown.
Sunbelt Archives.*

version, and that's what led me to the world of a slave trader named Theophilus Conneau.

His memoirs were first published in 1854, simultaneously in London by Richard Bentley and in New York by D. Appleton & Co. The British edition was titled *Revelations of a Slave Trader; or Twenty Years' Adventures of Captain Canot,* and the American edition was called *Captain Canot; Twenty Years as an African Slaver.* Both editions were edited by Brantz Mayer. Many years later, Conneau's original manuscript was found in the papers of Mayer's estate, and in 1976 the manuscript was published under the title *A Slaver's Log Book or 20 Years' Residence in Africa.* I have used all three editions here, but that's not the end of the story. A writer named Hevey Allen, searching for a marketable subject for a new novel to be published during the Great Depression, seized upon Conneau's story and transformed it into *Anthony Adverse* and it was published by Farrar and Rinehart in 1933 and became a best seller despite its three volumes and 1,220-page length. In 1936, the movie *Anthony Adverse,* directed by Mervyn LeRoy, was released by Warner Brothers. It starred Frederic March and Olivia de Havilland, and although because of its length it was not a big hit, it did win four Academy Awards, for Best Supporting Actress, Best Cinematography, Best Score, and Best Film Editing.

For a slave trader, Conneau was well educated (for his time and position), well read, and well spoken. Born in Florence, Italy, he was the son of a paymaster in Napoleon's Army, which had invaded Italy. After his father died at Waterloo, Conneau and five siblings were raised by his mother, who, Conneau tells us, "managed to keep me in school until near 12 years of age, where I was taught Latin, geography, arithmetic, and history." He also had a knack for languages and notes: "I was considered a marvel in languages, inasmuch as I spoke French, Italian, Spanish,

English, and professed a familiarity with Latin." He later learned SooSoo, a dialect of the Mandingo. In his memoirs, we have a rare opportunity, like we did with Mungo Park, to read the revelations of a primary source, a witness, as it were, turned food historian.

In the first half of his memoirs, Conneau was living in what is now Sierra Leone in West Africa working as a clerk for a trader and slaver, so he had opportunities to travel and observe native customs in the late 1820s. His attention to food and food customs seems to have started when he was captured by pirates and served them as a "cook's mate." Once he cooked up a "*déjeuner* (lunch) of codfish stewed in claret, snowy and granulated rice, delicious tomatoes, and fried ham" with "claret and followed up with brandy and cigars." He didn't much like the work, or the company, but he certainly liked the food. So did the pirates, and Conneau marvels that "[i]t is astonishing how well these wandering vagabonds know how to toss up a savoury mess, and how admirably they understand its enjoyment. A tickled palate is one of the great objects of their mere animal existence, and they

Captain Theophilis Conneau Examines a Slave. Only Known Illustration of Captain Conneau. Illustrator Unknown. From Revelations of a Slave Trader; or Twenty Years' Adventures of Captain Canot, 1854, by Theophilus Conneau, Back Cover.

are generally prepared with a mate who might pass muster in a second-rate restaurant." And that mate for a while was Conneau.

The captain, as he later became known, was interested in agriculture too, and his observations give us insight into the spread of New World crops in West Africa and how they fit into the existing pattern of other African crops grown for millennia. "It was the height of the dry season," he writes, "when everything was parched by the sun, yet I could trade the outlines of fine plantations, gardens, and rice-fields. Everywhere I found an abundance of peppers, onion, garlic, tomatoes, sweet potatoes, and cassava." Of the six crops he mentioned there, four were from the New World. And the food was inexpensive: "A leaf of tobacco purchased a fowl; a charge of powder obtained a basin of milk, or a dozen of eggs; and a large sheep cost only six cents, or a quart of salt."

He found that the main style of cooking was stewing together all kinds of crops and creatures, but he never knew what he would find in the stews he was served. Once he was given "a heavy ram-goat," which the Bager people (whom I've been unable to track down) he was staying with promptly turned into a stew. "As I lifted the lid from the vessel containing the steaming stew," he writes, "its powerful fragrance announced the remains of that venerable quadruped with which I had been welcomed." Showing his

African Bush Meat Dinner with Pit-Barbecued Trunk

"As a rule, there is only one principal meal, which is eaten in the early part of the evening. It mostly consists of parrot-soup, roasted or stewed monkeys, alligator eggs (also well liked by Europeans), and birds of every description. A great delicacy, so considered by Europeans and natives alike, is elephant's feet and trunk. They have somewhat the taste of veal, and have a very delicious flavor. To prepare them they dig a hole, about five feet deep, in the sand, and build in it a large fire. After the sand is thoroughly heated, the fire is removed, leaving only the ashes in the hole. They place the trunk and feet in this hole, covering them with leaves, and afterward with hot sand; they remain there about two hours, when they are considered done." –From *The Curiosities of Food*, by Peter Lund Simmonds, 1859.

sensitive side, Conneau could not force himself to eat it because the goat had apparently been something of a family pet. "Had starvation depended upon it, I could not have touched a morsel," he confesses. So Conneau's host sent one of his wives to bring her supper to his lodge instead of the goat stew. "A taste of the dish satisfied me that it was edible, though intensely peppered. I ate with the appetite of an alderman, nor was it till two days after that my trader informed me I had supped so heartily on the spareribs of an alligator!" He also notes that "I had never loved 'water fowl' of so wild a character."

Ever curious, Conneau inspected every stew he was served and was constantly surprised that no provider of needed protein was ignored in West Africa. "Many a time, when I was as hungry as a wolf, I found my vagabonds in a nook of the woods," he wrote, "luxuriating over a mess with the unctuous lips of aldermen; but when I came to analyze the stew, I generally found it to consist of a 'witch's cauldron' copiously filled with snails, lizards, iguanas, frogs, and alligators!" Usually, when he was quite hungry, he postponed his inspection until he had eaten his fill. "A long fast is a good sauce," he wrote philosophically, "and I need not assert that I started *sans façon* [unceremoniously]. My appetite was sharp, and the vapour of the liquid inviting . . . spoonful after spoonful was sucked in as rapidly as the heat allowed." Conneau asks for a second helping, and "[a]s the captain was helping me to the second ladle, he politely demanded whether I was 'fond of the thick;' and as I replied in the affirmative, he made another dive to the bottom and brought up the instrument with a heaping mass, in whose centre was a diminutive skull of an animal."

Even though English was not his first language—his childhood was spent in Italy—Conneau has a nice turn of phrase. In one example, he describes a particularly meager meal as "simple enough even for the most dyspeptic homoeopathist." A homoeopathist, defined by satirist Ambrose Bierce in *The Devil's Dictionary* as "the humorist of the medical profession," is one who believes that minute amounts of drugs can be administered as cures. A dyspeptic one is a person who suffers from indigestion, so what Conneau means in 1827 is that there was a small amount of very bland food. But most of the time, the food was quite spicy and he makes many comments about how "peppered" the food was, and on one occasion he tried some "stewed fowls, boiled to rags with rice, and seasoned with delicious 'palavra' sauce." I discuss that particular sauce in the chile pepper sections of this chapter, below.

There's a very simple reason stews are so popular in African cooking: The meats "seem to come from animals that have been trained all their lives as long-distance runners," in the words of African food expert Laurens van der Post. "Even chicken is rarely tender enough for roasting or grilling straightaway," he adds, so the meats need to be "boiled to rags" as Conneau put it, or minced into casseroles or highly marinated, as they are in Senegal. That's *yassa*-style cooking, with lemon-based, onion-chile pepper marinades for fish, fowl, or meat.

Many of the stews contained peanuts, of course called "ground-nuts" there, and Conneau waxed rhapsodic over a particular one he encountered often: "The savory steam of a rich stew with a creamy sauce saluted my nostrils, and, without asking leave, I plunged my spoon into a dish that stood before my entertainers, and seemed prepared exclusively for themselves. In a moment I was invited to partake of the *bonne-bouche* [mouth-watering]; and so delicious did I find it, that, even at this distance of time, my mouth waters when I remember the forced-meat balls of mutton, minced with roasted ground-nuts, that I devoured that night in the Mandingo town of Kya." This "Mandingo Stew" he referred to was, in his words, "mutton minced with roasted ground-nuts and rolled up into a shape of forced-meat balls, which when stewed up with milk, butter and a little malagueta pepper [*Afromomum melegueta*], is a rich dish if eaten with rice *en pilau*. Monsieur Fortoni of Paris might not be ashamed to present a dish of it to his aristocratic gastronomers of the Boulevard des Italiens." Such was the triumph of peanuts in the experience of Conneau, and he was not alone in this appreciation.

The Gooberization of Africa

Although they had not read what Captain Conneau wrote about peanuts, cooks all over Africa agreed with him in spirit, and the peanut became a major ingredient in the cuisines of the Sub-Saharan countries. Often peanuts were part of hors d'oeuvres served before the main dish. Mary Ellen Snodgrass, writing in her *Encyclopedia of Kitchen History* (2004), comments about early West African customs: "Central to the meal were platters and vessels of yams and sweet potatoes, leafy vegetables, peppers, peanuts,

tomatoes, and melon, all eaten with hands rather than served on individual plates or bowls. Hospitality was essential to the local social order, which welcomed guests with finger food." Another way peanuts were used was in the groundnut sauce (*ntwilo*) of the Bemba in the Congo. The peanuts were pounded into shreds and then the milky juice was squeezed out. This process was repeated until the result was lacking in any oil and was a thickish, milky cream. It was added to meat or fish stews, and McCann

Peanuts Piled High on a Truck Near Fatick, Senegal. Photographer Unknown. Sunbelt Archives.

Climbing to the Top of the Peanut Pyramid, Kano Nigeria. Photographer Unknown. Sunbelt Archives.

observes that it was "appetizing with stewed spinaches, locusts, or caterpillars."

Van der Post writes that there are a "score or more" peanut sauces in West Africa alone, from a simple one of pounded peanuts boiled in water that's added to thicken stews, to more complex ones for shrimp or prawns that also have chile peppers in them. He describes a chicken-groundnut stew that is made (with variations, of course) in Ghana, Nigeria, and Sierra Leone that combines the fowl with onions, garlic, tomatoes, and chile peppers and is thickened with peanut flour.

The semi-anonymous author of the Third Planet Food Blog (her first name is Liz) grew up in West Africa and commented on the peanut: "My favorite dishes using the peanut, however, come from West Africa. Peanuts took off as an African cash crop during the days of colonial occupation, and are a main ingredient in many West African dishes such as *mafe*, a peanut-based meat stew from Senegal and Mali, *tsire*, which are strips of beef rubbed with a peanut paste and grilled, or *couli-couli*, peanut pulp fried into a hard, nutty ring. Peanuts are a common thickener for sauces in many African countries, and in Nigeria we ate groundnut chop."

One of the earliest accounts I could find for groundnut chop ("chop" is slang for food or stew) dates to 1886 and I discovered it, of all places, in the *Scottish Geographical Magazine*. A writer for that publication, H. Nipperdey, commented: "The groundnut (the *n'guba* or *p'mta* of the Negro) occupies an important place in his housekeeping. He eats it sometimes raw, sometimes roasted, and makes of it, in conjunction with palm-oil, one of his favourite dishes—*maamba*, or palm-oil chop." That term is an alternative name of the recipe because it was one of the main original ingredients in the dish.

In later years, the peanut persevered. In the cookbook *The TIME Reader's Book of Recipes* (1949) by Florence Arfman, two African cooks commented on the chop. Lady Bettie Walker of Nyeri, Kenya, observed, "Since the Tanganyika ground nut scheme has made such a stir amongst the British tax-payers, I send this soup that we make at Treetops [Game-Watching Station]. It is actually made in the Outspan kitchens and then taken to Treetops where it is reheated without boiling and served to the big game animal watchers." And Mrs. Frances A. Sellars of Lagos, Nigeria, said, "This is one of our most popular menus out here in West Africa. It never takes place during the week, owing to its sleep-inducing nature, and is consequently taken at weekends when all business cares are forgotten. I must add that to enjoy this very delicious meal to the fullest extent, it must be preceded by the imbibing of a modest amount of alcoholic liquid in the form of beer or pink gins, and finished off by several hours of good sleep (which comes without any pain whatsoever!)."

According to Elizabeth Melville, author of *A Residence in Freetown* (1849), "Every country has its national dish, and 'ground nut soup', a rich white compound of boiled fowl and the almond-like kernel of the groundnut is one of the grand dishes is this part of the world [Sierra Leone]." Melville also commented on the market tables covered with "mounds of sand-coloured balls," which were sold "for a few pence each." Roasted peanuts were boiled in their shells, she noted, and then the shells were removed and the nuts were roasted. After they cooled, the peanut skins were removed and the nuts were ground on a grinding stone, mixed with salt, and fashioned into little balls, which were then added as needed to the groundnut soup. They were as convenient as today's jarred peanut butter.

Most modern versions of the recipe detail making a stew of chicken browned in (what else?) peanut oil, whatever chile peppers are available, onion, garlic, ginger, and often curry powder, and then a variety of vegetables and root crops: tomatoes, green beans, okra, and either potatoes, yams, or sweet potatoes.

Peanuts, either chopped or in butter form, are added during the last few minutes of cooking. After the stew is done, a wide variety of toppings are added and diners choose from cubed fresh mango, papaya, bananas, or pineapple; sliced onions or cucumber; chopped tomatoes; more chile peppers, usually chopped fresh; chopped hardboiled eggs; or even fried onion rings.

By far, the most unusual topping I found was this one from the 1950s: "Nuts were served to accompany drinks at most times and, delight of delights, they were used to make a soup most nights of the week. It was accompanied by sherry or gin peppers. The peppers, capsicums, or Nigerian Birdseye Chillies as they were known variously or officially, were put in the bottom of a bottle containing sherry or gin and left for a few weeks until the combination of the hot spice and the alcohol reached an optimum taste and sharpness. It was then ready to shake on to the soup." This topping produced some interesting reactions. One Nigerian, Ian McCall, recalls in his memoir, *A Personal History,* "Able Baker, an engineer in the Public Works Department, was staying in the Catering Rest House. There, he had his own bottle of sherry peppers which was placed on his table at lunch and dinner. A visitor from the United Kingdom leaned across Baker's table and snatched the bottle and applied a liberal dose to his

The Reintroduction of the Peanut to the Americas

"Protected by its shell, the peanut was the ideal transatlantic provender, able to survive extended sea voyages with minimal spoilage. So began the peanut's second Atlantic crossing— this time to mainland North America—aboard slave ships departing Africa. As the peanut could be eaten either cooked or raw, it quickly became a versatile staple of the Middle Passage. The nut arrived on so many slave ships that many English commentators thought of it as an African plant. . . For enslaved Africans the peanut provided an important source of protein to a diet monotonously dominated by starches. Expertise with the Bambara groundnut had encouraged African experimentation with the peanut when it was brought to Africa in the sixteenth century."
—Judith A. Carney and Richard Nicholas Rosomoff, *In the Shadow of Slavery*.

dish—and nearly choked. When the visitor had recovered from his paroxysm, Baker said to him: 'Maybe that'll teach you to say "by your leave" next time'."

Today, Nigeria is the third-largest peanut producer in the world, but when peanut cultivation exploded in that country in the 1950s and continued over the next two decades, there was difficulty in exporting them. That was because eight hundred thousand tons a year had to be shipped to either of two ports, Lagos or Port Harcourt, by rail, and that was a single line of eight hundred miles with limited rail cars—more peanuts than trains to carry them. So the peanut stocks were stored in Kano in gigantic and spectacular peanut pyramids. The peanuts eventually disappeared after supply caught up with demand, and the government of Nigeria focused its attention more on petroleum oil than peanut oil.

Two other former British colonies, Sudan and Ghana, today are numbers six and eleven in world peanut production. Former French colonies in Africa in top twenty countries for peanut production are Senegal (6), Chad (12), Guinea (15), Democratic Republic of the Congo (16), Mali (17), and Niger (20). And in Senegal, when peanut exports to France started an industry that lives on today, peanut cultivation is still very strong, accounting for about 40 percent of the cultivated land in the country, about two million hectares (7,718 square miles), providing employment for as many as one million people, and further strengthening the peanut's hold on African cooking.

A Continent of Chiles and Curries

The high priest of African chiles was Laurens van der Post, the South African author who wrote, "The man who has become hooked on piri-piri hungers for his favorite dish like a junkie for heroin, because the person who has once acquired a taste in the tropics for Indian curries, Oriental spices or African chillies becomes an addict. . . . My French and Chinese friends sometimes tell me that piri-piri and spice cooking are ruinous to a sensitive palate, and boast that they have created the world's two reigning academies of cuisine without recourse to such extremes in the kitchen." Van der Post goes on to question the truth of that belief by noting that fancy hotels in eastern Africa "are always full of piri-piri voluptuaries," so gourmets must love the spicy foods.

Pepe d' India. Engraving by M. Pietro Andrea Matthioli, in I discorsi di M. Pietro Andrea Matthioli, *Published by Vincenzo Valgrisi, 1563. Sunbelt Archives.*

I should have written *Sir* Laurens van der Post, because after taking Prince Charles on safari and consulting with Prime Minister Margaret Thatcher, he was knighted by Queen Elizabeth II in 1981. He wrote the addict comment in *First Catch Your Eland* (1977), in which he gives the background to his breakthrough book on African cuisine, *African Cooking* (1970). This book was significant because it was part of the Time-Life series "Foods of the World" and elevated African cuisine to the same level as the other books in the series, such as *The Cooking of Provincial France*

(1968) and *The Cooking of Vienna's Empire* (1968). After he had turned down a request by the Time-Life editors to go to Russia and write a "Foods of the World" title on Russian cuisine, he was struck by what seems to have been carpal tunnel syndrome, and his doctor told him to avoid writing with his right hand for six months (he didn't use a typewriter). But if he couldn't actually write, at least he could travel and have someone take notes for him.

He had an inspiration and wrote the editors "to ask if they had commissioned someone to do a book on the foods of Africa. They wrote back to ask: 'But is there such a thing?' Of course there was and to such an extent that my book on African food was chosen by *The New York Times* as the cookery book of the year and is still a world-wide bestseller." In order to complete *African Cooking*, van der Post traveled his native Africa extensively and will be our guide to its chile-dominated cuisine. But first, a little background.

Chile peppers are ubiquitous in Africa. We saw in Part 2 how they took over the entire country of Hungary, but here they conquered a continent. Not only are they produced commercially by every country on the continent, they have entered every possible niche in the complex cuisines in African countries that not only have their own culinary creations but also those of the colonizing countries of England, France, Portugal, Spain, Belgium, Italy, Netherlands, and Germany. Out of the fifty-four African countries and two disputed territories (Western Sahara and Somaliland), only two were never colonized: Ethiopia and Liberia.

According to the 2009 statistics provided by the Food and Agriculture Organization of the United Nations, seven African countries are among the world's top 20 producers of fresh chiles and peppers: Egypt (7), Nigeria (8), Algeria (11), Tunisia (12) Morocco (14), Ethiopia (16), and Ghana (18). Hungary finished at number 20. In the production of dried chiles and peppers, Hungary did a little better, finishing 19th to Morocco's number 20 position, but it was still beaten by six other African countries, Ethiopia (6), Ghana (10), Nigeria (12), Egypt (13), Benin (16), and Côte d'Ivoire (18).

Because the subject of chile peppers and cooking with them in Africa is so complex, the standard region-by-region examination will not suffice here. Rather, to show the depth of the chile

'Fatalii,' Capsicum chinense. *One of the Hottest African Chile Peppers. Photo by Dave DeWitt. Sunbelt Archives.*

pepper's adoption by the Africans, I'm going to use a cuisine-based model rather than the regional model simply because there are too many countries to cover for the geographical approach. From the pods themselves, I'm going to move on to spice mixtures and curries, hot sauces and pastes, and finally the most common types of other chile foods, from snacks to main dishes. Hopefully, this will be a better way to demonstrate the use of chiles with both native African ingredients and the imported New World foods.

Pili-Pili and the Pods Themselves

Since the Arabic countries north of the Sahara are linked culturally, economically, and gastronomically more closely with the Mediterranean region than with the rest of Africa, there is little doubt that chiles first appeared in North Africa. In the first place, the Strait of Gibraltar separates the Iberian Peninsula and North Africa by only a few miles, so it is a logical assumption that chiles would filter southward from Cadiz to Tangier by at least the early 1500s. In the second place, the Turks completed their conquest of North Africa in 1556, and since they had already introduced chiles into Hungary, it makes sense that they also carried them to Tunisia, Algeria, and Libya.

Although chiles probably appeared first in North Africa, they did not spread into the rest of Africa from that region but rather were brought by Portuguese explorers and traders. Even before Columbus, Portuguese exploration of Africa had proceeded down the west coast of the continent between 1460 and 1488. When Vasco de Gama rounded the Cape of Good Hope, crossed the Indian Ocean, and landed in India in 1498, he established the trade route for spices and other goods that the Portuguese controlled for more than a century.

By 1482, the Portuguese had settled the western "Gold Coast" of Africa, and by 1505 they had colonized Mozambique on the east coast. By 1510 they had seized Goa in India and had established a colony there. During this time, it is suspected that chile peppers were introduced by way of trade routes between Lisbon and the New World. By 1508, Portuguese colonization of the Pernambuco region of Brazil meant that both the *annuum* and *chinense* chiles prevalent there were made available for importation into Africa. The introduction of sugar cane into Brazil in the 1530s and the need for cheap labor were causes of the trade in slaves, and an active passage of trade goods between Brazil and Africa sprang up.

The most likely scenario for the introduction and spread of chile peppers into Africa south of the Sahara is as follows. Varieties of *Capsicum annuum* and *chinense* were introduced into all West and East African Portuguese ports during the forty years between 1493 and 1533, with the introduction into West Africa logically preceding that of East Africa. The chiles were first grown in small garden plots in coastal towns by the Portuguese settlers and later by the Africans. Although it has been suggested that chiles were spread throughout Africa by Europeans during their search for new slaves, the simplest answer is the best. The Portuguese may have been responsible for the introduction of chiles into Africa, but spreading them was for the birds. History—and evolution—repeated itself. Precisely in the same manner that prehistoric chiles spread north from South to Central America, chiles conquered Africa.

African birds fell in love with chile peppers. Attracted to the brightly colored pods, many species of African birds raided the small garden plots and then flew further inland, spreading the seeds and returning the chiles to the wild. Chiles thus became what botanists call a *subspontaneous* crop—newly established outside of their usual habitat, and only involuntarily spread by man. From West Africa, birds moved the peppers steadily east, and at some time chiles either reached the coast of East Africa or met the advance of bird-spread chiles from Mozambique and Mombasa. They also spread chiles south to the Cape of Good Hope. We must remember that these chiles were being spread by birds centuries before the interior of Africa was explored by Europeans. So when the early explorers encountered chiles, it was only natural for them to consider the pods to be native to Africa.

A nineteenth-century traveler to Angola, Joachim Monteiro, commented on the wild chiles he saw there: "It grows everywhere in the greatest luxuriance as a fine bush loaded with bunches of the pretty bright green and red berries. It seems to come up spontaneously around the huts and villages, and is not otherwise planted or cultivated. . . . It has a most violent hot taste, but the natives consume it in incredible quantities; their stews are generally of a bright-red colour from the quantity of this pepper added, previously ground on a hollow stone with another smaller round one. Their cookery is mostly a vehicle for conveying this chili pepper."

This bird-planting cultivation was still evident in 1956 when Pierre de Schlippe, a senior research officer at the Yambio Experimental Station in the Congo, reported that chiles had become the most important cash crop after cotton in the Zande district with, as he put it, "very little encouragement and no supervision whatsoever." When he asked a Zande tribesman whether he preferred chiles to cotton as a cash crop, the farmer replied, "Do the birds sow my cotton?" De Schlippe noted in his book on the Zande system of agriculture that the tribesman was suggesting that one should never do for oneself what others will do. "It is safe to assume that chiles as a cash crop had no influence on agricultural practice whatever," wrote De Schlippe.

The famous and notorious African bird's-eye chile is both wild and domesticated and is also known in English as "African devil chile," in Swahili as *pili-pili,* and in Kamba (a Bantu language) as *ndul.* It should be pointed out that *pili-pili* simply means "pepper-pepper" and is a generic term for any African chile that has two other spellings, *piri-piri* and *peri-peri.* Most sources state that the bird's-eye is *Capsicum frutescens,* making it a relative of the tabasco chile. It has grown wild in Africa for centuries but has been under commercial cultivation for many years in Uganda, Malawi, and Zimbabwe. Growing African bird's-eye chiles is very labor-intensive as they require hand-picking. Pungency can vary according to precise variety of bird's-eye, where it is grown, and environmental conditions. The bird's-eye, particularly the Ugandan variety, is thought to be the most pungent chile that is not of the *chinense* species (hence its notoriety), measuring up to 175,000 Scoville Heat Units (SHU). In a test of a variety provided by German chile gardener Harald Zoschke, the "Malawi Birdseye" variety from Africa was measured at 112,226 SHU, and the same variety grown in Harald's garden was measured at 99,579 SHU.

Reputedly, the hottest African chiles are those called "Mombassa" and "Uganda," which are *Capsicum chinense,* probably introduced by the Portuguese from Brazil. In some parts of Africa, these habanero-type chiles are called "crazy-mad" peppers, and "in Manyuema and Urua [in the Congo] there grows a pepper so excessively hot that Arabs who would eat bird's-eye chilies by handfuls were unable to touch it," writes Verney Lovett in his book, *Across Africa* (1877). "It is a small, round, red fruit about the size of a marble." One of the most notorious, the ominously named 'Fatalii' of the Central African Republic, is a superhot *chinense* that analytical chemist Marlin Bensinger has measured in his laboratory at 350,000 Scoville Heat Units.

Pili-pili has become the *de facto* common term for the chile pepper in Africa. There are hundreds of other names for the chile peppers of Africa because of the sheer number of languages spoken on the continent. The Portuguese there call the chile *pimento,* the English refer to it as *chilli* and *capsicum,* the Arabic words for it are *shatta* and *felfel*, and the French word for it is *piment*. Tribal names vary greatly: Chile is *mano* in Liberia, *barkono* in northern Nigeria, *ata* in southern Nigeria, *sakaipilo* in Madagascar, *pujei* in Sierra Leone, and *foronto* in Senegal. All of these names can be confusing, as well as the hot sauces and spice mixtures made with them, but I will try to sort them out.

From Harissa to Berbere: The Hot Sauces

A complex and powerful spice compound is the chile-based *harissa,* of Tunisian origin but found all over North Africa. It's a chile paste featuring red chiles for heat and color and curry spices such as cinnamon, coriander, and cumin for flavor. It is used in the kitchen and at the table to fire up soups, stews, and less spicy curries.

Harissa sauce is a classic North African condiment, which combines cayenne or other dried red chiles with cumin, cinnamon, coriander, and caraway. It is extremely hot and is used as a condiment, a marinade, a basting sauce, and a salad dressing. Harissa is often served on the side as a dipping sauce for grilled meats such as kebabs and is also served with couscous.

A similar spice paste, essential in Ethiopian cooking, is called *berbere,* which is made with the hottest chiles available, plus up to eleven spices, and is served as a side dish with meat or used as a

coating for drying meats and is an indispensable ingredient in the dishes known as *wat*, or *w'et* (depending on the transliteration), which are spicy, curry-like stews of lamb, beef, chicken, beans, or vegetables (never pork).

Laurens van der Post philosophized on *berbere* in 1970: "*Berbere* gave me my first inkling of the essential role played by spices in the more complex forms of Ethiopian cooking... It seemed to me related to that of Indian and of Indonesia, particularly Java; I suspect that there may have been far more contact between Ethiopia and the Far East than the history books indicate." Chile peppers are obviously extremely important in Ethiopian curries, and they have even inspired a derogatory expression, *ye wend alich'a*, meaning a man who has no pepper in him.

Identical to *berbere* in terms of ingredients, *awaze* takes the paste concept into a new dimension by creating a thinner hot sauce from it. The paste is spread thin and dried in the sun, combined with more cinnamon, salt, cardamom, and cloves, and is then ground to a fine powder. This powder is mixed with water and mashed cooked with garlic and onion to a thin consistency.

African Sauces and Braai, *South African Barbecue. Traditional Cuisine at the Restaurant, Lesedi Traditional Village, South Africa. Photograph by Kwang Cho, April 19, 2001. Sunbelt Archives.*

Pili Pili Pod,
Capsicum frutescens,
South Africa, 1997.
Photo by Dave DeWitt.
Sunbelt Archives.

As is typical with Ethiopian hot sauces, it is generally served over raw meats. Sometimes green chiles are used with basil to make a much milder version of *awaze*, but it's still used over raw meats.

Captain Conneau mentioned West African "palavra sauce," which is the same as the palaver sauce. The name is borrowed from the Spanish *palabra,* meaning "word" or "discussion," and in English it specifically means a discussion with or among African tribes. "Its hot, pungent ingredients mingle in the pot as heated voices mingle in the excitement of a palaver," wrote Carol Mac-Cormack, an anthropologist who studied the sauce-making techniques of the Sherbro tribe of southern Sierra Leone, where this sauce is called *pla'sas.* Red palm oil is a key ingredient in this sauce, as are chopped greens such as cassava leaves (called callaloo in the West Indies) or spinach. Locally grown leaves such as *platto, bologie,* and bitterleaf are often utilized.

Among the Yoruba of West Africa, "meat is always cut fine to be cooked," according to T. J. Bowen, author of *Central Africa* (1857). "Sometimes it is stewed, but it is usually made into *palave* sauce which the Yorubas called *obbeh,* by stewing up a small quantity of flesh or fish, with a large proportion of vegetables, highly seasoned with onions and red pepper. *Obbeh,* with *ekkaw* or boiled yam, pounded or unpounded, is the customary diet of all classes, from king to slave."

In Ghana, "[f]or a quick sauce, onions, peppers, tomatoes, and salt are ground together raw," writes Lynn Bryden, an anthropologist, "mixed with a tin of mackerel or sardines in oil, and served with other 'slices' (slices of boiled vegetables—yam, plantain, cocoyam [taro], cassava) or *kenkey* (steamed fermented maize dough)." Bryden also writes about the importance of these kinds of stews at a nubililty (coming of age) ceremony of the Avatime, a tribe living in the Togo hills. The girl sits on a low stool while her aunt from her father's side places porridge and stew in front of her. Eager children are then called, and they "wolf down the food." Water is poured over their hands and falls into the empty food dish. The children are sent away, and the father's sister gives the girl this water "three times to drink." I'm no anthropologist, but it seems to me that this ritual is the symbolic passing on of the essence of feeding children to the girl who is now ready for marriage and having children of her own.

A famous African food based on a hot sauce is *piri-piri*, Mozambique's "national dish." The same word describes small, hot, dried red chiles; a sauce or marinade made with those chiles; and the recipes combining shrimp, chicken, or fish with the piri-piri sauces. Such fiery combinations are so popular in Beira and Maputo that piri-piri parties are organized. The dish has even been introduced into Lisbon, where it is served with considerably less chile heat. Van der Post described the process of making the sauce:

> Of course, every cook in Mozambique had his own particular way of preparing piri-piri. I have chosen one provided by a Portuguese housewife of Mozambique. According to her instructions, one begins by squeezing out some lemons, passing the juice through a sieve, warming it in a pan, inserting peppers and chillies that must be red (and freshly picked, she emphasised). They are simmered on low heat for just five minutes. The mixture is then taken from the stove, separated from its juice and the peppers pressed into a fine paste. A pinch of salt is added, and the pounding continues until there are no lumps left in the pulp. The pulp is returned to the pan with the original lemon juice and further simmered while being constantly stirred. This then is the piri-piri sauce which can be eaten with steak, mutton, fowl, fish, and crustacean and always best I should say with rice of some kind to provide the exact civilising corrective to the pagan excitement of the sauce.

As we've seen, some distinctive sauces sprang up from numerous collisions of cultures, but there were some hot sauce duplications and amalgamations. A perfect example is South Africa. With its culinary influences from England, the Netherlands, India, and Malaysia, it's a place where *sambals* are not quite *sam-*

The Ingredients for Berbere Paste. Photo by Sergio Salvador, 2011. Sunbelt Archives.

bals and chutneys are *blatjangs*. South African food authority Renata Coetzee observed: "The Cape Malays are past masters at combining a variety of spices in one dish or at serving 'hot' dishes with a cool 'sambal' or, alternatively, hot chutney or pickles to add piquancy to bland foods."

Hot sauces take three forms in South Africa: *sambals*, *blatjangs*, and *atjars*. Because of the influence of the Cape Malays, the immigrants who first arrived as "indentured servants" from what is now Malaysia and Indonesia, there are the sambals. But these are not the original Malaysian and Indonesian sambals— they are more of a hot chile paste, while according to South African food expert Hilda Gerber, "Cape Malays today [1949] understand the term *sambal* to be a grated vegetable or fruit, notably quince, apple, carrot, or cucumber, salted and seasoned with vinegar and chiles. The same vegetables are called *slaai* or salad when they are not grated but shredded, although the dressing may be the same." Van der Post states that "[n]o Malay feast is complete wtihout a sambal of some kind."

Other sources revealed how far afield sambals had come: "Sambal is a mixture of gherkins cut small, onions, anchovies, cayenne pepper, and vinegar," according to a South African traveler known only as Lichtenstein. He added: "The natives, the South-African-born colonists, commonly season these dishes with the green pods of cayenne pepper, some of which they have lying by during winter." Hilda Gerber, author of *Traditional Cookery of the Cape Malays* (1949), commented: "This condiment might colloquially be described as a hot favourite. Some make it thin enough to pour, others make it rather thick, but whatever its consistency, it must be 'hot'."

The other two South African hot sauces are *blatjangs* and *atjars*, both of which are also served with curries and other main dishes. As with sambals, they had their origin in Java and were taken to South Africa by the Cape Malays. *Blatjangs*, though originally from Indonesia, are a South African version of Indian chutneys, and some of the same spices appear in them. *Blatjang* "acquired its name from a prawn and shrimp mixture that was sun-dried, pounded in a wooden mortar, and shaped into masses resembling large cheeses," wrote van der Post. "In this form it was imported to the Cape." *Blatjangs* eventually evolved and were combined with European fruits and vegetables grown in South Africa. Van der Post noted: "But the importance of *blatjang* is not in its modern complexities but in the fact that it became for South Africa what Worcestershire sauce became for the English." The South African poet and chef C. Louis Leipoldt described it as "bitingly spicy, pungently aromatic, moderately smooth and a very intimately mixed association of ingredients." The hot sauce is traditionally served with *bobotie* (see below).

Curiously, *blatjangs* contain vinegar but are not thought of as pickles, while *atjars* have no vinegar but are referred to as a type of pickle. Atjars consist of vegetables and/or fruits that are pickled in oil with chiles and certain curry spices. "The Cape colonists of the eighteenth and nineteenth centuries used a variety of atjars, as inventories show," wrote Hilda Gerber, who lamented the loss of knowledge of local recipes. "Although a number of Malay women

Spice Shop, Fez, Morocco. Illustrator Unknown. From Carpenter's Geographical Reader, *by Frank George Carpenter, 1905. Sunbelt Archives.*

know how to make several kinds of *atjar*, only very few bother to do so. Most of them are satisfied to use the two varieties they can get without difficulty from the Indian shops, viz. green mango *atjar* and lemon *atjar*, and quite a large percentage of Malay women do not even know that other varieties can be made."

Van der Post once described his family's atjar as "a wildly miscellaneous affair." The van der Post family combined as many as twenty miniature or immature vegetables from the garden, from "tiny cobs of corn" to "the youngest of cucumbers" and beans sliced thinly, cauliflower, carrots, peaches, apricots, and more. They were simmered together with many spices and garlic, until the vegetables were tender. They were then sorted to remove any inferior pieces, and the remainder was pickled in the usual oil and spice mixture with some curry powder added. Is this a pickle? A hot sauce? A condiment? All three, as the liquid was often used as a dressing after the fruits and vegetables were eaten. The old-style, homemade atjars were a thing of the past as recently as 1945, going the way of homemade chutneys as housewives just bought the jarred kind. "We do not find it anymore," lamented C. Louis Leipoldt. "And, my goodness, do not come and tell me it is still made; that in every Afrikaans cookbook and in some English ones you will find recipes for its preparation . . . that kind of atjar has disappeared completely. It has melted away like snow on the Cederberg mountains in August."

Pungent North African Spice Mixtures and Curries

"The North African housewife can choose from up to 200 different spices and herbs when she stops to replenish her supplies at a spice stall in the *souks* of the *medinas*," observed Harva Hachten. This diversity is reflected in the unique spice mixture *ras el hanout*, which is prepared with twenty to thirty spices ranging from the familiar to the downright weird. Paula Wolfert, in her book *Couscous and Other Good Food from Morocco*, states that "it is incorrect to think of *ras el hanout* as curry powder by another name" because it lacks sufficient amounts (or any, in some cases) of cumin, coriander, fenugreek, and mustard. However, most versions of *ras el hanout* contain other major curry spices, such as turmeric, ginger, cinnamon, nutmeg, black pepper, and chiles, so let's compromise and say that the mixture is a variation on curry powders. Some recipes for it call for using shiny green cantharides beetles called Spanish fly, which are reputed aphrodisiacs, and others call for additional iffy ingredients like belladonna berries (don't try this at home!), nigella (aka "black cumin" or "black onion seed"; it is neither), and orris root (a rhizome of an iris flower).

Less controversial curry mixtures found in North Africa include the basic Tunisian *tabil* mixture of coriander, caraway, garlic, and crushed red chile; *la kama*, a Moroccan blend of black pepper, turmeric, ginger, cumin, and nutmeg; *zahtar*, a combination of sesame seeds, ground sumac, and powdered thyme; and *qalat daqqa*, or Tunisian five-spice powder, which is another simple mixture—similar to a basic *masala*—of five curry spices, with cloves, black peppercorns, and nutmeg providing the dominant flavors.

The most famous North African curries, or curry-like dishes if you prefer, served from Morocco to Egypt, are called *tajines*, and they are named after the earthenware *tajine* pot in which they are cooked. Just about any meat—chicken, pigeons, mutton, beef, goat, and even camel—can be made into a *tajine* with the exception of pork. The meat is usually cubed, and, according to Harva Hachten, writing in *Kitchen Safari: A Gourmet's Tour of Africa*, "The cooking liquid is the secret of a tajine's tastiness. This is usually a combination of water and butter or oil (characteristically, olive oil) and seasonings to suit what's being cooked." The long cooking time allows the ingredients to become very tender and the cooking liquid to reduce to a thick, savory sauce.

In 1902, Budgett Meakin, a traveler in North Africa, described a recipe for the preparation of *couscous* (this time made with

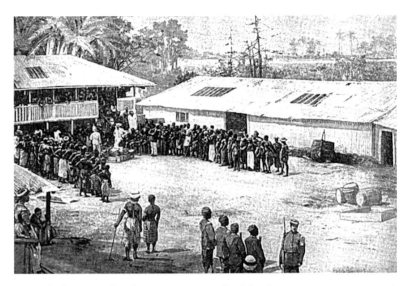

maize) that involved mutton curried with ginger, pepper, nutmeg, allspice, turmeric, and saffron. The mutton was sautéed in a *tajine* with butter and onions, the spices were added along with freshly chopped parsley, marjoram, and cilantro, and to the mixture water was added for stewing. When the meat was nearly done, a steamer filled with couscous was placed on top of the *tajine* and the rising steam finished the cooking. Meakin, writing in

What Sir Richard Burton Was Eating in Uganda in 1858

"Dinner was an alternation of fish and fowl, game and butchers' meat being rarely procurable and the fish were in two extremes, either insipid and soft, or so fat and coarse that a few mouthfuls sufficed; most of them resembled the species seen in the seas of Western India, and the eels and small shrimps recalled memories of Europe. The poultry, though inferior to that of Unyanyembe, was incomparably better than the lean stringy Indian chicken. The vegetables were various and plentiful, tomatoes, Jerusalem artichokes, sweet potatoes, yams, and several kinds of beans, especially a white haricot, which afforded many a *puree;* the only fruit procurable was the plantain, and the only drink—the toddy being a bad imitation of vinegar—was water." –From *The Lake Regions of Central Africa: a Picture of Exploration,* Volume 2, 1860.

The Moors, noted that: "A speciality of their kitchens is rather the use made of raisins, dates, etc. in their meat stews, with most excellent results. After *kesksoo* [*couscous*], their stews are their strong point, and right tasty and tender they are, whatever the age of the creature supplying the meat, as they needs must be, when they have to be carved with the fingers and thumb of one hand." He also commented that the Moors used some red pepper in their dishes but didn't like their curry meals really hot. Not so for the Nigerians and other West Africans.

West to East: Curries Get Hotter

Over in West Africa, particularly the former British colony of Nigeria, the curries are distinguished by an extra infusion of hot chiles. As Ellen Wilson, author of *A West African Cookbook*, has observed: "Learning to eat West African food means learning to enjoy [chile] pepper." She added: "West African dishes can be searing or simply warm, but it is noticeable that the [chile] pepper never conceals the other ingredients; in fact, it seems to enhance them."

Another distinguishing characteristic of Nigerian curries is that they are served with an inordinate number of accompaniments. In addition to the usual chutneys and raisins and shredded coconuts, the Nigerians offer as many as twenty-five condiments, including chopped dates, diced cucumber, diced citrus fruits, ground dried shrimp, diced mangoes and papayas, peanuts, grapes, fried onions, chopped fresh red chiles, and bananas. "Nigerians and old African hands," noted Harva Hachten, "spoon out a portion of everything so their plates become a mound of curry and rice completely hidden by a patchwork of color and tastes."

The famous African traveler and adventurer Sir Richard Burton, writing in *Wanderings in West Africa from Liverpool to Ferdinand Po*, Volume 2 (1863), maintained that "'Palm-oil chop' is the curry of the Western coast, but it lacks the delicate flavour which turmeric gives, and suggests coarseness of taste." Thus

Undated photograph of Sir Richard Burton. Note the Scar on His Upper Cheek from A Somali Spearpoint, 1854. Photographer unknown. From Men of Mark *(London, 1876). Sunbelt Archives.*

the "chop" is another African "almost curry." Burton continues, "After some time Europeans begin to like it, and there are many who take home the materials to Europe. Besides palm-oil, it is composed of meat or fowl, boiled yam, pepper, and other minor ingredients. I always prefer it with rice; pepper, however, is the general fashion." In the book Burton uses the generic term pepper to mean both chile peppers and malagueta pepper, so he probably means here that both peppers were used in the chop.

East African foods are as heavily spiced with chiles as are the West African dishes. Kenyans serve a stew called *kima*, which combines chopped beef with red chile powder and curry spices. It is obviously derived from the *keema*, or mincemeat curries, of India. East African cooking has been greatly influenced by Indian curries, which are usually not prepared from powders but rather from combinations of chiles and curry spices that are custom-mixed for each particular dish. Tanzanians are fond of combining goat or chicken with curried stews, or simply charcoal-broiling the meats after they have been marinated in a mixture of curry spices and chiles.

Curries are also important in the cookery of Mozambique, despite its history as a Portuguese colony. Its proximity to Natal in South Africa is probably the reason for that. Sometimes cashew nuts, a major crop in Mozambique, are added to their curries, much like candlenuts are added to Malaysian curries. Mozambique cooks are known for a chile paste that's almost a curry paste. *Piri-piri*, made not with bird's-eye chiles but with the long, thin and fiery African chiles that are probably cayennes, contains garlic, herbs, and oil too—but no curry spices. It is, however, analogous to curries in the native cuisines of East Africa that were not influenced by Arabs, Indians, or the British.

Ethiopia is one of those East African countries least influenced by British and Indian versions of curry—instead, they evolved their own unique curry tradition. According to Daniel Jote Mesfin, author of *Exotic Ethiopian Cooking*, "Marco Polo did not visit our country. And Ethiopia was never conquered. It came under brief Italian rule during Mussolini's time, but for the most part, we did not have direct and intimate dealings with foreign powers." Ethiopia was isolated from Europe but not from the spice routes. "Since Ethiopia was located at the crossroads of the spice trade," observed Michael Winn, owner of New York's

Blue Nile restaurant, "its people began to pay keen attention to blending spices. Fenugreek, cumin, red chiles, and varieties of herbs are used lovingly in creating meat, fish, and vegetable dishes."

Even the butter is curried in Ethiopia, with ginger, garlic, turmeric, basil, cardamom, and other spices combined to make a ghee-like concoction known as *nit'ir qibe*, or Ethiopian curried butter. But the most important spice mixture is a condiment called *berbere*, which is made with the hottest chiles available, plus other spices, and is served as a side dish with meat, used as a coating for drying meats, or is a major ingredient of curried meats. Tribal custom dictated that *berbere* be served with *kifto*, a warm, minced raw meat dish. According to legend, the more delicious a woman's *berbere* was, the better chance she had to win a husband. Recipes for *berbere* were closely guarded, as the marriageability of women was at stake.

Most *berbere* recipes contain about eleven curry spices in addition to garlic; notable for its absence is turmeric, a popular ingredient in Indian-influenced curries but not in Ethiopian ones. Some *berbere* recipes call for up to a cup or more of powdered hot chiles, so they are extremely important to *berbere*. Chile peppers are obviously extremely important in Ethiopian curries, and they have even inspired a derogatory expression, *ye wend alich'a*, meaning a man who has no pepper in him. The average daily consumption of chiles in Ethiopia is a little more than half an ounce per person, so they are as much a food as a spice. *Berbere* is an indispensable ingredient in the "national dishes" known as *wat*, or *w'et* (depending on the transliteration), which are spicy, curry-like stews of lamb, beef, chicken, beans, or vegetables (but never pork).

Ambrosia from the Cape

There is an oft-repeated quote from the South African poet, food historian, and chef C. Louis Leipoldt that concerns what is generically called "Cape curry" but is of Malaysian ancestry: "Do not assume that *penang* meat is just common curry . . . for there is reason enough to believe that the 'ambrosia' the old poets spoke of was nothing other than some kind of ginger-chilli-turmeric curried meat." In reality, the curries of the Cape came from two sources: the early Malayan slaves who served their

Dutch masters as farm workers, and Indian indentured servants who came first to work in the sugar fields of Natal around 1860 and later to work on South African railroads.

The Dutch had colonized South Africa because of its ideal position halfway between the Netherlands and their possessions in the Spice Islands. It was a perfect outpost for raising the vegetables and livestock necessary to replenish their ships. In 1652, the Dutch East India Company dispatched a party of officials to the Cape to establish a "revictualing station." Renata Coetzee, writing in *The South African Culinary Tradition*, observed: "Within fourteen days of their arrival these early settlers had laid out a vegetable garden." Their plantings included New World crops like chile peppers, sweet potatoes, pumpkins, and pineapples, plus Old World foods such as watermelons, cucumbers, radishes, and lemons and orange trees.

Sweet Potato. Engraving by Theodor Zwinger, 1696. Sunbelt Archives.

Curries in Southern Africa

"In the Indian area you could get a really hot chilli curry and rice, as opposed to the insipid Raj-English curry elsewhere in white cafes."
—Sylvester Stein, former editor of *Drum* magazine, describing his childhood in 1920s Durban, South Africa.

"Curries were perhaps the most distinctive food we ate. Indeed, strange though it may seem, I tend to think of curry as the closest to a national Rhodesian dish there is."
—Zimbabwe-born artist Trevor Southey.

"There are those who make curried meat from cooked or roasted cold meat. There are those who have mustard with milk tart! It is not for them that I am writing. May tinned food be their nourishment until the end of time."
—C. Louis Leipoldt, 1942.

Late in the seventeenth century, with the revictualing station in operation, commerce between the Dutch East India Company and the new Dutch colony of South Africa picked up considerably because of an important commodity: Malay slaves, referred to in South African literature as "the king of slaves." The men were utilized as farmers, carpenters, musicians, tailors, and fishermen, while the women were expert cooks who not only introduced exotic Spice Islands dishes but also imported the spices necessary to prepare them. Among the Malaysian spices transferred by the slaves to South Africa were aniseed, fennel, turmeric, ginger, cardamom, cumin, coriander, mustard seed, tamarind, and garlic.

The Cape Malays, as the slaves' descendants were called, developed a unique cuisine called, by some, "Old Cape Cookery." It evolved into a mixture of Dutch, English, and Malay styles and ingredients—with an emphasis on the Malay. Predominant among the numerous cooking styles were curries and their accompaniments. As early as 1740, "kerrie-kerrie" dishes were mentioned in South African literature. That terminology had changed by 1797, when Johanna Duminy of the Riviersonderend valley wrote in her diary: "When the evening fell I had the candles lit, the children were given their supper and put to bed. At nine o'clock we are going to have a delicious curry."

Johanna's curry probably was milder than that of today in South Africa, because for a time chiles and green ginger were greatly reduced for the Dutch palate. But the Cape Malays relished the heat, and Harva Hachten, author of *Kitchen Safari*, pointed out: "Curries are as much a part of Malay cooking as they are of Indian." But they also became English, too, for the British had seized the Cape in 1795 to prevent it from falling into French hands, then lost it for a few years to the Dutch, starting in 1803, before finally conquering it in 1806. British sovereignty of the area was recognized at the Congress of Vienna in 1815. As in India, the British settlers fell in love with curries.

At Last, a Professional African Food Historian

We have seen budding food historians in the ill-fated surgeon-adventurer Mungo Park and the peanut-loving slave trader Captain Conneau, but with C. Louis Leipoldt we have the real thing. Leipoldt's Restaurant in Brooklyn, Pretoria, refers to the inspiration of its name on its website as a "poet, playwright, pediatrician, botanist, journalist, novelist, cook and connoisseur of food and wine." The son of a preacher with a mother so strict she forbade her children from "mingling with the town folk," Leipoldt was confined to his house and began to hang around the kitchen, where he helped Maria, the Malay cook, prepare all the family means. She was his first culinary inspiration, and he wrote about her in *Leipoldt's Cape Cookery*: "She presided over a kitchen whose cleanliness could have served as model for an operating theatre of a modern hospital." She taught him the basic principles of Malay slow-cooked food "accompanied by a good-natured but nevertheless painful prodding of my juvenile person with the large wooden spoon that was her sceptre. [She] helped me to realise how any infringement of them impairs the excellence of all cookery." She also told him the secret of using curry spices and chiles: "My *basie* [little boss], it is to get the soul out of the spice and into the meat . . ."

Leipoldt left South Africa to pursue his medical career, and while studying medicine at Guy's Hospital in Chelsea in London in 1907, when Leipoldt had had enough of dissecting bodies, he went across to The Strand to wash dishes in the kitchen of one of the greatest of all chefs, Auguste Escoffier, at the Savoy. "Quite remarkably," writes Paul Murray in his online article "The C. Louis Leipoldt Trail," "it was not long before he sat for his exams in cookery under the maestro and returned successful, with an international qualification in cuisine." Now a chef as well as a doctor, he returned to South Africa to pursue his many careers simultaneously.

Dr. Peter Shields, who knew Leipoldt well because he grew up in his house in the Cape Town suburb of Kenilworth, told Trevor Emslie that Leipoldt was quite the jokester: "For instance, I re-member him telling us that in China it was considered a delicacy to take a live baby mouse by the tail, dip it in honey, put it in your mouth, and let it scamper down your throat!" Such infor-mation makes me think that some of his descriptions of unusual African foods may be with tongue in cheek, so to speak. "Giraffe meat is coarse and stringy, but parts of it are excellent, and the long succulent tongue, properly cooked, is not only eatable but delectable." I note for the record that a typical giraffe's tongue, as documented by the prestigious San Diego Zoo, measures between eighteen and twenty inches.

Brian Lello, who wrote the preface to the 1976 edition of *Leipoldt's Cape Cookery*, described the author as "an anti-pedant" who "eschews finicking precision about quantities. Let others write medical prescriptions for food instead of cultivating their flair." For one recipe, Leopoldt wrote: "Collect as many limpets off the rocks as your backache will allow." Once, when an editor questioned the meaning of one of his passages, he cried out testily: "How should I know what I meant; that is your job."

Leipoldt's cookbook *Kos vir die Kenner* (*Food for the Connoisseur*), first published in 1933, was republished in June 2011 by Human and Rousseau in Cape Town. It has two thousand South African and international recipes. In *Leipoldt's Cape Cookery*, written in the 1940s but not published until after his death in 1947, Leipoldt gives his philosophy about chiles in cookery: "What-ever it is that imparts this extraordinarily sharp, stimulating quality of chillies [capsaicin], also imbues them with distinctively individual merits that have long been ap-preciated by South African cooks. . . . It is also so stimulating, so valuable as a contrasting flavour, and so delicious when properly used, that other dishes, without it, are insipid and altogether lack distinction."

C. Louis Leipoldt. Photographer Unknown, Circa 1915. Sunbelt Archives.

Laurens van der Post, whom I quoted earlier as saying "the person who has once acquired a taste in the tropics for Indian curries, Oriental spices or African chillies becomes an addict," knew Leipoldt so well that they often discussed their philosophies about spicy South African specialties. And both of them agreed that curry manages to find its way into very unusual dishes. Take *bobotie*, for example, which Laurens van der Post says "is to South Africa what *moussaka* is to Greece," except for the fact that it contains both turmeric and curry powder, and those are only two of the variations of a dish about which van der Post observes: "There are as many boboties as there are homes in South Africa." Leipoldt points out that *bobotie* "was known in Europe in the middle ages when the Crusaders brought turmeric from the East." This of course was *bobotie* without chile peppers, which arrived centuries later. Essentially, *boboties* are spiced-up meat pies. Leipoldt explains the process of making a dish that is quite similar to *moussaka* but one spiced up with fresh ginger,

Cover of Kos Vir Die Kenner *(Food for the Connoisseur). Illustrator Unknown. Sunbelt Archives.*

chiles, and curry powder. It is what van der Post called the "the three great Cape Malay main dishes." The other two are *bredie* and *sosatie.*

Bredie is a spiced-up stew of meat, a starch like potatoes, and various vegetables that Leipoldt calls "intimately stewed so that the flesh is thoroughly impregnated with vegetable flavour." Van der Post adds that "the chosen vegetables, sliced or cubed, are placed on top of the meat with various seasonings, but always with chilies." *Sosaties*, or "curried kabobs," as Leipoldt calls them, are derived from two Malay words, *saté*, a spiced sauce, and *sésate*, which means meat skewered on a stick. Sosaties have "endless variations," according to van der Post, and Leipoldt in his typical lyrical manner writes that "[t]here is perhaps no other single dish that can be regarded as more genuinely Africaans than *sosaties*. . . . Sosaties, when properly made, should be tender and tasty, yet with a crispness that rivals a grilled chop, and bitingly spicy yet with a suavity that rivals the best made curry." In South Africa, it's all about getting back to curry.

How Curries Could Have Killed Apartheid

Trevor Emslie, in his online essay "Leipoldt, the Dostoevsky of South Africa," remarks on Leipoldt's legacy: "Leipoldt reminds us of the obligations we owe to the past . . . even as we face the future. . . . This is why Leipoldt continues, not only to charm, impress, entertain and fascinate us, getting under the skin, as it were, of his characters, and of South Africa and her problems, but also why he challenges our views and the way we live our lives in South Africa today, one and all."

Laurens van der Post, Leipoldt's culinary successor and the high priest of African chiles, was another Afrikaner by birth and, like Leipoldt, was liberal about racial and cultural issues. "The reappearance of curry in the fundamental and most conservative departments of the kitchen of the interior shows to what a depth the Indian influence spread," he wrote in *First Catch Your Eland* (1977). "The best place for curries was and remains Natal. Curry in all the forms in which it is done in India is served in hotels and homes and eaten with relish, however strong the colour prejudice of the household in which they are served. If only the heart in South Africa would be governed for a year or two by the national palate, there would be no apartheid or racial prejudice left in the land, because our cooking is the best advertisement the world could possibly have for a multi-racial society, free of religious, racial, and other forms of discrimination, if not even for immediate and unbridled miscegenation."

Since van der Post wrote that in 1976, apartheid has vanished in South Africa, and things have changed so much for the better that the 2010 FIFA World Cup was held there and was highly successful. So van der Post got his wish—sort of. The heart of South Africa is now governed by both the national palate and international sports.

PART 6

SIR GEORGE AND THE CURRY DIASPORA

Hunters Cooking Jungli Mans in the Jungle. Artist Unknown. Sunbelt Archives.

DICTIONARY

OF

THE ECONOMIC PRODUCTS OF INDIA.

BY

GEORGE WATT, M.B., C.M., C.I.E.,

REPORTER ON ECONOMIC PRODUCTS WITH THE GOVERNMENT OF INDIA.
OFFICIER D'ACADEMIE; FELLOW OF THE LINNEAN SOCIETY; CORRESPONDING MEMBER OF THE
ROYAL HORTICULTURAL SOCIETY, &c., &c.

(ASSISTED BY NUMEROUS CONTRIBUTORS.)
IN SIX VOLUMES.

VOLUME V.,

Linum to Oyster.

Published under the Authority of the Government of India,
Department of Revenue and Agriculture.

LONDON:
W. H. ALLEN & Co., 13, WATERLOO PLACE, S.W., PUBLISHERS TO THE
INDIA OFFICE.

CALCUTTA:
OFFICE OF THE SUPERINTENDENT OF GOVERNMENT PRINTING, INDIA,
8, HASTINGS STREET.

1891.

I F YOU CAN'T TRUST SOMEONE NAMED SIR GEORGE, WHO CAN YOU TRUST? WE CAN RELY UPON HIM AS YET ANOTHER ACCIDENTAL FOOD HISTORIAN BECAUSE OF HIS UNIQUE KNOWLEDGE OF THE FOOD PRODUCTS OF INDIA IN THE LATE 1880S. ANOTHER DOCTOR OF MEDICINE WHOSE INTERESTS RANGED FAR BEYOND THINGS MEDICAL, SIR GEORGE WATT WAS PART OF THE RAJ, AND HIS VARIOUS DUTIES, BEYOND BEING A PROFESSOR OF BOTANY AT CALCUTTA UNIVERSITY, INCLUDED HIS WORK AS SCIENTIFIC ASSISTANT SECRETARY OF THE GOVERNMENT OF INDIA, PRESIDENT OF PHARMACOLOGICAL SECTION OF THE INDIAN MEDICAL CONGRESS, AND MOST IMPORTANT TO OUR STORY OF NEW WORLD CROPS IN INDIA, THE REPORTER TO THE GOVERNMENT OF INDIA ON ECONOMIC PRODUCTS FROM 1887 TO 1903. DURING THAT TIME, WORKING WITH NUMEROUS AGENTS IN THE FIELD, HE ASSEMBLED THE *DICTIONARY OF THE COMMERCIAL PRODUCTS OF INDIA* (1889–90) IN TEN VOLUMES, WHICH WAS UNDOUBTEDLY THE MOST COMPLETE COMPILATION OF THE PLANTS OF INDIA EVER PUBLISHED. EVEN HIS ABRIDGMENT OF THAT WORK, *THE COMMERCIAL PRODUCTS OF INDIA: BEING AN ABRIDGMENT OF "THE DICTIONARY OF THE ECONOMIC PRODUCTS OF INDIA,"* PUBLISHED IN 1908, RAN TO 1,189 PAGES.

Sir George will be our Virgil as we explore the remarkable changes in Indian food and culture that resulted from the introduction of chile peppers, pineapples, potatoes, peanuts, tomatoes, sweet potatoes, and maize into the subcontinent. He was assisted in his duties, in his words, by the "Librarians of the India Office and of the Kew Herbarium for the limitless facilities afforded [him] in consulting the numerous works," and after he returned to Great Britain from India, he worked out of an office at the Royal Botanical Gardens at Kew, where he completed his abridgment.

Opposite: Frontispiece of Sir George Watt's Multi-Volume Dictionary of The Economic Products of India, *1891. Sunbelt Archives.*

Embracing a New Spice in the Land of Pepper

"There can be no doubt . . . that the Portuguese had very early introduced Capsicum into Goa, and very possibly commenced to export it, in competition with the true pepper," Sir George wrote his abridgment. He goes on to cite the early botanists Leonhart Fuchs and Charles Clusius that the two most common names given the Capsicums were "Calicut pepper" and "Pernambuco pepper." These two names give us a clue to the chile pepper's points of arrival and origin. Calicut was a city in southwest India on the Malabar Coast southwest of Bangalore, and Pernambuco was a region in the northeast part of Portuguese-held Brazil, now a state. Since there was no direct contact between Brazil and India, undoubtedly chiles moved through Lisbon on their way to Calicut and Goa.

When the Portuguese arrived in India, the Malabar Coast was one of the most important trading centers of the Old World. Huge camel caravans and shipping fleets were drawn there by the abundance of spices that were eagerly sought after in Europe. Vasco de Gama was the first European to visit the Malabar Coast, landing in Calicut in 1498. He brought back to Portugal an offer from the ruler of Calicut to trade spices and gems for gold, silver, and scarlet cloth. Such temptations were more than the Portuguese could bear, eager as they were to wrest the spice trade from Arab sailors, while at the same time outmaneuvering the Spaniards to the lucrative business. So they took the same action all the powerful European countries did to weaker nations: They took what they wanted.

Under the leadership of Alfonzo de Albuquerque, the Portuguese conquered the city of Goa on the Malabar Coast in 1510 and gained control of the spice trade. Goa was rich in spices—cloves, cinnamon, cardamom, ginger, and black pepper—which were shipped to Lisbon in return for silver and copper. These spices were essential to Indian *kari* cooking. Kari is a Tamil, or South Indian, word for sauce—or, more correctly, the combination of spices that are added to meat, fish, or vegetables to produce a stew. It was the word *kari* that was Anglicized to become the famous "curry." Before chiles, Indian cooks used black pepper and mustard seed to spice up their *kari* mixtures.

After their introduction into southwestern India, chiles spread to all parts of the subcontinent, but there are differing theories as to how that happened. In Africa, birds were responsible for much of the diffusion of chiles through the continent and the establishment of the semi-wild "bird's-eye" variety with its small, erect pods, which are still very popular there. But the chiles of India most evolved into pendant-podded plants more similar to cayennes than to bird chiles. Watt describes what he called *Capsicum minimum*: "Cultivated throughout India, but not extensively; closely resembles C. annuum, but is distinguished by . . . smaller seeds, and by the pod being erect, nearly cylindrical and yellow when ripe. It is generally known as Bird's-eye Chilli. This is found in many parts of India, principally in the southern districts, growing in waste places, gardens, &c, in an apparently wild state."

Sir George Watt. Photo courtesy of the Archives of the Dumfries and Galloway Health Board, Dumfries, Scotland.

In his abridgment of the dictionary, he adds: "This is often called 'Bird Pepper.' According to the *Pharmacographia Indica* (ii., 563), *C. minimum* exists as a weed of cultivation in most parts of India. This I personally have never observed, and hesitate to accept." He adds: "No Indian botanist has ever recorded having found a species of Capsicum in a wild condition." But his skepticism about this variety does not prevent him from quoting one of his correspondents in another book: "A very small 'chilly,' grown to a limited extent, and very hot. It is rarely used by natives, but by Europeans it is steeped in vinegar, mixed with salt, and used as a seasoning in stews, chops, &c." Similar uses are found in the West Indies for steeping very hot bird chiles with either vinegar or sherry.

K. T. Achaya, writing in *Indian Food: A Historical Companion* (1994), states that "other types of chilli are the tiny and very pungent bird chilli (so called because birds play a large part in seed dispersal)." What I believe occurred was that bird chiles existed in India after 1510 and still grow there today, but they are really minor in the overall picture of Indian chiles, and that the spread of chiles was the result of the deliberate cultivation of them. Achaya quotes "the great south Indian composer Purandaradāsa, who lived between 1480 and 1564, [and] was well aware of its qualities: 'I saw you green, then turning redder as you ripened, nice to look at and tasty in a dish, but too hot if an excess is used. Saviour of the poor, enhancer of good food, fiery when bitten, even to think of (the deity) Pānduranga Vittalā is difficult.'" This more accurately describes a cultivated cayenne type rather than a bird pepper.

Both Achaya and Lizzie Collingham, author of *Curry: A Tale of Cooks & Conquerors* (2006), speculate that Indians were attracted to Capsicums because they resembled the long pepper, *Piper longum*, but that's rather a stretch because the two fruits differ in color, size, and appearance, and the long pepper only vaguely resembles a chile pod. I think that chile expert Jean Andrews has a much better theory: "The pungent new American spice was welcomed by Indian cooks who, at home with biting black pepper and piquant ginger, were accustomed top sharp, spicy foods. The easily cultivated and naturalizing [chillies] were, for them, a lot more heat with less grinding and expense; they also grew readily and fruited abundantly in a sympathetic environment. Into curries they went."

The very observant Sir George noted: "The rapidity with which the species and races of this pepper became disseminated throughout the tropical and warm temperate tracts of the globe, following closely on the discovery of the West Indies and America, is one of the many examples of the marvellous powers of adaptability and endurance possessed by the plant-cohorts from the New World on their invading the Old." Achaya adds, "Here was a classic case of a new product eminently meeting a felt need."

Watt and Achaya both address a subject that many people don't realize about India: the adaptability of its cooks and their willingness to experiment with new ingredients. Chitrita Banerji, the author of *Eating India* (2007), comments on this: "The American motto I had fallen in love with and internalized during my years as an immigrant—change is good—could equally be a Bengali or even an Indian one when it came to food. The façade of unyielding tradition is just that—a façade. So is the idea of unmitigated regionalism. In reality, curiosity, experimentation, and metamorphosis all are at work. The only thing to fear is that the more artful elements of cuisine—whether on the street or in the kitchen—might vanish from lack of time, patience, and most of all, enthusiasm, which is crucial to the preparation of good food." She adds that "almost every cuisine in India had undergone a radical shift" when the Portuguese brought chile peppers into India, and "[n]ow the variety and ubiquity of chilies in India rivals that of countries like Mexico."

A Woman Collects Chillies in Khammam, India. Sunbelt Archives.

Despite that ubiquity, it took quite a while for them to spread throughout India, as Collingham notes: "Two centuries after the Portuguese at Calicut, the chilli had still not reached the northern plains of Hindustan." But in the south it was quickly adopted. "Indians were often slow to accept new foodstuffs," Collingham writes, "but only a few years after chillies had been introduced a south Indian poet declared them the 'Saviour of the Poor.' Ayurvedic physicians rarely advised the eating of foreign foods, but even they replaced black pepper with chiles in many of their cures." Garcia Orta, a Portuguese chronicler, wrote in 1593, "This Capsicum or Indian pepper is diligently cultivated in castles by gardeners and also by women in their kitchens and home gardens."

Three hundred years later, Sir George noted, "The consumption of chillies is very great, and both rich and poor daily use them; they form the principal ingredient in all chutnies and curries; ground into a paste, between two stones, with a little mustard oil, ginger, and salt, they form the only seasoning which the millions of poor can obtain to eat with their rice." A complete description of all the uses of chiles in the various cuisines of India would take hundreds of pages, so I'm going to give just a few examples of their ubiquity. The fact that chiles occur in the majority of Indian entrées, side dishes, snacks, and festival specialties is not really surprising. In India it is said, "The climate is hot, the dishes are hotter, and the condiments are the hottest." This saying supports the legendary Indian tolerance for hot chiles. In southern India, a typical meal for four persons can include the following amounts and types of chiles: a handful of soaked and drained whole red chiles, two tablespoons of cayenne powder, two tablespoons of freshly chopped green chiles, and a bowl of whole green chiles on the table for snacking. These chiles are, of course, in addition to the *masalas* and chutneys that are also used. And then there's Guntur, the chile capital of India.

In fiery south India, there is another saying, "Heat plus heat equals cool," an allusion to the gustatory sweating caused by hot chiles. The southern state of Andra Pradesh is the chile capital of the entire country, and, according to *The Wall Street Journal*, the city of Guntur is the hottest city in that state. In 1988, that financial newspaper sent reporter Anthony Spaeth to India to investigate rumors that chile peppers had completely conquered the local cuisine. His report was shocking, to say the least. "In Guntur," he wrote, "salted chiles are eaten for breakfast. Snacks are batter-fried chiles with chile sauce. The town's culinary pride are fruits and vegetables preserved in oil and chile, particularly its *karapo* pickles: red chiles pickled in chile." Another popular snack is deep-fried chiles dipped in chile powder.

Hot and spicy food is so predominant in Guntur that the agricultural market in town sells a single commodity: chile in its myriad forms. Legend and lore about chiles figure prominently in the culture of Guntur. The people often dream about them, and they believe that hot tempers arise from heavy chile eating and that chiles increase sexual desire. Children begin to eat chile at age five and quickly build up an incredible tolerance. In addition to culinary usage, the burning of red chile pods is said to ward off evil spells. In Guntur, as in other worldwide hotbeds of chile consumption, those who do not eat chile are viewed with concern, if not suspicion. The people of Guntur attribute the abnormal avoidance of chile to several causes: The offenders have lived abroad, are from out of town, or have married someone from a less-fiery state.

Other parts of India are not quite as addicted as the Gunturians, but it's close. Chitrita Banjeri kept track of the chile-infused dishes she ate as she journeyed around the country, revealing a great variety of different uses, including the commercially packaged, yogurt-cured chiles of Karnataka. In Bengali cuisine, a mixture called *panchphoron* ("five flavorings") features whole nigella, cumin, mustard, fennel, and fenugreek in equal proportions mixed together and tossed into chile-steeped oil (probably peanut oil or mustard oil). The resulting aroma "indicates the presence of a Bengali kitchen," as Banerji comments, and she adds that "today, it is hard to imagine almost any vegetable preparation without the green fire of fresh chilies, slit in the middle, the seeds left intact." Indeed, one Keralan recipe calls for green chiles and chicken in the ratio of one to seven, or a hundred grams to spice up seven hundred grams of chicken. And it also called for a generous amount of ground red chile added to that!

In Goa, one of the most popular dishes is vindaloo, a very spicy curry flavored with wine vinegar in which up to twenty red chiles are used in one preparation of it. The dish reflects the Goan love of hot peppers, which have become the central ingredient in nearly all the pork, fish, and vegetable dishes prepared there. In *dukar ani Batate*, a pork and sweet potato curry from Mangalore, a recipe that serves four calls for four fresh red chiles, four green chiles, and two teaspoons of black peppercorns.

Some four hundred years after chiles first entered India, the degree of their penetration into the various Indian cuisines was vividly illustrated by the cooking experiences of Robert H. Christie.

Christie, a British Army officer, collected recipes from India and used them to prepare elaborate banquets for his fellow members of the Edinburgh Cap and Gown Club in Scotland. In 1911, three years after Sir George came out with his abridgment, Christie published his landmark book, *Banquets of the Nations,* which contained an entire section on Indian and Afghani cookery. That section was published by Dover Publications as *Twenty-Two Authentic Banquets from India* (1975). It contained recipes for dishes from all parts of India and from neighboring regions that are today separate countries. An examination of the ingredients of these recipes reveals that fully two-thirds of the non-dessert and non-bread recipes contained some form of hot chiles.

In some regions, chiles totally dominated the food. In Christie's Bengal chapter, for example, twenty-two of twenty-three entrées contained chile peppers. In the Madras chapter, the count was eleven of thirteen, and in the Kashmir chapter, seven of eight recipes called for hot chiles in various forms, including fresh green and red plus dried red pods and powders. Christie's recipes from some regions, such as Punjab, were not nearly so hot, but still it is evident that in four hundred years chiles had completely conquered the cuisines of India, a land already rich in spices. They became an essential ingredient in both vegetarian and non-vegetarian cooking—imparting color, flavor, heat, nutrients, and religious lore. They are believed to ward off the "evil eye," and in many houses and offices, chiles are hung for just such a purpose. In the home, chiles are burned in the kitchen to intimidate the evil eye and protect children. "The smoke of a burning chile pepper," wrote Julie Sahni, "assures me that I am at home, warm and secure in my own culture wherever I may be."

And India is burning up the chile-pepper production statistics worldwide. For dried chile production it is first in the world, with 1.23 million metric tons in 2010. China was a distant second, with 253,800 metric tons. Because of the dominance of chiles in the agriculture and cuisines of India, to many it was no surprise that the hottest chile in the world (for a while) was found there.

How the Hottest Chile Pepper Reached India

It's fitting that a British Lord should be the one to carry one of the hottest chile peppers in the world from Trinidad to India in 1854. By stumbling on a key entry in an obscure Indian encyclopedia during a Google Books search, I believe I have unlocked a major mystery in the world of chile peppers: How was a New World crop, *Bhut Jolokia*, "the ghost chile," as some called it, introduced into India?

Here's the back story: Ever since the Bhut Jolokia first caused a media-induced ruckus because Indian plant scientists were claiming the title "World's Hottest Pepper," I've been tracking developments on the SuperSite. The question immediately arose: Where did this pepper originate? It was pretty clear to me: Trinidad, and my theory of plant transfer held that Indian immigrants to Trinidad, indentured servants replacing freed slaves in the sugar cane plantations, eventually were freed themselves and some became farmers. And some went back home to India carrying the *bhut* seeds. But all of this speculation was dead wrong.

'Bhut Jolokia' Chile. Photograph by Harald Zoschke. Sunbelt Archives.

I'm working on a major project to collect as many eighteenth- and nineteenth-century chile pepper descriptions as I can find to add to the ever-growing archive of chile pepper material posted on the SuperSite. During a search for Caribbean Capsicums between 1700 and 1910, this quote popped up: "One species called 'devil's pepper,' introduced by Lord Harris, from Trinidad, is so intensely hot that the natives can hardly manage to use it." It was from the *Cyclopædia of India and of Eastern and Southern Asia*, edited by Edward Balfour and published in Madras, India, in 1871 and 1885.

My first thought: Who was Lord Harris? It took me only a minute to discover that he was George Francis Robert Harris, Third Baron Harris, later Third Lord Harris, born in 1810. He was among the highest elite in England, but he still had a career, first, as governor of Trinidad, and second, as governor of Madras. The pieces were starting to fit together.

George Francis Robert Harris, the Third Lord Harris. Photographer Unknown. Sunbelt Archives.

Lord Harris was the most progressive and effective Trinidadian governor during the early days of British rule of the island. His accomplishments in his island paradise service to the crown (1846–54) range from establishing the postal system and creating the first library and public education system on the island to having piped water delivered to Port of Spain, the capital. He also coined the phrase "pearl of the Antilles" to describe Trinidad. But for our investigation, it is significant that he became the primary supporter of the Royal Botanic Gardens near the Queen's Park Savannah in Port of Spain.

I toured those sixty-two-acre gardens in 1991, but then I had no knowledge of Lord Harris's involvement in it. But I did notice that the garden was growing a number of chile peppers, including the Congo pepper, which has some of the largest pods of any of the varieties in the *chinense* species. I related the Congo pepper story in my article on Trinidad and Tobago. The gardens were in terrible shape in 1846 when Lord Harris became governor. But with his typical zeal and enthusiasm, Lord Harris "adopted" the gardens, finding a new director, William Purdie, and giving the garden many cash donations and other gifts like a Wardian

Case (a portable miniature greenhouse) in 1854 and at one time a gift of "£200 sterling, to be appropriated in prizes for the best specimens of native farming and garden produce brought forward at a public competition." That large sum of money illustrates Lord Harris's devotion to the gardens and reveals his British fascination with plant collecting and study. He lived in an era much influenced by the "Golden Age of Botany," the eighteenth century, which had alerted every intelligent Englishman to be on the lookout for unusual plants and to collect and preserve them.

I tried to discover what Capsicums the gardens were growing while Lord Harris was governor, but the only documentation I could find was a catalogue from 1865 to 1870, more than a decade after he left. That showed the gardens were growing *Capsicum annuum* L., the most common species of all, plus two other spices, the mysterious "*Capsicum frutescens*, L. India, Tropical America" and "*C. arboreum*, India." The location name "India" reveals a common mistake of the era—attribution of an Old World origin for some chile peppers. It is ironic to note that the garden undoubtedly provided the "Devil's pepper" seeds that Lord Harris carried to India the year he left Port of Spain for Madras, 1854.

Was the origin of the name Trinidadian or Indian? We probably will never know, but somehow the English name "devil" was translated into various Indian languages like Hindi and Assamese and became "ghost," or *bhut.* This is closely connected to Indian mythology and funeral practices, which hold that when a person dies, he or she leaves behind a ghost—the very rough equivalent to a Christian soul—and that ghost parallels the personality and manner of death of the deceased person. A cheerful, productive person will produce a mischievous ghost, while an evil person, or one killed violently by a tiger, will produce a ghost that turns into a demon, or devil. One source reported, "Amongst the evil *genii* of all India, is a being called Rakshasa, of giant bulk, terrible teeth, who feasts on dead bodies. The bhoot, acknowledged all over India, more resembles the ghost of Europe. The Rev. Dr. Caldwell in his work on the Devil-worship of the Shanar, has shown how continuously the people of India are making new deities or demons." Another source observes, "There is a fixed article of belief that when a man notorious for any particular vices dies, the man himself may become extinct, but his evil nature never dies, for every one of his vices then assumes personality and lives after him as a demon." In this sense, since ghosts can become devils, the words are roughly synonymous.

To prevent these ghosts from becoming demons and terrorizing the people, they take preventative action using hot peppers: "Villagers may put the *peppers* or ashes in the mouths of victims, but more often place the *peppers*, incense, and other substances in a fire. The victim breathes the fumes whose effect is to smoke out the ghost." The famous mythologist Sir James George Frazier reported in his book Psyche's Task (1913) that "[i]n Punjab, some people put pepper in the eyes of the corpse to prevent the ghost from seeing her way back to the house." I think the practice began with black pepper but the Indians switched to superhot chile peppers because of their superior heat, or power. And gradually, the superhot Bhut Jolokia became ingrained into the culture, especially in Assam, and were used—very carefully—in curries and other hot Indian foods.

Sir James George Frazer. Photographer Unknown. Sunbelt Archives.

All of the ghost speculation above is nonsense, according to Raktim Ranjan Bhagowati and Sapu Changkija, authors of "Genetic Variability and Traditional Practices in Naga King Chili Landraces of Nagaland." They claim "the term 'bhoot jolokia' could not be translated into English as 'ghost chili' . . . [because] the Assamese word 'bhoot' refers to the typical large pod size of the plant." This statement is contradicted by many sources, including Leena Saikia of Frontal Agritech, a major exporter of the chile, who told researcher Harald Zoschke in 2007, "In fact, 'Naga jolokia', 'Nagahari', 'Bhut jolokia', 'Bih jolokia' or 'Borbih jolokia' are the same chilli but named differently at different places. For example, the Assamese community call it as 'Bih jolokia' ('poison chilli'—'jolokia' means 'chilli' in Assamese), 'Bhut jolokia' (probably due to its ghostly bite or introduction by the Bhutias from Bhutan poison chilli) or 'Naga jolokia' (due to extreme hotness representing the aggressive temperament of the warriors of neighbouring Naga community). In Nagaland and Manipur states, it is known as 'Raja Mircha' or 'Raja chilli' ('King of Chillies')." I believe her rather than Bhagowati and Changkija because those two plant researchers from the School of Agricultural Sciences and Rural Development in Dimapur, Nagaland, also stated that another name for Bhut Jolokia is Saga Jolokia. In other words, they fell completely for Zoschke's pun: The title

PINEAPPLE SELLER ON ROAD TO KANDY, CEYLON

Pineapple Seller on the Road to Kandy, Ceylon. Postcard, c. 1930. Sunbelt Archives.

of his article on the Fiery Foods & Barbecue SuperSite is "Saga Jolokia," a pun on "Naga." This is another typically confusing chile-pepper nomenclature debate, but in this case I think the Nagaland researchers are mistaken.

I have tried in vain to discover how the "devil's pepper" went from Madras to Assam, so I think Sir George was very accurate when he wrote in 1908: "Very little information exists regarding the red pepper of Assam." That said, Balfour offers another link to the modern country of Trinidad and Tobago when he discusses another ghost pepper variation: "A kind called the Tobago red pepper is said to possess the most pungent properties of any of the species. It yields a small red pod, less than an inch in length, and longitudinal in shape, which is so exceedingly hot, that a small quantity of it is sufficient to season a large dish of any food. Owing to its oleaginous character, it has been found impossible to preserve it by drying; but by pouring strong boiling vinegar on it, a sauce or decoction can be made, which possesses in a concentrated form all the essential qualities of the vegetable. A single drop of this sauce will flavour a whole plate of soup or other food."

Today, researchers in Trinidad and the U.S. are discovering that the home of the devil's pepper is also the breeding ground for several other superhot chiles that equal or surpass the Bhut Jolokia's heat level, particularly the Trinidad Scorpion, with its dramatic "tail" that resembles a scorpion's stinger that has recently (as of 2012) replaced the Bhut Jolokia as the hottest chile in the world. I feel certain that the origin and transfer question of the Bhut Jolokia has now been answered, but solving one horticultural history mystery results in others: Why were all of the hottest chile peppers in the world found in Trinidad? And after one of them was taken to Madras, how did it end up in Assam and Nagaland about 1,600 miles away by air? To answer those questions I will have to travel to both Trinidad and India and track down some chile experts. Instead of doing that right now, I'm going to switch subjects to the bland but famine-busting New World crops.

An Apple That's Not an Apple, and Likewise for a Potato

To compile his *Dictionary of the Economic Products of India,* Sir George asked his far-flung correspondents to write and describe all the food products of India and how they were being used in the 1890s. I wonder if he was surprised to receive this information about *ananas,* or "pine-apples," as they were also called. Surgeon Major Jt. L. Dutt in Pubna wrote Sir George back: "Besides its value as an antiscorbutic, it seems to have an irritant action on the uterus, as it is reported to have caused abortion in weakly or predisposed women." Fortunately for the pineapple farmers, Dr. Dutt was referring to wild, bitter pineapples that contained cucurbitacins, which do, indeed, trigger abortions if eaten by pregnant women.

Indian food expert K. T. Achaya begins our tale of the pineapple in India and its early introduction: "By 1564 the fruit is described in India, nearly a hundred years before it was seen in England, and in 1616 Edward Terry describes its 'taste to be a pleasing compound, made of strawberries, claret-wine, rose-water and sugar, well tempered together. . . Jahangīr calls it a fruit of the 'European ports' in India, but adds that 'many thousands' were being grown in the royal plantations in Āgra [around 1600]." Like chile peppers, pineapples were quickly adopted by Indians.

Sir George tracked their spread: "The pine-apple was first introduced on the West-coast of India, but rapidly crossed the country and attained its greatest perfection in the Eastern Peninsula. From Calcutta through Eastern and Northern Bengal to Assam and Burma may be said to be its best Indian habitat, though it also occurs here and there throughout India." He was the first of many critics of the Indians' failure to cultivate it properly: "Little or no effort has been put forth either to improve the quality or to develop, on a commercial basis, the industry of pine-apple growing, which it would appear might be originated with advantage to India and profit to those concerned."

It was the flavor that drew people to the pineapple, as suggested by Edward Terry's description of it above, and stated by Sir George: "The pine-apple is generally regarded as one of the

Pineapple Sellers in Dhaka, Bangladesh. Photograph by Steve Evans, 2005. Sunbelt Archives.

most delicious fruits met with in tropical regions. To avoid the dangerous consequences attributed to it, however, many persons will only eat it when stewed, while others prefer to eat it fresh, with a little sugar or even salt. During the season in Calcutta good pine-apples can be purchased for a price each [of] less than a halfpenny." They were not only tasty but cheap and could be fermented, as one of Sir George's correspondents, L. Liotard, explained: "In Myanoung, Monsieur d'Avera is trying to make use of the large quantities that grow there to manufacture champagne. I am in correspondence with him on the subject, and he seems hopeful of success. Should the experiment succeed, it could be repeated on the Malabar coast."

I have not yet discovered if M. d'Avera succeeded or not, but Manjunath Hegade did in 2011. Hegade, a pineapple grower in the Shimoga District of Karnataka near Bangalore (now Bengaluru), in southwestern India, produced two barrels of pineapple wine and sent samples to the technical department of the state excise department for testing. He may become India's first commercial pineapple winery. If so, he would be imitating the success of Maui's Winery at Ulupalakua Ranch, which not only makes Maui Blanc ("aromas of candied lemon peel, white peach, ripe mango, and sweet ripe pineapple") but also Hula O'Maui, a sparkling pineapple wine like M. d'Avera was attempting, described as having "aromas of white grapefruit, lime zest, green pear, and fresh-cut pineapple."

Pineapples were popular home gardening fruits, and by 1872 there were six varieties available for gardeners around Calcutta. The "Ceylon" was regarded as "the finest in flavour of all procurable in Calcutta," according to Frederick Pogson, author of *Indian Gardening: A Manual of Flowers, Fruits, and Vegetables, Soils and Manures, and Gardening Operations of Every Kind in Bengal, the Upper Provinces, & the Hill Stations of India* (1872). The "Cayenne" (no relation to the Capsicum) Pogson described as "a variety much cultivated in Europe, and is esteemed for the best kind of winter fruiting." According to Sir George, the main method of consumption was "stewed, while others prefer to eat it fresh, with a little sugar or salt."

This comment might explain why, despite the popularity of the pineapple in India, there are surprisingly few recipes utilizing it in cooking. There are simple pineapple chutneys, of course, and while writing *A World of Curries*, I discovered a Pineapple Curry from Kerala that combines the usual curry spices with red and green chiles, shredded coconut, a large pineapple, and shrimp. Another pineapple curry combines the chopped fruit with ground coconut, peanuts, and chiles, and that combination is poured over *ghee* seasoned with cumin seeds. Also in Kerala, pineapples are common in desserts and are often simply combined with mangos, jackfruit, and bananas and served—another example of a very simple use. Apparently pineapples taste so good to the Indians that they don't need much preparation or cooking.

As with chile peppers, pineapples were another New World food that escaped Ayurvedic prohibitions against the use of foreign crops. Harish Johari, author of *Ayurvedic Healing Cuisine* (2000), writes that "pineapple cures both anxiety and a disturbed heart" and "the pulp of pineapple quenches thirst and increases mucus." Pineapple lovers will rejoice knowing that it "subdues excess Wind (Vata) and Bile (Pitta)" and aids in digestion. Johari also notes that sweet pineapple can be a substitute for tomatoes in cooked dishes.

Writers on Indian pineapple cultivation are not impressed with the agricultural methods used. Virendra Kumar Shrivrastava, author of *Commercial Activities and Development in the Ganga Basin* (1999), writes that "according to a survey conducted by the Indian Institute of Foreign Trade 'the pineapple industry in India has a long way to go to catch up with the advanced countries like USA and Philippines.'" The problem, in his opinion, is "there is no rapport between the grower and the canner, a very vital issue as far as quality control is concerned." Hans-Peter Brunner agrees in his book written ten years or so later, *North East India: Local Economic Development and Global Markets* (2010). He notes that "farmers do not understand the value-added applications of their pineapple and the industry is not organised, leaving little room for growth among small farmers." Despite these criticisms, India's pineapple production ranked seventh in the world in 2009, after that of the Philippines, Thailand, Costa Rica, Indonesia, China, and Brazil, respectively. The U.S. ranked nineteenth, with only a fourth of India's production, so the Indian farmers must be doing something right.

If Indians were confused about a fruit that is neither a pine nor an apple, just imagine what happened when they were confronted by two unrelated ground tubers with the same name: potato—one sweet and white. Plus, there are two types of sweet potato, *patata,* with an orange-colored tuber, and *batata*, the one with a white or pale yellow tuber. Further confusing the issue is the use of the generic term *batata* for both kinds of potatoes in India that makes it difficult for food historians to differentiate between the two ground tubers.

For example, the first western record of the potato in India is from 1615, when Sir Thomas Roe, the British ambassador to the Mughal court, was served potatoes at a banquet in Ajmer, Rajasthan. The traveler John Fryer noted that "potatoes were the usual banquet" when he was journeying though south-central India in the 1670s. In both cases it seems likely that they were observing sweet potatoes, because white potatoes were not a common crop in England at the time, but sweet potatoes were, and these Englishmen would have recognized the sweet potato.

Food historians pay a lot of attention to the sweet potato in India, with Sir George observing: "The sweet potato is eaten by all classes of the natives, either in curry or simply roasted as just stated, or cut in half, lengthwise, and fried. Another way of preparing it is to boil it, cut it in slices, and add rasped cocoanut, milk and sugar. In this way it becomes a good Indian dessert. It is also boiled, mashed, and made into pudding in the usual European style with sugar, egg, and milk."

Waverly Root writes: "On the mainland of Asia, India, which has had the sweet potato since at least 1616, probably appreciates it the most. It is widely cultivated in all parts of the subcontinent, where many varieties are grown." Yet in his book *Indian Food: A Historical Companion*, K. T. Achaya devotes only a single paragraph to it and ignores any discussion of its usage in cooking. In her bestselling cookbook, *Classic Indian Cooking*, Julie Sahni mentions it a single time when she says that it usually classified as a vegetable rather than a starch. Determined to check the sweet potato's status among other authors of Indian cookbooks, I used Amazon.com and Google Books to search the indices of ten major Indian cookbooks, including several by both Madhur Jaffrey and Pat Chapman, and found only an occasional mention and recipe using them. One, Sweet Potatoes and Tamarind (*Shakarkhandi Ki Chaat*), is simply sweet potatoes cooked in water with a little tamarind chutney, lemon juice, and cumin. This is in *The Everything Indian Cookbook* (2004) by Monica Bhide, and it's one of the few I found. Even in the massive cookbook *How to Cook Indian: More Than 500 Classic Recipes for the Modern Kitchen* (2011) by Sanjeev Kapoor, I found but two recipes containing sweet potatoes as an ingredient.

To my thinking, the only reason Indian cookbook authors ignore the sweet potato is simply that it's not very popular in Indian cooking, despite the words of Sir George and Root. In fact, the statistics of the Food and Agriculture Organization of the United Nations for 2004 reveal that India is not in the top twenty sweet-potato-producing countries, so it must be a minor crop in the country, unlike in China, the number one producer of the crop (see Part 7). However, the popularity of the potato that's not so sweet in India is a much different—and highly debated—story.

Aloo and Moongphali: More Delicacies from Beneath the Earth

Why did it take so long for most New World crops to become established in India? Food historian Sucheta Mazumdar believes that the delays in the foods' acceptance were caused by the

Indian Potato Farmer Shows Off the Day's Harvest. Photograph by Vishalsh521, 2008. Sunbelt Archives.

mobility of the pre-colonial society there, the availability of arable land, and the fact that most agriculture was on a small scale and not driven by economic factors. There was, in her words, "low demographic pressure to shape the seventeenth- and eighteenth-century responses to American crops." But after the British seized control of India, they rapidly began to commercialize the agricultural economy, and that of course would mean growing any crop that could turn a profit. For example, in the nineteenth century, the colonial government "discovered" sweet potatoes and both tomatoes and white potatoes as the population of India grew rapidly.

Sir George wrote about potatoes, of course: "Native of Peru and Chili [Chile], introduced into Spain in the beginning of the 16th century, whence it was introduced into India. The underground stem or tuber is in common use as an esculent. Coarse tasting brandy is also made from the potato. The potato is now cultivated in all parts of India in the plains and in the hills up to 9,000 feet. Potato is eaten by almost all classes. It enters largely into the manufacture of wheaten bread." The bread comment refers to the practice of adding potato flour to wheat flour to "stretch" it.

Potato historian R. N. Srivastava disagrees with Sir George and states that the potato was introduced into India by the Portuguese and the port was Surat in northwestern India in the state of Gujarat. This is because the potato was first known not as *aloo* (Hindi) but as *batata surrata* (Portuguese), or "potato of Surat." J. Fredrick Pogson, the author of *Indian Gardening* (1872), disagrees with both Sir George and Srivastava, writing that "the Potato . . . is a native of America, and was introduced into India by the English, and has been almost exclusively cultivated for the use of all classes of Europeans." There are arguments favoring all three countries, as well as Holland, so we will probably never know for sure how the introduction happened.

Srivastava explains how the potato spread throughout India: "In his 1675 descriptions of the gardens of Karnataka, [John] Fryer mentions potatoes among the vegetable crops grown, indicating that within a sixty year period potatoes had spread in the western part of India from Ajmer (in the north) to Karnataka (in the south)." Achaya disagrees, saying that it was sweet potatoes Fryer observed, thus setting off another one of those food history debates that probably will never be settled.

Governor-general Warren Hastings was given a basket of potatoes by the Dutch at a dinner in 1780, leading to the speculation that the Dutch introduced the potato into India, and in 1823, Lord Amherst, another governor-general, ordered that potatoes be planted in the park at Barrackpore, West Bengal, which is really in eastern India, and the Bengalis responded enthusiastically because the potatoes blended well with the flavors of cumin and mustard. Then they spread inland and most Indians loved the spuds, but of course there were some who were still suspicious of this new crop. They reached Madya Pradesh in central India around 1829, and by 1839 potato cultivation had become profitable in remote hill areas. However, they did not arrive in Madras (now Chennai) on the southeast coast until 1882.

In the twentieth century, Indian potato cultivation increased enormously with the application of modern agricultural techniques. M. S. Swaminathan, in his book *Science and the Conquest of Hunger* (1983), notes: "From a production of 1.5 million tonnes from 234,000 hectares [578,000 acres] in 1949–50, the production rose to 8.1 million tonnes from 664,000 hectares [1.6 million acres] in 1977–78. The yield per hectare has been nearly doubled during the last 30 years." By 2009, according to FAO statistics, Indian potato production was 34.4 million metric tons, making it number two in worldwide potato agriculture, after China. American production that year was 19.6 million metric tons, enough to be number four in the world, after Russia. But how were the Indians using the potato in cooking?

Pogson, writing in 1872, made this observation: "The Hindoos, strange to say, do not care much for the Potato, and the Mahomedans only use them in the form of vegetable curry. The cultivation of the Potato has been greatly extended, both in the Himalayas and plains, since the European troops have been supplied with them as part of their rations." Writing just thirty-six years later, in 1908, Sir George noted: "As an article of food, potatoes are now valued by all classes, especially the Hindus on days when forbidden the use of grain. At first potatoes were eaten by the Muhammadans and Europeans only, but for some years past they have got into universal usage, and it is now no uncommon circumstance to find cooked potatoes offered for sale at refreshment stalls, in various cold preparations, to be eaten along with so-called sweetmeats that form the midday meal of the city communities. The dried small tubers are also a common adulterant for the more expensive *salép* [dried orchid tubers]. Potatoes are also fairly extensively employed both in the manufacture of starch and in the distillation of alcohol." He also mentioned that potatoes were "used as food, either cooked in curry or boiled, roasted or fried."

In fact, those uses haven't changed very much in a century of Indian potato munching—they're just a bit more sophisticated. The simplest are the *burtas*, or mashes, which are generally used to accompany curries. Potato Burta is a simple mix of finely sliced onions and green chiles with lime juice mashed together with boiled potatoes and salt. There are several simple potato snacks, including *aloo chaat*, a simple potato salad flavored with *chaat masala* and tamarind; samosas filled with spicy boiled potatoes and other vegetables; and *aloo ki tikki*, fried potato patties offered by vendors at street food stalls in northern India, where they are served with tamarind or mint chutneys.

From around the states of India, there are additional dishes featuring potatoes. In Gujarat, potatoes are boiled and then tossed in peanut oil that has been seasoned with mustard seeds, curry leaves, and cayenne. In Punjab, *aloo methi* features potatoes that are sautéed in peanut or mustard oil to which fenugreek, garlic, green chile, turmeric, dill, and cilantro have been added. In Mararashtra, a popular dish is *dahiwalla aloo*, potatoes boiled with turmeric, then combined with a curry mixture made from coconut, onion, green chile, garlic, ginger, coriander, cumin, cayenne, mustard seed, cilantro, and yogurt. A favorite curry in Kashmir is *kashmiri dum aloo*, a bright red curry featuring Kashmiri chiles, yogurt again, boiled potatoes, tomatoes, and typical curry spices.

Another major underground crop in India is the peanut, called groundnut in English and *moongphali* in Hindi. Because it's often seen as merely a snack sold by street vendors, one might think that it's a minor crop like the sweet potato, but one would be mistaken, especially considering the fact that five and a half million metric tons were produced in India in 2009. That production makes the country the second-largest peanut growing nation, once again after China, and the U.S. places fourth, after Nigeria. The reason for India's prolific peanut production is simple: peanut oil.

Sir George had this to say about it in 1889: "In Europe, it is now extensively used as a substitute for olive oil or salad oil, both medicinally and for alimentary purposes. It has taken a distinct place in the soap manufacture, and it is largely consumed for lubricating machinery, as a lamp oil, and for dressing cloth." In his Abridgment he notes that "the nut made its first appearance in Europe as a commercial product about the year 1840." He was well aware of the oil's counterfeiting properties, writing that "the finer qualities are, however, used both in Medicine and as an article of Food, and there can be little doubt that large quantities are annually passed off as Olive oil and are made into a form of butter employed in cookery."

Indian Peanut Oil Mill. Engraved by Abel-François Poisson de Vandières, the brother of King Louis XV's mistress Madame de Pompadour, 1782. Sunbelt Archives.

Today in India, after the oil is extracted from the peanuts, what's left is pressed into groundnut cakes for farm animal fodder in southern India and any leftover chaff is used for field mulch. The shells are also used as a fuel and in the manufacture of particle board for the construction trade. The major growing states are Andra Pradesh, Karnataka, and Tamil Nadu, and they have what's called the "groundnut belt," a vast area of about twelve million acres or about twenty thousand square miles devoted to monoculture peanut production.

Sir George mentioned the culinary uses of the groundnut: "In India the nuts are sold in the bazaars or by the street hawkers either parched, with the shell on and put up in paper packets, or shelled and roasted in oil. They are eaten by natives of all classes and even by Europeans. In Bombay they are a favorite food of the Hindus during certain fasts." In another book he continues: "In Bombay they are a favourite food of the Hindus' certain fasts. . . . Hand-shelled nuts are sometimes made into confectionery." Oddly, he added, "the roasted seeds may be used as a substitute for chocolate."

Today, the culinary uses range from ground peanuts used as a thickening agent in curries to the same vendor snacks Sir George noted. Sometimes they are a flavoring ingredient for other dishes, like when they are sautéed in peanut oil with boiled potatoes, turmeric, green chile, cumin, and curry leaves. Groundnut chutneys are popular in southern India, and another use for them, mentioned first by Sir George, is as a simple dessert that combines peanut butter with ground dates to make balls that are then refrigerated. Another sweet dish combines peanuts with a jaggery (unrefined dark sugar) coating.

Although not a major factor in Indian cuisines, Robert Shilling, in his book *Groundnut* (2002), writes: "The groundnut or peanut is that rare thing in the economies of developing countries—a traditional cash crop with a bright future."

The Question of Pre-Columbian Maize and the Souring *Tamata*

When it comes to pre-Columbian representations of New World foods in India, the true believers are out in full force. Even at the university level there are fierce proponents who not only believe, but proselytize, that these sculptures are evidence for the existence of maize and pineapples in India going back to the eleventh century BC. One of these believers is Carl L. Johannessen of the University of Oregon, a professor emeritus of geography and the author of dozens and dozens of scholarly articles but no books that I could track down. There is absolutely no doubt in my mind that he is a true scholar but one who remains convinced that the "maize sculptures" in the Hoysala Temples in southern India, as he puts it, indicate that "humans were able to migrate between both hemispheres; more likely through trans-oceanic means of travel."

Hopefully, these humans had a Transporter à la *Star Trek* and could beam themselves back and forth between Mexico and India, because there is zero evidence for any "trans-oceanic" travel as described by Johannessen. Yes, these sculptures *look* like ears of maize, but that doesn't make them so. Paul C. Mangelsdorf, author of *Whence Came Maize to Asia*, notes that the same claims have been made for cotton, and he commented: "In the joint article with Oliver, I challenged the hypothesis on genetic and botanical grounds, concluding that the case for the trans-Pacific, pre-Columbian diffusion of Old World cultivated cottons is no better, in our opinion, than the case for an Asiatic origin or pre-Columbian diffusion of maize. To use the one as evidence to support the other is to assume that two guesses have, through some strange alchemy, a greater validity than one."

Other scholars have lined up to throw cold water on Johannessen's speculations. M. M. Payak and J. K. S. Sachan, writing in *Economic Botany* in 1993, state: "The contention that objects in the hands of male and female deities sculpted

Tomato Vendor, Bangalore, India. Photograph by Steve Evans, 2005. Sunbelt Archives.

on the exterior of the Kesav Temple at Somnathpur near the city of Mysore, Karnataka State, India, represent maize ears is rejected on linguistic, religious, sculptural, archaeological, and botanical grounds. . . . The wall images do not fully simulate in form and proportion the actual human figures. . . . We hold that these temple sculptures do not represent maize or its ear but an imaginary fruit bearing pearls known in Sanskrit as 'Muktaphala.'" Balaji Mundkur, writing in *Current Anthropology*, notes that "there is neither botanical or literary evidence from other lands to disprove the logical inference that this plant was confined to the New World until the Spanish conquests of the early 19th century." He concludes: "The research findings of Mangelsdorf (1974), Wilkes (1977), and Galinat (1978) clearly warrant the rejection of claims of 'evidence' for the occurrence of maize in any part of the Old World prior to 1492."

While this kind of speculation on the part of Johannessen and others is somewhat interesting, it reminds me of the conjectures—and the distinct lack of hard evidence—of Erich von Däniken in *Chariots of the Gods*. What Johannessen and the other proponents of pre-Columbian maize in India do not offer is any scientifically acceptable archaeological evidence of maize there dated before Columbus, undoubtedly because there is none. So these "theories" do not have a scientific basis and must remain mere speculation. An analogy would be an explorer finding sculpture in a pre-Incan tomb that resembles a carrot and theorizing that pre-European cultures introduced it into South America.

Maize was not immediately accepted into the Indian food culture like chile peppers. Sir George tells us that "so very little progress had, however, been made with maize cultivation that Roxburgh wrote, about the beginning of the 19th century, that Indian-corn was 'cultivated in various parts of India in gardens, and only as a delicacy; but not anywhere on the continent of India, so far as I can learn, as an extensive crop.' At the present day it would be more nearly correct, at any rate, to speak of maize as of equal value to the people of India collectively with wheat, instead of its being grown purely as a garden 'delicacy.' It is a field crop upon which at least the bulk of the aboriginal tribes of the hilly tracts of India are very largely dependent for subsistence. Thus its diffusion over India, during the present century, might almost be said to be one of the most powerful arguments against the statement often made that the Natives of India are so very conservative that they can scarcely be induced to change their time-honoured customs, even when these can be shown to be inimical to their best interests. So completely has India now appropriated the *makkai* that few of the village fathers would be found willing to admit that it had not always been with them, as it is now, a staple article of diet."

In his book *Economic Products of India Exhibited in the Economic Court, Calcutta International Exhibition, Part 6,* Sir George explains how this grain known as *makkai*, mostly cultivated in "Upper India" and the Himalayas, was utilized: "The cobs are either pulled while green and sold as vegetables to be roasted and the grains eaten; or they are allowed to ripen. In the latter case the grain is threshed out and either parched and eaten, or made into flour and converted into bread. A fine flour called *maizena* and corn-flour is made from this grain and extensively used as an article of diet for custards, light puddings, &c. But whether as a vegetable, or as a cereal, the maize is a common article of food of a very large section of the population of Northern, Central and Himalayan tracts of India; and it is more in use as a cereal than as a vegetable."

Today, India is fifth in worldwide maize production, after the U.S., China, Brazil, and Indonesia, respectively. It is cultivated in twenty-three of the twenty-eight Indian states, and the varieties grown are pop, flint, flour, Indian, and sweet. Its four categories of use are human consumption (35 percent), poultry feed (25 percent), cattle feed (25 percent), and processing into such commodities as corn flakes, flour, oil, and popcorn (15 percent). Maize is ground into several food products, and from coarse to fine they are corn meal (the *makkai* noted by Sir George, above) for use in making batters for fritters, cornstarch for thickening any liquid-based foods, and corn flour, which is often combined with wheat flour for baking.

I searched many Indian cookbooks for examples of maize in cooking and discovered that they are few and far between. Banerji notes that Bengali corn is "roasted over a charcoal fire, brushed with mustard oil, and seasoned with lime juice, hot chili powder, and black pepper." The Parsis, a small Zoroastrian religious group, enjoy *makki akoori*, maize kernels in scrambled eggs, and maize occasionally appears in some Indian soups, custards, and fritters. My conclusion is that maize is not a distinctive part of Indian cuisine.

Much more distinctive are tomatoes. If we turn once again to Sir George to guide us, he wrote in 1883: "At present cultivated in many parts of India for its large red or sometimes yellow fruits which are used for culinary purposes. . . . The natives are beginning to appreciate the fruit, but the plant is chiefly cultivated for the European population. The Bengalis use it in their sour curries." Two experts on Indian cooking, Pat Chapman and Madhur Jaffrey, disagree about who reintroduced tomatoes to India long after they first appeared when the Portuguese brought them in the sixteenth century, with Jaffrey giving credit to the British and Chapman stating: "Tomatoes . . . gained only limited acceptance in Indian cuisine until American missionaries reintroduced them in the 19th century."

By 1906, tomatoes were well established in India, and Ceylon's *Tropical Agriculturist* magazine reported: "In the memory of many now living the tomato was hardly known, except as a garden curiosity . . . and was of small size and full of seeds. Few people ate it, as the sterling qualities of the fruit were unknown. At the present time there are many scores of varieties, from the small 'grape' variety to the immense fleshy fruits, weighing a pound apiece or more. . . . No kitchen garden, even in India, is considered complete without it. . . . In India the tomato has become a very popular vegetable, and is cultivated on a fairly large scale, not only in private gardens, but by the market gardener, and the quality of the produce is very good indeed. Anyone who has visited the horticultural exhibitions held at various centres in this country must have been struck by the splendid quality of the tomato exhibits. A large number of varieties is cultivated."

As in Europe, it took tomatoes a long time to become popular in India, but with the Raj encouraging agricultural growth, they entered virtually every facet of Indian and Brit-Indian cookery. In *The Indian Cookery Book: A Practical Handbook to the Kitchen in India* (1880), published in Calcutta, the tomato is well represented with not only a chutney but a Love-Apple or Tomato Sauce requiring five hundred tomatoes, Tomato with Tamarind, Tomato Burta, and a Fresh Tomato Gravy Sauce for Made Dishes.

Nineteenth-century tomatoes in India were much more sour than they are today, so they fit in well with the sweet-and-sour dishes loved by the Bengalis, and after they gained respect, tomatoes were used mostly in chutneys and sauces. While researching

A *World of Curries* (1994), I found a quick tomato curry called Tomato Palya that is popular in the southern India coastal state of Karnataka, where it is eaten at breakfast and also as an accompaniment to meat curries. Its entire preparation takes only twenty minutes. In her book *Eating India* (2007), Chitrita Banerji encountered tomatoes all over India. They're combined with yogurt, garlic, ginger, and spices in Delhi's Butter Chicken and also stuffed into that city's flaky *parathas*; they're in a ketchup served with fried fillets of *bekti*, a fish popular in Bengal; in eggs served over tomatoes in Gujarat; and in sauce served over Fish Moily in Kerala, to name just a few uses.

The famous Indian chef and cookbook author Julie Sahni describes them not only as "tenderizing and souring agents" but also thickeners and coloring agents in sauces. In *Classic Indian Cooking* (1980) she uses them in a Fragrant Tomato

Tomato and Coconut Chutneys. Photograph by Ramesh NG, 2011. Sunbelt Archives.

331.—Tomato or Love-apple Chutnee.

Ingredients:—Two hundred large ripe love-apples, four ounces of raisins, seven ounces of salt, four ounces of sugar, eight ounces of chilies, finely sliced, four ounces of ground garlic, and seven ounces of ground mustard-seed.

Parboil the tomatoes in a quart of vinegar, add the other ingredients, and allow the whole to stand for ten to twelve hours; then boil it for twenty to thirty minutes over a slow fire; when cold, bottle it.

—From *The Indian Cookery Book*, Calcutta, 1880

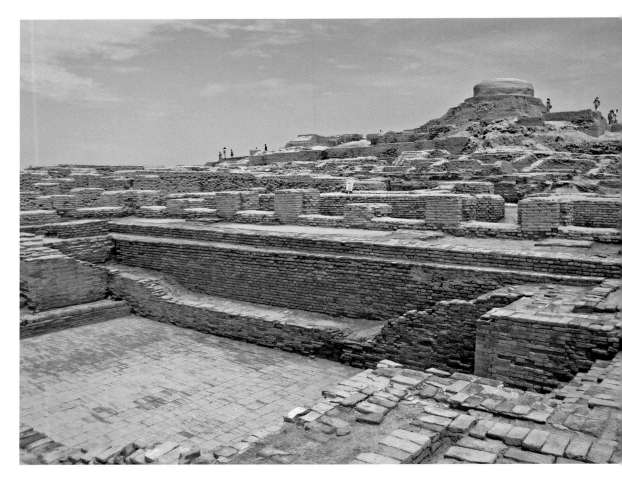

Ruins of Mohenjo Daro, Photograph by Grjatoi, 2006. Sunbelt Archives.

Sauce; an Onion Tomato Gravy, with a sauce that covers the most popular vegetarian egg dish in India, *ande ki kari*; and in several relishes including *tamatar* chutney, a sweet tomato relish, and Hot Hyderabad Tomato Relish, which is served as a side dish with meats in creamy curry sauces. Tomatoes are very prevalent in Pat Chapman's *India Food & Cooking: The Ultimate Book on Indian Cuisine,* and Madhur Jaffrey uses them in curries, soups, chutneys, relishes, sauces, and in lamb, rice, and eggplant dishes.

In 2009, India was the third largest producer of tomatoes, after China and the U.S., but most of these tomatoes are used fresh because, as J. M. Costa and Ed Heuvelink pointed out in 2005: "The processing industry is not well developed and only a minor proportion (6 percent to 10 percent) is used for processing into products such as purée, paste, ketchup, sauce and pickles.

The lack of suitable varieties for processing may be one of the reasons for this situation." Since tomatoes are used in so many curries, those particular dishes have become the focal point of New World crops in India.

Chitarita Banerji has trouble with two food terms, "curry" and "Indian food." She writes that curry is a term "whose regional application is so much at odds with the actual authenticity, regionalism, and idiosyncrasy of India's cuisines." Thus the term is "a slippery eel of a word, bent and stretched to cover almost anything with a spicy sauce, a king of misnomers, and yet, to those who use it, the perfect definition for whatever they are trying to describe at that given moment." It is rather like the term "Indian food," which Banerji admits is a misnomer, but she writes that "there is no other satisfactory term, since regional identities are in a permanent state of flux, all traditions subject to being reworked, while borrowing and adapting of technique and ingredients continue according to the perpetual migration of people within the country. Food in India has always been and still is fusion, and a fusion that remains unfinished."

One of the most intriguing theories about the ancestry of curry was advanced by Captain Basil Hall in his book *Travels in India, Ceylon, and Borneo* (1930). "It will surprise most people—old Indians inclusive—" he wrote, "to learn that the dish we call curry is not of India, nor, indeed, of Asiatic origin at all. There is reason to believe that curries were first introduced into India by the Portuguese." Hall reasoned that since the Portuguese had introduced chile peppers into India, and since hot peppers are a primary ingredient of curry, ergo the Portuguese must have introduced curries as well.

Hall was dead wrong, of course. Curry-like spice mixtures date back to at least 4,000 BC. In excavations of the ancient cities of Harpatta and Mohenjo-Daro in the Indus Valley in what is now Pakistan, grinding stones were found that contained traces of mustard seed, cumin, saffron, fennel, and tamarind. Since all of these spices appear in curries, it is not unreasonable to assume that the ancient Indus Valley people were cooking with curry spices six thousand years ago—although no recipes survive. Hall was just one of many writers with their own definitions of what curries are. Most of the curry controversies result from the belief that the original "Indian fashion" of curry has been stolen and ruined by the rest of the world, especially by the English.

Grinding Curry Stuff, Madras.

Other writers think that notion is nonsense, and they believe that cookery continues to evolve as the world shrinks. In fact, there are multitudinous definitions and beliefs about curry, and rarely do two writers agree on precisely what curry is.

"Curry in its twentieth century manifestation—a meat or occasionally vegetable stew flavoured with commercial curry powder—is essentially a British dish," wrote John Ayto, author of *The Glutton's Glossary* (1990). He was taking the oversimplified stance that all curries are made with commercial curry powder, which simply is not true, despite a plethora of commercial curry powders and other products. M. F. K. Fisher, the renowned gastronome, disagreed with the curry-powder-stew concept, believing the preparation of curries to be a high art: "Books about curries, for instance," she wrote in *With Bold Knife and Fork* (1968), "are published continually, with the success of a well-ticking clock. Special restaurants all over the world serve nothing but curries. Spice merchants grow rich on making their regional and private blends of curry powder. In other words, reputations can and do depend upon the authenticity of the recipe first and then of the powder that goes with the sauce, the skill with which the sauce is made, and in many cases the atmosphere in which the whole is served."

Such worship of curry irritates famed Indian chef and author Madhur Jaffrey, who wrote in her book *An Invitation to Indian Cooking*: "To me the word 'curry' is as degrading to India's great cuisine as the term 'chop suey' was to China's. If 'curry' is an oversimplified name for an ancient cuisine, then 'curry powder' attempts to oversimplify (and destroy) the cuisine itself." Jaffrey may call the word curry "degrading," but actually, it is not meant to be insulting. The term "curry" reflects the evolution of language, and the need to designate, in English, dishes that were based on various spice mixtures. Indeed, "curry" has come to mean, in English, different spice mixtures that are used in a similar manner in countries throughout the world. "Curry," explains Yohanni Johns, author of *Dishes from Indonesia* (1971), "is a word frequently used by foreigners to describe Indonesian dishes cooked with coconut milk." Santha Rama Rau, author of the Time-Life book on Indian cooking, says that the "proper sense" of the word curry is "a highly seasoned stew with plenty of sauce."

Perhaps the most outlandish (and obviously incorrect) belief about the origin of curry comes from Selat Elbis Sopmi of London's Punjab Restaurant, who wrote in *The Curry Club Magazine* that some centuries ago an Irish sea captain married into a wealthy family. The captain's gambling led to the demise of the family, which kept a large stable of racehorses. They were forced to sell the best of the horses and eat the rest. The Irishman used the word *cuirreach*, Celtic for "racetrack," and told everyone he had been reduced to eating *cuirreach gosht*, or racetrack meat. "Over the ages, this has become, through usage," claims Sopmi, "the word as we know it, curry."

Curries with the Crops of the New World

No one really knows precisely where in India curry was born, but to track its spread I'm going to start in the south because that's where the Portuguese landed and introduced most of the New World crops, particularly the chile pepper, potato, tomato, sweet potato, and pineapple. They were combined with the usual curry spices native to India, plus two key flavoring elements of the south, coconuts and tamarind. The Hindu scriptures refer to the coconut as the Sriphala—the holy or sacred fruit. However revered the coconut is in Hindu society, it is also an integral part of Muslim, Christian, Jewish, Buddhist, and Jain cuisines as well. The milk and purée derived from the coconut transform hundreds of ordinary fish, meat, and vegetable dishes into memorable curry treats. The tangy, sun-dried pods of tamarind often are sold in the form of a dried cake or in markets as paste, jars of concentrated pulp, syrup, and even powders.

The food of southern India is hardly known to most non-Indians who visit Indian restaurants outside India. Most of these restaurants serve what is known as Moghlai and Punjabi foods from India's north and northwest regions. The bias for this northern food is due largely to the fact that most of the early restaurant owners in the U.K. and U.S. were from those regions, and their success was widely emulated. Even in India, northerners have a limited idea of the incredible variety of delicacies found in the south and believe that most southerners are vegetarians. This is not true, and the myth has been spread by people from the two Indian states that are predominantly vegetarian. In Gujarat, in India's northwest, and in its neighboring state Rajasthan, at least 75 percent of the people are vegetarians because of the lingering influence of the Jain religion; with the rest of India, the reverse proportion is true.

New World crops shine in the curries of southern India. Karnataka has *tomato palya*, a tomato-based curry with the usual spices and fresh peas. Kerala has *pineapple kalan*, a pineapple-based curry with lots of coconut, fresh red and green chiles, yogurt, and shrimp, while Mangalore's *batate palya* is a potato-based curry with lots of tomatoes and lima beans. Even the spinach-based *keere kootu* of Tamil Nadu has four large tomatoes in it plus green chiles.

Curries developed in Sri Lanka probably simultaneously with those of southern India. Formerly known as Ceylon, the Isle of Gems, Sri Lanka has a very rich culinary tradition that has been influenced by traders, immigrants, and conquerors from India, Arabia, Malaysia, Portugal, the Netherlands, and Britain. Many people believe that Sri Lankan food is the same as southern Indian food, but there is one very large difference: the heat level. A Sri Lankan food importer, Anura Saparamadu, told me that no self-respecting Sri Lankan cook would ever buy Indian products because they are just too mild. "Their curries are cumin and coriander based," he said, "while our Sri Lankan curries are chile based." Food writer Tina Kanagaratnam, who grew up in Sri Lanka, agrees: "Hotter and more robustly flavored than Indian curries, the curries of Sri Lanka get their distinctive flavor from the roasting of whole spices until they are dark brown before grinding—and from extra chiles."

Sri Lanka's reputation for extremely hot curries rests with its red, white, and black curries. The color of the red curry is derived, not surprisingly, from a huge number of red chile pods. In one recipe for a Sri Lankan curry powder for fish and beef, Doreen Peiris, author of *A Ceylon Cookery Book*, calls for an entire pound of small dried red chiles! Fruits such as mangos are commonly curried in Sri Lanka, in both unripe and ripe forms. Another favorite fruit is jackfruit, the largest fruit that grows on trees—it weighs as much as seventy pounds! The unripe jackfruit meat is brined for about a month, then the salt is squeezed out, and the jackfruit is fried in lard and red chile powder. Jackfruit seeds, with a chestnut-like taste, are boiled and then curried. Both the fruit and the seeds are available canned in Asian markets.

White curries are considerably milder because the chiles are tempered with coconut meat and milk. One Sri Lankan recipe, Tamarind Chicken in White Curry Sauce, combines the tartness of tamarinds with the heat of chiles and the pungency of shallots, garlic, and spices. But it is the black curries, featuring darkly roasted curry spices, that give, according to Sri Lankan cooks, better aroma and flavor. Typically, a Sri Lankan black curry is

Market in Ceylon with Pineapples and Tomatoes. Photograph by W.L.H. Skeen, c. 1880. Sunbelt Archives.

Spices in Mapusa Market, Goa, India. Photographer Unknown. Sunbelt Archives.

made as follows: Coriander, cumin, fennel, and fenugreek seeds are roasted separately, then combined with whole cinnamon, cloves, cardamom seeds, and leaves from the curry tree. This mixture is then finely ground with mortar and pestle. The finishing touch is the addition of two types of chiles. Bush-ripened dried red chiles called *valieche miris* are added along with the tiny but deadly hot "bird's-eye" (see above) chile, a relative of chiltepins. The result is Ceylon Dark Curry Powder, which is used to make Black Lamb Curry.

Moving on to northern India, a joke goes that when two Indians meet, there are three opinions, four temples, five kinds of cuisines, and six different desserts. And since Hindus have more than thirty million gods and goddesses in their pantheon, the joke continues, there must be as many curry combinations, too. Curries in the northern region of India and the neighboring countries tend to be drier, thicker, and milder in heat than their counterparts in the southern part of the country. This cuisine tends to use yogurt rather than the coconut of the southern states. Also, in the curries of Pakistan there is a preponderance of nuts and dried fruits. And because these curries are fairly dry, diners use unleavened bread such as *naan* to scoop the thick gravy. Other breads to accompany curries are a deep-fried bread from Punjab called *bhatura*, *chapatti* (a griddle-baked flatbread), and *paratha* (a spicy spinach bread). Nuts figure prominently in northern curries and in Pakistan, and peanuts are commonly substituted for more expensive almonds, pistachios, and cashews. Tomatoes are used more than potatoes in northern curries and retain their universal popularity in curries with fruits like dried apricots or raisins as in biryani curries like Pakistan's *peshawari biryani* with *chana* (chickpeas), heavy cream, yogurt, milk, raisins, cashews, and almonds. But potatoes do make an appearance and are often added to fish curries. Ever-present are the chiles, but in lesser amounts than in the south.

West Bengal in the far eastern part of India has fairly dry, mustard-based curries. The Bengalis in West Bengal and in Bangladesh have great political and religious differences; most of the former are Hindus, and the latter are predominantly Muslims. Traditionally, the Hindus shun eating beef, while the Muslims consume it with great relish. But despite these differences, the two people agree on one thing: their passion for fish. Even the Brahmins eat fish as a part of their daily fare, calling it "the fruit of the sea" to avoid the stigma of eating flesh. A popular story in Calcutta illustrates the Bengali passion for fish. Swami Vivekananda, India's well-known philosopher and monk, continued eating fish even after joining a religious order that forbade it. His detractors went to his superior, Swami Ramakrishna Paramahamsa, and complained that Vivekananda was not a true ascetic. "Don't watch what goes into his mouth," Paramahamsa replied. "Listen to what comes out of it." A typical Bengali fish curry is *macher jhol*, which, in addition to firm fish, has potatoes, tomatoes, and fresh red chiles in it.

From eastern India, curries moved on to Bangladesh, Myanmar, and Southeast Asia. I track the spread and transformations of curries and New World crops throughout Asia in Part 7. More important to our story now is the migration of the Indian people who brought their curries—or at least their curry powders—with them to their new countries. We have seen the adoption of curries in Africa in Part 5, but there were three additional, major regions that developed curry traditions: the islands of the Pacific Ocean, Caribbean Sea, and what is now the United Kingdom.

The Curry Diaspora

Lizzie Cunningham, in her book *Curry: A Tale of Cooks and Conquerors*, makes this succinct observation: "When Indians travel, they take their food culture with them." A perfect example of this is the introduction of curries into the South Pacific, which was the result of both Indian immigration and the influence of the British, with their love of curries, that was transplanted from the Raj. As Cunningham put it, "Indentured labor took Indians and their food culture around the globe to Mauritius from 1843, British Guyana, Trinidad, and Jamaica from 1845, South Africa and Fiji from the 1870s. All these countries now demonstrate a strong Indian influence in their cookery." Fiji became a British colony in 1874 and began serious importation of Indian indentured laborers in two phases: first in 1879, and another large influx in 1900. Between 1879 and 1916, sixty thousand Indians arrived in Fiji, and for the most part these laborers worked for the Colonial Sugar Refining Company. After the indentured system was abolished in 1916, eventually the population reached more than ninety thousand Indians, and they started moving away from sugarcane labor and became shopkeepers and hawkers. Two Fijian curries feature New World foods: Shrimp with Cardamom and Almonds has typical curry ingredients and fresh green chiles, while Egg and Potato Curry has the same hot green chiles plus boiled potatoes and hard-boiled eggs.

Other Pacific locations with significant numbers of Indian immigrants were New Zealand, where the immigration came not from indentured laborers but simply from the fact that jobs and careers awaited Indians who could circumvent the tight immigration controls, and Hawaii, where curries migrated without much of a British or Indian influence. This is not unusual, though, for as food historian Howard Hillman has noted, "Hawaii has the most cosmopolitan admixture of cuisines, races, and cultural institutions in the world." However, the only New World ingredients in Hawaii's curries are just milled red chile in the curry powders, with the exception of some Hawaiian pineapple curries.

Another reason, of course, for the spread of curries in the Pacific was the British presence (and their love of curries), in such places as Australia. The curry blends used in Oz, as they call it, tend to be commercial rather than homemade, so it is the ingredients that are curried, rather than the curry spices, that make some of the curries strange indeed. Cunningham commented that curries have appeared on Pacific islands that have no history of Indian immigration, and "these curries are, however, so removed from anything that might be eaten on the subcontinent that they are almost unrecognizable as Indian food." And believe it or not, some Oz-dwellers love a dish called Curried Spaghetti, which in reality is an uninspired casserole of cooked spaghetti, ground beef, tomatoes, and a couple of teaspoons of commercial curry powder. Also in Australia, in a dish for organ meat lovers, ground lamb kidneys are combined with curry powder, ground lamb steak, tomato sauce, and bread crumbs

Curry Sign in Arima, Trinidad. Photograph by Dave DeWitt. Sunbelt Archives.

in a curry called *kolendo*; the ingredients are placed in a billycan, a can with a tight-fitting lid, and the billycan is boiled in water for five hours, which "sets" the curry mixture into a mold. Curries in the Caribbean are a step up from these bizarre Australian curry transformations.

Although curries in some form appear in the cuisines of most of the Caribbean, they are particularly prevalent in the countries where the East Indian population is the greatest: Jamaica, Martinique, and Trinidad and Tobago (T&T). In 1838, four years after slavery was abolished in T&T, the food history of the two islands began to change profoundly. (In the U.S. and the Caribbean, people of Indian heritage are called East Indians to distinguish them from the Indians of the Americas, who are now called, equally inaccurately, Native Americans.) That year, the mandatory, four-year post-slavery apprenticeship ended, and some twenty thousand slaves who worked the enormous sugarcane plantations left the estates and became squatters— resulting in an enormous labor shortage. That shortage was filled by freed slaves from other islands, plus a huge influx of indentured laborers from India. Beginning in 1845, a mass migration of workers from India over the next seventy-two years increased the population of Trinidad by a hundred and forty-five thousand. By the 1940s, the East Indian influence was so prevalent that travel writer Patrick Leigh Fermor wrote: "Wide tracts of Trinidad are now, for all visual purposes, Bengal."

Because the East Indians were thrown together in a strange land and were forced to share tasks equally, divisions of caste and

The Large 'Congo Pepper' in Trinidad, 1996. Photograph by Dave DeWitt. Hand Model, Mary Jane Wilan. Sunbelt Archives.

religion were soon dissolved. The Hindus, who formed the bulk of the diaspora, began to eat beef out of necessity. Unlike the Africans before them, the East Indian immigrants were allowed to keep their language, clothing, and food. Two animals that immigrated with them were the water buffalo—useful for heavy labor—and the white, humped cattle, which provided the milk for the beloved yogurt and butter, which was made into ghee. Many East Indian foods and cooking techniques were introduced into T&T, notably curries and rice (rice is still grown on Trinidad today). Curries have become enormously popular in the country, as noted by calypso writer Daisann McLane. "Without access to their curry," she wrote, "Trinidadian cooks would be as lost as Sicilians without fresh garlic."

The curry powder capital of Trinidad and Tobago is Tunapuna, a town about halfway between Port of Spain and Arima. Daisann McLane vividly described it in 1991: "Clouds of roasted cumin and turmeric, garlic, coriander, and those acidly hot Caribbean peppers . . . simply by breathing, one was exposed to hazardous levels of piquant longing." Most of the curry powders made today are much milder than those of India because the early cooks lacked powdered hot peppers. However, hot pepper sauces are often added to curried dishes at the table. Some cooks still use old-fashioned curry pastes, which usually have Congo peppers (a habanero relative) added to them.

Every imaginable foodstuff is curried in Trinidad and Tobago, including mangos, pumpkins, eggplants, potatoes, green tomatoes, okra, chicken, fish, shellfish, beef, pork, goat, and lamb. These curries are commonly served in roti shops, which dot the two islands. The curried mixture is placed upon the flat, thin roti bread and then is wrapped up into an easy-to-eat package of curry. My wife and I toured T&T in 1992 while researching our book *Callaloo, Calypso, & Carnival* (1993) and dined on nine different curried fillings for the roti bread at the Patraj Roti Shop in San Juan: fish, beef, chicken, goat, conch, shrimp, liver, duck, and potato. The fillings were wrapped in the bread or were served in bowls accompanied by torn-up bread called Buss-Up-Shut, which is slang for "burst up shirt," because the bread resembles torn-up cloth. The curry itself was not spicy, but the Congo pepper hot sauce served in squeeze bottles solved that problem.

Sophisticated citizens of Trinidad, who have traveled outside the country, realize that there is more to curry than just the T&T style, but any changes are unlikely. One restaurant owner told me she was quite disappointed when Gaylord's, a restaurant on Independence Square that served authentic East Indian curries, failed because the locals said "This isn't curry." Noted food writer Julie Sahni believes that "curry is such an integral part of Trinidadian cuisine that its Indian origin is actually being lost." She was amazed when a Trinidadian saleswoman in a curry factory asked her: "Are you from India? Do they have curry powder in India?"

The East Indian population of Jamaica is considerably smaller than that of T&T, but their curries are also esteemed. The first East Indians arrived in Falmouth aboard the *Athenium* in 1843, and within fifty years curries had risen to prominence on the island. The *Jamaica Cookery Book*, published in 1893, offered several curry recipes, including a simple but ingenious tropical curry sauce: Coconut jelly (the immature center of a green coconut) was boiled in coconut water with cinnamon and curry powder until thick.

The most popular curry dish in Jamaica is curry goat (not "curried goat"). In fact, according to Helen Willinsky, author of *Jerk: Barbecue from Jamaica*, it is "one of our national dishes." She wrote: "We always serve it for our special occasions, and it seems to be one of the best-remembered dishes by tourists." The first time I tasted curry goat in Jamaica, in a restaurant frequented

Curry Goat Over Fire, Jamaica. Photograph by Rick Browne. Sunbelt Archives.

by locals in Ocho Rios in 1984, I had to be careful not to swallow numerous sharp slivers of bone. In a truly authentic recipe, the goat meat is chopped up—bones and all—because Jamaican cooks believe that the marrow in the bones helps to flavor the dish. The goat was cooked in a large, cast-iron kettle over a wood fire in the backyard of the restaurant. The second time I tasted curry goat in Jamaica, in 1993, the venue was a bit fancier, but the flavor was the same. That time, the goat was prepared by the chef of the Ciboney resort (also in Ocho Rios) and was served at a rather elegant buffet at a beach party, and the bone slivers had been tediously removed.

In the early days, curry goat was considered to be a masculine dish, and there was a certain ritual involved with its serving. Zora Neale Hurston, an American anthropologist who traveled extensively in Jamaica in the 1930s, was fortunate enough to be invited to an all-male curry goat party. "On to the Magnus plantation and the curry goat feed," she wrote. "This feast is so masculine that chicken soup would not be allowed. It must be soup from roosters. After the cock soup comes ram goat and rice. No nanny goat in this meal either. It is ram goat or nothing."

In the French Antilles, the word for curry is *colombo*, named for the capital of Sri Lanka. A typical colombo, such as the Christmas specialty, Pork Colombo from Martinique, begins with a colombo paste that contains, in addition to some standard curry spices, crushed fresh garlic, ginger, and Scotch bonnet chiles, another habanero relative. As with curry goat, the fact that Old World animals are being curried in the New World with a combination of Old World spices and New World chiles adds another dimension to the curry diaspora. And New World foods are being curried as well, like the Aloo Curry of T&T with potatoes, West Indian *massala,* and Congo peppers. In Tobago, bananas, another Old World food that became, like sugar and coffee, a New World export, are curried and turned into a delicious dessert. Pineapples are also curried around the Caribbean, usually with shrimp but occasionally with chicken and/or bananas. New World pumpkins are curried in a soup in Guadeloupe.

The curry diaspora has also become a curry fusion in the West Indies, with curry spices blended with another spice mixture that's similar in concept: jerk seasoning that is based upon one of the most unique New World spices, allspice, a native of Jamaica. For example, in Helen Willinsky's book *Jerk from Jamaica* (1990), she offers a recipe for Pork and Mango Curry, which is a fascinating melange that has an Old World meat (pork) combined with an Old World fruit (mango) and New World peppers (fresh bells and Scotch bonnets), potatoes, and tomatoes seasoned with a combination of Old World curry powder and New World dry jerk seasoning that is essentially Old World spices (thyme, nutmeg, cinnamon, and black pepper), Old World alliums (onion powder and dried chives) with the New World twists of allspice and cayenne chile. This type of melding of ingredients proves Cunningham's main point: "While Indians tend to preserve their eating habits wherever they end up living, their hosts, no matter how hostile, frequently cannot resist their cooking."

The diaspora did not end with the Caribbean—it spectacularly transformed the food culture of England and the rest of the U.K. and, essentially, taught the non-Indian population how to appreciate and eventually come to love spicy foods. The curry revolution in the U.K. began in 1889 when James Sharwood found J.A. Sharwood & Co. Ltd. and began importing curry powder and chutney from India, which he repackaged. Sharwood's today has the largest market share of any U.K. Indian food manufacturer.

In the 1950s, immigrants from India began flooding into England, and when they began to arrive there were only six Indian restaurants in the entire country. By 1991 the total number of Indian, Pakistani, and Bangladeshis in the U.K. had exploded to 1.5 million and the number of Indian or curry restaurants as they're called, had mushroomed to seven thousand. The story of how this happened has been recorded in many books, a lot of those written by my good friend Pat Chapman, and I simply don't have the space here to go into all the details of the major transformation of a nation's cuisine. But even a cursory examination of British curry cookbooks will show that New World foods appear frequently in the curries and chutneys, with chiles and potatoes more dominant than the others, but with tomatoes, pineapples, sweet potatoes, and even turkeys holding their own. For more details on the curry phenomenon in the U.K., I recommend Pat Chapman's *Taste of the Raj* (1997) and Lizzie Cunningham's *Curry: A Tale of Cooks and Conquerors* (2006).

The Mating of the Old World with the New

Meanwhile, back in India, hundreds of years after the cuisines of India were transformed by three foreign arrivals into the country—the Portuguese, the Moghuls, and the British—we can observe how seamlessly and harmoniously the foods of the New World have blended with those of the Old in India with these dining descriptions from Bengali food expert Chitrita Banerji, who lives in Cambridge, Massachusetts, but made several culinary journeys to India between 2003 and 2006 and reported on them in *Eating India: An Odyssey Into the Food and Culture of the Land of Spices* (2007).

She describes these melded meals and their myriad ingredients, like "banana blossom cooked with diced potatoes, coconut chips, and tiny chickpeas, seasoned with bay leaf, cumin, whole green chilies, and garam masala" and notes: "Even the palate cleansers that followed—sweet and sour chutneys made with tomatoes, plums, or pineapples—glowed with deep jewel tones on the [banana] leaf in a way not possible on inorganic surfaces of porcelain, ceramic, or metal." Included in her descriptions are many foods that seemingly have not yet left India: "In Amritsar, the cooks serve *kulchas*, stuffed breads eaten only at breakfast or lunch. They are made with refined flour and are stuffed with a combination of potatoes, onions, chiles, black pepper, cumin, and pomegranate seeds and baked in a tandoor." Even more elegant is "the butter chicken of Delhi[,] first grilled and then cooked in a sauce that combines yogurt, garlic, ginger, ground spices, tomatoes, and butter."

My personal experience with the blending of old and new in India concerns, of course, chile peppers. A simple yet wonderful dish was served to Pat Chapman and me with our wives at the Rajasthan Painting Development School in Udaipur, where we were buying some fine paintings on camel bone. Pat and one of the directors there fixed *jungli mans*, one of the most basic chile pepper dishes in the world. All it took to make it was a pot and a small gas burner. They served it to us with no accompaniment except for a bottle of Super Strong Beer, with 8.7 percent alcohol. "Strong chiles call for strong beer," the director told us.

In the Mewari language of Rajasthan, *jungli mans* refers to a dish that would be prepared by a stranded hunter who had only the basics with him. It is amazingly tasty considering the limited ingredients. It is also quite hot, so serve it with some plain white rice. Two cups of ghee are heated in the pot, two pounds of chopped lamb are added and browned, then ten whole *lal mirch* chiles and a couple of teaspoons of salt go into the pot. Water is added as necessary to make sure that the meat neither fries nor boils but is essentially braised. Continue cooking until the meat is tender, about an hour more, stirring occasionally. The chiles are removed before serving, and the fact that they are whole means that their entire heat is not used. Still, the dish is quite hot, and I think the director was surprised by the fact that Mary Jane and I wolfed down the *jungli mans*, which was definitely not a dish designed for American tourists. But, lacking the traditional curry spices except for chiles, could you call it a curry?

Before leaving India and moving on to Asia, I would be remiss if I didn't mention that New World crops are comfortably

Domino's Pizza and KFC in New Market, Kolkata, India. Photo by Robin Banerji, 2008. Sunbelt Archives.

ensconced in the Indian transformations of American fast food operations. When McDonald's arrived in India, there was an attempt to transform the Big Mac into a chicken burger, but the company found that it had to go further, creating a spicy potato patty called McAlooTikki burger. There is also a vegetarian patty, the McVeggie, which contains a blend of Old and New World ingredients: peas, carrots, green beans, red bell pepper, potatoes, onions, rice, and seasonings. If you'd like a pizza that's not a pizza, you can order the Veg McCurry Pan, a rectangular-shaped crust that is topped with an eggless, creamy sauce containing broccoli, baby corn, mushrooms, and red bell pepper.

But if you want a pizza that *is* a pizza, complete with "plenty of chili flakes, ketchup, and other condiments," according to business writer Sheridan Prasso, "these pizzas at Domino's and Pizza Hut taste the same as in the U.S. What's different is the intensity of the competition. Pizza Hut has 134 locations across India (and 13,000 worldwide); Domino's, 149 (8,500). Both are adding about 50 stores a year—quadruple the average in other markets." And now, even in India, a pizza is not a pizza without tomato sauce.

My final reference to Sir George Watt has nothing to do with any of the New World crops he described above but rather one that played no role whatsoever in Indian food: cacao. In Arthur Knapp's book *Cocoa and Chocolate: Their History from Plantation to Consumer* (1920), he writes: "Sir George Watt has recently invented an ingenious machine for squeezing the beans out of the pod, but at present the extraction is done almost universally by hand, either by men or women." Apparently, he invented this device in Scotland after he retired from his duties in India.

PART 7

THE FIERY "VEGETABLE CIVILIZATIONS" OF ASIA

Vendor at a Floating Market in Thailand Displaying Her Tomatoes and Prik Kee Nu *Chiles. Photograph by Rick Browne. Sunbelt Archives.*

Terraced Rice Fields
in Yunan Province,
China. March 2003.
Photograph by
Jialiang Gao.

ALFRED W. CROSBY, THAT PESSIMISTIC EXPERT ON THE COLUMBIAN EXCHANGE, WROTE IN 1972: "NO LARGE GROUP OF THE HUMAN RACE IN THE OLD WORLD WAS QUICKER TO ADOPT AMERICAN FOOD PLANTS THAN THE CHINESE. WHILE THE MEN WHO STORMED TENOCHTITLÁN WITH CORTÉS STILL LIVED, PEANUTS WERE SWELLING IN THE SANDY LOAMS NEAR SHANGHAI; MAIZE WAS TURNING FIELDS GREEN IN SOUTH CHINA, AND THE SWEET POTATO WAS ON ITS WAY TO BECOMING THE POOR MAN'S STAPLE IN FUKIEN."

AND THEY COULDN'T HAVE ARRIVED AT A BETTER TIME, BECAUSE THE POPULATION GROWTH OF CHINA WAS STALLED; THE COUNTRY JUST COULDN'T PRODUCE ENOUGH FOOD FOR ITS EXISTING PEOPLE, MUCH LESS THE MILLIONS AND MILLIONS TO COME. AS IN INDIA, THE CHINESE READILY ADOPTED SOME UNFAMILIAR NEW WORLD FOODS FOR THE SIMPLE REASON THAT THEY WERE HUNGRY. I'M GOING TELL YOU THAT STORY, BUT FIRST, LET'S TAKE UP THE CURRY TRAIL THAT BEGAN IN THE LAST PART.

"Burn Your Lips and Remember My Dinner": Oriental Curries

In the early 1990s, I was the editor of *Chile Pepper* magazine and eager to track the history and culinary use of chiles around the world by publishing talented food writers. I received a query and sample article from a Berkeley-based, yet-unpublished author named Richard Sterling. His story was about the evacuation of Saigon to U.S. Navy ships during the Vietnam War and how he assisted in solving the problem of feeding the refugees. It still remains the most moving food article I've ever read, and there were tears in my eyes when I finished it. Needless to say, I published it and began a long relationship with Richard, who wrote mostly about his food adventures in Southeast Asia and Africa, and I published his articles on Vietnam, Cambodia, Thailand, Laos, and even Burma. He went on to become a very successful food and travel author of many books before going into semi-retirement and moving to Saigon. It is Richard who will be our guide to the chile-tomato-potato-laden curries of those countries.

Now called Myanmar, Burma remains mostly mysterious to Americans, but Richard had no qualms about sneaking into the country and sampling the delights of its chile-fueled curries. In his article "Party on the Irrawaddy," he wrote: "The Burmese cook approaches curry in a way as constant as the ancient past or the monsoon cycle." First, the Burmese make a curry paste out of their five basic ingredients: onions, garlic, chiles, ginger, and turmeric. Some Burmese cooks use other spices as well, including an occasional prepared curry powder, but the hallmark of the Burmese curry is its oiliness. The cooks use a combination of peanut oil and sesame oil, about a cup of each in a wok, and heat it until it smokes—this is called "cooking the oil." The curry paste is added, the heat is reduced, and the paste is cooked for fifteen minutes. Then some meat is added and cooked, and eventually the oil rises to the top. This state is called *see byan*, "the return of the oil." When the oil floats on top, the dish is done.

The oil is not skimmed off but rather is absorbed by the side dish of rice when it is served. Surprisingly, the curries, such as Swimming Chicken Curry, do not taste greasy—probably because of the light oil used. However, western cooks usually use less oil than the Burmese cooks. Richard noted, "This is a wet curry, or curry with gravy; it cries out for rice or even mashed potatoes to sop up the delicious sauce." Another Burmese chicken curry, quick to prepare, is Kyethar Peinathar Hin, or Chicken with Fenugreek and Chickpeas, which is heavily flavored with fenugreek. Sometimes chicken is curried with tomatoes, as in Kyethar Sipyan, one of the most basic of the Burmese curries. Duck is also popular in Burma, as indicated by Bairather Sepiyan, which uses the technique of the return of the oil and was a favorite of the writer George Orwell, who lived and worked in Burma for several years. In Chettiar Curry, also known as monsoon curry and one of the most highly treasured curries of Myanmar, New World potatoes, tomatoes, pumpkins, and paprika are combined with daikon radishes, ginger, tamarind, carrots, yellow split peas, and eggplant to make a surprisingly mild, tamarind-flavored vegetarian curry.

In contrast to the diminished pungency of some Burmese curries, Thai curries are extensively spiced with chiles. Contrary to popular belief, there is not just one "Thai chile" but rather dozens of varieties used in cooking. When I toured the wholesale produce market in Bangkok in 1991, I found literally tons of both fresh and dried chiles in baskets and in huge bales five feet tall. They ranged in size from piquin-like, thin pods barely an inch long to yellow and red pods about four inches long. But only fresh chiles are ground up with other ingredients to make the famous Thai curry pastes. Two key curry pastes are at the heart of Thai cooking: A red paste, called Nam Prik Gaeng Ped, uses red chiles, lemon grass, galangal, and a lot of cilantro plus traditional curry spices. The green curry paste (Gaeng Kiow Whan) is made with the smaller and very hot green Thai chiles. It looks deceptively mild, like a Mediterranean pesto, but is very spicy indeed. A yellow curry paste, colored with ground turmeric, is perhaps the mildest of all Thai curry pastes.

Culinary Adventurer Richard Sterling in Hanoi. Photograph Supplied by Richard Sterling. Sunbelt Archives.

The variety of Thai curries is astonishing. In the index of David Thompson's massive, 673-page *Thai Food* (2002) I counted forty-two different kinds beyond the powders and pastes. He writes: "Wherever you go in Thailand—province, region, or village—everyone has a favourite curry, which they believe to be superior to all others. Thai curries are diverse, and the range can be both bewildering and at time contentious. This huge array is the delicious outcome of the availability of ingredients, the changing seasons, regional variations, different techniques, personal tastes and local customs." Here are just a few of the Thai curries I am most familiar with.

Mussaman Curry Paste is so named after Muslim traders (or perhaps for Muslim harbor officials in the port of Bangkok) who first imported it from India. It is unique in that it uses curry spices most Thai dishes avoid, such as coriander, cloves, and cinnamon. It was first prepared in the court of King Rama I in the nineteenth century, and it's commonly combined with beef, potatoes, tamarind, and coconut milk to make a curry served at wedding feasts. Another ruler who loved such curries was Chulalongkorn, who reportedly had thirty-two wives competing for his favors. Each New Year he required each of his wives to prepare one new curry dish, and the wife who created the dish he liked the most would receive special gifts and elevated status.

New World crops are plentiful in Thai curries. Potatoes also make an appearance in Pannang Beef Curry (*Gaeng Pannang Nua*), where they are matched with red curry paste and coconut milk, while tomatoes are paired with green curry paste, chicken, coconut milk and eggplants in Green Chicken Curry (*Gaeng Kiow Whan Gai*). Pineapple stars in Fish Curry with Bamboo (*Gaeng Leuang Pahk Dat*), where a half of one is combined with catfish, red curry paste, bamboo shoots, and green beans. Undoubtedly, the popularity of pineapples in Thailand results from the fact that it is the second-largest producer of pineapples in the world, after the Philippines.

In Cambodia, which is now called Kampuchea, the Khmer cooks depend on chiles, lemongrass, galangal, and fish sauces in most of their curries. "The Cambodians are great eaters," Richard told me. "Their calendar is full of historical feasts, and any gaps are filled by weddings, births, funerals, and auspicious alignments of the stars. Theirs is a land of abundance and they enjoy regular harvests of rice, wild and cultivated fruits, fresh and saltwater fish, domesticated animals, and fowl and game. They love to eat meat. Pork is the most popular and it is excellent, as are all the meats. An English journalist we dined with said of her beefsteak that it was the best she ever had. We didn't tell her it was *luc lac*, or water buffalo." He added, "In Cambodia, as in India, there are as many curries as there are cooks. But all true Khmer curries have five constants: lemongrass, garlic, galangal, and coconut milk; the fifth constant is the cooking technique, dictated by the texture of lemongrass and the consistency of coconut milk." Chiles are a part of most Cambodian curries, but they are not as spicy as the ones served by the Thais.

Richard provided me with the recipe for basic Lemongrass Curry, which is an easy-to-prepare, coconut- and lemongrass-based dish using the cook's choice of meat; Cambodian cooks commonly use frog legs. Red Curry Cambogee features New World potatoes, peanuts, and bean sprouts combined with lemongrass again, beef or chicken, and both dried red chiles and paprika. Venison, dried shrimp, fish sauce, watercress, tomatoes, and the usual Southeast Asian spices make for a heady, aromatic curry combination in Cambodian Curried Venison (*Phan Sin Fahn*). "Curries have been popular since the days of the Hindu-inspired Angkor Wat," wrote Richard. "But, whereas the original Indian blend is based on onions and turmeric, I learned that the 'sons of Kambu' base theirs on lemongrass. The Chinese introduced the wok, but the Cambodian cook could not use it fully without such New World ingredients as chiles, peanuts, and squash. One of the most important aspects of Cambogee fare is the use of delicate aromatics, such as basil and mint, to provide a subtle counterpoint to robust flavors and heavy meats. And rather than cooking them into the dish, as other curry cooks might do, the Cambodian cooks often served us a plate of the sweet smelling leaves alongside the dish. We then used them according to our liking, just as we would use condiments."

In nearby Laos, two distinctive curry styles have emerged. One is that of the Laotians, whose cuisine is very similar to that of the Thais except that lemongrass and galangal are only rarely used in their curries. The other cooking style is that of the Hmong, a tribal people of southern Chinese origin. The Hmong cuisine, naturally, was inspired more by the Chinese, so soy sauce replaces fish sauces. Shallots, ginger, and chiles are common in Laotian curries. All of the ingredients are pounded together in a mortar until they are very smooth and then are cooked in coconut milk until a silky sauce is formed. "A good Laotian curry sauce is similar to the consistency of hollandaise," says Richard. Meats and fish are commonly curried in Laos, and Richard sent me his recipe for Laotian Catfish Curry, featuring the fish combined with eggplant, small green chiles, tomato, green beans, and coconut. He commented on this curry: "Maceration of the curry paste ingredients is critical and the ginger used for both its culinary and mystical value; in the currency of the spirit world it represents gold."

Laos represents a culinary division between Cambodia and Vietnam—the people of those two countries have little in common. Northern Vietnam was more influenced by China than by India, and heavy curry sauces are not common. However, other types of curries appear in the cuisine of Vietnam, especially in

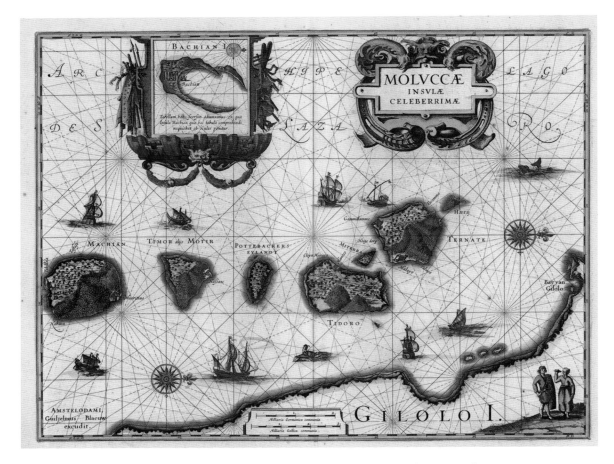

Map of the Moluccas by Jan Janssonius, 1638. Sunbelt Archives.

the south, where Indian traders and merchants made an impression. One of the most interesting Vietnamese curries is Curried Frog Legs (*Saigon Echnau Cari*), a mild, aromatic curry that is immensely popular where Richard lives now, Saigon. It combines frog legs, red curry paste, lemongrass, and cellophane noodles; this was understandably one of the curries beloved by the French, who occupied Vietnam between 1858 and 1954, except for the Japanese conquest during World War II. Other Vietnamese curries include *Saigon Cari*, a chicken curry combined with sweet potatoes and coconut milk, and another chicken curry, *Cari Ga*, in which the chicken is combined with taro root (potatoes or sweet potatoes are sometimes substituted), red curry paste, coconut milk, lemongrass, and ginger. When you begin preparing one of the Golden Triangle curries, remember the Burmese saying provided by Richard: "Eat hot curry, drink hot soup, burn your lips, and remember my dinner."

The Isles of Spice and Curries from "Excellent" to "Bizarre"

The original Spice Islands were the Moluccas, those remote isles of cloves and nutmeg that lie 1,500 miles east of Djakarta, Indonesia. But throughout history, the location of the Spice Islands gradually broadened to include all of the East Indies—now the countries of Malaysia, Indonesia, and Singapore. There was a simple reason for the broader definition: The spice-growing locations expanded as the region was conquered by one spice-seeking world power after another.

Today, Malaysia, Indonesia, and Singapore are separate, independent countries, and these "isles of spice" still live up to their name. Indonesia produces about 70 percent of the world's nutmeg and mace, plus large amounts of cassia, turmeric, black pepper, and cloves. Most of the cloves, incidentally, are not eaten but rather are smoked in cigarettes. Other curry ingredients grown in the region include chiles, ginger, galangal, lemongrass, kaffir lime, and coconuts, perhaps the most important single ingredient in the spice countries' curries. These culinary components, combined with the many ethnic influences on the region, have produced a fascinating and complex gastronomic stew that has become the most popular cooking style: currying. "Curries, easily the most common dish eaten with rice, are a definite mark of the Indian influence in Malay cooking," notes Singapore restaurateur Fawziah Amin. "For almost every meal, a dish of fish, prawn, or chicken curry has to be on the menu. While Indian curry is hot, rich, and fiery, with yogurt added, the Malays opt for a milder, delicate taste, with the creamy flavor of coconut milk in generous portions."

Harvey Day, author of *Curries of India* (1963), wrote, "No one with a discriminating palate would mistake a Malayan curry for an Indian curry." A quick glance at two recipes utilized in Malaysia reveals the differences. Singapore Curry Powder is typically Indian, and while Malaysian Curry Paste contains some Indian curry spices, it also shows the influence of Malay ingredients such as galangal, lemongrass, *blacan* (shrimp paste), coconut, candlenuts, and cinnamon. Such a blending reflects "three nationalities—Malays, Chinese, and Indians [living] together in a unique blending of culture and traditions," in the words of Jackie Passmore, author of *The Letts Companion to Asian Food & Cooking* (1991). She goes on to point out that "the harmony of this liaison is reflected in a unified cuisine which takes elements from each. The Indians contributed the art of spice blending. Shredded chili, for example, will give an extra bite to a mildly-flavored Chinese-style dish; a curry may gain depth by the addition of soy sauce and pickles." She also points out that Malaysia and Indonesia share ingredients, topography, and climate, so their cuisines are quite similar. Some of those common ingredients are coconut, chiles, ginger, galingal, and tamarind, in particular.

The basis of the Spice Islands' curries is the *sambals*, which are both fiery condiments in Malaysia and some cooked dishes in Indonesia. These *sambals* range from simple chile sauces to curry-like pastes and are primarily used to spice up other dishes, such as mild curries. The basis for most sambals is chiles, onions (or shallots or garlic), and citrus, but many other ingredients are used, including lemongrass, *blacan*, ginger, galangal, candlenuts, kaffir lime leaves, and coconut milk. Thus the sambals resemble a curry paste, but with a much greater number of chiles. Some of the sambals, such as *Buah Tomat*, incorporate a western ingredient—tomatoes. *Sambal Badjak*, or Indonesia Curry Paste, is one of the more complex sambals, being both hot and sweet at the same time, with up to ten fresh small red chiles similar to serranos combined with brown sugar and coconut milk. Prepared and packaged sambals are common. In 1991, while visiting Johore Baru, Malaysia, I stopped by a very modern supermarket and found both sides of an entire aisle were filled with sambal after sambal in all their various incarnations.

The sambals are the start for the curries, which have not changed much since William Marsden described them in his book, *The History of Sumatra* (1784): "Although the Sumatrans live, in a great measure, upon vegetable food, they are not restrained, by any superstitious opinion, from other aliments, and accordingly, at their entertainments, the flesh of the buffalo, goat, and fowls, are served up. Their dishes are almost all prepared in that mode of dressing, to which we have given the name of curry, (from an Hindostanic word) and which is now universally known in Europe. It is called in the Malay language, *goolye*, and may be composed of any kind of edible, but is generally of flesh or fowl, with a variety of pulse and succulent herbage, stewed down with certain ingredients, by us termed, when mixed and ground together, curry powder."

Marsden went on to describe how these curries are eaten: "A great diversity of curries is usually served up at the same time, in small vessels, each flavored, to a nice discerning taste, in a different manner; and in this consists all the luxury of their tables. Let the quantity or variety of meat be what it may, the principal article of their food is rice, which is eaten in a large proportion with every dish, and very frequently without any other accompaniment than salt and chili pepper." This is the earliest description I could find of the *rijsttafel,* or "rice table," in Dutch. It is not a dish but rather a feast of many dishes, including curries. The term derives from the Dutch settlers, who staged elaborate dinner parties in an attempt to upstage one another. It was up to the creative chef never to duplicate flavors, types of meat, or cooking styles, and for every dish that was spicy hot, there had to be a bland dish to offset it. Likewise, sweet dishes were offset by sour, warm dishes by cold dishes, wet by dry, and firm-textured by soft-textured.

Often, as many as fifty or sixty dishes were served, but despite such attention to detail, the food was not as important as the spectacle in a *rijsttafel,* and the quality of the party was judged by the number of servants it took to produce the affair. If fifty servants were required, the party was known as a "fifty-boy rijsttafel," which the Indonesians naturally found offensive. Today the term is considered to be a degrading holdover from colonial times; however, scaled-down rijsttafels are still staged for tourists—but without all those servants. Some of the curry dishes

The family of C.H. Japing partaking of a rijsttafel with Aunt Jet and Uncle Jan Breeman in Bandung, Indonesia, May 1936. Tropenmuseum of the Royal Tropical Institute (KIT).

included in early *rijsttafels* were the *gulais*, curried stews, and the *rendangs* (sometimes spelled *randang*), which are meat dishes cooked in coconut milk and spices. A popular rendang is one from Sumatra, which features either water buffalo or beef (beef is a minor meat in Indonesia), and Gulai Kambing, a classic goat curry from Sumatra; the very spicy Devil's Pork Curry, a liver curry called Rendang Limpa, and the very popular chicken curry, Gulai Putih, a Singapore favorite.

A wonderful description of the effects of Indonesian curries appeared in a nineteenth-century travel book, *The Boy Travellers in the Far East, Part Second* (1880), by Thomas Knox: "This is the famous Java curry; and if you have taken plenty of the pepper and chutney, and other hot things, your mouth will burn for half an hour as though you had drunk from a kettle of boiling water. And when you have eaten freely of curry, you don't want any other breakfast. Everybody eats curry here daily, because it is said to be good for the health by keeping the liver active, and preventing fevers."

Knox continued his Far East curry descriptions in the third part of his *Boy Travellers in the Far East* (1881) with this humorous tale set in Luzon, Philippines, in a section entitled "Bat Shooting in Luzon": "Mr. La Gironiere, who formerly owned Jala-jala, used to bring his guests over here for the same sport you have been enjoying. One day he had in his party a couple of Americans, and on the way back one of them said they would like to try the flesh of the bat and the iguana. Thinking they were in earnest, the host told his cook to make a curry of iguana, and a ragout, or stew, of bat, and serve them for dinner. The cook did as he was ordered, and the first dish on the table was the curry. Everybody ate heartily, and pronounced the curry excellent; and then the host ventured to remark, 'You see the flesh of the iguana is very delicate.' This was enough. Every plate was pushed aside, including that of the American who had made the proposal, and not a mouthful more of curry could any one eat. Some even fled from the table, and could not be prevailed on to return until the strange dish had been removed, and the order for the bat stew was countermanded. You see what prejudice is; they all thought the curry delicious till they knew what it was made of, and probably they would have said the same of the ragout."

Another humorous curry description was given by Frank Marryat, a midshipman aboard the survey vessel HMS *Samarang* in Brunei, Borneo, in 1847: "On the occasion of a dinner given to us by the Sultan of Bruni, the whole party were seized with a fit of very indecorous and immoderate laughter, by finding the centre dish, which was a curry, served up in a capacious vessel, which in Europe is only to be found under a bed. The curry, nevertheless, was excellent; and what matter did it make? 'What's in a name? A rose by any other name would smell as sweet.'"

In 1888, Mrs. Florence Caddy was entertained by the Sultan of Johore in the very Malaysian city I visited a little over a hundred years later: "Sometimes we had a Malay breakfast, beginning with a capital mayonnaise of fish and capers, and then a ponderous Malay curry, twenty courses in one, of about twenty-six dishes and 'sambals,' which are grated, shredded, chopped or powdered preparations of seven little dishes in each sambal-tray, of which you are expected to select several or nearly all. There are several sets of sambals. We enjoyed the curry, and made merry over it, counting the different dishes and flavourings we had heaped together on our hot-water plates. The Sultan piled his plate as high as possible with all the twenty-six varieties—and the sambals—enjoyed it, and came for more. Other curries after this will be sorrow's crown of sorrow, making us remember happier things."

This description is from her fascinating book *To Siam and Malaya in the Duke of Sutherland's Yacht "Sans Peur"* (1889). As the name of the yacht implies, Mrs. Caddy was fearless in her explorations of the culinary delights of Malaya, and she was a very careful observer of everything that was going on. She described how the elaborate twenty-six-course meals were prepared: "This masterpiece is compounded by the Babu—the Sultan's chef—under the Sultan's own eyes. Like a domesticated Frenchman, Sultan Abubekir likes poking about doing his housekeeping, looking after the 'perfectionating' of the *sambals*. When he comes to England, or goes anywhere on a visit, he can eat nothing that has not been prepared by his own cooks; of course, like all Moslems, he can only eat meat slaughtered by a Mohammedan butcher. Then the whole paraphernalia of dishes was handed round again to be eaten with the yellow glutinous rice, which they made a point of our tasting. This small-grained rice is a special sort. Yellow being the royal colour, it is received as an honour by the guests; but it is really not so good as the ordinary rice."

In all fairness, I should point out that not all visitors to the Spice Islands liked the curries they were served. A. Mackenzie Cameron visited Batavia in Java on business in 1885 and had this to say about what he was served for lunch.

> The midday meal, or curry and rice, comes on at about half after twelve, and consists only of rice, and any number of the most tasteless bizarre curries imaginable. I remembered with a sigh the delicious Ceylon curries when one could not only eat this horrid Oriental compound of turmeric and chillies, but even wish for a further acquaintance with tender chicken cooked with spices in cocoanut milk; but as for these Java curries they are evidently so bad, that even the Dutch so accustomed to them cannot get over them without the aid of nearly a dozen of "sambals," or preparations of the nature of pickled salads or mashes made up of any thing and every thing, from cocoanut chips to vegetable tops; but all loaded with chillies and oil. It requires considerable courage to venture into such nameless and worse than useless fare. To go without a proper English breakfast, and then without a lunch was bad enough; but to go without even a decent—mind, a moderately plain and decent dinner according to English ideas, filled up the cup of Dutch shortcomings in Java to the full. I can unhesitatingly say that my stays in Java were always of the nature of prolonged fasts, and I used to look forward to getting on board again just only to have a decent and "square" meal. On comparing notes with other English visitors, I found their experience at the hotels to have been precisely the same as my own. Only at respectable private houses can an eatable curry or a respectable joint of meat be seen.

Tiffin in Singapore, Rijsttafel in Sydney, and *Yohshoku* Curry Bars in Tokyo

Sir Thomas Stamford Raffles, the founder of Singapore, was curious about every aspect of life in his adopted country of Java (now Indonesia) and its capital, Dutch Batavia (now Jakarta). His description of the food of the natives in his book, *History of Java* (1817), shows the disdainful resistance of the European colonists to this cuisine:

Sir Thomas Stamford Bingley Raffles, 1817. Portrait Painted by George Francis Joseph. Sunbelt Archives.

> Indian corn is usually roasted in the ear, and offered for sale in the same manner. Other aliments are for the most part prepared in the manner of curry, termed by the *Maláyus gulai*: of these they have almost an endless variety, distinguished according to the principal ingredients. . . . Black pepper, as among the *Maláyus*, is scarcely ever used, on account of its supposed heating quality. The most common seasoning employed to give a relish to their insipid food, is the *lombok* [chile pepper]; triturated with salt, it is called *sámbel*, both by the *Maláyus* and Javans, and this condiment is indispensable and universal. It is of different kinds, according to the substances added to increase or diversify its strength or pungency; the most common addition is *trasi* [shrimp paste], denominated by the *Maláyus*, *bláchang*. The name *lálab* is given to various leaves and kernels, mostly eaten raw with rice and *sámbel*: many of these substances possess a pungency and odour intolerable to Europeans. . . . *Rújak* [now *rojak*] is prepared from unripe mangos and other fruits, which, being grated, receive the addition of capsicum and other spices, and thus constitutes a favourite dish with the natives, though very disagreeable to Europeans.

"There is no mention in Raffles' day of the now so famous Rijsttafel," notes Emily Hahn in her book *Raffles of Singapore*

Singapore. Raffles Hotel.

Postcard of the Raffles Hotel, Singapore, c. 1923. Sunbelt Archives.

(1946), and she points out that "the Europeans at Batavia as much as possible avoided eating rice until well on into the nineteenth century, and they always preferred their costly, difficult-to-get, half-sour or rancid, ill-preserved and unsuitable European foodstuffs." They also drank a lot. "In Batavia everybody drank a bottle of wine a day as a matter of course, quite apart from the beer, sake, spirits, and so on which were consumed on the side," she writes, adding that "the widow of Governor General van der Parra, who according to the contemporary witnesses was an exceptionally sober and strait-laced man, died long after her husband but still left 4,500 bottles of wine and over 10,000 bottles of beer." This behavior led to a Malay poem that went:

To do nothing but drink, every day of the year,
Port, Madeira, brandy and beer;
Naught accomplished save beefsteak and curry bitten,
Is a very bad thing indeed, Mr. Briton.

This bit of doggerel shows that at least some of the colonists were sampling curry, which led eventually to the British Tiffin light lunches so popular in Sir Raffles's eventual home: Singapura, or Singapore. The tradition of "tiffin," derived from the obsolete English slang "tiffing," not surprising meaning "taking a little drink or sip," was transferred from British India to Singapore and eventually became famous at Raffles Hotel, the hotel named after him much later. The Tiffin lunches were first served at Raffles Hotel in 1899, but about a decade before that, Rudyard Kipling was recommending the food there, as reported in newspaper dispatches that were eventually published in his book *From Sea to Sea* (1899): "Providence conducted me along a beach, in full view of five miles of shipping,—five solid miles of masts and funnels—to a place called Raffles Hotel, where the food is as excellent as the rooms are bad. Let the traveller take note. Feed at Raffles and sleep at the Hotel de l'Europe."

I learned more about tiffin while visiting Raffles Hotel in 1991. As mentioned, the "tiffin curry lunches," still served at Raffles in its main dining room, called, of course, the Tiffin Room, originated in India, where men went to work carrying a tiffin carrier, a stacked series of containers (enamel or stainless steel) held together by a metal frame. The concept was brought to Singapore by the British, because they were loathe to dine in local establishments for fear of tropical diseases such as typhoid, cholera, and dysentery. One of the main ingredients of a tiffin lunch was a tiffin curry, which went easy on the chiles and spices so as not to offend British tastes. Tiffin curries were served by the best hotels, and a famous tiffin room was Emerson's Tiffin, Billiards, and Reading Room, which opened in 1866 near Cavenagh Bridge. Tiffin curries became popular partly because the moderately spicy curries were believed to aid in curing hangovers, a typical affliction of the British, who as we have seen dearly loved to carouse. Early tiffins usually featured curry puffs, curried eggs, chicken, prawns, or eggplants accompanied by rice, sambals, and a mango chutney. A typical later tiffin curry lunch, as served by the Europe Hotel in 1932, consisted of curried fish and rice accompanied by iced consommé, veal, ham, fruits, and a watercress salad.

Nearly all of the curries in the Spice Islands these days have chile peppers in them, but that's about it for the New World crops, and the potatoes, tomatoes, peanuts, and pineapples used in the curries of the subcontinent have been replaced with coconut, lemongrass, galangal, eggplants, candlenuts, and okra—all Old World crops. But Indonesia grows many New World crops and is the eighth largest producer of peanuts in the world and comes in fourth for pineapples, chiles, sweet potatoes, and maize. What are they used in? Well, we've seen the chiles in action, and maize is used nearly exclusively for livestock feed, but the other three crops are firmly ensconced in other non-curry dishes.

Sir Stamford Raffles, as he liked to be called, also wrote about peanuts in his *History of Java*: "The *káchang góring* of the oil-giving Malay countries, or, as it is indifferently termed by the Javans, *kachang china, penden, or tana*, is cultivated almost exclusively for the purpose of obtaining its oil, near the capitals of the principal districts, both central and maritime." Today, peanut oil is commonly used in the cooking of both Malaysia and Indonesia. Peanuts make a notable appearance in Sambal Kacang, a peanut sauce used to dress *gado gado*, a salad from Bali of green beans, cauliflower, sprouts, eggs, and potatoes. Perhaps their most common use is in sauces to dress *satays*, those tasty kebabs that are commonly said to be the "national dishes" of both countries.

Peanuts are found in the sauces of *satay padang*, made with water buffalo, where they are combined with garlic, onion, small fresh chiles, sugar, ginger, tamarind, lime juice, and coconut so the pieces of meat are basted with it. Chicken often replaces the buffalo, and it is sometimes placed on the skewers alternating with shrimp and pineapple chunks, or steak and pork cubes. They are combined again with pineapple in at least one curry, Pakari, an Indonesian sweet specialty that's loaded with coconut but is completely lacking in chiles.

Pineapples also make an appearance in Rojak (sometimes "Rujak"), a salad with cucumber, green mango and lots of red chile flakes that's dressed with a Lemongrass Sambal to which shrimp paste, sugar, vinegar, and lemon juice have been added. Another version of Rojak from Padang, Indonesia, replaces the cucumber with grapefruit and tart apples and is dressed with a syrup made with brown sugar, fresh small, hot chiles, tamarind pulp, and peanut butter. The Wikipedia listing for Rojak lists fourteen different variations, and not all contain fruits. Rujak Juhi, for example is made with fried *takwa* tofu, fried boiled potatoes, fried shredded salted cuttlefish, cucumber, noodles,

Raffles Hotel,

2, BEACH ROAD, SINGAPORE.

TELEGRAPHIC ADDRESS : RAFFLES—SINGAPORE.

This First-Class Motel,

WHICH has been enlarged and entirely renovated, is facing and commanding an extensive view of the harbour, close to the Public Offices, Mercantile quarters, and the Esplanade.

SUITES, consisting of Sitting-room, Bed-room, Dressing-room, with Private Bath-room attached.

A most spacious Dining-room facing the sea.

BAR, BILLIARD and READING ROOM in separate block and fitted up with all modern improvements.

Four First-class Billiard Tables.

The Table d'Hote is always supplied with every delicacy in season, and is open to non-residents.

Breakfast, 9 a.m.; Tiffin, 1 p.m.; Dinner, 7.30 p.m.

Boarders and Visitors of the Raffles Hotel can have their Lunch at the Raffles Tiffin Rooms in Raffles Square, without extra charge.

Wines, Spirits, & Liquors of the best qualities & brands.

ELECTRIC BELLS THROUGHOUT THE BUILDINGS.

TERMS—MODERATE.

BRANCH HOTELS :
EASTERN & ORIENTAL HOTEL, PENANG.
SARKIES' HOTEL, RANGOON.

SARKIES BROTHERS,
Proprietors.

lettuce, cabbages, peanut sauce, vinegar, chile, and fried garlic. These is even an Indonesian relish devoted to pineapple, Petjili Nanas, in which chopped pineapple is combined with onion, fresh red chiles, cinnamon, and brown sugar and used to accompany curries.

Advertisement for the Raffles Hotel, 1899. Sunbelt Archives.

Sweet potatoes are even sweeter in Spice Islands cooking because they are sugared and turned into fritters like Buah Jingah, or stuffed pancakes, Martabak Kubang, from west Sumatra. They are also popular in the Philippines in an appetizer called Ukoy, once again in cake form but this time mixed with whole shrimp, chiles, green onions, and another little-used New World crop, grated acorn squash.

White potatoes are a minor crop in Indonesia, but they still make an appearance in cooking in Sambal Ubi Kentang, a potato sambal with the ubiquitous fresh chiles, green onions, lime juice, nutmeg, and cilantro. The British also used them in the very refined, mild curry puffs, an appetizer often served at tiffin lunches. Lean ground meat is mixed with diced boiled potatoes, minced onion, curry power, and paste and then used as the filling for a standard flour pastry.

Finally, tomatoes have at least one *sambal* devoted to them, Malaysian Sambal Buah Tomat, a simple combination of crushed fresh chiles, prawn paste, tomatoes, and deep-fried, crushed onions. They also make an appearance in Indonesian Mutton Soup, which I was served in Singapore. This could easily be called a curried soup, for it contains all the usual curry spices, fresh chiles, lemongrass, mutton or goat meat, and four diced tomatoes. Korma A yam, His Majesty's Chicken, uses two ripe, sliced tomatoes and chicken segments stewed together with chiles, curry spices, shallots, and coconut milk. Popular condiments to serve with Spice Islands curries include sliced raw bananas, fried bananas, sliced pineapple, chopped peanuts, grated coconut (either raw or roasted), fried eggplant, and even deep-fried anchovies topped with chile powder.

I finally became a guest at a Rijistafel Banquet, and it didn't happen in either Malaysia or Singapore but rather in Sydney, Australia, in 2000. It was a serendipitous occasion that I just lucked into. I was making an appearance as one of the guests of honor at the Australian National Fiery Food Festival, along with Diana Kennedy, the famous Mexican food expert. I was also a judge at their Australian Fiery Food Challenge, a food-tasting contest modeled after the Scovie Awards, which are produced in the U.S. by my company. Another judge was Carol Selva Rajah, a noted Australian food writer, cookbook author, a Malaysian food expert. She promptly adopted my wife and me and gave us a copy of her latest book, *Makan-lah!: The True Taste of Malaysia*. One of her projects during the Taste of Sydney, the umbrella food event, was to produce the Batavia Rijistafel Banquet, a fourteen-course spice dinner held at the National Maritime Museum. Because of our intense interest in spices of all kinds, she really wanted us to attend this exclusive dinner. The main problem was that the museum had sold all the tickets in a matter of hours and there were no seats left. So Carol gave me her seat at the banquet! Unfortunately, there was no room for Mary Jane, so she was on her own back in Manly while I hobnobbed with the museum elite.

Cocktails and starters were served aboard the *Batavia*, a full-size reproduction of the original Dutch spice ship that wrecked off the coast of Western Australia in 1629. It was moored at the museum, and I was fascinated to go aboard the remarkable replica. The ship was built by the Dutch government (it took ten years) and was transported to Sydney for the Olympic celebrations aboard a floating dock ship, and then it was released to cruise into Sydney harbor under sail, accompanied by fireworks and the booming of its own cannons. Sipping on a Heineken (what else?), I went down the ladders to the spice storage deck and was amazed at how cramped it was, with ceilings only about five feet off the deck. Here, the sacks of spices were stored—black pepper, long pepper, nutmeg, mace, cloves, and cinnamon. The sailors— all three hundred of them—slept among the spice sacks because of the lack of room on the 193-foot-long ship.

The Batavia Rijistafel Banquet was a bit overwhelming, and I had to pace myself when trying something particularly tasty and spicy, like the Rendang Bambu Sapi, her beef and chile dish loaded with spices, or the Sambal Goreng Udang Karing, a delicious prawn *sambal*. There were Bali dancers performing, but at this *rijistafel* the food was just as important as the spectacle. It remains, along with the curry feasts Pat Chapman took us to at restaurants from London to Bath to Mumbai, one of the most memorable meals of my life.

Later, Carol took us to Cabramatta, a small city outside Sydney where many of the Asian immigrants live. It was rather like being in Singapore and its ethnic diversity, with Vietnamese soup shops, Cambodian discos, Chinese grocery stores, and Thai herb shops. We all ate the Vietnamese Beef Soup with chilli-garlic sauce, and it was unforgettably good. Carol also took us to one of the largest distributors of Indian food, herbs and spices in Australia and also referred us to Herbies Spices in nearby Rozelle.

Matsuya, *Fresh Tomato Curry and Rice, Popular in Japan. Photographer Unknown. Sunbelt Archives.*

Herbie, as Ian Hemphill is nicknamed, recognized me because he sells dried chiles in addition to literally hundreds of varieties of spices. It was there that I bought the wild spicy mountain pepper that is gaining in popularity in Australian gourmet circles. The Malaysians have a saying, "Good food and happiness go hand in hand." Even for transplanted Malaysians like Carol Selvah Rajah, that maxim still holds true.

The Philippines and Japan don't really qualify as spice islands, but all of these islands are, indeed, getting more spicy as they adopt not only foods of the New World but also the cooking ingredients and techniques of the other regions that have melded together the crops of the new and old, like the curry countries I've covered earlier. There are several incarnations of Filipino cuisine because of the influences of the Spice Islands, China, and the Spanish occupation that lasted for four hundred years. Asian cuisine expert Jennifer Brennan observes: "The dishes of Manila and most of Luzon reflect the Spanish heritage, being substantial and somewhat bland, with few spices. In the Muslim and tropical south, pork is not eaten and the spicing is closer to the Indonesian, including the use of hot peppers."

Here's how that happened. The Philippines rival Indonesia in the length and diversity of its archipelago. Indonesia is vaster, with 17,508 islands that stretch for 3,181 miles, while the Philippines have 7,107 islands that span only 1,093 miles, but there is great diversity between the north and south portions of the archipelago. New World crops arrived in the north through direct transport from Mexico aboard the "Manila galleons," on a trade route that was established in 1565 by Andrés de Urdaneta. So the food in the north was heavily influenced by the Spanish tradition while the south reflects the spread of the Spice Islands curries, particularly on the island on Mindanao, which is only 1,640 miles from Malaysia.

Joshua Ligan, writing online at Examiner.com, notes that "Filipino Muslim cuisine is the liberal use of herbs and spices that most Christian Filipinos are wont to avoid, such as cumin, coriander, turmeric, galangal, cornflower, roasted coconut powder, and an Allium species locally called *sakurab* in the Maranao language." The typical curried food eaten in Mindanao is *kulma*, a word derived from the Indian "korma," and "is based on nuts and coconut milk, but contains no yogurt or cream." It is peanut-based and the meat is stewed in a rich sauce in the manner of curry. Ligan gives as an example a recipe for Davao-style Beef Kulma in which the blending of Old World and New World crops is quite important. The Old World typical curry ingredients—shallots, garlic, ginger, turmeric, cumin, coriander, coconut, and anise—are combined with New World peanut oil, peanut butter, tomato paste, *annatto* (achiote), and green chiles to make the basic sauce. To that, more Old World foods are added: *patis* (Filipino fish sauce), Chinese eggplant, carrots, and taro roots. When done, the dish is served accompanied by Old World bananas and New World papayas.

Curries are much more pervasive and important in Japan, but of course, they have a new identity. Marc Matsumoto describes them in his online article "Homemade Japanese Curry": "Typically the mix comes in segmented bars like chocolate that you break off and add to a pot of meat, veggies and water. Japanese curry is sweeter, milder and thicker than Indian curries and used to be one of my favourite dishes growing up." It belongs to a group of foods with origins outside the country called *yohshoku*. Makiki Itoh, writing on the Just Hungry Blog, notes: "Curry is tremendously popular in Japan—it's on the menu at just about every 'family' restaurant and department store restaurant, and there are curry-only restaurants as well as ones that specialize in high class *yohshoku* in general." Called in English "curry rice" because it's always served with rice, she describes it as an "English stew with curry," and totally unlike those in Britain today, which are Indian or Pakistani-based.

"If you've ever been to a Japanese grocery store," she writes, "you've probably seen the blocks or bags of curry base taking up an inordinate amount of shelf space. Competition amongst curry base makers in Japan is fierce." The restaurant leader of Japanese curries is the CoCo Ichibanya chain, with more than 1,200 restaurants around the world, including not only Japan but also China, Taiwan, South Korea, Thailand, and the U.S. Miles Clements, writing about the chain in the *Los Angeles Times*, comments: "Japanese curry is globalization ladled onto a plate, a dish that seeped into the Japanese cookbook not from curry-rich South Asia but from the United Kingdom. There, of course, curry is part of Britain's adoptive identity, still the culinary Indian jewel in its post-colonial crown. Japanese curry is a peculiar hybrid, relatively mild and as thick as gravy yet as recognizable as any from the subcontinent."

Unlike with most Japanese curries, Clements continues, the CoCo Ichibanya chain focuses squarely upon the level of chile heat in ten different gradations based upon the diner's proven ability to enjoy the pungency-giving chemical capsaicin. "The restaurant reserves spice levels six through ten for those with truly masochistic constitutions," he writes, "each of which can be ordered only after you've proved you've finished its predecessor. (You'll be subject to a sincere questioning by a server.)" Other than a tomato garnish and a version of *keema* with bell peppers, chiles are the only New World crops to be found in Japanese curries, which are mostly served over squid, stewed chicken, fried pork *katsu* (a cutlet), tofu, okra, *natto* (fermented soybeans), or eggplant.

The spread of curries comes to a screeching halt in the two Koreas and China. Curries are unheard of in Korea, except, of course, in the occasional Indian restaurant, and so are most New World foods, with the exception of chile peppers and tomatoes, which are the only American crops in the top twenty food products of South Korea, ranked by value. It's far different in North Korea, where potatoes and maize are crops numbers three and four, respectively, and sweet potatoes eighth. South Korea, a far more spicy place, ranks ninth in the world in the production of fresh chiles, probably because it is number one in the world in the per capita consumption of chiles, with an astonishing ten pounds of dried chiles per person, per year.

"Ages to Prepare, Seconds to Consume"

In 2008, *Health* magazine published its brief list of the five healthiest foods in the world, and four out of the five were fermented foods: Japanese soy sauce, Greek yogurt, Indian lentils, and Korean kimchi. (The other was the unfermented Spanish olive oil.)

The author of the article, Joan Raymond, wrote that "[k]imchi (or kimchee) is loaded with vitamins A, B, and C, but its biggest benefit may be in its 'healthy bacteria' called lactobacilli, found in fermented foods like kimchi and yogurt. This good bacteria helps with digestion, plus it seems to help stop and even prevent yeast infections, according to a recent study. And more good news: Some studies show fermented cabbage has compounds that may prevent the growth of cancer." Fermentation is a preservation process that takes a lot of time, hence the Korean expression that reflects how time-intensive many of their recipes are: "Ages to prepare, seconds to consume."

Kimchi, for example, is fermented for weeks, months, or even years, and the longer it ferments, in the words of Mei Chin in "The Art of Kimchi," in *Saveur* magazine, "the stronger its aroma and flavor; stinky is a word we English-speaking kimchi lovers use for the most intense versions, and we say it with the same affection a cheese aficionado feels for a ripe Taleggio. If you can eat it and love it, you are part of the tribe." And the tribe in both Koreas is large and hungry for it: The typical South Korean eats forty pounds of kimchi each year! And that's why in South Korea

Jeotgal, Fermented Seasoned Seafood, and Cubed Radish Kimchi on a Serving Tray in Korea, 2007. Photographer Unknown. Sunbelt Archives.

Chefs Prepare a Huge Amount of Bibimbap at the Festival in Jeonjuk, South Korea. Photographer Unknown. Sunbelt Archives.

their number two crop, after rice, is fresh vegetables used to make this fermented health food, since there are nearly two hundred versions of the dish. And it's not just cabbage used to make it; the ingredients range from oysters to pumpkins to mushrooms to pomegranate.

Chin points out that "as a general rule, kimchi gets saltier and more pungent as you travel from north to south across the Korean peninsula. This makes sense, because in the north the climate is cooler, and it's therefore always been easier to preserve vegetables without heavily salting them and fermenting them for long periods." The cooler climate of North Korea also means that it's a lot easier to grow potatoes, maize, and sweet potatoes that do not thrive further south. Maize is essentially a feed grain for livestock and is not a part of the North Korean diet except as corn flour, but potatoes are because the late ruler, Kim Jong Il, was convinced that new potato varieties would solve his country's food problems much like they did in Germany and Russia. Potato production has increased more than four-fold since 1995, according to the International Potato Center in Lima, Peru, and it occupies half a million acres of farmland in the north.

The New World crops have one thing in common in North Korean cuisine: noodles. Cellophane noodles called *dangmyeon* are made with sweet potato starch, while *olchaengi guksu* noodles are composed of dried corn flour and the chewy *gamjanongma guksu* noodles are made from potato starch.

The best-known dish made from these noodles is *japchae* or *chapchae*, composed of *dangmyeon* stir- fried in sesame oil with such vegetables as sliced carrots, onion, spinach, and mushrooms combined sometimes with beef, sweetened with sugar, flavored with soy sauce, and garnished with thin slivers of fresh chiles.

Because the food in the north is not nearly as spicy as it is in the south, basic dishes made with potatoes and sweet potatoes tend to be bland. Recipes for dishes popular in Gangwon Province, like *kamja guk* (potato soup) and *gamjajeon* (potato pancake), are quite basic and do not contain chiles. Copeland Marks, in his book *The Korean Kitchen*, comments that "Cogumn Boiled Sweet Potatoes are . . . a popular side dish in restaurants and homes" and that sweet potatoes are often eaten as a snack. One unusual sweet potato dish, *goguma chilge muchim*, does not use the tubers but rather sweet potato vines, stripped of their leaves and stir-fried with or without mushrooms as a "side dish that mercifully does not contain hot chili," according to Marks.

Moving south, Marks writes, "[o]ddly, the red color furnished by the chili predominates in Korean food, yet the tomato, which also originated in Central America, did not make the same headway in the Korean lexicon of ingredients and is hardly ever used." If that's true, why is it in the top twenty South Korean food products? I think the answer to that question is that tomatoes are eaten raw in South Korea and are not used in cooking. According to blogger Drew, writing on the TOJ blog, "[T]he only Korean food I've seen them applied to is Kongguksoo, a cold soy bean noodle dish, and they are an arbitrary addition at that; the only other way Koreans really eat slicing tomatoes is by serving them in wedges, sprinkled with sugar, at bars and in brothels and like establishments."

And they are also served at one celebration of the fruit, the Toechon Tomato Festival. Blogger Cindy, writing on the Seoul Adventurer Blog, describes it: "About forty foreigners gathered for a day trip to Gwanju to witness Korea's version of a tomato festival. Korea's Toechon Tomato Festival is child friendly, relatively contained with a mere ton of tomatoes and hosts . . . 10,000 people for the weekend." Tomatoes are a local specialty in Gwanju, and the festival is designed to promote them with displays of different varieties, tasting booths, and a tomato cooking contest. But Marks is right—they're not a popular ingredient in cooking as chile peppers totally dominate New World foods in South Korea cuisine.

"The chili is seen everywhere, drying on the roofs in major cities, or on a bridge crossing a river, on museum grounds in a southwest Korean town," Marks writes. "No spot is sacrosanct when drying the chili." The basic and standard Korean seasoning is *gochu jang*, a fermented chile paste composed of glutinous rice, fermented soybean cake, hot red chiles, salt, and a malt syrup made of barley and water. These ingredients are cooked together, then placed in a jar for a three-month fermentation process. Marks notes that "*gochu jang* provides a sting and a rich red color to the food. Korean cooking without this indispensable condiment is unthinkable."

Gochu jang makes appearances in a wide range of dishes, including *ten chang chigae*, a thick stew of fish, meat, bean curd, and squash; *udong*, a wheat noodle soup with onions, bean curd, and egg; and *bibimbap,* a bowl of warm white rice topped with *namul* (sautéed and seasoned vegetables), a raw or fried egg, and sliced beef. It also is a key ingredient in a snack food sold by street vendors called *tteokbokki.* This is the modern version of a very old dish that is essentially rice cakes stir-fried with a variety of ingredients such as beef, mung bean sprouts, green onions, shiitake mushrooms, carrots, onions, and soy sauce. Further variations of this complicated dish include the addition of boiled eggs.

Tall jars of homemade *gochu jang*, fermenting and mellowing in the sun, interspersed with the kimchi jars, line terraces all across Korea. Although traditional households still prepare their seasonings in this way, the making of *gochu jang* is now a dying art. Today, Korean grocery stores carry small jars of *gochu jang* made from furnace-dried peppers and filled with preservatives and MSG. However, these mass-produced pastes are fairly good, especially when cooks add other spices to them. Commercial *gochu jang* is available in Asian markets in the United States.

And not forgetting the curry diaspora, there is only one province in China with any kind of curry tradition, and that's Yunnan, which shares its southern border with Myanmar, Laos, and Vietnam—all of which have their own versions of curry. Calvin and Audrey Lee, authors of *The Gourmet Chinese Regional Cookbook*, state simply that "[c]urry came to Yunnan from Burma" and give as an example a recipe for Yunnan Lamb with Curry and Black Beans, which shows how Yunnanese cooks flavored their curries with beans and bean sauces.

In the rest of China, E. N. and Marja Anderson observe: "Curry powder and other non-Chinese spices, have, of course, come into Chinese cuisine in the last few decades or even centuries, but they remain very much an alien phenomenon, and Chinese cooks are not comfortable or skilled with them." However, the situation regarding the importance of New World crops is radically different in China as compared to in Korea.

Another Chinese food historian, Frederick C. Simoons, quoted what he says is a common expression in Southeast Asia: "The way to contentment is to live in an American house, to have a Japanese wife, and to employ a Chinese cook." And American foods have played a huge role in why this quote is so common, beginning with a lowly, unpopular root crop that is considered to be "the most marginal of foods," according to Simoons.

The Triumph of the Southern Barbarian Tuber

The unsung sweet potato (*Ipomoea batatas*) beat the real potato (*Solanum tuberosum*) to Europe by nearly a century but was already well established in Polynesia before the round-the-world voyage by Magellan in 1521. From New Zealand to Hawaii to Easter Island, the most remote outposts of Polynesia, the first European explorers to arrive found the sweet potato was the basic food plant grown and eaten in all three locations, much to the bewilderment of later food historians. As with the possible appearance of maize in the Old World prior to Columbus, the sweet potato is even more certainly flaunting the rules of the Columbian exchange. "The sweet potato's pre-Magellanic introduction into Polynesia now seems beyond doubt," writes Jennifer Wolfe in *Sweet Potato: An Untapped Food Resource*. "There are still many conflicting opinions, however, as to exactly how the sweet potato arrived there and to what extent it spread to the west . . . without European influences."

Columbus dined on sweet potatoes on the island of St. Thomas in the Caribbean and noted that they looked like radishes and a kind of bread was made with them. The confusion that exists between the two potatoes can be blamed on two rather famous historical figures. The first, Peter Martyr d'Anghiera, chaplain to the court of Ferdinand and Isabella, called it simply "potato" when he described the nine varieties of it cultivated in Honduras in 1514. The other was John Gerard, who called it the same thing in his *Herball* of 1597.

Around this time the sweet potato entered China through three channels: from Vietnam into two parts of Guangdong province and from Manila into Fujian province in the 1590s. It was called *chin-shu* ("golden tuber") or *fan-shu* ("southern barbarian tuber") and was made widely known in Fukien during the famine

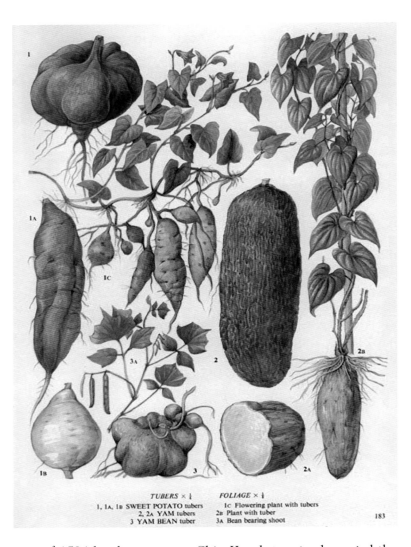

TUBERS × ⅓   FOLIAGE × ⅓
1, 1A, 1B SWEET POTATO tubers   1C Flowering plant with tubers
2, 2A YAM tubers   2B Plant with tuber
3 YAM BEAN tuber   3A Bean bearing shoot

183

Vintage Sweet Potato Botanical Print. Artist Unknown. Sunbelt Archives.

year of 1594 by the governor, Chin Hsueh-tseng, who urged the locals to grow a crop that would feed them when their grain cops failed during times of drought, and sweet potatoes were perfect because they could be prepared in a number of ways for people and also could be fed to chickens, pigs, and dogs, all of which were being eaten. Sweet potatoes were drought- and locust- resistant, and their cultivation took about one-tenth of the work of growing rice. By the middle of the seventeenth century they had spread extensively throughout Guangdong, Taiwan, and Fujian, and they became the primary staple, after rice. They were baked or boiled whole, dried and made into a flour for noodles and steamed cakes that have lasted to this day as a New Year's treat. They were also turned into what was probably a very strange-tasting wine. Other uses included a simple gruel with barley flour and peanut powder, or stirred into a hash with chopped turnips and soybean juice.

Sweet potatoes were valued because they provided more calories than white potatoes or rice—an eight-ounce cup of rice provided 185 calories, while the same amount of sweet potatoes contained 291 calories. The sweet potato became, like the white potato in northern Europe, the basic staple of the small land holder. Anderson states that "sweet potatoes moved from an exotic local-famine relief crop to the staple food of tens of millions in the east and elsewhere." This new crop allowed the population that had reached the limits of its natural resources to expand greatly. The population explosion during the Ch'ing Dynasty began with a population of about one hundred and fifty million people in the early 1700s to triple that by the mid-nineteenth century. Jonathan Spence, in his essay on the Ch'ing, noted that "maize, sweet potatoes, Irish potatoes and peanuts all became basic crops during the Ch'ing and . . . along the rocky Shantung coast sweet potatoes often accounted for nearly half a year's food for the poor." Thus China's rapidly expanding population during this time was similar to that of both Germany and Russia in later times in that they all depended upon New World root crops as their basic food, with the later addition in China of maize.

A budding food historian by the name of Li Hua-nan was a magistrate in Checkiang during the 1750s who took notes on the foods of the time and how the locals prepared them. He recorded the uses of "pork products, fowl, game, fish, eggs, milk and cheeses, sweet dishes and dumplings, sweet potatoes, mushrooms and squash, ginger, preserved plums, and a variety of vegetables such as garlic and radishes, peanuts, greens, and dates," according to Spence. Hua-nan scrupulously recorded all the ways that pig meat could be preserved, and although he didn't single out New World crops for particular attention, he did describe how sweet potatoes were peeled, steamed, and pressed through a rice strainer to remove the fibers. Then the mash was rolled into strips or dried in cake form to preserve them. Peanuts were boiled, reboiled in salted water and stored in it, or were drained and stored in pickle juice.

According to Yi Wang of the International Potato Center in Lima, Peru, there were three major uses of sweet potatoes in China: "as an industrial raw material, as a livestock feed, and as a food in China." He adds that most production areas are in low income, nutritionally poor mountain areas. As grain production has developed rapidly in most regions of China, they are becoming less important as a main food but remain the "major energy source" for the very poor people. Wang adds, "Generally speaking, most sweet potato is used for industrial processing and animal feed and a small portion for human food."

Although the Chinese readily admit that New World crops greatly assisted the population growth and staved off famines, that fact does not mean that the Chinese like to eat all these foods. For example, sweet potatoes were—and still are in many regions—the food of the poorest classes, and to be called a "barbarian tuber eater" was an insult in pre-Communist China. Now, in polite speech, the name has been changed to *kan shu*, or "sweet tuber," but sweet potatoes remain a subsistence food and one that has only found its way into gourmet cooking in a limited manner. Anderson sums it up about these tubers: "Sweet potatoes have never become popular in China; they are regarded as the worst of all foods almost everywhere they grow. They are eaten only in desperation; prosperous families feed their sweet potatoes to pigs."

That was published in 1988; since then, Frederick Simoons, in his book *Food in China: A Cultural and Historical Inquiry* (1991), tracked an increasing usage of sweet potatoes in urban culture, which is food evolution in action. Steamed or roasted sweet potatoes are a common snack sold by street vendors in Beijing and other large cities, and Cantonese Sweet Potato Balls are an appetizer in which the sweet potatoes are boiled, mashed mixed with sugar and flour, made into balls, and deep-fried in peanut oil until golden brown. There are similar recipes for Sweet Potato Croquettes. Simoons even cites a dish formerly served in the imperial court, Fragrant Duck Braised with Sweet Potatoes, and the fact that the Li people of Hainan distill the versatile tuber into a liquor.

I searched a number of Chinese cookbooks listed on Amazon.com and found that dried sweet potatoes are a common ingredient in various dishes, especially soups, stews, and combination dishes where they are cooked with pork or duck in various sauces, and, yes, occasionally curries. I should point out, though, that many of the cookbooks had no mention at all of sweet potatoes or white potatoes, so I would not say that cooks are devoted to them— they are more of a basic ingredient like carrots.

Simoons observes that a number of food historians, including Martin Yang, have noted a progression as families became more affluent: The poor ate sweet potatoes all year long and at every meal; as their family progressed, millet joined sweet potatoes as the staples; and then they quickly went to all millet, then all wheat without any other staples when the family became middle class or even wealthy. A 1956 study of rural communities showed that sweet potatoes accounted for only 12 percent of crop area, but 84 percent of all farm families ate them regularly, and it provided 8.2 percent of their total caloric intake.

Still, the Food and Agriculture Organization of the United Nations statistics for sweet potato production show that China is by far the largest producer in the world, harvesting 81.2 million metric tons in 2010, twenty-eight times the production of the number two harvester, Uganda, with 2.9 million metric tons. The U.S. came in eighth, with 1.1 million metric tons. Sweet potatoes were definitely a needed addition to the calorie supply, but they alone were not completely responsible for the incredible growth of the Chinese population.

A Street Vendor's Handy Sweet Potato Roaster in Qingdao, China. Photograph by Brücke-Osteuropa, 2011. Sunbelt Archives.

White Potatoes, Maize, and the Infinitude of Babies

After the arrival of the New World foods, Chinese food historian E. N. Anderson wrote that "for the first time in Chinese history, root crops became important." He added: "White potatoes, virtually unknown in the Ming, became abundant [in the Ch'ing], owing much of their spread to French missionary activity in the eighteenth and nineteenth centuries." This is contradicted by several food historians who credit the Dutch with their importation, citing the fact that in the south they are still called *ho-lan-shu*, or "Holland tuber."

By the end of the Ming Dynasty (1644), New World crops were important even in the most remote parts of China. Hsü Hsia-ko, who traveled to the remote inland mountains of southern China, reported that the Yao people there were dependent on both potatoes and sweet potatoes. Most food historians agree with the observation that the history of the white potato in China has been local, sporadic—isolated rather than national—and a backup crop at times when grain crops have failed. That said, potato flour is a common thickener in Chinese cooking, and the Chinese eat potatoes much the same way Americans do—roasted, fried, baked, boiled, and french-fried. But wait a minute—are those french fries sold at the hundreds of McDonald's and KFC locations grown in China? Ironically, the answer is no; they're imported frozen from the U.S. because China does not have adequate frozen-potato processing facilities, and it is easier for fast-food franchise owners to import them ready-for-deep-frying.

The importation of American frozen potatoes began in 1997 and has grown very rapidly, with the U.S. supplying 70 percent of China's frozen potatoes in 2006–2007, according to the United States Potato Board. This number is contradicted by the prestigious *American Journal of Potato Research*, which claims the U.S. has a 97 percent share of the Chinese frozen potato market. Whichever number is correct, it is obvious that the U.S. dominates the fast-growing Chinese love for this particular method of potato consumption. Of potatoes produced in China, only about 6 percent go into processing for ingredients like potato flour, 50 percent is used for human consumption, and the rest as animal feed.

That human consumption includes potatoes that are steamed, boiled, or baked, as well as processed into stir-fried potato threads that are probably the most common usage, especially among the elderly. The per capita consumption of potatoes is about 126 pounds, which is high by world standards. This number is contrasted with the U.S. at 138.9, and Belarus with the highest, at an astonishing 379.1 pounds per year. In terms of total production, China leads the world, with total production in 2010 of 74.8 million metric tons. India comes next, with about half that, Russia and Ukraine follow; the U.S. is in fifth place, with about 18 million metric tons. But the growth in Chinese population, much as it was aided by root crops, needed a grain crop to continue expansion.

Alfred W. Crosby, citing Ping-ti Ho's book *Studies on the Population of China, 1368–1953* (1959), notes that although rice production doubled between the years of 1000 to 1850, "the problem of diminishing returns became more and more apparent." Chinese farmers could not keep up with the demand for rice because "China's mothers seemed to have a capacity to produce an infinitude of babies," Crosby writes, "but her land did not have the capacity to produce an infinitude of rice." There was a solution, however, because "even as late as 1700 the Chinese farmer had left largely untouched the dry hills and mountains of the northern two-thirds of China."

Vintage Botanical Print of Maize by Leonhart Fuchs, 1543. Sunbelt Archives.

It was maize that filled the lands empty of crops, and "by the late eighteenth and early nineteenth centuries maize had become the primary food crop in large areas of the uplands of southwest China," writes Crosby. "As the valleys of the Yangtse River and its tributaries filled up with people in the eighteenth century, the excess population, forced up into the hills and mountains, found that maize was the key to extract subsistence from the previously barren highlands." In the northern regions the process took longer, and maize cultivation didn't really take off until the nineteenth century. But the result was the same: a population boom, because maize was feeding the people instead of their livestock, as in the United States but not in countries like Egypt, India, and Indonesia.

Ping-ti Ho noted that rice accounted for perhaps 70 percent of China's total food output in the early seventeenth century, but that percentage changed radically after the introduction of New World crops. "By 1937 the percentage had dropped to about thirty-six percent," notes Crosby. "In the last three centuries the dry land crops, such as wheat, millet, maize, and sweet potatoes, in contrast to rice," in the words of Ho, "have increased to about sixty-four percent, and American food plants alone to approximately twenty percent of the total national food production." And the result has been "a continual growth of population."

This growth is detailed by several historians, and Simoons tracks it: "Early in the Ming period, China's population is estimated to have been about 60 million, virtually the same as at the beginning of the Christian era. Yes, aided by American plants, which arrived late in Ming times and became staples in Ch'ing times, population increased rapidly, to 431 million in

---

Modern Chinese Maize Recipes

Here are some examples of the contemporary uses of maize in Chinese cooking.

Sōng rén ù mǐ, Pine Nuts with Sweet Corn, is a simple, representative dish from the northeast.

Sù mǐ gēng, Sweet Corn Soup, is popular all over the country. I found hundreds of variations of this, so it is probably the most popular incarnation of maize in China.

Yù mǐ lào, Flat Corn Pancakes, one Chinese food blogger writes, is "a popular 'junk food' served at many restaurants."

Also, maize is now incorporated into many mainstream Chinese recipes that previously did not use it, like Sichuan Beef Stir-Fry. Corn oil is one of the most popular vegetable oils, and corn starch is a favored thickener.

1951, and once again, maize was the main food of families with the lowest incomes. Later, maize increasingly became food for livestock." In addition, the increase in the affluence of middle-class Chinese because of industrialization caused a great increase in meat consumption. In 1978, China fed 7 percent of its grain to livestock; in 1990 the percentage was up to 20 percent. The average person in China ate 42 pounds of meat per year in 1980, and that was up to an average of 110 pounds per person by 2007, thanks to maize. China was in second place to maize in worldwide production after the U.S., but it is closing fast as the country's population grows.

Crosby concludes: "It seems more likely that the number of human beings on this planet today would be a good deal smaller but for the horticultural skills of the neolithic American." Since Crosby wrote those words more than forty years ago, the prevalence of New World foods in China has increased beyond his wildest dreams, and the country now exports much of what it grows back to the New World, as we shall soon see.

Dropping Flower Gives Birth and *Lo Chiao* Hot Stuff

Another "lowly" crop that received a warm welcome in China was the peanut, but that welcome took centuries to develop. Various food historians have tried to discover when and where the peanut entered the country, and the theories come down to two possible scenarios: into Fujian (formerly Fukien) in southeastern China through Malaysia or the Philippines, or directly into the southeast China mainland from the port of Macao. The Portuguese would have been the traders who introduced it in either theory. The precise date is not known, but the early sixteenth century is the most likely since by 1700 the peanut was being served as a delicacy at banquets in the region.

It was called *lo hua sheng*, which means "dropping flower gives birth," a reference, as Anderson puts it, to the fact that "the flower produces a pod that plants itself by growing into the earth. The phrase is confusingly shortened to *hua sheng* in ordinary speech." The Chinese grew to like and respect the peanut because it filled niches in the environment not suited for other crops like rice and maize, notably sandy soils, and because it added needed nitrogen to the soil, which is important in crop rotation. They spread slowly, but by end of the nineteenth century, peanuts were common in agriculture and diet throughout the country. They eventually became the most commonly consumed edible nut, even though they're not botanically a nut but rather a legume. Ping-ti Ho included them with white potatoes, sweet potatoes, and maize as the New World crops responsible for the second agricultural revolution in China, the one that led to the "striking increase in population" that continues to this day.

Although there are at least ten varieties of peanut grown in China, the Chinese usually classify them as either large or small. The large ones arrived later and are called, of course, foreign peanuts, and they were the snack foods, usually prepared by roasting and salting or by frying, steaming, or boiling, while the smaller ones were consumed in their raw form, or used as an ingredient in a number of dishes. The peanut stars in one of the most familiar Chinese restaurant dishes in Western culture, the Sichuan *gōng bǎo jī dīng,* or Kung Pao Chicken, in which peanuts, chile peppers, and corn starch are the New World Crops that help create it. Peanuts are commonly used in making candy, cookies, pastries, cakes, and other sweets, and as the Chinese love soups, there are many variations on peanut soup, often quite sweet. Simoons tracked down quite a number of dishes with peanuts combined with other New World crops and found such dishes as Cantonese Duck with Peanut Butter and Pineapple. Spicy peanut sauces are also very popular in China, which brings up the subject of chile peppers.

Of all the New World crops that changed Chinese cuisine—rather than assisting in population growth—the most important by far was the chile pepper. "Brought to the Orient by the Portuguese in the 1500s," writes E. N. Anderson, "these [chiles] did not remain a minor and local part of the diet, as did tomatoes, but swept through the Far East with epochal effect. Perhaps no culinary advance since the invention of distilling had more effect than the propagation of chili peppers in the Old World." Like the Indians with their black pepper, the western Chinese were pre-conditioned to like chiles because they were accustomed to *fagara* (*Zanthoxylum* spp.), the mouth-numbing but spicy, brown "Sichuan pepper" so prevalent in western Chinese dishes. Other common ingredients used to assist *fagara* in spicing up dishes were ginger, cassia, cinnamon, black pepper, star anise, and the superstar of them all.

We cannot underestimate the importance of the chile pepper in China, and no one explains that better than Anderson: "Not only did [*Capsicum annuum*] incalculably benefit the cuisine of all those people civilized enough to accept it, it is also high in vitamins A and C, iron, calcium, and other minerals; is eminently storable and used in pickles; can be grown anywhere under any conditions as long as the growing season is long and warm; and thus is now the world's ubiquitous high-vitamin supplement to grains and other staples, providing what they lack in both taste and nutritional qualities."

Unlike most New World crops, chiles were immediately accepted, particularly in mountainous regions where other high-vitamin crops did not grow well.

The two most probable scenarios for the introduction of chiles into China are either the Portuguese bringing them to Macao from Singapore, perhaps as early as 1515, or, as I wrote in 1990: "[m]ore likely is the theory that chiles were introduced into Sichuan by sixteenth-century Indian Buddhist missionaries traveling the 'Silk Route' between India and China. After all, western Sichuan is closer to India than to either Macao or Singapore." However

Recently Harvested Peanut Plants Stacked by a Village House in the Southern Jiangxia District, City of Wuhan, with Chickens. Photograph by Vmenkov, 2008. Sunbelt Archives.

Kung Pao Chicken Dish Served at a Sichuan Restaurant in Shanghai. Photograph by Steven G. Johnson, 2008. Sunbelt Archives.

they arrived, they rapidly spread throughout southwestern China until they arrived in Hunan, Sichuan, and Yunnan, where according to Anderson again: "Only in these western provinces did chilis achieve the importance they have enjoyed in Korea, Southeast Asian, and India." He added: "Nowhere [else] have they penetrated into ordinary cuisine." That may have been true in the mid-1980s when Anderson was researching his book *Food in China*, but again, the westernizing of Chinese food in the decades since then has changed everything.

Called simply *lo chiao*, or hot pepper, chiles dominated the foods of the region. They were boiled in vegetable oils to make chile oil condiments for stir-frying; they were incorporated with soybeans, garlic, and various spices to make the popular dip, marinade, and condiment known as hoisin sauce that is popular all over China; and as a basic ingredient they were incorporated into many of the most popular dishes of the southwest. In addition to the aforementioned Kung Pao Chicken, they appear in the Hunanese *duò jiāo yú*, Steamed Fish with Chopped Red Chile; in simple dishes like the Sichuanese Sliced Pork with Chile Peppers and *hǔ pí jiān jiāo*, or Pan-Seared Green Chile Pepper; and are prominent in *là zi jī dīng*, or Diced Chicken with Chiles, and *shuǐ zhǔ niú ròu*, Sliced Beef in Hot Chile Oil.

Contrary to Anderson's assertion, chiles appear in northern China in condiments served with staple dishes such as *jiǎo zi*, Chinese Dumplings; Steamed Prawns with Chile Dipping Sauce popular in Canton; and as a main ingredient in *hóng shāo chāng yú*, Braised Pomfret. More commonly in all parts of China,

"Lantern Chile"
(Capsicum chinense)
Purchased at the
Market in Haikou,
Hainan, China. Photo
by Anna Frodesiak,
2005.

commercial chile sauces are found in markets as condiments, and there are quite a few of them that first originated in Sichuan or Hunan. Many of these sauces are available all over China in food markets as packaged products manufactured by companies like Lee Kum Kee. This international Chinese food manufacturer was established in 1888 in Nanshui, Zhuhai, Guangdong Province, and is now headquartered in Hong Kong. It provides more than 220 varieties of sauces and condiments to more than 100 countries and regions across five continents. Here's how that company keeps the spicy traditions of the southwest available all over the country.

Dou ban sauce from Sichuan is made from broad bean or soybean paste with a liberal number of chiles and is called chile bean sauce in English. Lee Kum Kee's version is *toban djan*, or Chili Bean Sauce with identical ingredients. *La jiao* is red chile oil with *fagara* used mainly in cold dishes, and Lee Kum Kee's Chiu Chow Chili Oil is a very similar oil that originated in Chiu Chow. And *guìlín làjiāojiàng* is another oil made of fresh chile, garlic and fermented soybeans that is also called soy chile sauce. Lee Kum Kee's version of this is not an oil but rather Guilin Chili Sauce from Guilin that uses the very hot bird's-eye chiles and is designed for use in stir-frying.

Another factor driving the spread of chile peppers in China is American and Chinese fast-food operations, which Anderson probably couldn't observe in the mid-1980s. McDonald's has opened up 1,100 restaurants in China, second to KFC, who leads all fast-food franchises, with 3,200 locations. There are plenty of other ones, including Pizza Hut, but to give two examples of spiced-up fast food, there are Hot Wings on the KFC menus and Hot and Spicy Chicken Kebabs in Pizza Huts. In terms of Chinese fast food, in Harbin in far northeastern China there is a chain called Oriental King of Dumplings, and on their English menu under "Fresh Vegetables" are the mystifying dishes "Oleaster with Pepper Sauce," "Seald Lettuce with Pepper Sauce," and "Scalding Cymbidium." Oleaster is the species name of wild olive, so maybe these are olives in chile sauce? Maybe "seald lettuce" is a lettuce wrap covered in chile sauce. And since Cymbidium is a genus of orchid, I have no idea what that dish is. But the point is that chile peppers and sauces have traveled from the southwest of China all the way to the far northeast.

But there is another dimension to Chinese chiles. China is now the largest producer of fresh chile peppers in the world, with production nearly seven times that of the next country, Mexico, while with dried peppers China is second, after India. China is exporting massive quantities of dried chiles all over the world, and I was told by food experts in Singapore that most of the chiles in their markets are Chinese. A few years ago I reported on the problems in Mexico caused by Chinese chiles that are nearly identical to popular Mexican favorites such as ancho and pasilla, and *USA Today* reported in 2005 that Chinese chiles now account for one-third of all such peppers consumed in Mexico, according to the National Council of Chile Producers. And there's even more of a problem when we consider Chinese tomatoes.

The Chinese Tomato Paste Scandal

The Chinese food experts E. N. and Marja Anderson tell us how significant New World crops have become in China: "The New World vegetables [and fruits like tomatoes and chiles] stand out as a special class because of their common and recent origin in China and their extreme importance." They go on to point out that white and sweet potatoes have become staples, as has maize. The peanut has become the number one oil-producing crop throughout southern China and was readily accepted into the cuisines. The Andersons explain, "Two other New World crops have transformed southern Chinese (and, indeed, most Old World cooking), the tomato . . . only adopted in the last hundred years ago, and the [chile] pepper [described above]." They add that tomatoes and chiles provided rich sources of vitamins A and C, improving the diet and also contributing "to the rise of China's population and wealth."

When tomatoes first arrived in China in the 1500s, introduced by the Portuguese at their port of Macao, they were called *fan chich*, or "barbarian eggplant," as the originally isolationist Chinese

Tomato Botanical Print by Basilius Besler, c. 1613. Sunbelt Archives.

were wont to do. Simoons notes that there was nothing to suggest that tomatoes were feared in China as they were in Europe, but still it took the Chinese a long time to get accustomed to this crop. And it's only been in the last hundred years that the tomato has been fully embraced by Chinese cooks, especially in the south. Anderson points out that "Western foods were not accepted mindlessly" and that tomatoes and potatoes were gradually worked into various Chinese cuisines, and peanuts were eventually found to be acceptable in baked goods and spicy dishes such as Kung Pao Chicken.

Once again, one of Anderson's observations of the mid-1980s is not particularly accurate today, as China rapidly embraces modern agricultural techniques. "It continues to spread and become more widely accepted in cooking," he wrote of the tomato. "At present, however, it is still primarily a part of urbanized Cantonese cuisine—the area that has been longest and most intimately in contact with foreigners." Obviously, what happened was something Anderson could not predict: that Chinese farmers would move the tomato far beyond a mere addendum to Chinese cookery dependent upon the demand of foreigners and into

another realm—that of a commodity.

Don Cameron, manager of the Terranova Ranch in Helm, California, visited Chinese tomato growers in 2007 and observed then that China was a force to be reckoned with in world tomato production. "They have been only growing processing tomatoes since the mid- to late 1970s," he told Brenda Carol, a reporter for *Western Farm Press*. "They now produce between four and five million tons per year, primarily for paste production. They are the third largest producer, and they are committed to increasing production."

And that they have. The 2010 statistics from the Food and Agriculture Organization of the United Nations reveals that the Chinese producers are now number one in the world in growing tomatoes, and a brief glance at those stats show an astonishing fact: They are not only number one, they are dominant. While the United States produces a respectable 12.9 million metric tons of tomatoes, the Chinese more that tripled that figure, with 41.8 million metric tons! And what do they do with all that production? In the parlance of agriculture, they dump it on the world tomato market. Here's how that works.

In the first place, there are only three areas that are able to process tomatoes: the central valley of California, the Mediterranean coast, and China's Xinjiang province (along with small parts of Inner Mongolia). According to the World Processing Tomato Council, the output of these three areas accounts for 85 percent of the world's total processing capacity. Ninety percent of China's tomatoes are for export, and where would you imagine they export them to? Why not Italy, a country that now worships the tomato in all its forms? And it's not just the Chinese who initiated this "grave and preoccupying phenomenon," in the words of the Calabrian newspaper *Gazzetta de Sud*.

"In the 1990s," writes Arthur Allen in *Slate*, the online magazine, "searching for a cheap product for the export markets,

Italian companies began setting up tomato-processing plants in China to produce paste, which Italian packers repackaged, slapped with 'Made in Italy' stickers, and shipped to Africa." But that backfired when the Chinese noticed, and they were quick to cut the Italians out of the African market by shipping paste directly and cutting the cost to the Africans. They also began flooding the European markets with cheap tomato paste, and in 2002, customs agents in Bari, Italy, seized 160 tons of rotting, worm-infested imported paste. The situation got so bad in 2005 that the headlines in the paper *Corriere della Sera* screamed: "Italy—Invaded by Chinese Tomatoes!" That year, Italian tomatoes rotted in the fields because Chinese paste had lowered the price so much that the tomatoes were not worth harvesting.

China countered by attempting to convince the world that their young people were consuming more tomatoes all the time in ketchup they put on their burgers and the tomato sauce on their pizzas from the burgeoning industry of thousands of American fast-food outlets. Arthur Allen, who heard this comment at a meeting of the World Processing Tomato Council in Beijing in 2007, said to his interpreter: "So the way to save the world's tomato industry is by getting the Chinese to eat more junk food?" His interpreter responded, "You weren't supposed to notice that."

The situation with Chinese tomatoes is just a microcosm of what's happening with Chinese worldwide domination of New World crops. Using the FAO statistics from 2010, the latest available to me in 2012, I examined the major New World crops covered in this book: sweet potatoes, maize, white potatoes, tomatoes, peanuts, pineapples, turkeys, green chiles and peppers, and dried chiles. China dominated seven of those nine crops, with the U.S. number one with just maize and turkeys. I added up the total tonnage of Chinese and U.S. crops and their relative value in international dollars, and the result was shocking. A glimpse at the table in the appendix shows what I mean. China is not just narrowly ahead of the U.S. in terms of most crops; the country is clobbering the U.S. For example, in white potato production, China beats the U.S. 74.8 million metric tons to 18.0. In peanuts, China wins, 15.7 million metric tons to 1.9, and so on with all the crops except maize and turkeys. China will probably never match U.S. turkey production, but with maize, the gap is down to 316.1 million metric tons for the U.S. to 177.5 for China.

What all this means for the economy of both countries and for the world I will leave to experts to squabble over, because I'm not qualified to make any predictions. All I know is that in 520 years, we have progressed from the Columbian exchange to China's throttlehold on the very crops that transformed world cuisines, economies, and histories. At the very least, that's quite an accomplishment for the People's Republic of China.

The Odd New World Crop in China

"Chocolate came into widespread use in China only recently. In June 2004, China's first Salon de Chocolat, an international exposition of fine chocolates was held in Beijing. Chocolate, however, has met significant resistance, especially outside large cities. World Trade Organization figures show Chinese chocolate imports growing from $17.7 million in 1999 to 49.2 million in 2003. The average annual per capita consumption in China is estimated at 0.7 kilogram, below the average of 5.7 kilograms for consumers in the European Union countries. Clearly, chocolate's penetration into Chinese cuisine has historically been peripheral at best and remains problematic even today." —Bertram M. Gordon, writing in *Chocolate: History, Culture, and Heritage*

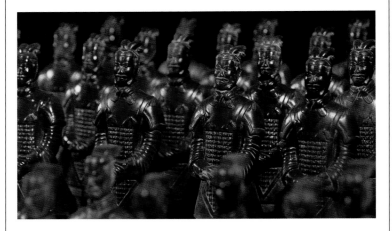

Chocolate Soldiers on Display at Beijing's World Chocolate Wonderland, a Theme Park Dedicated to Chocolate. Photographer Unknown. Sunbelt Archives.

AFTERWORD

The Fate of the Minor Foods

At least Columbus knew his beans. He was the first European to notice that the natives of the New World "have beans of kinds very different from ours." Yet the similarity of New World beans to the beans of the rest of the world, like fava beans, chick peas, lupines, and lentils, initially baffled the herbalists. Historian Lawrence Kaplan noted, "Had herbalists and botanical authors of the succeeding three centuries taken account of Columbus' recognition that these New World legumes were different from those of Europe, some of the confusion might have been avoided."

And the only country where American beans were readily adopted into the cuisine was Columbus's native Italy, although France does have dishes with green beans, *haricots verts*. In Britain, seventeenth- and eighteenth-century cookbooks make no mention of dried New World—or even Old World—beans.

Except for the turkey's popularity in France, Italy, and England, American meats played no roles in world food history, and except for maize, other New World grains and nuts had little impact around the world either. The only American nut that factors into other cuisines is the cashew, a popular ingredient in Indian, Thai, and Chinese cooking. The Chinese love our unique pecans, and China is the number one importer of them. But they've been planting tens of thousands of pecan trees in the past few years since the unshelled nuts became a fad—their resemblance to eggs has some sort of symbolic meaning. Once those trees start producing, after eight years of growth, prices will fall precipitously in the United States. This sort of agricultural cycle has been repeated endlessly.

American fruits like papayas, guavas, and cherimoyas are now grown in the tropics around the world, yet none of them are significant crops like the avocado, with a million tons grown in Mexico, large crops in other parts of the Americas, and cultivation that has spread to Vietnam, Indonesia, parts of southern India, Sri Lanka, Australia, New Zealand, the Philippines, and Malaysia. The U.S. still produces over one-third of all the world's strawberries, and only Spain has a really significant crop of them.

Of the herbs, spices, and flavorings, allspice remains an American crop based in Jamaica, although it is very popular in Middle Eastern cooking. Of the minor foods, only vanilla has achieved worldwide fame because it is such a versatile ingredient and flavoring for ice cream, sweets, and chocolate, and the major world producers, in order of crop size, are Madagascar, Indonesia, China, and Mexico. It is also used in baking, perfume manufacturing, and aromatherapy. But it is not a major crop, just one of the many transferred to the Old World during the Columbus exchange.

And of course, the Columbus exchange is just history now. It's been supplanted by mass globalization because of the incredibly efficient worldwide transportation systems. The quick and easy movement of nearly everything internationally has created an exchange far more complex than the first one. These complicated invasions go beyond food and can be tracked to a certain degree. Think of human, animal, and plant diseases, and invasive species from kudzu to feral hogs.

The story of *Precious Cargo* is just part of the Columbian exchange saga, because the changes went in both directions. We now realize the vast impact of New World foods on the rest of the planet. But the complete story of the monumental effects of European foods on the Western Hemisphere has yet to be told.

ENDNOTES

Prologue: Discovery, Botany, and Food Evolution
"Proponents of localized food production . . . " Kiple, xiv.
"The quest for spices . . ." DeWitt, *Spicy Food Lover's Bible*, 93; Wikipedia,
    "Age of Discovery," online; Williams, 6–8; Bown, 1494, 4–5.
"In 1497–99, Vasco da Gama . . . ." Bernstein, 172–76.
"Technology played a large role . . . " Culver, 71–72; Bernstein, 158.
"Columbus's three ships were caravels . . . " Bernstein, 176; Bown, 3.
"Running parallel with the Age . . . " Egmond, 2.
"Right on the heels of Clusius . . . " Phelps, 76–80.
"Botany was still in its infancy . . . " Ibid.
"Both Clusius and Gerard . . . " Egmond, 3.

Part 1
Spanish Invasions and Strange Foods of the New World

Out of the Ash: The Prehistoric Cuisine of Cerén
"On an August evening . . . " DeWitt, "Out of the Ash," online.
"In 1976, while leveling ground . . . " Ibid.
"Using techniques that were developed . . . " Ibid.
"Dr. Sheets and his students . . . " Ibid.
"Dr. Sheets wrote me back . . . " Ibid.

The Taming of the Wild Chile
"But what kind of chile . . . " Ibid.
"Paleoethnobotanists . . . " Ibid.
"Because chiles cross-pollinate . . . " Ibid.
"It was exciting to think . . . " Ibid.
"The first conclusion I reached . . . " Ibid.

The Cuisine of Cerén
"In addition to the vegetable crops . . . " Ibid.
"Linda Brown, who wrote the 1996 . . . " Ibid.
"It is always a challenge . . . " Ibid.

Columbus and Peppers
"Considering the food that Columbus and his men . . . " Bown, 19–22, 45.
"The ship's biscuit . . . " Bown, 19–22.
"After a diet like that . . . " Cohen, 181.
"Colón continued, 'The Indians. . .' " Cohen, 78, 81, 132.
"Maize, the central ingredient in tamales . . . " Root, *Food*, 235; Sturtevant,
    610; Cohen, 78; Pilcher, 1–23; Cohen, 213–14; Coe, 1994, 12.
"The Spaniards seemed to like sweet potatoes . . . " Cohen, 78, 153.
"Another crop they immediately appreciated . . . " Columbus, 203–04; Cohen,
    121, 156.
"There are several mentions . . . " Cohen, 162.
"Columbus was the first European . . . " Coe, 1994, 43.
"The pineapple moved in the best social circles . . . " Coe, 1994, 42.
"In addition to the pineapple . . . " Coe, 1994, 54.

"And the Columbian Exchange. . . " Smith, 2004, Vol. 2, 175.

Cortés and Turkeys
"Bernal Díaz was excited as the Cortés expedition . . . " *Wikipedia*, "Historical urban community sizes," online; Levy, 106; Thomas, 614; Díaz, 216–219.
"Díaz gushes, 'With such wonderful sights . . . ' " Díaz, 216–219.
"Chronicler of Conquest: Bernal Díaz del Castillo . . . " Cohen, 1963, 7–13.
"The Aztec world revolved around maize . . . " Coe, 1994, 88–94.
"The chile seller . . . sells mild red chiles . . . " Sahagún, quoted in Coe, 1994, 89–93.
"Tomatoes had a similar number of varieties . . . " Ibid.
"Other seafood dishes were common . . . " DeWitt, 1990, 81–83.
"Sahagún, one of the first behavioral scientists . . . " Ibid.
"Aztec cookery was the basis . . . " Ibid.
"The salsas were usually made . . . " Ibid.
"Montezuma's feasts took Aztec cuisine . . . " Díaz, 225–27.
"One of the most popular meats in the Aztec kitchens . . . " Quoted in Eiche, 15.
"Peter Martyr, who wrote a history . . . " Eiche, 12.
"Sahagún wrote that turkeys are . . . " Quoted in Coe, 1994, 96; Eiche, 13.
"The turkey was honored in a festival . . . " Quoted in Coe, 1994, 96; Davis, 35.
"Food historian Andrew F. Smith . . . " Smith, 2006, 8–9.
"In 1541, Francisco de Orellana . . . " Mann, 316–19.
"Mann explains: 'Physical scientists . . . ' " Mann, 320–21.

Pizarro and Potatoes
"'This city is the greatest and finest . . . " MacQuarrie, 110, 113, 123; "Cuzco," 177; Reader, 59.
"At the heart of the Incan Empire . . . " DeWitt, 1990, 74.
"Although farming was the top vocation . . . " MacQuarrie, 45.
"It has been estimated that more kinds of foods . . . " DeWitt, 1990, 74.
"Maize, an ancient crop . . . " Von Hagen, 64; Reader, 57.
"The potato . . . " Zuckerman, 5; Reader, 37–38, 29–30.
"Potatoes might store well . . . " Reader, 38; Zuckerman, 6.
"The great Inca civilization . . . " DeWitt, 1990, 75.
"The Incas worshipped the chile pepper . . . " Ibid.
"According to El Inca, the Incas . . . " Ibid.
"Garcilaso also collected . . . " DeWitt, 1990, 76.
"But food was not the only . . . " Ibid.
"The Incas decorated bowls . . . " Ibid.
"About AD 900, a sculptor . . . " Ibid.
"El Inca, the Historian . . . " Library of José Durand, online.

Between New World and Old
"People who want to rewrite history . . ." Dunmire, 112–13.
"But what the Spanish settlers of Mexico . . ." Dunmire, 113; Super, 32.
"The next Spanish food necessity was meat . . ." Crosby, 1972, 76–77.
"Pork was the first Old World meat . . ." Coe, 1994, 230; Dunmire, 115.

Cortés, Party Animal of New Spain
"After the news of peace . . ." Coe, 1994, 241–42.
"On the morning of the first party day . . ." Ibid.

"The next day the plaza became the island . . ." Ibid.
"Marzipan, candied citron . . ." Coe, 1994, 243–44; DeWitt, 2006, 154–55.

The Lord of Sipán and His Golden Peanuts
"The peanuts of South America . . ." Radthorne, online.
"The peanuts were three . . ." Ibid.
"Alva, who was the director . . ." Ibid.
"The police chased away . . ." Ibid.; Bourget, 227.
"Archaeologists, of course . . ." Bourget, quoted in Anon., *Sex*, online; Anon., *Lord*, online; Stone-Miller, 96–97.
"Supporting Stone-Miller's . . ." Bourget, 148; Jackson, 140–41; Towle, 43.
"In 1988 . . ." Anon., *Lord*, online; Anon., *Order*, online.
"Another theory was unknowingly advanced . . ." Anon., *Alpheus*, online; Verrill, 98.

Between New World and Old
"People who want to rewrite history . . ." Dunmire, 112–13.
"But what the Spanish settlers of Mexico . . ." Dunmire, 113; Super, 32.
"The next Spanish food necessity was meat . . ." Crosby, 1972, 76–77.
"Pork was the first Old World meat . . ." Coe, 1994, 230; Dunmire, 115.

Cortés, Party Animal of New Spain
"After the news of peace . . ." Coe, 1994, 241–42.
"On the morning of the first party day . . ." Ibid.
"The next day the plaza became the island . . ." Ibid.
"Marzipan, candied citron . . ." Coe, 1994, 243–44; DeWitt, 2006, 154–55.

Part 2
The Culinary Century: Turkish Wheat, Indian Chickens, and False Pepper

"The enslaved peoples . . . " Foster and Cordell, xiii.
"What was Europe like . . ." Sokolov, 91–92.
An Exchange Becomes Globalization
"The sixteenth century and a little beyond . . ." Crosby, 1972, 219.
"On the other hand . . ." Weatherford, 102.
"Gradually, scholarly opinion . . ." Kiple, 162.
"These days, the term . . ." Grew, 5; Bernstein, 14.
"So, again, we need a new term . . ." Kiple, xiv.

The Maize Mystery in Europe
"The word 'corn' was a generic term . . ." DeWitt, 2006, 171.
"The Old World reception of New World crops . . ." Foster and Cordell, xiii.
"The national cuisines we find in European countries . . ." Sokolov, 91–92.
"One is Alfred W. Crosby . . ." Crosby, 219.
"On the other hand . . ." Weatherford, 102.
"Gradually, opinion has shifted . . ." Kiple, 162.
"These days, the term . . ." Grew, 5; Bernstein, 14.
"So again, we need a new term . . ." Kiple, xiv.
"There is a commonly held belief . . ." Langer, 59–60.
"Thus maize was eaten . . ." Root, 1980, 238; Tannahill, 205.
"Chile pepper expert Jean Andrews . . ." Andrews, 1999, 15; McCann, 2005, 25.

"Andrews's findings further confuse the issue . . ." DeWitt, 2006, 171.
"In the fall of 1495 . . ." Ibid.
"The appearance of maize in Leonardo's notebook . . ." DeWitt, 2006, 172.
"M. D. W. Jeffreys, in his article . . ." Jeffreys, 23–66.
"Jeffreys believes that . . ." Davidson, 472.
"Or, was maize already established . . ." DeWitt, 2006, 172.

"Turkish Wheat" Enters Society
"It took longer for maize to be recognized . . ." Ibid.; Root, 1992, 76; Tannahill, 205.
"Maize gradually arrived in other parts of Italy . . ." McCann, 67–69; Gentilcore, 19.
"Surprisingly, maize quickly entered the realm . . ." McCann, 69.
"Initially, farmers grew maize because . . ." DeWitt, 2006, 173.
"Maize was being eaten by peasants . . ." Ibid.
"Scappi's Recipe . . ." Ibid.

The Power of Polenta
"Initial resistance to America crops . . ." Root, 1980, 238.
"After the introduction of buckwheat . . ." Ibid.
"But there was a downside to the peasant polenta . . ." Ibid.
"Polenta is an extremely simple dish . . ." Del Conte, 253; Root, 1971, 280.
"And that's what it is . . ." Root, 1992, 280; Del Conte, 253.
"Noted Italian chef Lidia Bastianich observes . . ." Bastianich, 128.
"When the polenta is thick and creamy . . ." Root, 1992, 281.
"Other polenta variations include . . ." Del Conte, 253–54; Root, 1992, 281–82.
"The most unusual polenta recipe recounted . . ." Root, 1992, 281.
"But like many Italian dishes . . ." Kostioukovitch, 296.

Europeans Adopt the "Indian Chicken"
"The 2009 statistics from the Food and Agriculture Organization . . ." Online at http://faostat.fao.org/site/339/default.aspx.
"Historians endlessly debate about when turkeys arrived . . ." Eiche, 15; Smith, 2006, 16.
"Rather, Smith continues . . ." Smith, Ibid.
"Further complicating this issue . . ." Smith, 2006, 17, 15.
"Once turkeys arrived in Europe . . ." Smith, 2006, 15–21; Eiche, 15–17; K. Davis, 28–31, 24.
"That said, the simplest explanation . . ." World Wide Words, www.worldwidewords.org/articles/turkey.htm; Devlin, online.
"Despite the fact that no one knew . . ." Eiche, 22, 26, 71.
"That said, it is no wonder . . ." Eiche, 70–96.
"In this gorgeous and satirical painting . . ." Eiche, 93.

They're Also Good To Eat
"The flavor of turkey meat was first mentioned . . ." Smith, 2006, 9; Coe, 1994, 124.
"Eiche wrote that her research indicated . . ." Eiche, 20; Smith, 2006, 22.
"In 1549, Catherine de' Medici hosted . . ." Flandrin, 359.
"But not everyone was as enthusiastic . . ." Eiche, 49.
"However, Estienne was in the minority . . ." Root, 1992, 538.

"Bartolomeo Scappi, the chef for Pope Pius V . . ." DeWitt, 2006, 44–45; Scappi, 209, 193.

"After Scappi's book appeared . . ." Smith, 2006, 20, 17.

The National Bird and Tales of Truffled Turkeys

"Benjamin Franklin was a champion . . ." DeWitt, 2010, 115.

"But Franklin was a lightweight . . ." Brillat-Savarin, 1854, 105–108.

"In his essay on truffles . . ." Brillat-Savarin, 1854, 126, 108.

"And that's an astonishing figure . . ." Drouard, 264, 273, 266.

"Besides these noble aims . . ." Drouard, 264–66, 274.

"*Chefs de cuisine* originally worked . . ." Shore, 305; Anon., "The Chef," online.

"Turkey Roasted with Truffle . . ." Beauvilliers, 154.

"Thus the turkey played a key role . . ." Eiche, 42.

"And Alexander Dumas . . ." Ibid.

"Dumas did not stop . . ." Eiche, 43.

"Even musicians were touched . . ." Anon., "Tasting Truffles," online.

Turkey Traditions Today

"The United Kingdom is seventh in the world . . ." FAO, 2009, online; Wilson, 130; Anon., "Christmas Dinner," online.

"These days, approximately ninety percent . . ." Anon., "UK Christmas Traditions," online; Devlin, online.

"For Christmas in 2008, holiday revelers . . ." Anon., "Christmas Statistics and Traditions," online; Anon., "Christmas Facts," online.

"In Italy, the world's fifth largest producer . . ." Di Conte, 100, 207; Root, 1992, 437.

"A town in the province . . ." Root, ibid.; Di Conte, 207.

"In northern Italy, the turkey is known . . ." Di Conte, 335, 191.

"Perhaps the interesting turkey roasting . . ." Field, 238–39.

"Since turkey breasts are far more common . . ." Anon., "Involtini alla salvia," online.

"Moving on to the number three. . ." Zoschke, personal communication; Zentralverband der Deutschen Geflügelwirtschaft, online.

"German food expert Harald Zoschke. . ." Zoschke, ibid.

"We can trace the heritage of a recipe like this . . ." Grasse, online; Zoschke, ibid.

"He went on to tell me that stuffing . . ." Zoschke, ibid.; Eiche, 25.

"Ever since 150 turkeys . . ." Eiche, ibid.

"But they're not so aggressive . . ." Barrell, ibid.

"However, Licques is not the epitome of French . . ." Ibid.

"But even that event . . ." Ibid.

"During the 1960s . . ." Black, 90.

"Bantam Books published . . ." Garvin, 81.

"*Dinde aux marrons* . . ." Garvin, 81–82.

How Paprika Conquered Hungary

"As impressive as the turkey's infiltration. . ." Halász, 33.

"Since Columbus was working for the Spanish royalty . . ." DeWitt, 1984, 171; Katz, 214; Lang, 128.

"It was at this point that paprika appeared . . ." Halász, 14; DeWitt, 1999, 219.

"Tomatoes, however, made an early appearance. . ." Lang 30, 32, 315–16.

"The most likely scenario . . ." DeWitt, 1999, 220.
"So, sometime between 1538 and 1548 . . ." DeWitt, ibid.; Halász, 30.
"In 1569, an aristocrat named Margit Szechy . . ." DeWitt, ibid.; Halász, 25–26.
"After the settlement of this dispute . . ." Halász, 26; Lang, 130.
"During this time . . ." Lang, ibid.
"Capsaicin, the chemical that makes chile peppers hot . . ." Lang, 131.
"Lang notes that the nobility . . ." Lang, 131–32.
"It wasn't until 1844 . . ." Ibid.
"Around this same time . . ." Gentilcore, 79–80, 92, 97–98.
"Today, the great pepper-growing areas . . ." Hudgins, 24.
"Types of Hungarian Paprikas . . ." DeWitt, 1999, 222.
"In Kalocsa, the annual harvest . . ." Ibid.
"With regards to paprika . . ." Lang, 133.
"So how do those tons of newly picked peppers . . ." Hudgins, 25–27.
"But until the mid-1800s . . ." Ibid.
"The Palfys' invention made possible . . ." Ibid.
"Ferenc Horvath of Kalocsa . . ." Ibid.
"In the Hungarian countryside . . ." DeWitt, 1999, 221.
"Food authority Craig Claiborne has noted . . ." Ibid.
"Paprika has exerted a great influence . . ." DeWitt, 1990, 176–77.
"For a country of just ten million people . . ." FAOSTAT, online.

The Peperoncino-Eating Contest: A Burned-Out Theater of the Absurd
"It took a long time . . ." DeWitt, Da Vinci, 169.
"Since Columbus was responsible . . ." DeWitt, Da Vinci, 189.
"The Accademia Italiana del Peperoncino . . ." DeWitt, Peperoncino, online.

Part 3
Exotic, Strong, and Often Intoxicating: New Drinks and Flavorings

Sugar's Possible Origins
"During the fifteenth century . . . " Bernstein, 205; Root, 1980, 494, 488; Schumann, 13.
"And the history of sugar . . ." Mintz, 113, 139; Bernstein, 267; Wilson, 303; Root, 1980, 488.
"That fuzziness is directly related to the fact . . ." Root, 1980, 488–90; Mintz, 140; Macinnes, xix.

Columbus and Cane
"In 1424, Henry the Navigator . . ." Ponting, 482; Macinnes, 25.
"It was only natural that the Portuguese . . ." *Wikipedia*, "Sugar," online; Macinnis, 31.
"Columbus reported that the cane . . ." Root, 1980, 490; Mintz, 35.

When Sweetness Sours: Sugar and Slavery
"The European 'invasion' of the Americas . . ." Mann, 2011, 11–12.
"One thing the Europeans . . ." Root, 1980, 491; Heuman and Walvin, 78.
"Africans were the obvious choice . . ." Macinnes, 35; Mintz, 43.
"As the development of sugar plantations grew . . ." Tannahill, 219; Mintz, 36, 53, 33.
"Barbados was nearly completely cleared . . ." Bernstein, 269; Tannahill, 219.

"The complicated trade patterns . . ." Mintz, 43.
"These triangular trading scenarios . . ." DeWitt, 2010, 33; Bernstein, 271.

Rumbullion: The Value-Added American Liquor
"The story of rum begins and ends. . ." Barty-King and Massel, 68.
"The origin of the word 'rum'. . ." Schumann, 12.
"Although most West Indies planters . . ." Barty-King and Massel, 82; Parker, 82;
    Ligon, 80; Schumann, 13.
"Rum had other uses . . ." Standage, 108.
"All visitors remarked on the planters' heavy drinking . . ." Kupperman, 26;
    Macinnis, 58.
"While visiting the Mount Gay Visitor Center . . ." DeWitt, "Bonney Barbados,"
    online.
"Rum was also a signature value-added product . . ." Higman, 126.
"Its power to intoxicate quickly . . ." Bernstein, 271, 274; Standage, 104–05,
    111; Coulombe, 3.
"Because rum, unlike beer and wine, . . ." Macinnis, 101; Schumann, 12;
    Standage, 108–09.
"It's nearly impossible to write about rum . . ." English, online; Wilson, 400.
"Pirates, on the other hand, . . ." English, online.
"Charles Coulombe, the author of *Rum, ...*" Coulombe, 75–77.
"Far away from the Royal Navy . . ." Parker, 297.

Queen Elizabeth's Teeth and the Sugar Poet
"And these luxury stimulants . . ." Mintz, 38–39.
"The popularity of sugar . . ." Tannahill, 219; Mintz, 44, 45, 73, 39.
"One of features of the English sugar-eating character . . ." Macinnis, 45;
    Barham, 31–33.
"Sugar's rise to glory inspired poetry . . ." Macinnis, 89–91.

The "White Spice" in British Cookery
"From early on, cooks in England . . ." Wilson, 298–99.
"In the 1570s . . ." Flandrin, 384; Wilson, 300–01; Mead, 56.
"But there were more practical uses . . ." Wilson, 301; Mintz, 125.
"Two factors delayed this transformation . . ." Mintz, 125–26; Wilson,
    301–02.
"The ever-increasing popularity of sugar . . ." Macinnis, 82–83.
"To make little fine Cakes . . ." Glasse, 284.
"Soon after Glasse's cookbook was published . . ." Mintz, 133, 6.
"In 1772, Lord Chief Justice Mansfield declared . . ." Macinnis, 117–19.
"Slavery in the British Empire was officially abolished . . ." Macinnis,
    123–27; Mintz, 197.

The Ultimate Flavors: Chocolate and Vanilla
"In 1921, archaeologist Neil M. Judd . . ." Edgar, 24–25; Bower, online.
"Crown's next step was to team up . . ." Ibid.

Chocolate for Turquoise?
"By studying ancient North American trade routes . . ." DeWitt and Gerlach,
    1990, 137.
"The *pochteca* established . . ." Ibid.

"The connection between the Southwest . . ." Ibid.
"Archaeologist Dorothy Washburn . . ." Bower, online.

Aztec Origins, New Spanish Drinks
"An evergreen tree that produces . . ." Root, 1980, 550.
"Bernardino de Sahagún, the Spanish chronicler . . ." Coe, 1996, 91–92.
"The cacao beans were not only used . . ." Coe, 1996, 98–99.
"In the Aztec world, both cacao and vanilla . . ." Bray, 88, 149–50; Coe, 1996, 89–93, 101.
"The conquering Spanish adopted . . ." Abbott, 74; Coe, 1996, 108–09, 115, 112.

A New Medicine for Spain
"Contrary to popular belief . . ." Coe, 1996, 130–133.
"To the Spanish in Spain . . ." Coe, 1996, 126; Weinberg and Bealer, 55.
"Historian Marcy Norton notes . . ." Norton, 666–67.
"Between 1544, when chocolate first arrived . . ." Weinberg and Bealer, 55; Norton, 670.
"And this accident enabled the Spanish . . ." Weinberg and Bealer, 56.

Italy's Perfumed Chocolate
"Italy was next for chocolate the conquerer . . ." Coe, 1996, 140.
"But the introduction of chocolate into Italy . . ." Coe, 1996, 141–42.
"Meanwhile, in 1664, a Roman physician . . ." Coe, 1996, 142–43; Weinberg and Bealer, 56.
"In Florence, Redi was tending . . ." Coe, 1996, 146–47.
"Redi was a busy man . . ." Coe, 1996, 147–49; Rain, 54.

The Chocolate Seduction of France
"When the Spanish princess Maria Theresa . . ." Coady, 30; Coe, 1996, 158; Abbott, 74.
"But is this story of chocolate history in France . . ." Gordon, "Chocolate in France," 570–71.
"His protestation was countered . . ." Ibid.
"And the 'secrecy' of chocolate . . ." Ibid.
"Chocolate was making gains in popularity in Versailles . . ." Gordon, "Chocolate in France," 571–72.
"Louis XIV was forced to end . . ." Coady, 31–32; Gordon, "Chocolate in France," 172.
"In 1657, a Frenchman opened a shop . . ." Root, 1980, 72; Weinberg and Bealer, 57–58; Schivelbusch, 92.
"The chocolate parlors in London . . ." Coady, 36; DeWitt, 2010, 41 ff.
"Hannah Glasse's famous cookbook . . ." Root, 1980, 552; Hess, vii.
"How to Make Chocolate, by Hannah Glasse . . ." Glasse, 357.
"Chocolate arrived in Hanover . . ." Coady, 32; Weinberg and Bealer, 57.

Cacao Becomes Cocoa
"In the 1854 translation of the French edition . . ." Brillat-Savarin, "Physiology," 143; Weinberg and Bealer, 59.
"Food chemist Harold McGee . . ." McGee, 696.
"Before this invention . . ." Weinberg and Bealer, ibid.; Schivelbusch, 93.

"Chocolate technology evolved quickly . . ." McGee, ibid.; Weinberg and Bealer, ibid.; Gordon, "Commerce," 589–90.

"The Coes wrote that 'Baroque Europe' . . ." Coe, 1996, 177–78; Weinberg and Bealer, 60; FAOstat, online.

"In 2008, the International Cocoa Organization . . ." One Golden Ticket, online.

"Chocolate is certainly one . . ." Harald Zoschke, personal communication, October 10, 2011.

"When it comes to chocolate bars . . ." Ibid.

"A smaller but increasing . . ." Ibid.

Chocolate vs. Vanilla

"To complete the story of chocolate . . ." National Confectioners Association, online.

"Focusing just on ice cream consumption figures . . ." NPD Group, online; Adwan, Euromonitor, online.

"Synthetic Vanilla . . ." Vanilla and Spices of PNG online.

"So it would appear that within the huge ice cream market . . ." FAOstat, 2009, online.

American Coffee, Featuring the Return of Slavery

"The tale of coffee as an adopted American crop . . ." Ukers, 6–9.

"The date was 1723 . . ." Ibid.

"In Paris, he discovered . . ." Allen, 161; Weinberg and Bealer, 241; Ukers, ibid.

"De Clieu and the coffee plant . . ." Allen, 161–62; Ukers, ibid.;Weinberg and Bealer, 242.

"Historian Wild points out . . ." Wild, 124; *Wikipedia*, "History of Martinique," online.

"Another romantic account . . ." Weinberg and Bealer, 242; Wild, 172–73.

The Great Soberer

"Before coffee was transferred . . ." Davidson, 201.

"Coffee, via Venetian merchants . . ." Weinberg and Bealer, 68; Pendergrast, 8.

"After that, the exact date . . ." Ibid.

"It's popularity in Paris . . ." Davidson, ibid.

"The first coffeehouse in London . . ." Weinberg and Bealer, 77, 154; Pendergrast, 9; Visser, 297.

"But that was not always the case . . ." Snodgrass, 236; Pendergrast, 13.

"This was the 'first wave' of coffee . . ." Schivelbusch, 21–22, 35.

The Second Wave of Coffee

"Around the time that de Clieu . . ." "History of Coffee," online; Grant, 37; Pan American Union, 56.

"Slavery expert David Brion Davis . . ." Davis, David, 112; Allen, 1999, 173.

"Mark Pendergrast in *Uncommon Grounds* . . ." Pendergrast, 18.

"But the tide was slowly turning . . ." Ullathorne, online; Cowper, 202.

"Cowper was part of the coffeehouse scene . . ." Webb, 169; Ukers, 88.

"If the coffeehouses had one outstanding achievement . . ." Standage, 163–65.

Goethe and the Discovery of Caffeine

"Most people know that Johann Wolfgang von Goethe . . ." Anon., "Goethe," online; Weinberg and Bealer, xvi.

"Goethe was friendly with the famous chemist . . ." Weinberg and Bealer, xvii.
"At Goethe's house . . ." Weinberg and Bealer, xvii–xix.
"'You are forgetting your *famulus*. . .'" Weinberg and Bealer, xix.
"Inspired by his meeting with Goethe. . ." Weinberg and Bealer, xix–xxi.

The Decline of Coffee in England
"Much is made over the dates . . ." Davis, David, 233–34; Bernstein, 278.
"In England, tea from China . . ." Schivelbusch, 81; Allen, 1999, 198.
"England didn't possess any tea-producing colonies . . ." Allen, ibid.;
    Schivelbusch, 83.
"The price of tea . . ." Schivelbusch, ibid., 79; Burnett, 77.
"Coffee's decline was further exacerbated . . ." Schivelbusch, 62; Weinberg and
    Bealer, 173–74.
"England turned to tea . . ." Weinberg and Bealer, 180; Anon., "Coffee
    Consumption," online.
"And if we examine the top ten . . ." FAOstat, online.

Part 4
Venerous Roots, Poisonous Love Apples, and the King of Fruits

"New World foods like maize . . . " Ollivander, 208.
"As for the tomato . . ." Cohen, online; Root, 1980, 511.
"He is gentler with the potato . . ." Heiser, 33; Smith, *Potato*, 22; Root, 1980, 386.
"With reputations like those . . ." Root, 1980, 378.

The Spud Migration East
"As with many of the New World plants . . ." Hawkes and Francisco-Ortega, 1–7.
"Since several other researchers had suggested . . ." Ibid.
"As the potato arrived in the various ports . . ." Smith, Potato, 22; Reader,
    77–78, 111; Root, 1980, 383.
"The French didn't see anything erotic . . ." Allen, Devil's Garden, 133; Root,
    1980, 378.
"The Italians considered the potato . . ." Gentilcore, 18; Root, 1992, 36.
"John Reader, in his book *Potato*. . ." Reader, 108–09, 111.
"It wasn't until the eighteenth century . . ." Reader, 114–17.
"Wars were another reason . . ." McNeill, 72; Reader, 118.
"In England, potatoes slowly . . ." Wilson, 217; Root, 1980, 383.
"It was a far different story in Ireland . . ." Root, 1980, 382.

Ireland's "Lazy Roots" Rot
"The story of how potatoes arrived in Ireland . . ." Reader, 136; Root, 1980,
    380.
"To corroborate the tale . . ." Lee, 190; Reader, 84.
"Then I noticed that many historians . . ." Anon., Notes and Queries, 195; Root,
    1980, 380.
"But we do know that sometime . . ." Anon., *The Independent*, 389; Zuckerman,
    29–30.
"And the biggest racist of all . . ." Allen, Garden, 134–35; Zuckerman, 98–99.
"Cobbett believed that wheat bread . . ." Ibid.
"What was really happening behind the scenes . . . " Allen, Garden, 135–36.
"By 1815, Ireland's population had swelled . . ." Reader, 161.

"In September of 1845 . . ." Reader, 163; Zuckerman, 194.

"I don't have the space here . . ." Anon., Monoculture, online; Anon., Industrial Agriculture, online.

"Considering flavor first, in his famous . . ." Brillat-Savarin, Gastronomy, 177–92.

"Brillat-Savarin found potatoes so insipid . . ." Ibid., 271.

"He charms his way into joining . . ." Ibid.; Turgeon, 766, 913.

Parmentier: From Prisoner to Potatohead

"In 1762, the foremost potato promoter . . ." Anon., "Introduction of the Potato," 622; Anon., "The Potatoes of Parmentier," 280.

"Parmentier was born in 1727 . . ." Ibid.; Zuckerman, 82.

"In 1748, the Besançon *parlement* . . ." Toussaint-Samat, 717; Zuckerman, 82; Reader, 120.

"By this time Parmentier was a pharmacist . . ." Touissaint-Samat, 718; Anon., "Introduction of the Potato," 623.

"Louis XVI visited the field . . ." Ibid.; McNeill, How the Potato, 78.

"Farmers descended upon the field . . ." Anon., "The Potatoes of Parmentier," 280; Reader, 122; McNeill, 78.

"Parmentier continued his promotion . . ." Anon., "Introduction of the Potato," 623; Reader, 121; DeWitt, *Foodies*, 118.

"The King told Parmentier that . . ." Reader, 122; Touissant-Samat, 723.

"Parmentier was among the first . . . " Reader, 122; "The Potatoes of Parmentier," 280; Zuckerman, 85.

"Even his recipes live on . . ." Touissaint-Samat, 723.

"Perhaps the ultimate form . . ." Touissaint-Samat, 723, 725–26.

Tubers of War

"In his essay . . ." McNeill, "How the Potato," 82.

"Between 1750 and 1850 . . ." Langer, 51–54.

"The timing of the potato . . ." Mann, Eyes, 94–96.

"But that didn't mean that people . . ." Reader, 119; Langer, 54; Anon., "The Potato," online.

"The invading countries began . . ." Reader, 119, 124, 129.

"When the Habsburg monarchy in Prussia . . ." Anon., "War of the Bavarian," online.

"Russia was the last major country . . ." Munro, 37; Langer, 54, 58; Kiple and Ornelas, online.

"That happened in Russia . . ." Langer, ibid.; Kiple and Ornelas, online; Croddy and Wirtz, 10.

"The story was quite different . . . " Grivetti, et al., Food, 130.

"In the 1930s, Russia . . ." Langer, 58; Kiple and Ornelas, online.

"Based on the experiences . . ." Salaman, 576; Dowling, 67.

"Meanwhile, the British army . . ." Dowling, ibid.

"According to Walter Moss . . ." Moss, 224.

"A wartime magazine call *Rabotsna* . . ." Moss, 225, 80, 59.

"Even the German prisoners of war survived . . ." Spiller, 161.

"When the potatoes ran out . . ." Moskoff, 348; Anon., "Soviet Union," online; Anon., "World War II Casualties," online.

"One of the Soviet Republics . . ." FAOStat, 2005; Anon., "World War II Casualties," ibid.

Naples, the Birthplace of the Italian Tomato
"'Tomato sauce,' writes John Dickie . . ." Dickie, 172.
"When the Italian *scalco* Antonio Latini . . ." Gentilcore, 50–52.
"Just sixty-three years before . . ." Gentilcore, 14, 50.
"Dickie is not as impressed . . ." Dickie, 172–73.
"An unpublished manuscript of a recipe collection . . ." Gentilcore, 52–54; Grewe,
    74.
"The next time tomatoes appear . . ." Gentilcore, 55–56; Dickie, 173.
"Pomidori alla Napolitana . . ." Gentilcore, 61.
"Religious orders continued Corrado's . . ." Gentilcore, 56–57.
"Interestingly, Corrado wrote another book . . ." Dickie, 175–76.
"On the island of Sardinia . . ." Gentilcore, 58–59.

Tomatoes Meet Pasta and Pizza
"Food historian Silvano Serventi . . ." Serventi, 165; Gentilcore, 89–90.
"The next step took place . . ." Gentilcore, 78, 90.
"Tomato sauce recipes started appearing . . ." Serventi, 266.
"It was Artusi who broke free . . ." Gentilcore, 97–98.
"Waverly Root notes that . . ." Root, Italy, 499–500; qtd. in Pollack, 15; Dickie,
    199–200; Riley, 270–271.
"Such practices probably led to . . ." Capatti and Montanari, 27.
"Other the other hand . . ." Dickie, 200; Gentilcore, 94.
"Toward the end of the nineteenth century . . ." Gentilcore, 91–92.
"That's because she has her own pizza . . ." Gentilcore, 92–93; Dickie, 200–01.
"Margherita loved the last one . . ." Ibid.
"Despite unification, pizza was slow . . ." Dickie, 202–09.
"But soon it was King Umberto . . ." Dickie, 209–10, 208.
"But Margherita's hygiene . . ." Dickie, 209–10.
"We all know what happened . . ." Baugniet, 6–7.
"So, finally, what hath the tomato wrought . . ." Capatti and Montanari, 33.

Lust for Plants
"Human beings are collectors of every object . . ." Anon., "Tulip Mania," online.
"The lust for this particularly beautiful plant . . ." Ibid.; Frankel, online; Benschop,
    et al., online.
"Other plant manias over the centuries . . ." Smith, *The Tomato*, 132–34.

"It Tastes like a Raspberry—No, Make That a Melon."
"So I completely understand what the Europeans . . ." Root, 1980, 356; Beauman
    2005, 22, 52–53, 127.
"The best thing he ever tasted . . ." Coe, 42.
"After the pineapple arrived in Europe..." Beauman, 2005, 52–53.
"David Hume said essentially the same thing . . ." Beauman, 2005, 53, 76; Ripley, 528.
"Pineapples fit neatly . . ." Conniff, 196–97.
"By the mid-1720s . . ." Beauman, 2005, 76, 78, 85, 87, 97; Okihiro, 89.

The Pineapplehead Politician
"John Murray, the Fourth Earl of Dunmore . . ." Anon., "John Murray," online.
"In 1730 (some sources say 1750) . . ." Okihiro, 164; Beauman, 2005, 86.
"A year after a pineapple was installed . . ." Okihiro, ibid.; Root, 357; Beauman,
    2005, 131–32.

"The appeal of the fruit spread . . ." Olmert, online.

"Back in Scotland . . ." Anon., "Dunmore Pineapple," online; Okihiro, 86.

"Around this same time . . ." Beauman, 2005, 111; Olmert, online.

"In 1767, William Wrighte's . . ." Beauman, 117, Okihiro, 164; Anon., "Jeffersonian Dinners," online; Kimball, 89.

"A year later, George Washington . . ." Washington, online; DeWitt, *Foodies*, 80, 87.

"Back in England . . ." Beauman, online; Weston, 78; Blackley, 35.

"Lord Dunmore didn't spend all his time . . ." Anon., "John Murray," online; Guy, online; Anon., "Dunmore's Proclamation," online.

"As the violence increased . . ." Ibid.; Anon., "Battle of Great Bridge," online.

"Dunmore fled to New York . . ." Anon., "John Murray," online.

Symbol of Status, Faith, or Hospitality? Or All of Them?

"Fran Beauman commented . . . " Beauman, online; Beauman, 2005, 89.

"Since money is power . . . " Beauman, 2005, 88, 92, 114.

"The pineapple was also a symbol . . ." Olmert, online.

"In 1666, with St. Paul's Cathedral . . ." Weaver, online.

"The pineapples at the tops . . ." Anon., "St. Paul's Cathedral," online; Hogarth, 23.

"The pineapple in America . . ." Beauman, online; Anon., "Myth #12," online.

"And what was the sign . . ." Beauman, 2005, 115; Lausen-Higgins, online; Beauman, online.

"Beauman explains . . ." Beauman, online.

Part 5
Of *Kenkey*, Chop, *Piri-Piri*, and the Testicle Tree

"The importance of American foods in Africa . . . " Crosby, 1972, 185.

Mungo Park Meets Mealie

"In 1795, Mungo Park, a Scottish surgeon . . ." Maclachlan, 50.

"But he couldn't get home . . ." Park, 271–72.

"Food historians reading this . . ." Park, 15–16.

"Park was correct—the *kouskous* . . ." Mous, 157; McCann, 2009, 48.

"In terms of corn's cultivation . . ." Park, 14; McCann, 2005, 50.

"Park continues his agricultural description . . ." Park, 280; McCann, 2005, xi.

"And corn was grown differently . . ." McCann, 2009, 47–50; McCann, 2005, 46.

"Not only did the tribal woman . . ." Park, 296.

"The hospitality enabled Park . . ." Anon., "Mungo Park," online; Maclachlan, 128.

"Another one of Park's biographers . . ." Thomson, 255, 282; Boyle, back cover.

Flying Under the Cookbook Radar

"Today in South Africa . . ." Osseo-Asare, 60; McCann, 2009, 49–50; McCann, 2005, 197.

"And this was a process . . ." McCann, 2009, 139; McCann, 2005, 198–99.

"McCann points out that . . ." McCann, 2009, 139; Weinzweig, online.

"I checked the recipes . . ." Binns 118–119; Harris 173–77.

"Even my coauthors and I . . ." DeWitt, *Africa*, 65, 204; McCann, 2009, 49.

"*Green Corn*, by Emily G. Bradle . . . " Bradley, n.p.

From *Kenkey to Ablemamu*: The Gold Coast Goes Gourmet
"In order to describe the many uses . . ." Sandler, 148, 101.
"Purees sound primitive . . ." Sandler, 49; Osseo-Asare, 119, 74; Snodgrass,
    291–92.
"The evolution of maize . . ." Anon., Ghana, online; McCann, 2009, 49.
"Fran Osseo-Asare firmly believes . . ." Osseo-Asare, "Ghana-ktyle," online;
    Anon., "Kenkey," online; Anim-Antwi, online.
"Writing in *The World Is a Kitchen* . . ." Polgreen, 139–40.
"But why was the *kenkey* . . ." Bartle, online; Mollison, 20.
"The next evolutionary stage . . ." Anon., "Maize Flour," online.
"Miss Spears's Ablemamu Baking Powder Bread . . ." Saffery, 284.
"*The Ghana Cookery Book* was originally . . ." Anon., *The Ghana Cookery
    Book, Books for Cooks*, online; Anon., *The Ghana Cookery Book*, amazon.
    com, online.
"Another review more clearly explains . . ." Anon., "Complete Guide to Ghana,"
    online; Osseo-Asare, "Update," online; Canvin, online.
"What the book reveals . . ." Saffery, xii–xv; Leipoldt, *Food & Wine*, 289.
"Maize or 'miele' bread . . ." Leipoldt, *Food & Wine*, 289, 291.
"In Darkest Chocolate . . ." FAOStat, online; Anon., "Chocolate Facts," online;
    L Pierre, 59.

How the Testicle Tree Reinvented African Salads
"What, you ask . . ." Montgomery and Nabwire, 40.
"David Saffery observes . . ." Saffery, xxix; Ali, x.
"But the food of the colonizers . . ." Sellick, 10.
"Mayonnaise is the perfect example . . ." Harris, 119.
"Harris writes that . . ." Harris, 102–03; FAOStat, online.
"Commercial avocado-growing . . ." Whiley, et al., 3; "Tropical Fruit GIS," online.
"Patrick Karanja is such a farmer . . ." Koigi, online.
"And how are Karanja's avocados . . ." Anon., "Salads," online.
"Other avocado salads include . . ." Harris, 116; Anon., "Kachumbari," online.

Bathurst, the Pineapple Capital of South Africa
"To celebrate its favorite fruit . . ." Anon., "Big Pineapple," online.
"Locals claim that . . ." Anon., "Bathurst," online.
"This is all very nice . . ." FAOStat, online.

When Senegal Struck Peanut Oil
"When the peanut farmer . . ." Root, 1980, 329; Anon., "Goober Pyle," online.
"But sources differ . . ." Root, 1980, 330; Anon., "Goober Pyle," online; Anon.,
    "Chocolate-coated," online; Hamilton, 2; Flandrin and Montanari, 459.
"The French soap-making industry . . ." Smith, *Peanuts*, 66; Klein, 37; Flandrin
    and Montanari, ibid.; Hamilton, 2.
"Gorée and St. Louis . . ." Smith, *Peanuts*, 66–67; Anon., "Introduction of the
    Groundnut," online; Klein, ibid.; Johnson, 95.
Captain Conneau, the Slave-Trading Food Historian
"I am no longer surprised . . ." Campbell, *Edible*, 236.
"His memoirs were first published . . ." Google Books, online; Mouser, 101;
    Dirks, online.
"For a slave trader . . ." Conneau, *A Slaver's Log Book*, 1; Conneau,
    Revelations, 10, 81.

"In the first half . . ." Conneau, *Revelations*, 34.

"The captain, as he later became . . ." Conneau, *Revelations*, 144, 132.

"He found that the main style . . ." Conneau, *Revelations*, 102.

"Ever curious, Conneau . . ." Conneau, *Revelations*, 124, 176–77.

"African Bush Meat Dinner Menu . . ." Simmonds, 78.

"Even though English was not . . ." Conneau, *Revelations*, 140, 143; Bierce, 135.

"There's a very simple reason . . ." Van der Post, *Cooking*, 67–69,

"Many of the stews contained peanuts . . ." Conneau, *Revelations*, 115; Conneau, *A Slaver's Log Book*, 117.

The Gooberization of Africa

"Although they had not read . . ." Snodgrass, 251; McCann, 2009, 146.

"Van der Post writes . . ." Van der Post, *Cooking*, 64.

"The semi-anonymous author . . ." Quinn, "A World of Nutrition in Peanuts," online.

"One of the earliest accounts . . ." Nipperdey, 484.

"In later years . . ." Arfman, online.

"According to Elizabeth Melville . . ." Melville, n.p.

"Most modern versions . . ." Anon., "The Toppings," online.

"By far, the most unusual topping . . ." Anon., "Our Reporter", online.

"Today, Nigeria . . ." FAOStat, online; Anon., "Our Reporter", online.

"Two other former British colonies . . ." FAOStat, online; Anon., "Agriculture in Senegal," online.

A Continent of Chiles and Curries

"The high priest of African chiles . . ." Van der Post, *Eland*, 243–44; van der Post, *Cooking*, 122.

"I should have written . . ." Anon., "Laurens van der Post," *Wikipedia*, online; van der Post, *Eland*, 1–2.

"He had an inspiration . . ." Ibid.

"Chile peppers are ubiquitous . . ." Anon., "Africa," Wikipedia, online.

"According to the 2009 . . ." FAOStat, online.

Pili-Pili and the Pods Themselves

"Since the Arabic countries . . ." DeWitt, *Africa*, 2–3.

"Although chiles probably . . ." DeWitt, *Whole Chile*, 178–81.

"By 1482 . . ." Ibid.

"The most likely scenario . . ." Ibid.

"African birds fell in love . . ." Ibid.

"A nineteenth-century traveler . . ." Monteiro, 293.

"This bird-planting cultivation . . ." DeWitt, *Whole Chile*, 182–83.

"The famous and notorious . . ." Anon., African Birdseye, online."

"Reputedly, the hottest . . ." Cameron, 263.

"*Pili-Pili* has become . . ." DeWitt, *Africa*, 2.

From Harissa to Berbere: The Hot Sauces

"A complex and powerful . . ." DeWitt, *Whole Chile*, 191.

"A similar spice paste . . ." DeWitt, *Whole Chile*, 198

"Laurens van der Post . . ." Van der Post, *Cooking*, 37; DeWitt, *Encyclopedia*, 7.

"Identical to *berbere* . . ." DeWitt, *Bible*, 125; DeWitt, *Africa*, 26.

"Captain Conneau mentioned . . ." DeWitt, *Bible*, 122.

"Among the Yoruba . . ." Bowen, 300.

"In Ghana..." Bryden, 93.

"A famous African food . . ." Van Der Post, *Eland*, 244–45.

"As we have seen . . ." DeWitt, *Bible*, 122–23.

"Hot sauces take three forms . . ." Ibid.; van der Post, *Cooking*, 141.

"Other sources revealed . . ." DeWitt, *Bible*, 123.

"The other two South African . . ." Ibid.; van der Post, *Cooking*, 140–41; Snyman, online.

"Curiously, *blatjangs* . . ." DeWitt, *Bible*, 123–24.

"Van der Post once . . ." Van der Post, *Cooking*, 140; Leipoldt, *Food & Wine*, 391.

Pungent North African Spice Mixtures and Curries

"The North African housewife . . ." DeWitt, *Curries*, 170–72, 180; Hemphill, 347–48; 367.

"Less controversial curry mixtures . . ." DeWitt, *Curries*, 172–73.

"The most famous North African . . ." Ibid.

"In 1902 . . ." Meakin, 91.

West to East: Curries Get Hotter

"Over in West Africa . . ." DeWitt, *Curries*, 173.

"Another distinguishing characteristic . . ." DeWitt, *Curries*, 173–74.

"The famous African traveler . . ." Burton, *Wanderings*, 145–46.

"What Sir Richard Burton . . ." Burton, *Regions*, 88.

"East African foods . . ." DeWitt, Curries, 176.

"Curries are also important . . ." Ibid.

"Ethiopia is one of those . . ." Mesfin, xix; Winn, personal communication.

"Even the butter . . ." DeWitt, *Curries*, 177.

"Laurens van der Post . . ." Van der Post, *Cooking*, 37–38; DeWitt, ibid.

Ambrosia from the Cape

"There is an oft-repeated quote . . ." Leipoldt, *Food & Wine*, 241; van der Post, *Cooking*, 132–33; Wikipedia, "Indian South Africans," online.

"The Dutch had colonized . . ." DeWitt, *Curries*, 166–67; Leipoldt, *Cape*, 13.

"Late in the seventeenth century . . ." DeWitt, ibid.; van der Post, *Cooking*, 153–54.

"The Cape Malays . . ." DeWitt, *Curries*, 167–68.

"Johanna's curry probably . . ." DeWitt, ibid.; Anon., Wikipedia, "South Africa," online.

"Curries in Southern Africa . . ." Sellick, 73, 215; Leipoldt, *Food & Wine*, 240.

At Last, a Professional African Food Historian

"We have seen budding . . ." Anon., "Leipoldt," online; Leipoldt, *Cape*, 11.

"Leipoldt left South Africa . . ." Murray, online.

"Dr. Peter Shileds . . ." Emslie, online; Leipoldt, *Cape*, 129; San Diego Zoo, online.

"Brian Lello . . ." Lello, 10.

"Leipoldt's cookbook . . ." Lello, 9; Human and Rousseau, online; Leipoldt, *Cape*, 34–35.

"Laurens van der Post . . ." Van der Post, *Eland*, 283, 286; Leipoldt, *Cape*, 73–74.

"*Bredie* is a spiced-up stew . . ." Leipoldt, *Cape*, 71–76; van der Post, 136–37, Leipoldt, *Food & Wine*, 347.

How Curries Could Have Killed Apartheid
"Trevor Emslie . . ." Emslie, online.
"Laurens van der Post . . ." Van der Post, *Eland*, 435–36.

Part 6. Sir George and the Curry Diaspora

"If you can't trust . . ." Anon., "George Watt (Botany)," online.
"Sir George will be our Virgil . . ." Watt, Abridgment, viii.

Embracing a New Spice in the Land of Pepper
"There can be no doubt . . ." Watt, *Abridgment*, 265; Collingham, 51.
"When the Portuguese arrived . . ." DeWitt, *Whole*, 204.
"Under the leadership . . ." Ibid.
"After their introduction . . ." Watt, *Dictionary*, 139.
"In his abridgment . . ." Watt, *Abridgment*, 267, 266; Watt, *Exhibited*, 43.
"K. T. Achaya . . ." Achaya, 227–28.
"Both Achaya and Lizzie Collingham . . ." Achaya, 228; Collingham, 53;
   Andrews, *Trail*, 25.
"The very observant Sir George . . ." Watt, *Abridgment*, 266; Achaya, 228.
"Watt and Achaya both . . ." Banerji, 25, 58.
"Despite that ubiquity . . ." Collingham, 71, 53; DeWitt, *Curries*, 33.
"Three hundred years later . . ." Watt, *Dictionary*, 137; DeWitt, *Whole*, 211.
"In fiery south India . . ." DeWitt, *Whole*, 211–212; Spaeth, n.p.
"Hot and spicy food . . ." Ibid.
"Other parts of India . . ." Banerji, 64, 11; Collingham, 53.
"In Goa . . ." Collingham, 68–69; DeWitt, *Curries*, 46.
"In some regions . . ." DeWitt, *Whole*, 206–207; DeWitt, *Curries*, 33.
"And India is burning. . ." FAOStat, online.

How the Hottest Chile Pepper Reached India
"I'm working on . . ." Balfour, Vol. 1, 577.
"My first thought . . ." Anon., "George Harris," online.
"Lord Harris was the most . . ." Ibid.
"I toured those 62-acre gardens . . ." Ibid., "Pemberton," online.
"I tried to discover . . ." Prestoe, online.
"Was the origin of the name . . ." Balfour, Vol. 2, 46; Monier-Williams, 240.
"To prevent these ghosts . . ." Frazier, 133.
"All of the ghost speculation . . ." Bhagowati, 171; Zoschke, online.
"I have tried in vain . . ." Watt, Products, 267; Balfour, Vol. 1, 682.
"Today, researchers in Trinidad . . . " See complete coverage of these superhot
   chiles in numerous articles at www.fiery-foods.com.

An Apple That's Not an Apple, and Likewise for a Potato
"To compile his *Dictionary* . . ." Watt, *Dictionary*, 238; Small, 408.
"Indian food expert . . ." Achaya, 233.
"Sir George tracked their spread . . ." Watt, *Abridgment*, 67.
"It was the flavor . . ." Watt, Products, 13.
"I have not yet discovered . . . " Sharma, online; Anon., "Maui's Winery,"
   online.
"Pineapples were popular . . ." Pogson, 172; Watt, *Dictionary*, 238.

"This comment might explain . . ." DeWitt, *Curries*, 54; Bladholm, 209; Banerji, 210.

"As with chile peppers . . ." Johari, 31.

"Writers on Indian pineapple cultivation . . ." Shrivastava, 110–11; Brunner, 197; FAOStat, online.

"If Indians were confused . . ." Mazumdar, 60.

"For example . . ." Mazumdar, 60–61.

"Food historians pay a lot of attention . . ." Watt, *Exhibited*, 100.

"Waverly Root writes . . ." Root, *Food*, 498; Achaya, 199; Sahni, 93; Bhide, 22; Kapoor, 606.

"To my thinking . . ." FAOStat, online.

Aloo and Moongphali: More Delicacies from Beneath the Earth

"Why did it take so long . . . " Mazumdar, 62, 71.

"Sir George wrote about the potato . . ." Watt, *Exhibited*, 173.

"Potato historian R.N. Srivastava . . ." Srivastava, 4; Pogson, 82.

"Srivastastava explains how . . ." Srivastava, ibid.; Achaya, 226.

"Governor-general Warren Hastings . . ." Collingham, 165; Srivastava, ibid.

"In the twentieth century . . ." Swaminathan, 169; FAOStat, online.

"Pogson, writing in 1872 . . ." Pogson, ibid.; Watt, *Abridgment*, 688, 1030.

"In fact, those uses . . ." *Indian Cookery*, 33; Murdoch Books,16, 23, 40.

"From around the states of India . . ." Panjabi, 148, 166. 168.

"Another major underground crop . . ." FAOStat, online.

"Sir George had this . . ." Watt, *Dictionary* 1, 283; Watt, Abridgment, 74, 82.

"Today in India . . ." Krishna, 419–22; Shilling, ix.

"Sir George mentioned . . ." Watt, *Dictionary* 1, 287; Watt, *Exhibited*, 17.

"Today, the culinary uses . . ." Krishna, 422.

"Although not a major factor . . ." Shilling, ibid.

The Question of Pre-Columbian Maize and the Souring *Tamata*

"When it comes to pre-Columbian . . ." Johannessen, "Pre-Columbian," online; Johannessen, "Vita," online.

"Hopefully, these humans had Transporters . . ." Mangelsdorf, 413–22.

"Other scholars have lined up . . ." Payak and Sachan, 202; Mundkur, 676.

"Maize was not immediately accepted . . ." Watt, *Abridgment*, 1133.

"In his book *Economic Products* . . ." Watt, *Exhibited*, 194.

"Today, India is fifth . . ." FAOStat, online; Anon., "Maize," online; Anon., "Maize Basic," online; Bladholm, 50–51.

"I searched many Indian cookbooks . . ." Banerji, 69; Batra, n.p.

"Much more distinctive . . ." Watt, *Exhibited*, 105; Jaffrey, 231; Chapman, India, 189.

"By 1906, tomatoes . . ." Willis, 399.

"As in Europe . . ." *Indian Cookery*, 82, 30, 35, 77.

"331.—Tomato or Love-apple Chutnee . . ." *Indian Cookery*, 77.

"Nineteenth-century tomatoes . . ." Collingham, 166,149; DeWitt, *Curries*, 53; Banerji, 115–16, 119, 82, 182, 207.

"The famous Indian chef . . ." Sahni, 4, 266–67, 208, 233, 440–41; Chapman, *India*, 189 ff.; Jaffrey, 252.

"In 2009, India . . ." FAOStat, online; Costa and Heuvelink, 10.

Curry Defined, Over and Over Again

"Chitarita Banerji has trouble . . ." Banerji, 38, 79, 260.
"One of the most intriguing theories . . ." DeWitt, *Curries*, 2.
"Hall was dead wrong . . ." Ibid.
"Curry in its twentieth century . . ." DeWitt, *Curries*, 3–5.
"Such worship of curry . . ." Ibid.
"Perhaps the most outlandish . . ." Ibid.

Curries with the Crops of the New World

"No one really knows . . ." DeWitt, *Curries*, 34.
"The food of southern India . . ." Ibid., 34–35.
"New World crops shine . . ." Ibid., 53–55.
"Curries developed in Sri Lanka . . ." Ibid., 37–38.
"Sri Lanka's reputation . . ." Ibid., 38–39.
"White curries are considerably milder . . ." Ibid., 38.
"Moving on to northern India . . ." Ibid., 68–69; 97.
"West Bengal, in the far eastern part . . ." Ibid., 71.

The Curry Diaspora

"Lizzie Cunningham, in her book . . ." Cunningham, 245–246; DeWitt, *Curries*,
    197, 222, 226.
"Other Pacific locations . . ." DeWitt, *Curries*, 197.
"Another reason, of course . . ." Ibid., 198; Cunningham 248–49.
"Although curries in some form . . ." DeWitt, *Caribbean*, 5.
"Because the East Indians . . ." DeWitt, *Curries*, 199.
"The curry powder capital . . ." Ibid., 200.
"Every imaginable foodstuff . . ." DeWitt, *Callaloo*, 25.
"Sophisticated citizens . . ." Ibid.
"The east Indian population of Jamaica . . ." DeWitt, *Curries*, 201–202.
"The most popular curry dish . . ." DeWitt, *Curries*, 202–203.
"In the early days . . ." DeWitt, *Curries*, 203.
"In the French Antilles . . ." Ibid, 202.
"And the curry diaspora . . ." Cunningham, 247; Willinsky, 7, 37.
"The diaspora did not end . . ." Keane, online.
"In the 1950s . . ." DeWitt, Curries, 209.

The Mating of the Old World with the New

"Meanwhile, back in India . . ." Banerji, xi.
"She describes these melded meals . . ." Banerji, xvi; xv; 94; 115.
"My personal experience . . ." DeWitt, *Fiery Fast Food*, online.
"In the Mewari language . . ." Ibid.
"Before leaving India . . ." Benerji, 260;
"But if you want a pizza . . ." Prasso, online.
"My final reference to Sir George Watt . . ." Knapp, online.

Part 7
The Fiery "Vegetable Civilizations" of Asia

"Alfred W. Crosby, that pessimistic expert . . . " Crosby, Columbian, 199.

"Burn Your Lips and Remember My Dinner": Golden Triangle Curries
"Now called Myanmar . . . " DeWitt, *Curries*, 106–07.
"The oil is not skimmed off . . . " Ibid., 107–08, 123–25, 133.
"In contrast to the diminished pungency . . . " Ibid., 109–110, 115–16.
"The variety of Thai curries . . . " Thompson, 274.
"Mussaman Curry Paste . . . " DeWitt, *Curries*, 110, 116.
"New World crops are plentiful . . ." Ibid., 109–110, 121, 124, 130; FAOStat,
    online.
"In Cambodia . . . " Ibid., 112–13, 117, 120.
"Richard provided me . . . " Ibid., 112, 120, 122.
"In nearby Laos . . . " Ibid., 113–14, 129.
"Laos represents a culinary division . . . " Ibid., 114, 126, 132.

The Isles of Spice and Curries from "Excellent" to "Bizarre"
"The original Spice Islands . . . " DeWitt, *Curries*, 136.
"Today, Malaysia, Indonesia, and Singapore . . . " Ibid., 138–39, 142.
"Harvey Day, author of *Curries of India* . . . " Ibid., 142; Passmore, 172, 246.
"The basis of the Spice Islands' curries . . . " Ibid., 142, 149.
"The *sambals* are the start . . . " Marsden, 56.
"Marsden went on to describe . . . " Marsden, ibid.; DeWitt, *Curries*, 143.
"Often, as many as fifty or sixty dishes . . . " DeWitt, *Curries*, 143.
"A wonderful description . . . " Knox, Second, 348.
"Knox continued his Far East . . . " Knox, Third, 99.
"Another humorous curry description . . . " Marryat, 129.
"In 1888 . . . " Caddy, 241–42.
"This description is from . . . " Ibid.
"In all fairness . . . " Cameron, A. Mackenzie, 28.

Tiffin in Singapore, Rijsttafel in Sydney, and *Yohshoku* Curry Bars in Tokyo
"Sir Thomas Stamford Raffles . . . " Raffles, 98.
"There is no mention . . . " Hahn, 225–26, 190.
"This bit of doggerel . . . " Anon., "Tiffin," online; Anon., "Tiffin Room," online;
    Kipling, 234.
"I learned more about tiffin . . . " DeWitt, *Curries*, 146.
"Nearly all of the curries . . . " FAOStat, online.
"Sir Stamford Raffles . . . " Raffles, 123; Owen, *passim*; DeWitt, Asian, 52.
"Peanuts are found . . . " DeWitt, *Asian*, 146, 173, 66, 138; DeWitt, *Curries*,
    226.
"Pineapples also make an appearance . . . " DeWitt, *Asian*, 56, 58, 25; Anon.,
    "Rojak," online.
"Sweet potatoes are even sweeter . . . " Owen, 201; 211; DeWitt, *Asian*, 72, 237,
    242; DeWitt, *Curries*, 150.
"Finally, tomatoes . . . " DeWitt, *Asian*, 23, 108, 175.
"I finally became a guest at a Rijistafel Banquet . . . " DeWitt, *OZ*, online.
"Cocktails and starters were served . . . " Ibid.
"The Batavia Rijistafel Banquet . . . " Ibid.
"Later, Carol took us to Cabramatta . . . " Ibid.
"The Philippines and Japan . . . " Brennan, 58.
"Here's how that happened . . . " Anon., "Geography of Indonesia," online;
    Anon., "Geography of the Philippines," online.
"Joshua Ligan, writing online . . . " Ligan, online.

"Curries are much more pervasive . . . " Matsumoto, online; Itoh, online.
"If you've ever been to . . . " Itoh, ibid.; Clements, online.
"Unlike most Japanese curries . . . " Clements, ibid.
"The spread of curries . . . " FAOStat, online; Park, *Korean*, online.

"Ages To Prepare, Seconds To Consume"
"In 2008 . . . " Raymond, online.
"Kimchi, for example . . . " Chin, online; Raymond, ibid.; FAOStat, online.
"Chin points out . . . " Chin, ibid.; Kim, 80; Anon., "Potatoes," online.
"The New World crops . . . " Anon., "Korean Noodles," online; Anon.,
    "Japchae," online.
"Because the food in the north . . . " Anon., "Gamjajeon," online; Marks, 54, 66.
"Moving south . . . " Marks, 4; Anon., Drew, online.
"And they are also served . . . " Anon., Cindy, online.
"The chili is seen everywhere . . . " Marks, 4, 9.
Gochu jang makes appearances . . . " Popham, 52; Anon., "Bibimbap," online;
    Anon., "Tteokbokki," online.
"Tall jars of homemade . . . " DeWitt, *Encyclopedia*, 177; Marks, 26.
"And not forgetting the curry diaspora . . . " Lee and Lee, n.p. (ebook).
"In the rest of China . . . " Anderson, *Modern China*, 332; Simoons, 43, 122.

The Triumph of the Southern Barbarian Tuber
"The unsung sweet potato . . . " Wolfe, 17.
"Columbus dined on sweet potatoes . . . " Root, 1980, 496–98.
"Around this time . . . " Anderson, 79; Mazumdar, 66–67; Spence, 262.
"Sweet potatoes were valued . . . " Mazumdar, 68; Anderson, 94; Spence, 263.
"A budding food historian . . . " Spence, 265.
"According to Yi Wang . . . " Wang, 4–5.
"Although the Chinese readily admit . . . " Anderson, 122.
"That was published . . . " Simoons, 123.
"Frederick Simoons observes . . . " Simoons, 122.

White Potatoes, Maize, and the Infinitude of Babies
"After the arrival . . . " Anderson, 94; Simoons, 124.
"By the end . . . " Anderson, 80; Simoons, 124.
"The importation of American . . . " Anon., "Anything Is Possible," online; Cee
    and Theiler, online.
"That human consumption . . . " Anon., "Anything Is Possible," online;
    FAOStat, online.
"Alfred W. Crosby . . . " Crosby, 1972, 198–99.
"It was maize that filled . . . " Ibid.
"Ping-ti Ho noted . . . " Crosby, 1972, 201–02.
"This growth is detailed . . . " Simoons, 77; Anon., "Land," online; FAOStat,
    online.
"Modern Chinese Maize Recipes . . . " Anon., "Chinese Food," online; Anon.,
    Chris, online.
"Crosby concludes . . . " Crosby, 1972, 202.
Dropping Flower Gives Birth and *Lo Chiao* Hot Stuff
"Another lowly crop . . . " Anderson, 125; Simoons, 280; Chang, 27.
"It was called . . . " Anderson, ibid.; Simoons, 280–81.
"Although there are at least ten . . . " Simoons, 281–82.
"Of all the New World crops . . . " Anderson, 131; Simoons, 52.

"We cannot underestimate . . . " Anderson, ibid.
"The two most probable . . . " Simoons, 386; DeWitt, *Whole Chile*, 275; Anderson, 131–32.
"Called simply *lo chiao* . . . " Anderson, 132; Simoons, ibid.; Anon., "Chinese Food," online.
"Contrary to Anderson's assertion . . . " Anon., ibid.; Anon., "Hot Sauce," online; Anon., "Lee Kum Kee," online.
"*Dou ban* sauce . . . " Anon., "Hot Sauce," online; Anon., "Lee Kum Kee," ibid.
"Another factor driving . . . " Anon., "KFC," online; Anon., Karen, "Foraging," online.
"But there is another dimension . . . " FAOStat, online; Hawley, online.

The Chinese Tomato Paste Scandal
"The Chinese food experts . . . " Anderson and Anderson, 328–29.
"When tomatoes first arrived . . . " Anderson, 129, 131; Anderson and Anderson, 328–29.
"Once again . . . " Anderson, 131.
"Don Carmeron, manager . . . " Carol, online.
"And that they have . . . " FAOStat, online.
"In the first place . . . " Anon., "Analysis of Tomato," online; Allen, Arthur, online.
"In the 1990s . . . " Allen, Arthur, ibid.
"China countered . . . " Ibid.
"The situation with New World tomatoes . . . " FAOStat, online.
"The Odd New World Crop in China . . . " Gordon, 600–01.

Afterword: The Fate of the Minor Foods

"At least Columbus . . . " Abala, 135–36.
"And the only country where American beans . . . " Abala, 139–148.
"Except for the turkey's popularity . . ." *Wikipedia* online, FAO crop reports.
"Of the herbs, spices, and flavorings . . . " Ibid.

BIBLIOGRAPHY

Abala, Ken. *Beans: A History*. Oxford: Berg, 2007.

Abbot, Elizabeth. *Sugar: A Bittersweet History*. New York: Penguin Books, 2010.

Achaya, K. T. *Indian Food: A Historical Companion*. Delhi: Oxford University Press, 1994.

Adwan, Lyla. "Vanilla—Ice Cream's Enduring Flavour." Online at the Euromonitor Blog, http://blog.euromonitor.com/2002/08/vanilla-ice-creams-enduring-flavour.html.

"African Society." *Journal of the African Society*, Vol. 1 (October). London: Macmillan & Co., 1901.

Ali, Barlin. *Somali Cuisine*. Bloomington, IN: AuthorHouse, 2007.

Allen, Arthur. "Kitchen Diplomacy in Red China." *Slate*, Nov. 12, 2007, www.slate.com/id/2177831.

Allen, Stewart Lee. *The Devil's Cup: A History of the World According to Coffee*. New York: Ballantine Books, 1999.

—. *In the Devil's Garden: A Sinful History of Forbidden Food*. New York: Ballantine, 2002.

Anderson, E. N. *The Food of China*. New Haven, CT: Yale University Press, 1988.

Anderson, E. N., Jr., and Marja L. Anderson. "Modern China: South." *Food in Chinese Culture*. Ed. K. C. Chang. New Haven: Yale University Press, 1977.

Anderson, Edgar. *Plants, Man, and Life*. Berkeley: University of California Press, 1967.

Andrews, Jean. "Diffusion of the Mesoamerican Food Complex to Southeastern Europe." *Geographical Review*, Vol. 83, No. 2 (Apr. 1993) 194–204.

—. *The Pepper Trail*. Denton, TX: The University of North Texas Press, 1999.

Anim-Antwi, Benjamin. "Taste of Africa: Kenkey." *C.R.E.A.T.I.V. Blog*, online at http://creativafrica.weebly.com/1/post/2011/10/taste-of-africa-kenkey.html.

Anon. "Agriculture in Senegal." *Wikipedia*, online at http://en.wikipedia.org/wiki/Agriculture_in_Senegal.

Anon. "Alpheus Hyatt Verrill." *Wikipedia*, online at http://en.wikipedia.org/wiki/Alpheus_Hyatt_Verrill.

Anon. "Analysis of Tomato Sauce Industry in China, 2008." *Fresh Plaza*, online at www.freshplaza.com/news_detail.asp?id=32820.

Anon. "Batata." *The Free Dictionary*, online at www.thefreedictionary.com/batata.

Anon. "Battle of Great Bridge." *Wikipedia*, online at http://en.wikipedia.org/wiki/Battle_of_Great_Bridge.

Anon. "Bibimbap." *Wikipedia*, online at http://en.wikipedia.org/wiki/Bibimbap.

Anon. "Big Pineapple." Online at www.bathurst.co.za/Interest.htm.

Anon. "'The Chef' (Encyclopedia of Food & Culture)." *eNotes*, online at www.enotes.com/food-encyclopedia/chef.

Anon. "Chinese Food." *Travel China Guide*, online at www.travelchinaguide.com/intro/cuisine_drink/cuisine.

Anon. "Chocolate-coated Peanut." *Wikipedia*, online at http://en.wikipedia.org/wiki/Chocolate-coated_peanut.

Anon. "Chocolate Facts." *Divine Chocolate*, online at www.divinechocolate. com/about/resources/facts/ghana.aspx.

Anon. "Christmas Dinner." *Wikipedia*, online at http://en.wikipedia.org/wiki/ Christmas_dinner.

Anon. "Christmas Statistics and Traditions." *I Love British Turkey*, online at www.britishturkey.co.uk/turkey-bytes/christmas-facts.shtml.

Anon. "Coffee consumption Per Capita." *EarthTrends*, online at http:// earthtrends.wri.org.

Anon. "Complete Guide to Ghana." *Squidoo.com*, online at www.squidoo. com/ghana.

Anon. "Dunmore Pineapple." *Wikipedia.*, online at http://en.wikipedia.org/ wiki/Dunmore_Pineapple.

Anon. "Dunmore's Proclamation." *Wikipedia*, online at http://en.wikipedia. org/wiki/Lord_Dunmore%27s_Proclamation.

Anon., Chris. "Flat Corn Pancake." KungFuEats. Online at www.kungfueats. com/2010/02/flat-corn-pancake.

Anon., Karen. "Foraging for Food in Harbin, China." *Meathook Blog*, Mar. 30, 2011, online at http://offthemeathook.com/tag/winter.

Anon. "Gamjajeon." *Wikipedia*, online at http://en.wikipedia.org/wiki/ Gamjajeon.

Anon. "Geography of Indonesia." *Wikipedia*, online at http://en.wikipedia. org/wiki/Geography_of_Indonesia.

Anon. "Geography of the Philippines." *Wikipedia*, online at http:// en.wikipedia.org/wiki/Geography_of_the_Philippines.

Anon. "George Harris, 3rd Baron Harris." *Wikipedia*, online at http:// en.wikipedia.org/wiki/George_Harris,_3rd_Baron_Harris.

Anon. "George Watt (Botany)." *Wikipedia*, online at http://en.wikipedia.org/ wiki/George_Watt_(botany).

Anon. "Ghana." *Wikipedia*, online at http://en.wikipedia.org/wiki/Ghana.

Anon. "The Ghana Cookery Book." *Books for Cooks*, online at www. booksforcooks.com.au/ghana-cookery-book-p-22548.html.

Anon. "Goober Pyle." *Wikipedia*, online at http://en.wikipedia.org/wiki/ Goober_Pyle.

Anon., Cindy. "Gwanju Toechon Tomato Festival." *Seoul Adventurer Blog*, Aug. 16, 2011. http://seouladventurer.wordpress.com/2011/08/16/gwanju-toechon-tomato-festival.

Anon. "History of Coffee." *Food Info*, online at www.food-info.net/uk/ products/coffee/hist.htm.

Anon. "Hot Sauce." *Wikipedia*, online at http://en.wikipedia.org/wiki/Hot_ sauce.

Anon. "In China Anything is Possible." *United States Potato Board*, June 24, 2008, online at www.potatoesusa.com/articleDetail.php?id=6.

Anon. "Indian South Africans." *Wikipedia*, online at http://en.wikipedia.org/ wiki/Indian_South_Africans.

Anon. "Industrial Agriculture: Features and Policy." *Union of Concerned Sciences*, online at www.ucsusa.org/food_and_agriculture/science_and_ impacts/impacts_industrial_agriculture/industrial-agriculture-features. html.

Anon. "The Introduction of the Groundnut to the Gambia." *Afrol News*, online at http://afrol.com/archive/groundnuts_gambia.htm.

Anon. "Introduction of the Potato into France." *Harper's New Monthly*

Magazine, Vol. IV (Dec. 1851–May 1852). New York: Harper Brothers, 1852, 622–24.

Anon. "Involtini alla salvia." *MyCityCuisine.org*, online at www.mycitycuisine.org/wiki/Involtini_alla_salvia.

Anon. "Japchae." *Wikipedia*, online at http://en.wikipedia.org/wiki/Japchae.

Anon. "Jeffersonian Dinners." *Monticello.org*, online at www.monticello.org/site/research-and-collections/jeffersonian-dinners.

Anon. "Johann Wolfgang von Goethe." *Wikipedia*, online at http://en.wikipedia.org/wiki/Johann_Wolfgang_von_Goethe.

Anon. "John Murray, 4th Earl of Dunmore." *Wikipedia*, online at http://en.wikipedia.org/wiki/John_Murray,_4th_Earl_of_Dunmore.

Anon. "Kachumbari." *Wikipedia*, online at http://en.wikipedia.org/wiki/Kachumbari.

Anon. "Kenkey." *Wikipedia*, online at http://en.wikipedia.org/wiki/Kenkey.

Anon. "KFC and Pizza Hut." *WeninChina*, online at www.weninchina.com/Food/KFC_Pizza_Hut.html.

Anon. "Korean Noodles." *Wikipedia*, online at http://en.wikipedia.org/wiki/Korean_noodles.

Anon. "Land." *Oregon State University*, online at http://people.oregonstate.edu/~muirp/landlim.htm.

Anon. "Laurens van der Post." *Wikipedia*, online at http://en.wikipedia.org/wiki/Laurens_van_der_Post.

Anon. *Lee Kum Kee*, online at http://us.lkk.com/en.

Anon. "Lord of Sipán." *Wikipedia*, online at http://en.wikipedia.org/wiki/Lord_of_Sip%C3%A1n.

Anon. "Maize." *Indiamart, Indian Agro Industry*, online at http://agro.indiamart.com/agricultural-commodities/maize.html.

Anon. "Maize Basic." *PNB Krishi*, online at www.pnbkrishi.com/maize.htm.

Anon. "Maize Flour." *African Foods*, online at www.africanfoods.co.uk/maize-flour.html.

Anon. "Manila Galleon." *Wikipedia*, online at http://en.wikipedia.org/wiki/Manila_galleon.

Anon. "Monoculture and the Irish Potato Famine: Cases of Missing Genetic Variation." *Understanding Evolution*, online at http://evolution.berkeley.edu/evolibrary/article/agriculture_02.

Anon. *Notes and Queries, A Medium for Intercommunication for Literary Men, General Readers, Etc.* Vol. 11 (Jan.–June 1867). London: Oxford University Press, 1867.

Anon. "Order of the Sun (Peru)." *Wikipedia*, online at http://en.wikipedia.org/wiki/Order_of_the_Sun_(Peru).

Anon. "Our Reporter". "Why You Won't See the Pyramids Again." *Matori, Nigeria: The Nation*, Nov. 28, 2009. Online at http://thenationonlineng.net/web2/articles/26922/1/Why-you-wont-see-the-pyramids-again/Page1.html.

Anon. "Patata." *The Free Dictionary*, online at www.thefreedictionary.com/patata.

Anon. "Pepper Profile: African Birdseye." *Fiery Foods & Barbecue SuperSite*, online at http://fiery-foods.com/pepper-profiles/152-baccatum-pubescens-and-frutescens-species/107-pepper-profile-african-birdseye.

Anon. "Pineapple." *Maui's Winery at Ulupalakua Ranch*, online at www.mauiwine.com/pineapple.

Anon. "Pineapples." Online at www.bathurst.co.za/Pineapples.htm.

Anon. "Potatoes: A North Korean Obsession." *Fueling Growth, Health, and Prosperity*. Lima, Peru: International Potato Center, 2003.

Anon. "The Potato—Its Unexpected Historical Impact." Online at http://h2g2.com/dna/h2g2/A18740522.

Anon. "The Potatoes of Parmentier." *The Independent*, Vol. LXXVIII (Apr.–June, 1914). New York: The Independent Weekly, 1915, 280.

Anon. "Raleigh's Lazy Root." *The Independent* (Mar. 5, 1917). New York: The Independent Weekly, 389.

Anon. "Rojak." *Wikipedia*, online at http://en.wikipedia.org/wiki/Rojak.

Anon. "Salads." *South African Avocado Grower's Association*, online at www.avocado.co.za/recipes.html.

Anon. "Sex, Death and Sacrifice in Paris." *Museum Views*, Mar. 2010, online at http://museumviews.com/2010/03/sex-death-and-sacrifice-in-paris.

Anon. "South Africa." *Wikipedia*, online at http://en.wikipedia.org/wiki/South_Africa.

Anon. "St. Paul's Cathedral." *London Tourist Attractions*, online at http://populartouristattractions.co.uk/london/st_pauls_cathedral.html.

Anon. "Sugar." *Wikipedia*, online at http://en.wikipedia.org/wiki/Sugar.

Anon. "Tiffin." *Wikipedia*, online at http://en.wikipedia.org/wiki/Tiffin.

Anon. "Tiffin Room." *Raffles Website*, online at www.raffles.com/singapore/restaurants-and-bars/tiffin-room.

Anon., Drew. "Tomatoes. Why Food in Korea Is So Bad." *Toj Blog*, Feb. 27, 2010. Online at http://foodandsteez.blogspot.com/2010/02/tomatoes-ie-why-food-in-korea-is-so-bad.html.

Anon. "The Toppings." *Africanchop.com*, online at www.africanchop.com/groundnutchop.htm.

Anon. "Tropical Fruit Global Information System." *Avocado Marketing—General Information*, online at www.itfnet.org/gfruit/Templates%20English/avocado.market.info.htm.

Anon. "Truffle History." *T.A.S.T.E. Truffles*, online at www.truffles.net.au/6.html, Oct. 15, 2011.

Anon. "Tteokbokki." *Wikipedia*, online at http://en.wikipedia.org/wiki/Tteokbokki.

Anon. "Tulipmania." *University of Chicago*, online at http://penelope.uchicago.edu/~grout/encyclopaedia_romana/aconite/tulipomania.html.

Anon. "UK Christmas Traditions." *I Love British Turkey*, online at www.britishturkey.co.uk/turkey-bytes/uk-christmas.shtml.

Anon. "War of the Bavarian Succession." *Wikipedia*, online at http://en.wikipedia.org/wiki/War_of_the_Bavarian_Succession.

Anon. Noreen. "What You Can and Can't Get at McDonalds India . . . " *Indiamarks*, online at www.indiamarks.com/guide/What-You-Can-and-Can-t-Get-at-McDonalds-India-/1739.

Anon. "Who was C. Louis Leipoldt?" *Leipoldt's Restaurant*, online at www.leipoldtsrestaurant.co.za/aboutus.htm.

Anon. "World War II Casualties." *Wikipedia*, online at http://en.wikipedia.org/wiki/World_War_II_casualties#Third_Reich.

Anon. "World War II Casualties of the Soviet Union." *Wikipedia*, online at http://en.wikipedia.org/wiki/World_War_II_casualties_of_the_Soviet_Union.

Arfman, Florence. *The TIME Reader's Book of Recipes*. New York: E. P. Dutton & Co., 1949. (Excerpts used are online at www.congocookbook.com/rare_recipes/florence_arfmann.html.)

Aymler, Thomas. "How is McDonald's in America Different from McDonald's in China?" *Tom's China Blog*, Mar. 10, 2011. Online at www.tomschinablog. com/how-is-mcdonalds-in-america-different-from-mcdonalds-in-china.

Balfour, Edward. *The Cyclopædia of India and of Eastern and Southern Asia*. Vol. 1. Madras: B. Quaritch, 1885.

—. *Cyclopædia of India and of Eastern and Southern Asia*. Vol. 2 and 4. Madras: Scottish and Adelphi Presses, 1871.

Bancroft, Hubert Howe. *The Native Races of the Pacific States of North America*. London: Longmans, Green & Co., 1875.

—. *A Popular History of the Mexican People*. San Francisco: The History Company, 1887.

Banerji, Chitrita. *Eating India: An Odyssey into the Food and Culture of the Land of Spices*. New York: Bloomsbury USA, 2007.

Barham, Andrea. *Queen Elizabeth's Wooden Teeth and Other Historical Fallacies*. London: Michael O'Mara Books, 2007.

Barrell, Sarah. "In Search of . . . Turkeys in France." London: *The Independent (Europe)*, Nov. 30, 2003, online at www.independent.co.uk/ travel/europe/in-search-of-turkeys-in-france-737475.html.

Bartle, Phil. "Kwasi Bruni: Corn and the Europeans." *Akan Studies*, online at www.scn.org/rdi/kw-brun.htm.

Barty-King, Hugh, and Anton Massel. *Rum Yesterday and Today*. London: Heinemann, 1983.

Bastianich, Lidia. *La Cucina di Lidia*. New York: Doubleday, 1990.

Bates, Oric. *Varia Africana, Vol. 1*. Cambridge, MA: African Department, Harvard College, 1917.

Batra, Neelam. *AARP 1,000 India Recipes*. New York: John Wiley & Sons, 2011 (Digital Edition).

Baugniet, Rebecca. *500 Pizzas & Flatbreads: The Only Pizza & Flatbread Compendium You'll Ever Need*. Portland, ME: Sellers Publishing, 2008.

Beauman, Fran. *The Pineapple, King of Fruits*. London: Chatto & Windus, 2005.

—. "The King of Fruits." *Cabinet Magazine*, Issue 23, "Fruits," Fall, 2006. Online at www.cabinetmagazine.org/issues/23/beauman.php.

Beauvilliers, Antoine B. *The Art of French Cookery*. London: Longman, 1827.

Benschop, Maarten. "The Global Flower Bulb Industry: Production, Utilization, Research." *Horticultural Reviews*, Vol. 36, 2010. Online at http://media.wiley.com/product_data/excerpt/06/04705052/0470505206. pdf.

Bernstein, William J. *A Splendid Exchange: How Trade Shaped the World*. New York: Grove Press, 2008.

Bhagowati, Raktim Ranjan, and Sapu Changkija. "Genetic Variability and Traditional Practices in Naga King Chile Landraces of Nagaland." *Asian Agri-History*, Vol. 13, No. 3 (2009), 171–180.

Bhide, Monica. *The Everything Indian Cookbook*. Avon, MA: Adams Media, 2004.

Bierce, Ambrose. *The Enlarged Devil's Dictionary*. Ed. Ernest Jerome Hopkins. Garden City, NY: Doubleday & Co., 1967.

Binns, Brigit Legere. *Polenta: Over 40 Recipes for All Occasions*. San Francisco: Chronicle Books, 1997.

Black, Colette. *The French Provincial Cookbook*. New York: Collier Books, 1963.

Blackley, Pat, and Chuck Blackley. *Virginia's Historic Homes and Gardens*. Minneapolis: Voyageur Press, 2009.

Bladholm, Linda. *The Indian Grocery Store Demystified*. New York: Macmillan, 2000.

Bourget, Steve. *Sex, Death, and Sacrifice in Moche Religion and Visual Culture*. Austin: University of Texas Press, 2006.

Bowen, T. J. *Central Africa*. Charleston, SC: Southern Baptists Publication Society, 1857.

Bower, Bruce. "Pueblo traded for chocolate big-time." *Science News*, Mar. 17, 2011, online at www.sciencenews.org/view/generic/id/71308/title/Pueblo_traded_for_chocolate_big-time.

Bown, Stephen R. *Scurvy: How a Surgeon, a Mariner, and a Gentleman Solved the Greatest Medical Mystery of the Age of Sail*. New York: St. Martin's Griffin, 2003.

—. *1494: How a Family Feud in Medieval Spain Divided the World in Half*. New York: St. Martin's Press, 2011.

Boyle, T. C. *Water Music*. New York: Penguin Books, 1983.

Bradley, Emily B. *A Household Book for Tropical Colonies*. London: Oxford University Press, 1948.

Bray, Warwick. *Everyday Life of the Aztecs*. New York: Dorset Press, 1968.

Brennan, Jennifer. *The Cuisines of Asia*. London: Macdonald & Co., 1984.

Brillat-Savarin, Jean-Anthelme. *Gastronomy as a Fine Art: or, The Science of Good Living*. A translation of the "Physiologie du goût" of Brillat-Savarin. Trans. R. E. Anderson. London: Chatto and Windus, 1877.

—. *The Philosopher in the Kitchen*. New York: Penguin Books, 1981.

Brown, Robert. *The Story of Africa and Its Explorers*. London: Cassell & Co., 1892.

Brunner, Hans-Peter. *North East India: Local Economic Development and Global Markets*. New Delhi: SAGE Publications, 2010.

Bryden, Lynn. "Snacks and Stews from Ghana." *The Anthropologists' Cookbook*. Ed. Jessica Kuper. New York: Universe Books, 1977.

Burnett, John. *Liquid Pleasures: A Social History of Drinks in Modern Britain*. London: Psychology Press (Routledge), 1999.

Burton, Sir Richard Francis. *Wanderings in West Africa from Liverpool to Ferdinand Po*. Vol. 2. London: Tinsley Brothers, 1863.

—. *The Lake Regions of Central Africa: A Picture of Exploration*. Vol. 2. London: Longman, Green, Longman, and Roberts, 1860.

Caddy, Mrs. Florence. *To Siam and Malaya in the Duke of Sutherland's Yacht "Sans Peur."* London: Hurst and Blackett, Ltd., 1889.

Cameron, A. Mackenzie. "Business Journies [sic] Through Java." *Calcutta Review*. Vol. 80–81. Calcutta: University of Calcutta, 1885.

Cameron, Verney Lovett. *Across Africa*. Vol. 2. Leipzig: Bernhard Tauchnitz, 1877.

Campbell, Cheryl, ed. *Edible: An Illustrated Guide to the World's Food Plants*. Washington, DC: The National Geographic Society, 2008.

Campbell, Dawn, and Janet Smith. *The Coffee Book*. Gretna, LA: Pelican Press, 1993.

Canvin, Maggie. *SocioLingoAfrica*, online at www.sociolingo.com/2009/10/cookery-in-ghana.

Capatti, Alberto, and Massimo Montanari. *Italian Cuisine: A Cultural History*. New York: Columbia University Press, 2003.

Carney, Judith A., and Richard Nicholas Rosomoff. *In the Shadow of Slavery: Africa's Botanical Legacy in the Atlantic World.* Berkeley: University of California Press, 2009.

Carol, Brenda. "China's Processing Tomato Industry Moving into the World Market." *Western Farm Press,* Oct. 20, 2007, online at http://westernfarmpress.com/chinas-processing-tomato-industry-moving-world-market.

Carpenter, Frank George. *Carpenter's Geographical Reader.* New York: American Book Company, 1905.

Cee, Jacob, and Susan Theiler. "U.S. French Fries Heat Up China's Fast Food Industry." *American Journal of Potato Research,* Mar. 2, 2009, online at www.fas.usda.gov/info/agexporter/1999/usfrench.html.

Chang, K.C. "Ancient China." *Food in Chinese Culture.* New Haven: Yale University Press, 1977.

Chapman, Jeff. "The Impact of the Potato." *History Magazine,* online at www.history-magazine.com/potato.html.

Chapman, Pat. *Pat Chapman's Curry Bible.* London: Hodder & Stoughton, 1997.

—. *India Food & Cooking: The Ultimate Book on Indian Cuisine.* London: New Holland Publishers, 2009.

Chin, Mei. "The Art of Kimchi." *Saveur Magazine,* Oct. 14. 2009, online at www.saveur.com/article/Kitchen/The-Art-of-Kimchi.

Christie, Robert H. *Twenty-Two Authentic Banquets from India.* New York: Dover Books, 1975. A reprint of the Indian and Afghanistani sections of Christie's 1911 *Banquets of the Nations,* published by J. & J. Gray and Co.

Clements, Miles. "The Find: CoCo Ichibanya in Torrance." *Los Angeles Times,* Apr. 14, 2011, online at http://articles.latimes.com/2011/apr/14/food/la-fo-find-coco-ichibanya-20110414.

Coady, Chantal. *Chocolate: The Food of the Gods.* San Francisco: Chronicle Books, 1993.

Coe, Sophie D. *America's First Cuisines.* Austin: University of Texas Press, 1994.

Coe, Sophie D., and Michael D. Coe. *The True History of Chocolate.* New York: Thames and Hudson, 1996.

Coetzee, Renata. *The South African Culinary Tradition.* Cape Town: C. Struik Publishers, 1977.

Cohen, J. M. Introduction. *The Conquest of New Spain.* By Bernal Díaz. New York: Penguin Books, 1963.

Cohen, J. M., ed. and trans. *The Four Voyages of Christopher Columbus.* New York: Penguin, 1969.

Cohen, Sharon. "Love, Death, or Mere Curiosity? The Tomato in Renaissance Europe." Online at http://wwwflorilegium.org.

Collingham, Lizzie. *Curry: A Tale of Cooks and Conquerers.* New York: Oxford University Press, 2006.

Columbus, Christopher, and Bartolomé de las Casas. *Personal Narrative of the First Voyage of Columbus to America: From a Manuscript Recently Discovered in Spain.* Boston: B. Wait and Son, 1827.

Conneau, Theophilus. *Revelations of a Slave Trader; Or, Twenty Years' Adventures of Captain Canot.* London: Richard Bentley, 1854. (This is the British edition heavily edited by Brantz Mayer.)

—. *Captain Canot; Twenty Years as an African Slaver.* New York: D.

Appleton & Co., 1854. (This is the American edition heavily edited by
Brantz Mayer.)

——. *A Slaver's Log Book of 20 Year's Residence in Africa.* Sheffield, MA:
Howard S. Mott, Inc., 1976. (This is the unedited version.)

Conniff, Richard. *The Species Seekers: Heroes, Fools, and the Mad Pursuit
of Life on Earth.* New York: W. W. Norton & Co., 2011.

Connor, Mary E. *The Koreas.* Santa Barbara, CA: ABC-CLIO, 2009.

Cortés, Hernán. *The Five Letters of Relation from Fernando Cortes to the
Emperor Charles V.* Ed. and trans. Francis Augustus MacNutt. Vol. 1. New
York: G. P. Putnam's Sons, 1908.

Costa, J. M., and Ed Heuvelink. "Introduction: The Tomato Crop and
Industry." *Tomatoes: Volume 13 of Crop Production Science in
Horticulture.* Ed. Ep Heuvelink. Cambridge, MA: CABI, 2005.

Coulombe, Charles A. *Rum: The Epic Story of the Drink That Conquered the
World.* New York: Citadel Press, 2004.

Cowper, William. *The Poems of William Cowper.* Vol. 2. Chiswick: Press of
C. Whittingham, 1822.

Croddy, Eric, and James J. Wirtz, eds. *Weapons of Mass Destruction: An
Encyclopedia of Worldwide Policy, Technology, and History.* Santa
Barbara, CA: ABC-CLIO, 2005.

Crosby, Alfred W. *The Columbian Exchange: Biological and Cultural
Consequences of 1492.* Westport, CT: Greenwood Press, 1972.

——. "Columbian Exchange." *Food & History,* Vol. 7, No. 1 (2009), 225–226.
Turnhout, Belgium: Brepols Publishers NV.

Culver, Henry B. *The Book of Old Ships: From Egyptian Galleys to Clipper
Ships.* New York: Dover Publications, 1992.

"Cuzco." *The New American Cyclopaedia: A Popular Dictionary of General
Knowledge,* Vol. 6. New York: D. Appleton & Co., 1867. 177.

Davidson, Alan. "Maize." *The Oxford Companion to Food, 2nd Edition.* New
York: Oxford University Press, 2006.

Davis, David Brion. *Inhuman Bondage: The Rise and Fall of Slavery in the
New World.* New York: Oxford University Press, 2008.

Davis, Karen. *More Than a Meal: The Turkey in History, Myth, Ritual, and
Reality.* New York: Lantern Books, 2001.

Day, Ivan. "Royal Sugar Sculpture." *HistoricFood.com,* online at www.
historicfood.com/Royal-sugar-Sculpture.htm.

de Marees, Pieter. *Description and Historical Account of the Gold Kingdom
of Guinea.* Trans. Albert van Dantzig and Adam Jones. New York: Oxford
University Press, 1987.

de Sade, Marquis. *Letters from Prison.* Trans. Richard Seaver. New York:
Arcade Publishing, 1999.

——. *The Complete Marquis de Sade.* Vol. 1. Trans. Paul J. Gillette and John S.
Yankowski. Los Angeles: Holloway House Publishing, 2005.

Devlin, Vivien. "How to Cook the Classic Christmas Turkey," *Luxury
Scotland,* online at www.luxuryscotland.co.uk/turkeyarticle.

DeWitt, Dave. "Bonney Barbados: A Travel Retrospective, 1996." *Fiery Foods
& Barbecue SuperSite,* online at http://fiery-foods.com/chiles-around-the-
world/76-caribbean/1869-a-baja-occasion, 2011.

——. *The Chile Pepper Encyclopedia.* New York: William Morrow & Co., 1999.

——. "Fiery Fast Food–Indian Style: A 1996 Retrospective." *Fiery Foods &
Barbecue SuperSite,* 1996, online at www.fiery-foods.com/chiles-around-

the-world/78-india/2808-fiery-fast-food-indian-style-a-1996-retrospective.

—. "Out of the Ash: The Prehistoric Chile Cuisine of Cerén." *Fiery Foods & Barbecue SuperSite*, online at www.fiery-foods.com/article-archives/85-chile-history/1822-out-of-the-ash-the-prehistoric-chile-cuisine-of-ceren, 2005.

—. *Da Vinci's Kitchen: A Secret History of Italian Cuisine*. Dallas: Ben Bella Books, 2006.

—. *The Founding Foodies: How Washington, Jefferson, and Franklin Revolutionized American Cuisine*. Naperville, IL: Sourcebooks, 2010.

—. "The Peperoncino-Eating Contest: Could You Eat a Chihuahua's Weight in Chiles?" *Burn! Blog*, Feb. 12, 2012, online at www.burn-blog.com/2757/the-peperoncino-eating-contest-could-you-eat-a-chihuahuas-weight-in-chiles.

—. "Tasting the Heat in OZ." Fiery Foods & Barbecue SuperSite, online at www.fiery-foods.com/chiles-around-the-world/75-australia/1783-tasting-the-heat-in-oz.

DeWitt, Dave, and Arthur Pais. *A World of Curries*. Boston: Little, Brown and Company, 1994.

DeWitt, Dave, and Mary Jane Wilan. *Callaloo, Calypso & Carnival: The Cuisines of Trinidad and Tobago*. Freedom, CA: The Crossing Press, 1993.

DeWitt, Dave, Mary Jane Wilan, and Melissa T. Stock. *Hot and Spicy Southeast Asian Dishes*. Rocklin, CA: Prima Publishing, 1995.

—. *Hot & Spicy Caribbean*. Rocklin, CA: Prima Publishing, 1996.

— *Flavors of Africa Cookbook*. Rocklin, CA: Prima Publishing, 1998.

DeWitt, Dave, and Nancy Gerlach. *The Whole Chile Pepper Book*. Boston: Little, Brown and Company, 1990.

Díaz, Bernal. *The Conquest of New Spain*. Trans. J. M Cohen. New York: Penguin Books, 1978.

Dickie, John. *Delizia! The Epic Story of Italians and Their Food*. London: Hodder & Stoughton, 2007.

Dirks, Tim. "The Oscars 1930s." *Filmsite*, online at www.filmsite.org/aa36.htm.

Dowling, Timothy C., ed. *Personal Perspectives: World War II*. Vol. 2. Santa Barbara, CA: ABC-CLIO, 2005.

Drouard, Alain. "Chefs, Gourmets and Gourmands." *Food: The History of Taste*. Ed. Paul Freedman. Berkeley: University of California Press, 2007, 263–300.

Du Chaillu, Paul Belloni. *Lost in the Jungle*. London: Sampson Low, Son and Marston, 1870.

Dunmire, William W. *Gardens of New Spain: How Mediterranean Plants and Foods Changed America*. Austin: University of Texas Press, 2004.

Ecott, Tim. *Vanilla: Travels in Search of the Ice Cream Orchid*. New York: Grove Press, 2004.

Edelstein, Sari. *Food, Cuisine, and Cultural Competency for Culinary, Hospitality, and Nutrition Professionals*. Sudbury, MA: Jones & Bartlett Publishers, 2011.

Edgar, Blake. "The Power of Chocolate." *Archaeology*, Nov.–Dec. 2010, 20.

Egmond, Florike. *The World of Carolus Clusius: Natural History in the Making, 1550–1610*. London: Pickering & Chatto, 2010.

Eiche, Sabine. *Presenting the Turkey: The Fabulous Story of a Flamboyant and Flavourful Bird*. Florence: Centro Di, 2004.

Emslie, Trevor. "Leipoldt, the Dostoevsky of South Africa." *New History*, online at http://newhistory.co.za/leipoldt.

English, Rich. "Yo Ho Ho and a Bottle of Rum." Modern Drunkard Magazine, online at www.moderndrunkardmagazine.com/issues/10_04/10-04-pirates.htm.

FAO (Food and Agriculture Organization, United Nations), "World Crop Statistics, Commodities by Country, 2009." Online at http://faostat.fao.org/site/339/default.aspx.

Field, Carol. *Celebrating Italy*. New York: William Morrow & Co., 1990.

"Brits Top European Chocolate Rankings," Dec. 15, 2003, *Food&Drinkeurope.com*, online at www.foodanddrinkeurope.com/Products-Marketing/Brits-top-European-chocolate-rankings.

Foster, Nelson, and Linda S. Cordell. *Chilies to Chocolate: Food the Americas Gave to the World*. Tucson: University of Arizona Press, 1992.

Frankel, Mark. "When the Tulip Bubble Burst." *Bloomberg Business Week*, Apr. 24, 2000, online at www.businessweek.com/2000/00_17/b3678084.htm.

Frazier, Sir James George. *Psyche's Task: A Discourse Concerning the Influence of Superstition on the Growth of Institutions*. London: Macmillan & Co., 1913.

Garvin, Fernande. *The Art of French Cooking*. New York: Bantam Books, 1965.

Geddie, John. *The Lake Regions of Central Africa: A Record of Modern Discovery*. London: T. Nelson & Sons, 1892.

Gentilcore, David. *Pomodoro! A History of the Tomato in Italy*. New York: Columbia University Press, 2010.

Glasse, Hannah. *The Art of Cookery Made Plain and Easy: Which Far Exceeds Any Thing of the Kind Yet Published*. London: W. Strahan [and 25 others], 1784.

Goldblith, Samuel A. "The Legacy of Columbus, with Particular Reference to Food." *Food Technology*, Vol. 46, No. 10 (Oct. 1992), 62–85.

Gordon, Bertram M. "Chinese Chocolate: Ambergris, Emperors, and Export Ware." *Chocolate: History, Culture, and Heritage*. Eds. Louis Evan Grivetti and Howard-Yana Shapiro. Hoboken, NJ: John Wiley & Sons, 2009, 595–604.

—. "Chocolate in France: Evolution of a Luxury Product." *Chocolate: History, Culture, and Heritage*. Eds. Louis Evan Grivetti and Howard-Yana Shapiro. Hoboken, NJ: John Wiley & Sons, 2009, 569.

—. "Commerce, Colonies, and Cacao: Chocolate in England from Introduction to Industrialization." *Chocolate: History, Culture, and Heritage*. Eds. Louis Evan Grivetti and Howard-Yana Shapiro. Hoboken, NJ: John Wiley & Sons, 2009, 580.

Grant, Reg. *Slavery: Real People and Their Stories of Enslavement*. New York: Penguin Books, 2009.

Grasse, M. From *Marx Rumpolt, Ein New Kochbuch, c. 1581*. Transliteration and translation. Online at http://clem.mscd.edu/~grasse/GK_Rumpolt1.htm.

Grew, Raymond. *Food in Global History*. Boulder, CO: Westview Press, 1999.

Grewe, Rudolph. "The Arrival of the Tomato in Spain and Italy: Early Recipes." *The Journal of Gastronomy*. Vol. 3, No. 2 (Summer, 1987), 67–83.

Grivetti, Louis Evan. "Chocolate, Crime, and the Courts: Selected English

Trial Documents, 1693–1834. *Chocolate: History, Culture, and Heritage*. Eds. Louis Evan Grivetti and Howard-Yana Shapiro. Hoboken, NJ: John Wiley & Sons, 2009, 243.

—. "Dark Chocolate: Chocolate and Crime in North America and Elsewhere." *Chocolate: History, Culture, and Heritage*. Eds. Louis Evan Grivetti and Howard-Yana Shapiro. Hoboken, NJ: John Wiley & Sons, 2009, 255.

—. "From Bean to Beverage: Historical Chocolate Recipes." *Chocolate: History, Culture, and Heritage*. Eds. Louis Evan Grivetti and Howard-Yana Shapiro. Hoboken, NJ: John Wiley & Sons, 2009, 99.

Grivetti, Louis Evan, and Howard-Yana Shapiro, eds. *Chocolate: History, Culture, and Heritage*. Hoboken, NJ: John Wiley & Sons, 2009.

Grivetti, Louis Evan, Jan L. Corlett, and Cassius T. Lockett. *Food in American History, Part 8: Potatoes in World War II, Home Front and Abroad (1941–1945). Nutrition Today*, Vol. 41, No. 3 (May/June), 2006, 125–130.

Grogan, Edward Scott, and Arthur Henry Sharp. *From the Cape to Cairo: The First Traverse of Africa from South to North*. London: Hurst and Blackett, 1900.

Groth, B. H. A. "The Sweet Potato." *Contributions from the Botanical Laboratory of the University of Pennsylvania*. Vol. IV, No. 1. New York: D. Appleton & Co., 1911.

Guy, Louis L. "Norfolk's Worst Nightmare." *Norfolk Historical Society Courier*, Spring 2001. Online at www.norfolkhistorical.org/insights/2001_spring/nightmare.html.

Hachten, Harva. *Kitchen Safari: A Gourmet's Tour of Africa*. New York: Atheneum, 1970.

—. *Best of Regional African Cooking*. New York: Hippocrene Books, 1970.

Halász, Zoltán. *Hungarian Paprika Through the Ages*. Budapest: Corvina Press, 1963.

Hamilton, Cherie Y. *Cuisines of the Portuguese Encounters*. New York: Hippocrene Books, 2008.

Harris, Jessica B. *The Africa Cookbook: Tastes of a Continent*. New York: Simon & Schuster, 1998.

Harvey, Mark, Stephen Quilley, and Huw Beynon. *Exploring the Tomato: Transformations of Nature, Society, and Economy*. Northampton, MA: Edward Elgar Publishing, 2003.

Hawkes, J.G., and J. Francisco-Ortega. "The Early History of the Potato in Europe." *Euphytica*. Vol. 70, 1993, 17.

Hawkins, Sir John. *The Hawkins' Voyages During the Reigns of Henry VIII, Queen Elizabeth, and James I*. Issue 57. London: The Hakluyt Society, 1878.

Hawley, Chris. "Chinese Chili Pepper Invasion Making Some Mexicans Hot." *USA Today*, online at www.usatoday.com/news/world/2005-11-21-pepper-war_x.htm.

Hemphill, Ian. *The Spice and Herb Bible*. Toronto: Robert Rose, Inc., 2006.

Hedrick, U.P., ed. *Sturtevant's Edible Plants of the World*. New York: Dover Publications, 1872.

Heiser, Charles B. *The Fascinating World of the Nightshades*. New York: Dover Publications, 1987.

Hess, Karen. "Historical Note." *The Art of Cookery Made Plain and Easy*. By Hannah Glasse. Bedford, MA: Applewood Press, 1998.

Heuman, Gad J., and James Walvin. *The Slavery Reader*. Routledge Readers in History Series. London: Psychology Press, 2003.

Higman, B.W. *Jamaican Food: History, Biology, Culture.* Kingston: University of the West Indies Press, 2008.

Hillman, Howard. *The Book of World Cuisines.* New York: Penguin Books, 1979.

"History of Martinique," *Wikipedia,* online at http://en.wikipedia.org/wiki/History_of_Martinique.

Ho, Ping-Ti. "The Introduction of American Food Plants into China." *American Anthropologist,* New Series, Vol. 57, No. 2 (Apr. 1955), 191–201.

Hobhouse, Henry: *Seeds of Change: Five Plants that Transformed Mankind.* New York: Perennial Library, 1987.

Hogarth, William. *The Analysis of Beauty: Written with a View of Fixing the Fluctuating Ideas of Taste.* London: Printed by W. Strahan, for Mrs. Hogarth, 1772.

Hudgins, Sharon. "Harvest-Time in Kalocsa: Hungary's 'Red Gold,'" *Fiery Foods & BBQ,* May–June 2004, 24–40.

Human and Rousseau. "Kos vir die Kenner." Online at www.humanrousseau.com/Books/11371.

Itoh, Makiki. "Japanese Beef Curry (Curry Rice)," *Just Hungry Blog,* online at www.justhungry.com/japanese-beef-curry.

Jackson, Margaret Ann. *Moche Art and Visual Culture in Ancient Peru.* Albuquerque: University of New Mexico Press, 2008.

Jaffrey, Madhur. *From Curries to Kebabs: Recipes from the Indian Spice Trail.* New York: Random House Digital, 2003.

Jeffreys, M. K. W. "Pre-Columbian Maize in the Old World: An Examination of Portuguese Sources." *Gastronomy.* Ed. Margaret L. Arnott, The Hague: Mouton, 1975. 23–66.

Jenkins, J. A. "The Origin of the Cultivated Tomato." *Economic Botany.* Vol. 2, No. 4 (Oct.–Dec., 1942), 379–392.

Johannessen, Carl J. "Pre-Columbian Maize in China and India?" Online at http://geography.uoregon.edu/carljohannessen/research.html.

—. "Vita." Online at http://geography.uoregon.edu/carljohannessen/cv.html.

Johari, Harish. *Ayurvedic Healing Cuisine: 200 Vegetarian Recipes for Health, Balance, and Longevity.* Rochester, VT: Bear & Co., 2000.

John, G. Wesley. *The Emergence of Black Politics in Senegal: The Struggle for Power in the Four Communes, 1900–1920.* Stanford, CA: Stanford University Press, 1971.

Kapoor, Sanjeev. *How to Cook Indian: More Than 500 Classic Recipes for the Modern Kitchen.* New York: Stewart, Tabori & Chang, 2011.

Katz, Esther. "Chili Pepper, from Mexico to Europe: Food, Imaginary and Cultural Identity." *Estudios de Hombre,* No. 24. Guadalajara, Mexico: Universidad de Guadalajara, 2009.

Keane, Michael J. "The Sharwood's Story." *Local History: Offley Works,* online at www.ovalpartnership.org.uk/kennington-oval-vauxhall-history/notable-buildings/offley-works/sharwoods-story.html, Aug. 2011.

Kim, Jae so. *Korean Agriculture 1995.* Venezuela: Inter-American Institute for Cooperation on Agriculture, 1995.

Kimball, Marie. *The Thomas Jefferson Cook Book.* Greenville, MS: Lillie Ross Productions, 2004.

Kiple, Kenneth F. *A Movable Feast: Ten Millennia of Food Globalization.* New York: Cambridge University Press, 2007.

Kiple, Kenneth F., and Kriemhild Coneè Ornelas, "Potatoes—White." *The Cambridge World History of Food*, online at www.cambridge.org/us/books/kiple/potatoes.htm.

Kipling, Rudyard. *From Sea to Sea*.Vol. 1. Leipzig: B. Tauchnitz, 1900.

Klein, Martin A. *Islam and Imperialism in Senegal: Sine-Saloum, 1847–1914*. Stanford, CA: Stanford University Press, 1968.

Knapp, Arthur W. *Cocoa and Chocolate: Their History from Plantation to Consumer*. London: Chapman and Hall Ltd., 1920. Online at www.gutenberg.org/files/19073/19073-h/19073-h.htm.

Knox, Thomas Wallace. *The Boy Travellers in the Far East, Part Second: Adventures of Two Youths in a Journey to Siam and Java, with Descriptions of Cochin-China, Cambodia, Sumatra and the Malay Archipelago.* New York: Harper & Brothers, 1880.

—. *The Boy Travellers in the Far East, Part Third: Adventures of Two Youths in a journey to Ceylon and India, with Descriptions of Borneo, the Philippine Islands, and Burmah. New York: Harper and Brothers*, 1881.

Koigi, Bob. "Kenya Takes to the Sweet Taste of the Avocado Market." *Webaraza Farmer*, online at http://webarazafarmer.com/index.php?option=com_content&task=view&id=228&Itemid=28.

Kostioukovitch, Elena. *Why Italians Love To Talk About Food*. New York: Farrar, Straus and Giroux, 2006.

Krise, Thomas W. "James Grainger," *Cengage Learning,* online at http://college.cengage.com/english/lauter/heath/4e/students/author_pages/eighteenth/grainger_ja.html.

Krishna, K. R. *Agroecosystems of South India: Nutrient Dynamics, Ecology, and Productivity.* Boca Raton, FL: BrownWalker Press, 2010.

Kupperman, Karen Ordahl. Introduction. *A True and Exact History of the Island of Barbados*. By Richard Ligon. Indianapolis: Hackett Publishing Co., 2011, 1–35.

Lang, George. *The Cuisine of Hungary*. New York: Bonanza Books, 1971.

Langer, William. "American Foods and Europe's Population Growth 1750–1850." *Journal of Social History*, Vol. 8 (1975), 51–66.

Lappé, Frances Moore, Joseph Collins, and Peter Rosset. *World Hunger: Twelve Myths*. New York: Grove Press, 1998.

La Pierre, Yvette. *Ghana in Pictures*. Minneapolis: Twenty-First Century Books, 2004.

Lausen-Higgins, Johanna. "A Taste for the Exotic: Pineapple Cultivation in Britain." *Building Conservation*, 2010, online at www.buildingconservation.com/articles/pineapples/pineapples.htm.

Lee, Calvin B. T., and Audrey Evans Lee. *The Gourmet Chinese Regional Cookbook*. Menlo Park, CA: Askmar Publishing, 1979.

Lee, Sir Sidney. *Dictionary of National Biography,* Vol. XLVII. New York: Macmillan, 1896.

Leipoldt, C. Louis. *Leipoldt's Cape Cookery*. Cape Town: W. J. Flesch & Partners, 1976.

—. "Culinary Treasures." *Leipoldt's Food & Wine*. Eds. T. S. Emslie and P. L. Murray. Cape Town: Stonewall Books, 2003.

Lello, Brian. "A Note on the Author." *Leipoldt's Cape Cookery*. By C. Louis Leipoldt. Cape Town: W. J. Flesch & Partners, 1976.

Levy, Buddy. *Conquistador: Hernan Cortés, King Montezuma, and the Last Stand of the Aztecs*. New York: Bantam Books, 2009.

Library of José Durand. "Garcilaso Inca de la Vega." University of Notre Dame Rare Books and Special Collections, online at www.library.nd.edu.

Ligan, Joshua. "Tired of Adobo and Pancit? The Undiscovered Kulma of the Southern Philippines." *Examiner.com*, Aug. 13, 2010, online at www.examiner.com/ethnic-foods-in-san-jose/tired-of-adobo-and-pancit-the-undiscovered-kulma-of-the-southern-philippines.

Macinnes, Peter. *Bittersweet: The Story of Sugar*. Crows Nest NSW, Australia: Allen & Unwin, 2002.

Maclachlan, T. Banks. *Mungo Park*. Edinburgh: Oliphant, Anderson & Ferrier, 1898.

MacQuarrie, Kim. *The Last Days of the Incas*. New York: Simon & Schuster, 2007.

Mandeville, Bernard. *The Fable of the Bees: or, Private Vices, Publick Benefits*. Edinburgh: T. Ostell & Mundell, 1806.

Mangelsdorf, Paul C. "Review of *Agricultural Origins and Dispersals*, by Carl O. Sauer." *Prehistoric Agriculture*. Ed. S. Struever. Garden City, NJ: Museum Source Books in Anthropology, 1971.

Mann, Charles C. *1491: New Revelations of the Americas Before Columbus*. New York: Vintage Books, 2006.

—. "The Eyes Have It." *Smithsonian*. Vol. 42, No. 11 (Nov. 2011), 86–106.

Marrayat, Frank. *Borneo and the Indian Archipelago*. London: Longman, Brown Green, and Longmans, 1848.

Marks, Copeland. *The Korean Kitchen: Classic Recipes from the Land of the Morning Calm*. San Francisco: Chronicle Books, 1999.

Marks, Robert. *Tigers, Rice, Silk, and Silt: Environment and Economy in Late Imperial South China*. New York: Cambridge University Press, 2006.

Marsden, William. *The History of Sumatra: Containing an Account of the Government, Laws, Customs and Manners of the Native Inhabitants*. London: Thomas Payne & Son, 1784.

Matsumoto, Marc. "Homemade Japanese Curry Rice," *No Recipes Blog,* online at http://norecipes.com/blog/karei-raisu-japanese-curry-rice.

Mazumdar, Sucheta. "The Impact of New World Food Crops on the Diet and Economy of China and India, 1600–1900." *Food in Global History*. Ed. Raymond Grewe. Boulder, CO: Westview Press, 1999.

Mead, William E. *The English Medieval Feast*. London: George Allen and Unwin, 1967.

McCabe, James Dabney. *Our Young Folks in Africa*. Philadelphia: J. B. Lippincott & Co., 1882.

McCann, James C. *Maize and Grace: Africa's Encounter with a New World Crop*. Cambridge: Harvard University Press, 2005.

McCann, James. *Stirring the Pot: A History of African Cuisine*. Athens: Ohio University Press, 2009.

McGee, Harold. *On Food and Cooking*. New York: Scribner, 2004.

McKee, Brian R. "Household Archaeology and Cultural Formation Processes: Examples from the Cerén Site, El Salvador." *The Archaeology of Household Activities*. By Penelope Mary Allison. Oxford (U.K.) and New York: Psychology Press, 1999.

McNeill, William H. "Mythistory, or Truth, Myth, History, and Historians." *Mythistory and Other Essays*. By William H. McNeill. Chicago: University of Chicago Press, 1986.

—. "How the Potato Changed the World's History." *Social Research*, Vol. 66, No. 1 (Spring 1999) 67–83.

Meakin, Budgett. *The Moors: A Comprehensive Description*. London: S. Sonnenschein & Co., 1902.

Melville, Elizabeth. *A Residence in Freetown*. London: John Murray, 1849.

Mesfin, Daniel J. *Exotic Ethiopian Cooking*. Falls Church, VA: Ethiopian Cookbook Enterprises, 1990.

Miley, Mary. *Myth #12, History Myths Debunked. WordPress.com*, online at http://historymyths.wordpress.com/tag/pineapple-symbol-of-hospitality.

Miller, Philip. *The Gardeners Dictionary: Containing the Methods of Cultivating and Improving the Kitchen, Fruit and Flower Garden, as also the Physick Garden, Wilderness, Conservatory, and Vineyard, Vol. I*. London: Printed for the Author, 1735.

Mintz, Sidney W. *Sweetness and Power: The Place of Sugar in Modern History*. New York: Penguin Books, 1985.

Miracle, Marvin P. *Maize in Tropical Africa*. Madison, WI: The University of Wisconsin Press, 1966.

Mollison, Bill. *Ferment and Human Nutrition*. Tyalgum, NSW, Australia: Tagari Publications, 1993.

Monier-Williams, M. A. *Religious Thought and Life in India,* Part I. London: J. Murray, 1883.

Montgomery, Bertha Vining, and Constance R. Nabwire. *Cooking the East African Way*. Minneapolis: Lerner Publications, 2002.

Monteiro, Joachim John. *Angola and the River Congo*. Vol. 1. London: Macmillan, 1875.

Morphy, Countess (Marcelle Azra Forbes). *Recipes of All Nations*. New York: William H. Wise & Co., 1935.

Moskoff, William. *The Bread of Affliction: The Food Supply of the USSR During World War II*. New York: Cambridge University Press, 2002.

Moss, Walter. *A History of Russia: Since 1885*. London: Anthem Press, 2004

Mote, Frederick W. "Yüan and Ming." *Food in Chinese Culture*. Ed. K. C. Chang. New Haven: Yale University Press, 1977.

Mous, Maarten. "Loss of Linguistic Diversity in Africa." *Language Death and Language Maintenance*. Eds. Mark Janse and Sijmen Tol. Amsterdam: John Benjamins Publishing Co., 2003.

Mouser, Bruce L. "Theophilus Conneau: The Saga of a Tale." *History in Africa*, Vol. 6, 1979, 97–107.

Mundkur, Balaji. "On Pre-Columbian Maize in India and Elephantine Deities in Mesoamerica." *Current Anthropology*, Vol. 21, No. 5 (Oct. 1980).

Munro, George E. "Food in Catherinian St. Petersburg." *Food in Russian History and Culture*. Eds. Musya Glants and Joyce Toomre. Bloomington: Indiana University Press, 1997.

Murdoch Books. *World Kitchen India*. Sydney, NSW, Australia: Murdoch Books, 2010.

Murray, Paul. "The C. Louis Leipoldt Trail." *Murray's Food Trails,* Dec. 12, 2007, online at www.litnet.co.za/cgi-bin/giga.cgi?cmd=cause_dir_news_item&news_id=29679&cause_id=1270

NPD Group. Food and Beverage Market Research, online at www.NPDGroup.com.

National Confectioners Association. *International Trade Statistic and Regulation Database*. Online at www.candyusa.com/Sales/TradeRegulations.cfm?navItemNumber=2783.

Nipperdey, H. "The Industrial Products and Food-Stuffs of the Congo." *Scottish Geographical Magazine*, Vol 2. Eds. Hugh A. Webster and Arthur

Silva White. Edinburgh: Royal Scottish Geographical Society, 1886.

Norton, Marcy. "Tasting Empire: Chocolate and the European Internalization of Mesoamerican Aesthetics." *American Historical Review*, Vol. III, No. 3 (June 2006), 660–691.

Olmert, Michael. "The Pineapple in Colonial Williamsburg." *ColonialWilliamsburg.org*, online at www.history.org/almanack/life/christmas/dec_pineapple.cfm.

Ollivander, Holly, and Huh Thomas, eds. *Gerard's Herbal, or The Generall Historie of Plantes: Selections from the 1633 Enlarged & Amended Edition*. Velluminous Press, 2008.

"One Golden Ticket." *Chocolate Consumption Statistics*, Jan. 27, 2011, online at http://onegoldenticket.blogspot.com/2011/01/chocolate-consumption-statistics.html.

Osseo-Asare, Fran. *Food Culture in Sub-Saharan Africa*. Westport, CT: Greenwood Press, 2005.

—. "Update on African Cookbook Project." *BetumiBlog*, online at http://betumiblog.blogspot.com/2010/05/update-on-africa-cookbook-project.html.

—. "Ghana-style Kenkey." *BetumiBlog*, online at www.betumi.com/2009/08/recipe-12-kenkey-ghanas-challenge-to.html.

Owen, Sri. *Indonesian Regional Food and Cookery*. London: Frances Lincoln, Ltd., 1994.

Pan American Union. *Coffee: Extensive Information and Statistics*. Washington, D.C.: Government Printing Office, 1902.

Panjabi, Camellia. *The Great Curries of India*. New York: Simon & Schuster, 1995.

Park, Jae Bok. "Present State and Prospect of Korean Red Pepper Industry." *Korean Food Research Institute*, Sept. 2010, online at www.chilepepperinstitute.org/files/tiny_mce/file_manager/2010_IPC_jbpark.pdf.

Park, Mungo. *Travels in the Interior Districts of Africa: Performed Under the Direction and Patronage of the African Association in the Years 1795, 1796, and 1797*. London: W. Bulmer (printer), 1807.

Parker, Matthew. *The Sugar Barons: Family, Corruption, Empire, and War in the West Indies*. New York: Walker & Co., 2011.

Passamore, Jacki. *The Letts Companion to Asian Food & Cooking*. London: Charles Letts & Co., 1991.

Payak, M. M., and J. K. S. Sachan. "Maize Ears Not Sculpted in 13th Century Somnathpur Temple in India." *Economic Botany*. Vol. 47, No. 2 (Apr. 1,) 1993.

Pemberton, Rita A. "The Trinidad Botanic Gardens and Colonial Resource Development, 1818–1899." Online at www.sg.inter.edu/revista-ciscla/volume29/pemberton.pdf.

Pendergrast, Mark. *Uncommon Grounds: The History of Coffee and How It Transformed Our World*. New York: Basic Books, 1999.

Phelps, W. H. "John Gerard, the Herbalist." *The Library*. Vol. 6, No. 2. 76–80.

Pilcher, Jeffrey M. *Food in World History*. New York: Routledge, 2006.

Pogson, J. Frederick. *Indian Gardening: A Manual of Flowers, Fruits, and Vegetables, Soils and Manures, and Gardening Operations of Every Kind in Bengal, the Upper Provinces, & the Hill Stations of India*. Calcutta: Wyman & Co., 1872.

Polgreen, Lydia. "A Taste of Ghana." *The World Is a Kitchen: True Stories of Cooking Your Way Through Culture*. Eds. Michele Anna Jordan and Susan

Brady. Berkeley, CA: Travelers' Tales, 2006

Pollack, Penny, and Jeff Ruby. *Everybody Loves Pizza: The Deep Dish on America's Favorite Food.*
Cincinnati: Clerisy Press, 2005.

Ponting, Clive. *World History: A New Perspective.* London: Chatto & Windus, 2000.

Popham, Peter. *The Insider's Guide to Korea.* Edison, NJ: Hunter Publishing, 1987.

Prasso, Sheridan. "India's Pizza Wars." *Fortune Online,* Sept. 25, 2007, online at http://money.cnn.com/magazines/fortune/fortune_ archive/2007/10/01/100398841/index.htm.

Prestoe, Henry. *Catalog of Plants Cultivated in the Royal Botanic Gardens, Trinidad from 1865–1870.* Port of Spain: The Chronicle Printing Office, 1870.

Quinn, Elizabeth. "A World of Nutrition in Peanuts." Thirdplanetfood.com, online at http://thirdplanetfood.com/tidbits/?p=1223.

Radthorne, Daniel. "Poverty, Pots, and Golden Peanuts." *Culture,* University of California at San Diego, Oct., 2011, online at http://prospectjournal. ucsd.edu/index.php/2011/10/poverty-pots-and-golden-peanuts-looting-and-the-destruction-of-archaeological-sites-on-the-north-coast-of-peru.

Raffles, Sir Thomas Stamford. *The History of Java.* Vol. 1. London: Black, Parbury, and Allen, 1817.

Rain, Patricia. *Vanilla: The Culinary History of the World's Favorite Flavor and Fragrance.* New York: Jeremy P. Tarcher/Penguin, 2004.

Randall, Gary, "Williamsburg, Christmas, and the Pineapple." *Faith and Freedom Network,* Dec. 26, 2004, online at http://faithandfreedom.us/ weblog/2004/12/williamsburg-christmas-pineapple.html.

Raymond, Joan. "World's Healthiest Foods." *Health,* Feb. 1, 2008, online at www.health.com/health/article/0,,20410299,00.html.

Reader, John. *Potato: A History of the Propitious Esculent.* New Haven, CT: Yale University Press, 2009.

Riley, Gillian. *The Oxford Companion to Italian Food.* New York: Oxford University Press, 2009.

Ripley, George, ed. *The American Cyclopaedia: A Popular Dictionary of General Knowledge.* Vol. 13. New York: D. Appleton & Co., 1875.

Roland, Jacques, and Carol Sherman. *The Food Encyclopedia.* Toronto: Robert Rose Inc., 2006.

Root, Waverly. *Food.* New York: Simon & Schuster, 1980.

—. *The Food of Italy.* New York: Vintage Books, 1992.

—. *The Food of France.* New York: Vintage Books, 1992.

Rebora, Giovanni. *Culture of the Fork: A Brief History of Food in Europe.* New York: Columbia University Press, 2001.

Saffery, David, ed. *The Ghana Cookery Book.* London: Jeppestown Press, 2007.

Sahagún, Berardino de. *General History of the Things of New Spain: Florentine Codex.* Ed Charles E. Dibble. Santa Fe: Arthur J.O. Anderson School of American Research, 1,950–82.

Salaman, Redcliffe N. *The History and Social Influence of the Potato.* Ed. J. G. Hawkes. New York: Cambridge University Press, 1985.

"Mammals: Giraffe." *San Diego Zoo,* online at www.sandiegozoo.org/ animalbytes/t-giraffe.html.

Sandler, Bea. *The African Cookbook*. New York: Citadel Press, 1993.

Scappi, Bartolomeo, and Terrence Scully. *The Opera of Bartolomeo Scappi (1570): L'arte et Prudenza d'un Maestro Cuoco*. Trans. Terrence Scully. Lorenzo Da Ponte Italian Library. Toronto: University of Toronto Press, 2008.

Schivelbusch, Wolfgang. *Tastes of Paradise: A Social History of Spices, Stimulants, and Intoxicants*. New York: Vintage Books, 1993.

Schumann, Charles. *Tropical Bar Book*. New York: Stewart, Tabori & Chang, 1989.

Sellick, Will. *The Imperial Africa Cookery Book*. London: Jeppestown Press, 2010.

Serventi, Silvano, and Françoise Sabban. *Pasta: The Story of a Universal Food*. New York: Columbia University Press, 2000.

Sharma, Anisha. "Pineapple Wine from Shimoga, Karnataka, India–Bangalore Mirror." *Indian Wine*, online at http://indianwine.com/cs/blogs/indian_wine_news_and_messages/archive/2011/07/24/pineapple-wine-from-shimoga-karnataka-india-bangalore-mirror.aspx.

Sheets, Payson D. *Before the Volcano Erupted: The Ancient Cerén Village in Central America*. Austin: University of Texas Press, 2002.

Shilling, Robert, and R. Gibbons. *Groundnut*. The Tropical Agriculturist Series. London: Macmillan Education, Ltd., 2002.

Shrivrastava, Virendra Kumar. *Commercial Activities and Development in the Ganga Basin*. New Delhi: Concept Publishing Company, 1999.

Shore, Elliott. "Dining Out." *Food: The History of Taste*. Ed. Paul Freedman. Berkeley: University of California Press, 2007, 301–332.

Simoons, Frederick J. *Food in China: A Cultural and Historical Inquiry*. Boca Raton, FL: CRC Press, 2001.

Small, Ernest. *Top 100 Food Plants*. Ottawa: NRC Research Press, 2009.

Smith, Andrew F. *The Tomato in America: Early History, Culture, and Cookery*. Columbia: University of South Carolina Press, 1994.

—. *The Turkey: An American Story*. Urbana-Champaign: University of Illinois Press, 2006.

—. *Potato: A Global History*. London: Reaktion Books, 2011.

—. *Peanuts: The Illustrious History of the Goober Pea*. Urbana: University of Chicago Press, 2002.

Snodgrass, Mary Ellen. *Encyclopedia of Kitchen History*. New York: Taylor and Francis, 2004.

Snyman, Lannice. "Blatjang." *Epicurious*, online at www.epicurious.com/recipes/food/printerfriendly/Blatjang-231247?printFormat=4x6.

Sokolov, Raymond. *Why We Eat What We Eat: How Columbus Changed the Way The World Eats*. New York: Touchstone, 1991.

Spaeth, Anthony. "In Guntur, India, Even at 107 Degrees, It's Always Chili, Chili and More Chili." *Wall Street Journal*, June 30, 1988.

Spence, Jonathan. "Ch'ing." *Food in Chinese Culture*. Ed. K. C. Chang. New Haven: Yale University Press, 1977.

Spiller, Harry. *Prisoners of Nazis: Accounts by American POWs in World War II*. Jefferson, NC: McFarland & Co., 1998.

Srivastava, B.N. *Potato in the Indian Economy*. Lima, Peru: International Potato Center, 1980.

Standage, Tom. *A History of the World in 6 Glasses*. New York: Walker & Co., 2005.

Stedman, John Gabriel. *Narrative of a Five Years' Expedition Against the Revolted Negroes of Surinam*, Vol. II. London: J. Johnson, 1806.

Stone-Miller, Rebecca. *Art of the Andes: From Chavín to Inca*. New York: Thames and Hudson, 1995.

Super, John C. *Food, Conquest, and Colonization in Sixteenth-Century Spanish America*. Albuquerque: University of New Mexico Press, 1988.

Swaminathan, Monkombu Sambasivan. *Science and the Conquest of Hunger*. New Delhi: Concept Publishing Company, 1983.

Tannahill, Reay. *Food in History*. New York: Crown Publishers, 1989.

The Indian Cookery Book: A Practical Handbook to the Kitchen in India (A Thirty-Five Years' Resident). Calcutta: Thacker, Spink, and Co., 1880.

Thompson, David. *Thai Food*. Berkeley, CA: Ten Speed Press, 2002.

Thomson, Joseph. *Mungo Park and the Niger*. London: G. Philip & Son, 1890.

Towle, Margaret A. *The Ethnobotany of Pre-Columbian Peru*. Piscataway, NJ: Transaction Publishers, 2007.

Turgeon, Charlotte, and Nina Froud, eds. *Larousse Gastronomique*. New York: Crown Publishers, 1966.

Ukers, William Harrison. *All About Coffee*. New York: The Tea and Coffee Trade Journal Company, 1922.

Ullathorne, Graham. "How Could We Do Without Sugar and Rum?" *History in Focus: Slavery*, online at www.history.ac.uk/ihr/Focus/Slavery/articles/ullathorne.html.

"Vanilla and Spices of PNG (Papua New Guinea)." Online at www.agriculture.org.pg/vanilla&spice.htm.

Van der Post, Laurens. *African Cooking*. New York: Time-Life Books, 1970.

—. *First Catch Your Eland*. Leicestershire: F.A. Thorpe, 1982.

Verrill, A. Hyatt. *Foods America Gave to the World*. Boston: L.C. Page & Co., 1937.

Von Hagen, Victor. *Realm of the Incas*. New York: The New American Library, 1975.

Walker, Timothy. "Cure or Confection: Chocolate in the Portuguese Royal Court and Colonial Hospitals, 1580–1830." *Chocolate: History, Culture, and Heritage*. Eds. Louis Evan Grivetti and Howard-Yana Shapiro. Hoboken, NJ: John Wiley & Sons, 2009, 561.

Wang, Yi. "Overview of Sweet Potato Production in China." International Potato Center, Lima, Peru. Online at www.eseap.cipotato.org/MF-ESEAP/Fl-Library/SP-China.pdf.

Walsh, Joseph M. *Coffee: Its History, Classification and Description*. Philadelphia: The John C. Winston Co., 1894.

Washington, George. "George Washington to Lawrence Sanford, September 26, 1769, Account Book 2." The George Washington Papers at the Library of Congress, 1741–1799, online at http://memory.loc.gov/ammem/gwhtml/gwhome.html.

Watt, Sir George. *Economic Products of India Exhibited in the Economic Court, Calcutta International Exhibition, Part 6, 1883–84: Foods, Food–stuffs, and Fodders*. Calcutta: Superintendent of Government Printing, 1883.

—. *A Dictionary of the Economic Products of India*. Vols. 1 and 2. Calcutta: Superintendent of Government Printing, 1889.

Watt, Sir George. *The Commercial Products of India: Being an Abridgment of "The Dictionary of the Economic Products of India."* London: John Murray, 1908.

Weatherford, Jack. *Indian Givers: How the Indians of the Americas Transformed the World*. New York: Fawcett Columbine, 1988.

Weaver, Lawrence. *Sir Christopher Wren, Scientist, Scholar and Architect*. Online at www.ebooksread.com/authors-eng/lawrence-weaver/sir-christopher-wren-scientist-scholar-and-architect-vae/page-4-sir-christopher-wren-scientist-scholar-and-architect-vae.shtml.

Webb, William Trego, ed. *Selections from Cowper's Letters*. London: Macmillan, 1895.

Weinberg, Bennett Alan, and Bonnie K. Bealer. *The World of Caffeine: The Science and Culture of the World's Most Popular Drug*. New York: Psychology Press (Routledge), 2001.

Weinzweig, Ari. "Grits Verus Polenta: What's the Difference?" *Zingerman's Food Tours*, online at www.zingermansfoodtours.com/2011/07/grits-versus-polenta-whats-the-difference.

Weston, Richard. *Tracts on Practical Agriculture and Gardening*. London: S. Hooper, 1769.

Whiley, Antony, and Bruce Schaffer, and B. Nigel Wolstenholme. *The Avocado: Botany, Production, and Uses*. Cambridge, MA: Cabi Publishing, 2002.

Wild, Anthony. *Coffee: A Dark History*. New York: W. W. Norton & Co., 2005.

Williams, Brian, and Brenda Williams. *The Age of Discovery*. New York: Peter Bedrick Books, 1994.

Willinsky, Helen. *Jerk from Jamaica: Barbecue Caribbean Style*. Berkeley, CA: Ten Speed Press, 1990.

Willis, J. O., ed. *The Tropical Agriculturist and Magazine of the Ceylon Agricultural Society*. Colombo, Ceylon: The Ceylon Board of Agriculture, 1906.

Wilson, C. Anne. *Food and Drink in Britain*. Chicago: Chicago Academy Publishers, 1991.

Wink, Michael. "A Short History of Alkaloids." *Alkaloids: Biochemistry, Ecology, and Medicinal Applications*. Eds. Margaret F. Roberts and Michael Wink. New York: Plenum Press, 1998.

Winn, Michael. Personal communication, Aug.1993.

Wolfe, Jennifer A. *Sweet Potato: An Untapped Food Resource*. Cambridge: Cambridge University Press, 1992.

Wood, Peter. *The Seafarers: The Spanish Main*. Alexandria, VA: Time-Life Books, 1979.

Zentralverband der Deutschen Geflügelwirtschaft. "Daten und Fakten der einzelnen Verbände." Online at www.zdg-online.de/presse/daten-fakten.

Zoschke, Harald. "Saga Jolokia." *Fiery Foods & Barbecue SuperSite* (Nov. 17, 2006–Dec. 31, 2007), online at http://fiery-foods.com/chile-pepper-gardening/127-other-stories-about-growing-chile-peppers/2363-saga-jolokia.

—. Personal communication, Oct. 10, 2011.

Zuckerman, Larry. *The Potato: How the Humble Spud Rescued the Western World*. New York: North Point Press, 1998.

INDEX

blatjangs (South African hot sauce), 235–236, 237–238

Bock, Hieronymus (author), 59

Book of the Art of Cooking (Libro del arte de cocina), 71

Bourg-en-Bresse (town that has a movable feast), 81

Bowels of Naples (Il ventre di Napoli), 178

Bradley, Emily G. (author), recipe for green corn, 203, 359, 377

Bradley, Richard (author), 184

Bread of Affliction, The, 170, 387

breads
    cassava bread, 24, 201–202

Bridge of Sighs (notable for ears of maize artwork featured on), 60

Brillat-Savarin, Jean Anthelme (gourmand), 72, 73, 128, 158, 159, 349, 353–54, 356, 373

Brueghel, Pieter (artist), 67

Bruning National Archaeological Museum (Peruvian artifacts stored here), 40

Buonassisi, Rosario (pizza expert and author), 176

Burton, Sir Richard (famous adventurer/author)
    curries and, 241 (il.) –243
    palm oil chop (food dish), 241–242

cacao. *See also* chocolate
    cacao beans used for currency, 25

Cadbury, John and Benjamin (chocolate company founders), 129

caffeine, discovery of by Goethe, 143–144

Cambridge World History of Food, The, 54, 384

Campi, Vincenzo (author), 67

Capatti, Alberto (author), 179, 357, 358, 377

Capodilista, Emo (owner of a hunting lodge), 60

Capsicum annuum (chile pepper), 229, 262, 335

Capsicum chinense (African chile pepper), 228 (il.), 229, 232, 337 (il.)

Carlyle, Thomas (pro-slavery pamphleteer), 113–114

Carvajal, Gaspar de (author), 34

cassava bread, 24, 201–202

Castelgomberto (province that holds an annual turkey fair), 77

Castello, Villa di, 59, 67

Catherine de' Medici, 69, 349

Cavalcanti, Ippolito (author), 174

Cerén (located in present day El Salvador), 16 (il.) –19
    cuisine of, 21–22
    prehistoric cuisine of, 16–19
    remains of Maya Village, 16 (il.)
    type of cooking utensils used, 22
    website, 17

Chachalaca (New World bird),65

Chanca, Diego (court physician), 23, 24

Charles V (Spanish ruler), 34, 69, 83, 119, 120, 379

Charles VI (Holy roman Emperor), 127

Chavín (Peru), 39, 43, 391

chía, 27

chicahuatl, (drink made of chocolate & chiles), 29

chicha (beer made from fermented corn), 36, 38

Chichen Itza (Maya site), 117

chile de agua (irrigated chile), 28

chiles de árbol (tree chiles), 28

chile mollis (tamale), 29

chiles and chile peppers
    African food culture and, 225–228
    anecdotes about medicinal qualities, 38
    birds, role of in spreading seeds, 229–230
    ceramics featuring chile pepper designs, 39
    Ceren and, 18 (il.) –21
    chile stem, 18 (il.) –19
    development of Heirloom varieties, 28–29
    hottest chile peppers and, 18–19, 230, 232
    North Africa and, 228
    seafood dishes, adding to, 29
    seeds and, 20
    shapes of, 20
    spice seasoning, 24
    taming of wild, 19–21, 28–29